EUROPEAN CENTRAL BANK

EUROSYSTEM

THE EURO AT TEN –
LESSONS AND CHALLENGES

**FIFTH
ECB CENTRAL BANKING
CONFERENCE
13-14 NOVEMBER 2008**

**EDITORS
BARTOSZ MAĆKOWIAK
FRANCESCO PAOLO MONGELLI
GILLES NOBLET
FRANK SMETS**

© **European Central Bank, 2009**

Address
Kaiserstrasse 29
D-60311 Frankfurt am Main
Germany

Postal address
Postfach 16 03 19
D-60066 Frankfurt am Main
Germany

Telephone
+49 69 1344 0

Internet
http://www.ecb.europa.eu

Fax
+49 69 1344 6000

ISBN 978-92-899-0375-2 (print)
ISBN 978-92-899-0376-9 (online)

CONTENTS

INTRODUCTION
by Bartosz Maćkowiak, Francesco Paolo Mongelli,
Gilles Noblet and Frank Smets 6

OPENING ADDRESS
by Lucas Papademos 16

SESSION 1
EUROPEAN MONETARY UNION (EMU) AFTER TEN YEARS –
WHAT HAS EMU BROUGHT TO CONSUMERS AND THE
CORPORATE SECTOR? PRICES AND QUANTITIES

The euro at ten – unfulfilled threats and unexpected challenges
by Francesco Paolo Mongelli and Charles Wyplosz 24

Comments
Francesco Caselli 58
Vítor Constâncio 66

General Discussion 78

SESSION 2
EUROPEAN MONETARY UNION (EMU) AFTER TEN YEARS –
WHAT HAS EMU BROUGHT TO CONSUMERS AND
THE CORPORATE SECTOR? THE EVOLUTION AND THE ROLE
OF FINANCIAL MARKETS

EMU and financial integration
by Philip R. Lane 82

Financial integration, macroeconomic volatility and risk sharing –
the role of the monetary union
by Sebnem Kalemli-Ozcan, Simone Manganelli, Elias Papaioannou
and José Luis Peydró 116

Comments
Marco Pagano 156
Axel A. Weber 159

General Discussion 165

KEYNOTE ADDRESS
by Jean-Claude Trichet 168

SESSION 3
CHALLENGES FOR MONETARY POLICY AND FINANCIAL STABILITY FROM GLOBALISATION

The global roots of the current financial crisis and its implications for regulation
by Anil Kashyap, Raghuram Rajan and Jeremy Stein 180

Comments
Stephen G. Cecchetti 210
Seppo Honkapohja 217

General Discussion 222

SESSION 4
PANEL
THE EURO AND THE ENLARGEMENT – CHALLENGES AHEAD

INTRODUCTION
by Francesco Giavazzi 226

PANEL STATEMENTS
Vítor Gaspar 228
Athanasios Orphanides 233
András Simor 237

General Discussion 241

SESSION 5
PANEL
OPTIMAL CURRENCY AREAS – ACADEMIC VIEWS

INTRODUCTION
by Wolfgang Schill 244

PANEL STATEMENTS
Martin Feldstein 246
Andrew K. Rose 251
André Sapir 263
Jaume Ventura 268

General Discussion 274

SESSION 6
PANEL
INTERNATIONAL INTERDEPENDENCIES AND MONETARY POLICY –
POLICY MAKER'S VIEWS

INTRODUCTION
by Lucrezia Reichlin 278

PANEL STATEMENTS
Ben S. Bernanke 279
Stanley Fischer 283
Su Ning 288
Guillermo Ortiz Martínez 291
Jean-Claude Trichet 300

General Discussion 303

CLOSING ADDRESS
by Jürgen Stark 306

PROGRAMME 312

INTRODUCTION[1]

BY BARTOSZ MAĆKOWIAK, ECB
FRANCESCO PAOLO MONGELLI, ECB
GILLES NOBLET, ECB
FRANK SMETS, ECB

The European Central Bank was established on 1 June 1998. It began operating the single monetary policy the day on which the euro came into existence, 1 January 1999. The Fifth ECB Central Banking Conference took place in November 2008, a few months after the tenth anniversary of the establishment of the ECB, and a few weeks before the tenth anniversary of the launch of the euro. Not surprisingly, four out of six sessions of the conference focused on the challenges of and the lessons from the first decade of EMU. Charles Wyplosz (Graduate Institute of International Studies) presented a paper, written jointly with Francesco Paolo Mongelli (ECB), assessing the evolution of main macroeconomic variables in the first decade of EMU. Philip Lane (Trinity College Dublin) and José Luis Peydró Alcalde (ECB) presented papers evaluating the evolution of financial markets in the first decade of EMU. Peydró's presentation was based on the joint paper with Sebnem Kalemli-Ozcan (University of Houston), Simone Manganelli (ECB), and Elias Papaioannou (Dartmouth College). Two panels focused on the tenth anniversary of the euro. The panel chaired by Francesco Giavazzi (Università Bocconi) and comprising Erik Berglöf (EBRD), Vítor Gaspar (European Commission), Athanasios Orphanides (Central Bank of Cyprus), and András Simor (Magyar Nemzeti Bank) discussed enlargement of the euro area, in the past and in the future. The theory of optimal currency areas was the topic of the panel chaired by Wolfgang Schill (ECB) and comprising Martin Feldstein (Harvard University), Andrew Rose (University of California at Berkeley), André Sapir (Université Libre de Bruxelles), and Jaume Ventura (CREI).

2008 turned out to be not only the year of the tenth anniversary of the ECB, but also the year in which a global financial crisis unfolded. Therefore, the other two sessions of the conference focused on the global financial crisis. Raghuram Rajan (University of Chicago) presented a paper, written together with Anil Kashyap (University of Chicago) and Jeremy Stein (Harvard University), in which the authors discuss the roots of the global financial crisis and put forth a proposal for regulatory reform meant to prevent a future financial crisis from escalating. A stimulating exchange of views led by the paper's discussants followed Rajan's presentation. At the end of the conference the panel chaired by Lucrezia Reichlin (London Business School) and comprising several central bankers (Ben Bernanke, Federal Reserve; Stanley Fischer, Bank of Israel; Su Ning, People's Bank of China; Guillermo Ortiz, Banco de México; and Jean-Claude Trichet, ECB) discussed international interdependency in the

---

1   We would like to thank all participants in the 5th ECB Central Banking Conference, and all those who helped organise this conference. Furthermore, we wish to thank Werner Breun, Susanne Buchinger, Patricia Kearns-Endres and Maria Mileva for their help in editing this volume.

conduct of monetary policy, especially during the current crisis. The tenth anniversary of the euro and the global financial crisis intertwined in the speeches delivered at the conference by the ECB Board members: in the opening address by Lucas Papademos, in the keynote speech by Jean-Claude Trichet, and in the closing address by Jürgen Stark.

This volume contains the papers presented at the Fifth ECB Central Banking Conference as well as the discussions and the speeches. As the volume's editors, we believe that the texts published here contain a rich combination of materials. The reader will find in this volume a documentation of what has actually happened in the first decade of EMU, surveys of EMU related literature, but also new empirical studies concerning EMU. Moreover, the volume gives a snapshot of what renowned economists and leading central bankers thought in November 2008 about the global financial crisis, about EMU, and about which ideas appear most promising for future research in macroeconomics and financial economics. In the rest of this Introduction, we would like to summarise the contributions to this volume.

The main message of the paper by Mongelli and Wyplosz is that the essentials of a monetary union have gone well in the first decade of the euro, perhaps as well as anyone could have hoped ten years ago. Inflation in the euro area has been low and stable. Low inflation, low inflation expectations, and, in general, low macroeconomic variability have supported trade in goods and services, financial integration, risk-sharing, and efficiency. The dispersion of inflation rates across the euro area countries is now comparable to the dispersion of inflation rates across regions of the United States. The convergence of inflation rates has been achieved despite not fully synchronised fiscal policies, not fully integrated labour markets, the diversity of initial conditions, and despite the Balassa-Samuelson effects due to the catching up of some countries.

Mongelli and Wyplosz discuss three concerns that were popular among sceptics prior to the launch of the euro. The threats identified by the sceptics at that time have remained unfulfilled. The ECB quickly gained credibility, without having to resort to repeated interest rate hikes or intervention in the foreign exchange market. Furthermore, national fiscal policies have largely avoided pro-cyclicality, which could have exacerbated the differences in economic outcomes among the euro area countries. It is difficult to determine to what extent the observed fiscal outcomes are due to the existence of the Stability and Growth Pact. Finally, there appears to be no evidence of divergent real interest rates among the euro area countries, as one could have feared based on the Walters critique.

While the expected risks failed to materialize, unexpected challenges arose in the first decade of EMU. One challenge has been the emergence of current account imbalances, in both directions, in some member countries of the euro area. Financial integration has made it possible to borrow and lend on a large scale worldwide. Within the euro area, this process has been accelerated by the absence of exchange rate risk. The current account imbalances have been accompanied by persistent changes in real exchange rates between member countries of the euro area. Another challenge is discussed in the section of the paper reflecting only the views of Charles Wyplosz. Wyplosz points to data from the ECB's survey of professional forecasters showing that the proportion of forecasters who expect inflation to be between zero and two percent has fallen gradually since 1999. The conclusion Wyplosz draws from this development is that there could be a need for improvement in the communication strategy of the ECB.

The paper by Lane and the paper by Kalemli-Ozcan, Manganelli, Papaioannou, and Peydró Alcalde survey the evolution of financial markets in the first decade of EMU. The two surveys are complementary and, in our judgment, can be a starting point for anyone interested in what happened in the financial markets in the euro area between 1999 and 2008. The main message of both surveys is that a substantial increase in the degree of financial integration between euro area countries has been taking place. Within-euro-area cross-border holdings of debt and equity have risen remarkably. On the other hand, retail banking and lending to non-bank entities remaing largely in the national domain. This asymmetric pace of integration suggests a need for removing the remaining barriers to competition and to trade in financial services within the European Union. Integrated financial markets help insure against country-specific shocks: Countries can then maintain a stable path of consumption in the face of idiosyncratic fluctuations in income. As a result, the cost of not having country-specific monetary policy decreases and the net benefits of the monetary union rise.

Both papers review the empirical research suggesting that at least some of the increase in the degree of financial integration within the euro area would not have happened without the euro. In particular, Kalemli-Ozcan et al. refer to the recent empirical work on banking integration by Kalemli-Ozcan, Papaioannou, and Peydró. This analysis suggests that cross-border banking activity between the euro area countries increased by about 40 percent compared to a control group consisting of otherwise similar countries not in EMU.

Lane reviews the recent empirical literature on the effects of financial integration within EMU on macroeconomic volatility. In this literature, the main question is whether the increase in the degree of financial integration in the first decade of EMU has allowed more sharing of country-specific consumption risks. The lessons from this literature are still unclear, Lane concludes. One interpretation is that too little time has passed since the launch of the euro for an econometrician to be able to detect an increase in the sharing of country-specific consumption risks in the euro area. On the other hand, Kalemli-Ozcan et al. present new econometric evidence to suggest that greater banking integration has indeed led to more sharing of country-specific consumption risks. Using banking integration data for twenty developed countries over the past thirty years, Kalemli-Ozcan et al. find that a country with larger external assets experiences less consumption volatility. The authors quantify the degree of international risk sharing due to greater banking integration. They find that 38 percent of country-specific consumption risk is diversified away, on average across the twenty developed countries in the sample, through cross-border bank activity. Furthermore, Kalemli-Ozcan et al. find that a country that doubles its external assets, relative to population, diversifies away an additional 17 percent of country-specific consumption risk. Why do Kalemli-Ozcan et al. find that financial integration allows more sharing of country-specific consumption risks, while other studies – including those surveyed by Lane – fail to obtain this finding? A plausible explanation has to do with the unique nature of the dataset used by Kalemli-Ozcan et al. Their dataset·is detailed and it covers more countries and more years than the datasets of others.

The paper by Kashyap, Rajan, and Stein discusses the causes of, and the lessons from, the current financial crisis. The authors argue that the roots of the crisis lie in the global macroeconomic environment of the last several years. An important difference between the most recent period of sustained growth and previous such periods is the low level of long-term real interest rates over the last several years. After the emerging market crises in the late 1990s and the bursting of the information technology bubble in 2001, saving grew to very high levels in emerging markets (particularly in Asia) while, at the same time, corporate investment and public investment declined in many countries. Excess savings were channelled toward residential investment, and this process led to an increase in housing prices. Furthermore, demand arose among financial institutions such as pension funds and insurance companies for assets that would simultaneously appear safe and offer a real return higher than the long-term interest rate. Other financial institutions, mainly based in the United States, managed to satisfy this demand. They did so by transforming sub-prime mortgages into securities with AAA ratings, acceptable to pension funds, insurance companies, and banks throughout the world.

Kashyap, Rajan, and Stein argue that banks are being hit especially hard by the global financial crisis, because the problem of governance and the problem of short-term leverage are especially serious in banks. Importantly, the two problems interact: Agency problems between outside investors and bank managers are the reason why banks rely on short-term debt. Furthermore, the authors argue that it is difficult to solve the problem of governance and, therefore, to wean banks from leverage. Direct regulatory interventions, such as mandating more capital, may simply exacerbate private sector attempts to get around regulation. Direct regulatory interventions may also damage financial intermediation, and thereby decrease economic growth.

Kashyap, Rajan, and Stein advocate a specific reform of bank capital structure, capital insurance, meant to prevent a future financial crisis from escalating. In a nutshell, capital insurance would work as follows. A bank with $500 billion in risk-weighted assets would be given the following choice by regulators: It could either accept an upfront capital requirement that is, for example, 2 percent higher, meaning that the bank would have to raise $10 billion in new equity. Or the bank could acquire an insurance policy that pays off $10 billion in the event of a systemic "event". The insurer, a pension fund or a sovereign wealth fund, would at inception put $10 billion in Treasuries into a custodial account. If no adverse event occurs over the life of the policy, the $10 billion would be returned to the insurer, together with the insurance premium from the bank and the interest paid by the Treasuries. If there is an event, the $10 billion would be transferred to the balance sheet of the insured bank. Capital insurance is meant by the authors as a complement to other possible regulatory reform measures.

The paper's discussants, Stephen G. Cecchetti (BIS) and Seppo Honkapohja (Bank of Finland), welcome the idea of capital insurance. However, both discussants raise questions concerning specific aspects of the proposal.

The contribution by Giavazzi serves as an introduction to the panel on enlargement of the euro area. Giavazzi formulates several questions that he believes are important in thinking about enlargement: Should the EMU entry criteria be modified to include a measure of the health of the banking system? How should policy react to large capital inflows? Does enlargement strengthen the case for centralized euro area banking supervision? What is the optimal monetary policy regime in the transition to EMU, an exchange rate peg or inflation targeting with a flexible exchange rate? Berglöf, the first of the four panellists, emphasizes that those interested in enlargement can learn a great deal from the current crisis. He argues that the euro can be a mechanism to prevent a financial crisis from escalating. Furthermore, a commitment to joining the euro area can speed up institutional reform.[2] The second panellist, Gaspar, describes enlargement – not just of the euro area, but of the European Union in general – as a success. Enlargement spreads prosperity and democracy across Europe, he argues. Gaspar believes that it is a bad idea to speculate about modifying the EMU entry criteria. Such speculation can only increase the uncertainty associated with the transition to EMU. He offers a number of principles to guide policy-makers during this transition. The other two panellists, Orphanides and Simor, both central bank governors, describe the recent experiences of Cyprus and Hungary, respectively. According to Orphanides, the optimal mix of monetary policy and exchange rate policy during the transition to EMU is country-specific. Furthermore, Orphanides believes that it is important for prospective EMU entrants to achieve sufficient real and nominal convergence with the euro area before joining the Exchange Rate Mechanism. Simor's contribution focuses on the optimal timing to join EMU. From the recent turmoil in his country, Simor draws the lesson that a country should not try to join the euro area before implementing structural reform to scale back the overly generous welfare state.

Introducing the panel on the theory of optimal currency areas, Schill asks the panellists to re-evaluate this theory from the viewpoint of 2008, after ten years of EMU. The first panellist, Feldstein, describes the euro as a success. He stresses that continuous fiscal responsibility of the euro area countries is necessary to make the success of EMU permanent. According to Feldstein, some fiscal rule of the type embodied in the Stability and Growth Pact is a prerequisite for a successful currency union. More generally, what is required is the willingness of each member of the currency union to accept, at times, short-term losses in exchange for long-term gains.

The second panellist, Rose, reviews the recent literature linking monetary union, international trade, and business cycle synchronisation. He surveys this literature using the quantitative technique of meta-analysis, which allows him to estimate the effects of EMU taking into account the entire extant empirical literature. Twenty-six recent studies have investigated the effects of the introduction of

---

2   The text of Erik Berglöf's panel intervention could not be included in this volume.

the euro on trade (i.e., using European data only). Taking all these studies into account, Rose finds that EMU has raised trade inside the euro area by at least eight percent, and perhaps by as much as twenty-three percent. Twenty different studies have estimated the effect of trade on the synchronisation of business cycles. Aggregating across these studies estimates, Rose finds that an increase of bilateral trade between two countries raises the synchronisation of their business cycles by an economically and statistically significant effect. He estimates that a one percent increase in bilateral trade increases the correlation coefficient of de-trended output by 0.02. Rose concludes that EMU has created a virtuous circle. By increasing trade and the synchronisation of business cycles, EMU has reduced the need for national monetary policies.

In his panel contribution, Sapir observes that the authors of the Maastricht treaty chose different criteria for joining EMU than those emphasized by the theory of optimum currency areas. Sapir argues that the reasons for this choice were threefold. A large fraction of asymmetric shocks prior to monetary integration in Europe were considered to be national monetary policy shocks. National monetary policy shocks would automatically disappear in a monetary union. Furthermore, the launch of the euro was expected to create an optimum currency area endogenously, by fostering economic integration. Finally, national fiscal policies were seen as potential absorbers of asymmetric shocks. According to Sapir, the viewpoint that the criteria emphasized by the theory of optimum currency areas are unimportant is being challenged today. In the face of the global financial crisis, the "core" countries such as Germany, France, the Benelux, and Austria are doing better than the "periphery" countries such as Greece, Ireland, Portugal, and Spain. The core countries are precisely those that would have qualified for EMU ten years ago based on the criteria emphasized by the theory of optimum currency areas; the periphery countries would not have qualified.

Ventura begins his panel contribution with sceptical remarks concerning whether the theory of optimum currency areas is of practical relevance in today's world. He goes on to argue that economists need to develop a new theory of why international cooperation in monetary policy, a monetary union in particular, can be optimal. He observes that, in a set of interdependent economies, lending of last resort entails externalities. A monetary union can be modelled as an institution that allows internalization of these externalities.

The contributions to the panel of central bankers discuss international interdependency in the conduct of monetary policy, especially during the current crisis. Chairman Bernanke emphasizes the importance of cooperation among central banks. He notes that unprecedented cooperation among central banks of sovereign nations took place in the run-up to the establishment of EMU and is taking place continuously within EMU. He goes on to argue that the global financial crisis has been an occasion for unprecedented policy coordination among central banks globally. The same theme returns in President Trichet's panel contribution. Trichet emphasizes that international coordination can help strengthen domestic objectives of monetary policy. International cooperation is likely to be particularly beneficial at a time of a global financial crisis, such as the current one, or at a time when uncertainty prevails in global financial markets, such as after 11 September 2001. In the words of Trichet, central banks have established "intimate confidence" and they have "built a remarkable common ground of shared experience, mutual understanding, and trust (…). The world can count on a continuation of this fruitful cooperation among central banks (…)." In his panel contribution, Governor Ortiz agrees with Trichet that international cooperation in monetary policy, while apparently less important in "normal times", becomes crucial at a time of a global crisis. Ortiz believes that the global financial crisis is showing the need for improving institutional arrangements for international cooperation in monetary affairs.

Governor Fischer's panel contribution focuses on the question whether the recent increase in global financial integration has moved, or should be moving, the desirable monetary policy regime of a small open economy, such as Israel, in any particular direction. Fisher's answer to this question in the case of Israel is a qualified yes. He believes that policy-makers in a small open economy face the choice between a pegged exchange rate regime, joining a monetary union being a special case, and a regime of flexible inflation targeting with a flexible exchange rate. If the latter option is chosen, policy-makers must recognize that the real exchange rate matters for monetary policy in a small open economy, and that having a flexible exchange rate does not necessarily imply that the exchange rate is totally free floating.

The panel contribution by Governor Su has two themes. Su describes the People's Bank of China's view of how the challenges from globalisation affect China and China's monetary policy. Furthermore, he discusses how the People's Bank of China and the government of China have responded to the challenges from globalisation, in particular to the challenges associated with the current financial crisis.

We would like to conclude the Introduction with a brief summary of the speeches delivered at the Fifth ECB Central Banking Conference by the ECB policy-makers. The text of each speech is included in the volume. The opening address by Vice-President Papademos has two parts. The first part contains reflections on the economic performance of euro area in the first decade of its existence and on the policy challenges faced by the ECB in that period. The second part is devoted to the lessons for central banks from the global financial crisis. The reader may want to pay particular attention to the discussion of benefits and costs of central banks "leaning against the wind".

The keynote speech of the conference, by President Trichet, discusses the sources of, and the lessons from, the global financial crisis, both for monetary policy and for regulation of financial institutions. In addition, Trichet outlines the policy response of the ECB to the crisis, in particular the policy response in cooperation with other central banks.

In the closing address of the conference the Executive Board Member Stark emphasises that the first decade of EMU has not been calm: The ECB had to confront the aftermath of the Asian crisis, the bursting of the dot-com bubble, the attack of 11 September 2001, and the recent sharp rise in commodity prices.

The ECB has done well in those rough times. However, the magnitude and the global nature of the current crisis pose an unprecedented challenge to the ECB and to EMU. Stark believes that the ECB and EMU will meet also this challenge, and he speaks about the core principles which will help, in his view: the focus of the ECB on price stability in the medium-term and ECB's independence. Stark's speech also addresses enlargement of the euro. EMU membership has helped countries protect macroeconomic stability in the face of the global financial crisis. Therefore, it is not surprising that many countries would like to join the euro area on a fast-track procedure. However, Stark emphasizes that "there is no shortcut". The fast introduction of the euro would not resolve the underlying structural problems of the candidate countries and moreover, could weaken EMU. Structural adjustments as well as real and nominal convergence are necessary before the adoption of the euro.

Lucas Papademos opening the 5th ECB Central Banking Conference

OPENING ADDRESS

OPENING ADDRESS

BY LUCAS PAPADEMOS, VICE-PRESIDENT OF THE ECB

I   INTRODUCTION

On behalf of the Executive Board, I would like to welcome you to the Fifth ECB Central Banking Conference, taking place in the tenth year of the ECB's establishment. We are delighted that this year's conference has attracted many distinguished participants from academia, central banks, governments, international institutions and the financial sector. Your contributions will ensure that this conference will provide insightful and thought-provoking analysis and generate debate on many policy issues of relevance to central banking.

As we will be celebrating the 10th anniversary of the introduction of the single European currency in a few weeks' time, the theme of this conference is, of course, focused on "The Euro at ten: lessons and challenges". The introduction of the euro was a historic milestone in the process of European monetary, economic and political integration, with wide-ranging implications for the European and global economies. Accordingly, this conference will concentrate on several issues of relevance to the performance of the euro area economy and financial system and on the challenges for the conduct of monetary policy and the performance of other central banking tasks in an increasingly integrated global economy.

2   THE EURO: ECONOMIC PERFORMANCE AND POLICY CHALLENGES

The first session will examine the macroeconomic performance of Economic and Monetary Union, its achievements and challenges, over the past ten years. There are several key questions to be addressed. First, has the euro and the single monetary policy established a zone of monetary stability as envisaged, with all the direct and indirect benefits this entails for the 320 million citizens of the euro area? The evidence unambiguously provides a positive answer. The euro has been a resounding success: it has established itself as a stable and credible currency, which has become the second most important currency in the world after the US dollar. A deeper analysis, however, should reveal the contribution of monetary policy, and of other factors, to this achievement and the challenges that lie ahead and must be effectively addressed in order to ensure the preservation of price stability in the years to come.

A second key question is whether – or to what extent – the euro has contributed to boosting the trend growth of the euro area economy by strengthening competition, enhancing market efficiency, raising productivity growth and increasing labour utilisation. The answer to this question if less straightforward and the evidence seems, at first sight, to be rather mixed. On the one hand, average annual economic growth in the euro area has remained virtually the same (2.18%) over the ten years following the introduction of the euro (1999-2007) as in the two preceding decades (2.14% (1990-1999) and 2.27% (1980-1989)). On the other hand, employment grew impressively, namely by 18.67 million, or 1.36% per annum, over the past ten years, compared with 5.99 million, or 0.49% per annum, in the previous decade. A deeper analysis could reveal how the euro has contributed to strengthening the performance of the real economy, but also how other factors constrained and partly offset its positive impact, and it will also point to important challenges ahead, parts of which stem from the divergences in the performance in terms of growth and competitiveness across the member countries in the euro area. We are looking forward to the paper by Wyplosz and Mongelli, and to the discussion that will follow, for answers to these and other relevant questions.

Another important set of issues, which will be addressed in the second session, concerns the role of the euro in fostering the integration of financial markets in Europe and in promoting the efficiency and stability of the European financial system – and through it – of the broader economy in the euro area. Assessing the impact of the euro on the integration, efficiency and stability of the European financial system requires careful analysis in order to disentangle its contribution from the influence of other factors that have simultaneously affected the development and functioning of the financial system.

Indeed, the globalisation of financial markets and institutions, which was fostered by financial innovation and technological advances, has played a key role in shaping the overall environment and influencing the processes that determine financial market efficiency and stability. Moreover, the increasing interconnectedness and interdependence of our economies and financial systems have important implications both for the conduct of monetary policy and for the performance of the central banking task of safeguarding financial stability. These implications – and there are many – will be examined and assessed in the third session on the basis of the paper by Kashyap, Rajan and Stein and in the concluding policy panel. And, in between, two other panels will address – from both an analytic and a policy point of view – other important challenges confronting the euro area, in particular those stemming from its future enlargement and its evolution towards an optimal currency area.

3   THE ONGOING FINANCIAL CRISIS: LESSONS AND CHALLENGES FOR CENTRAL BANKS

Over the past ten years, the ECB has performed its tasks in an often difficult economic and financial environment that was adversely affected by sizeable and persistent shocks; and it has had to face some extraordinary challenges. The first was the unique, historically unprecedented challenge of conducting the single monetary policy successfully so as to preserve price stability in a newly established monetary union of politically independent, though economically well-integrated, member countries. The other major and exceptional challenge is the one we are still facing today: the preservation of price stability and the safeguarding of financial stability in the euro area during the worst financial crisis in decades.

The ongoing financial crisis which is, in many respects, unprecedented in intensity, scope and complexity has highlighted the role of the ECB in safeguarding financial stability. The events of the past year allow us to draw a number of conclusions concerning the responsibilities and actions of central banks in general, and of the ECB in particular, in contributing to preserving price stability through both crisis management and crisis prevention. And they have also shown how the conduct of a monetary policy aimed at the preservation of price stability and the performance of tasks aimed at safeguarding financial stability require the appropriate use of available policy instruments. Let me briefly elaborate on a number of pertinent lessons learnt and on the challenges to be faced.

It is by now widely accepted that a main underlying cause of the current global financial crisis was the same one that had fuelled similar episodes in earlier times: the excessive growth of credit globally over a long period of time and the associated high leverage in the financial system and in the non-financial sectors of some countries. Central banks, through their monitoring and analysis of monetary and credit developments, can provide early warning signals about the building-up of financial imbalances that may lead to excesses in the financial markets – through various channels involving an under-pricing of risk and an increase in market liquidity that can fuel asset price bubbles which will eventually be followed by market corrections. And such corrections will be the more severe, the higher the degree of leverage and the more prolonged the period of excessive credit growth. There is substantial empirical evidence across countries and over different periods in support of this proposition. The ECB's monetary policy strategy, which includes a comprehensive analysis of developments in money and credit, is well-suited to provide useful information about monetary risks to financial stability that can have longer-term implications for price stability and output volatility.

A second related policy issue is whether – or to what extent – central banks should "lean against the wind" of financial market excesses that can be expected to turn into a financial storm and whether they can do this both in a manner that is consistent with the preservation of price stability and by effectively using the single policy instrument at their disposal, the interest rate. In principle, this can be done, and should be done, under certain circumstances. This would require the monetary policy stance to be tightened in periods of booming financial markets, so as to contain the risk of instability to the price level over a longer-term horizon (when the boom could turn into a bust); in other words, in order to buy insurance against the risk of a financial crisis in which financial intermediation could grind to a halt. Such a policy could also help address the problem of moral hazard that may be created by policies that aim only to mitigate the impact of adverse shocks to financial stability, and thus treat asset booms and busts asymmetrically. In practice, however, a policy of "leaning against the wind" is not always feasible; it may by itself not be an effective means to contain unsustainable asset price bubbles in the presence of exuberant expectations and it may not be compatible with the maintenance of price stability over the medium term.[1]

Consequently, the single instrument of monetary policy – the central bank interest rate – cannot always be used, cannot be used systematically, to simultaneously achieve the price stability objective (over the medium and longer term) and effectively safeguard financial stability. Clearly, additional tools must be employed to this end. Central banks can further strengthen their analytical tools and methodologies that can help identify risks and vulnerabilities in the financial system and provide early warning signals of emerging imbalances and potential instabilities. And central banks – via their financial stability reviews and other means – have done so fairly successfully. But the recent experience has also shown that, despite the communication of such early warnings, the financial markets did not hear, or did not want to hear them for several reasons, including the influence of inappropriate incentive structures at different stages of the financial intermediation and securitisation chain. What is, therefore, needed is a more effective use of regulatory policy instruments by supervisory authorities that can help contain procyclicality in risk assessment and the increase in leverage that is characteristic of asset market booms. Pre-provisioning measures during the upswing phase of the cycle and more effective and longer-term oriented risk management can contribute to this end.

More generally, and this a third important lesson learnt from the ongoing financial crisis, the effective safeguarding of financial stability – both in preventing and in managing a financial crisis – requires parallel and complementary action by central banks and supervisors, and an enhanced cooperation and exchange of information between them. It is evident that this can be achieved most effectively and efficiently when central banks are responsible for banking supervision, or are actively involved in the performance of supervisory tasks – as well as have access to pertinent information – in collaboration with a separate supervisory authority. However, irrespective of the organisational structure and the institutional responsibility, effectively reducing the likelihood of a recurrence of financial crises affecting markets and institutions requires the fruitful cooperation of the central banks and supervisory functions.

Let me now conclude by briefly pointing to two other important lessons and associated challenges that have been highlighted by the ongoing financial crisis: the first concerns the role and actions of central banks in mitigating the impact of financial turbulence on the financial system and the broader economy; the second is related to the need to strengthen the cross-border financial stability arrangements globally and in Europe.

---

1   An overvaluation of asset prices can occur – and has occurred – in an environment of relatively stable consumer prices. In such an environment, a significant change in the policy interest rate to contain credit growth and asset price dynamics could be inconsistent with the preservation of consumer price stability over the medium term. An alternative means of containing bank credit expansion by reducing the rate of growth of central bank money – at a given policy interest rate – would effectively entail a rise in market interest rates and could pose similar problems of potential inconsistency.

The recent experience has demonstrated the crucial role of central banks in crisis management through the provision and management of liquidity in the money markets and, in exceptional cases, by providing emergency liquidity assistance to individual institutions. Since the eruption of the market turmoil, central banks in advanced economies have used various policy instruments to limit its effects. The ECB's operations in the money markets have been based on a fundamental principle: the separation of the monetary policy stance from liquidity management. The monetary policy stance is defined by the level of the key ECB interest rates and is determined with a view to achieving the primary objective of preserving price stability over the medium term. Liquidity management aims at ensuring the orderly functioning of money markets and at mitigating financial stability risks.

The provision and management of liquidity by central banks has alleviated pressures in the money markets and has kept spill-over effects on the credit markets and the real economy contained. In particular, the provision of unlimited liquidity by the ECB to the euro area banking system against an expanded list of eligible collateral since mid-October should effectively eliminate concerns about liquidity risk and further reduce pressures in the term money market. Central banks, however, cannot address some of the underlying causes of money market tensions, such as concerns about counterparty credit risk and the continuing uncertainty regarding banks' other funding sources and capital positions. The measures being taken by governments should address these problems over time.

The separation principle that guides the conduct of monetary policy and the management of liquidity during a financial market correction implies that the policy interest rate is not employed to alleviate stresses in the financial system if upside risks to price stability prevail. Only if the preservation of price stability is secured over the medium term, and will not be jeopardised by a change in the monetary policy stance, can the policy interest rate be employed to mitigate the impact of financial market stresses in the economy, including their potential effects on medium-term price developments.

Finally, I would like to stress that the financial crisis has underscored the importance of international cooperation and concerted action in addressing the liquidity needs of cross-border financial institutions and ensuring the efficient distribution of liquidity at a global level. In particular, the Federal Reserve, the ECB and other major central banks cooperated closely and their concerted liquidity provision enhanced the effectiveness of liquidity management globally. There is an emerging consensus on the need to strengthen cooperation between the supervisory authorities responsible for major cross-border institutions and to promote a more convergent and consistent application of regulations. In the European Union, the implementation of measures to improve supervisory cooperation, and to accelerate the convergence of supervisory rules and practices, has gained momentum. And there is a growing understanding of the need to strengthen the pan-European character of financial stability arrangements for crisis prevention and crisis management. Regardless of the institutional framework that may be adopted, what is essential is to ensure the effective cooperation and the sharing of relevant information between central banks and supervisors in a timely and efficient manner.

4   CONCLUDING REMARKS

Over the past ten years, the euro has established itself as a stable and credible currency and the single European monetary policy has preserved price stability, and thus the purchasing power of the euro, in the euro area. In addition, the euro has played an important role in insulating euro countries from other adverse effects that the financial crisis could have had on their economies, via the foreign exchange markets and other channels, if the euro had not existed. And some Member States that have not yet adopted the euro as their currency have indeed experienced such effects. Therefore, the euro and the liquidity management of the ECB have also played an important role in safeguarding financial stability in the euro area.

With these thoughts on some lessons that could be learnt from our experience with the euro, from the ongoing financial crisis and from the contribution of the ECB and central banks to the preservation of financial stability, I wish us all a fruitful and enriching conference.

Francesco Paolo Mongelli, Vítor Manuel Ribeiro Constâncio, Gertrude Tumpel-Gugerell, Francesco Caselli and Charles Wyplosz (from left to right)

SESSION I

EUROPEAN MONETARY UNION AFTER TEN YEARS – WHAT HAS EMU BROUGHT TO CONSUMERS AND THE CORPORATE SECTOR? PRICES AND QUANTITIES

THE EURO AT TEN – UNFULFILLED THREATS AND UNEXPECTED CHALLENGES[1]

BY FRANCESCO PAOLO MONGELLI, ECB
CHARLES WYPLOSZ, GRADUATE INSTITUTE OF INTERNATIONAL STUDIES, GENEVA

ABSTRACT

The first ten years of the euro may well have been as good as many had hoped. Price stability has been broadly attained and interest rates are very low. These achievements are serving the citizens of the euro area well. A remarkable feature is that recent inflation dispersion in the euro area is already as low and as stable as in the United States. We might, understandably, have expected inflation dispersion to have remained higher in the euro area due to differences in national fiscal policies and supply shocks, adjustments to equilibrium exchange rates and the ongoing catching up of incomes. Three concerns raised prior to the launch of the euro have been broadly dispelled: first, the ECB has established its own credibility and has anchored inflation expectations; second, national fiscal policies are no longer pro-cyclical; and third, there is no evidence of the growing divergence predicted by the Walters critique, which states that real interest rates could act as asymmetric transmission channels. However, we may be witnessing a transmutation of the Walters critique that operates through eventually self-equilibrating external current account deficits

1   We are grateful to Vítor Manuel Ribeiro Constâncio and Francesco Caselli for their excellent discussion of our paper. We would also like to thank Frank Smets, Chiara Osbat, Manfred Kremer, Renate Dreiskena, Aidan Meyler, Luca Benati, Irina Bunda, Malin Andersson, Christine Elding, Luca Dedola, Viviene Petit, Javier Perez, Joan Peredes and Joachim Schroth for their assistance, suggestions and comments. Irene Mühldorf and Karen Forbes-Baeyens provided editorial assistance.

I   INTRODUCTION

More than ten years ago, many economists were sceptical about the wisdom of monetary union in Europe. Some even characterised it as a project that was doomed to failure and that could actually tear the European Union apart.[2] This foreboding has not materialised. On the contrary, a whole new generation of Europeans is growing up with, at most, a distant memory of Belgian and French francs, Deutsche Mark, Italian lire and other predecessor currencies. An anniversary is a time to take stock. Accordingly, our aim is to review what has been achieved, recall the various threats to monetary union that did not materialise during this period, and address a number of unexpected challenges.

Given some of the early concerns, the smooth functioning of the euro area should not be taken for granted. In Section 2, we illustrate that in spite of the recent hiccup in inflation, price stability has been broadly achieved, with average inflation having been close to or slightly above 2% since January 1999. Furthermore, the absence of exchange rate risk, low current and expected inflation, low interest rates and low macroeconomic variability more generally are supporting other beneficial dynamics such as additional trade in goods and services as well as deeper financial integration. These achievements are undoubtedly serving the citizens of the euro area well.

Many of the debates in the 1990s foresaw difficulties and threats to the successful functioning of EMU. As it turns out, most of them have not materialised, at least not to a significant extent (see Section 3). First, there was a fear that a new supranational central bank would have to earn its credibility the hard way. Would the new ECB feel compelled to be systematically over-restrictive in its early years? In fact, various measures indicate that the ECB was literally "born credible". Even though the euro soon depreciated, it became clear that this was mainly a dollar event. Second, there was a concern that countries with higher inflation rates would also have relatively lower real interest rates, which could have a pro-cyclical impact and could foster a cyclical de-coupling from the rest of the euro area. In this case, a single monetary policy would have polarising, destabilising effects on inflation and growth (this argument is also known as the Walters critique). While the pattern of national real interest rates to some extent conforms to the Walters critique, there is no evidence of a destabilising effect. Third, there was a fear that some national authorities would display a bias towards running budget deficits that could threaten price stability. The Stability and Growth Pact was designed with that concern in mind. Although fiscal discipline remains an elusive objective and the Pact had to be amended once, the quality of fiscal policies has generally improved and there is no indication that they have been destabilising. Finally, there was also concern that once changes in the nominal exchange rate had been ruled out, real exchange rates would not be sufficiently flexible, meaning that the euro would thwart necessary changes in competitiveness within the euro area. This did not happen either.

---

2   See, for example, Feldstein (1997), *"Instead of increasing intra-European harmony and global peace, the shift to EMU and the political integration that would follow it would be more likely to lead to increased conflicts within Europe and between Europe and the United States"*.

At the same time, a number of difficulties that were not widely expected have arisen. This is the topic of Section 4. First, to a surprising extent, the ECB has found itself criticised for its lack of transparency. The ECB's monetary policy strategy was designed with a view to establishing credibility. It was inspired by the highly successful German model, which combined a prominent role for monetary aggregates with great pragmatism in executing policy. But the growing popularity of the inflation targeting strategy, which emphasises transparency and coherence between medium-term forecasts and policy actions (the ECB's two-pillar approach), has come to be seen by some as too complicated. Second, attention is gradually focusing on the tendency for current account imbalances, both positive and negative, to become relatively large in some countries. To some extent, this may reflect the increased financial integration the single currency has spurred. However, current account imbalances may also have grown because persistent inflation differentials, albeit smaller than in the past, have accumulated over time and have led to a loss of competitiveness. We examine this pattern and its potential causes, including the possibility that it is an expected effect of the Walters critique.

2   THE ECB'S ACHIEVEMENTS

In this section, we briefly review some evidence on price stability, growth, economic integration and the international role of the euro. We then turn to the benefits that the euro is bringing to consumers and the corporate sector.

2.1   PRICE STABILITY

The first and foremost objective of the ECB, as stated in the Treaty on European Union (Maastricht Treaty), is price stability. Table 1 shows that over the first five post-war decades, with a few exceptions, inflation in all euro area countries was never as low as it was during the first ten years of the euro. One of these exceptions is Ireland, which has gone through a decade of extraordinary growth, catching up with and then passing the richer European countries.[3]

Table 1 also shows that inflation rates have been quite similar, but not identical, across the euro area member countries. Some degree of dispersion is unavoidable and possibly even desirable. We will deal with this issue at greater length below. At this stage, we only wish to establish a few facts and suggest some interpretations. Chart 1 shows a measure of dispersion, the standard deviation across euro area member countries. Dispersion has steadily declined since 1999 and is now of the same order of magnitude as within the United States, a monetary union of similar size but with a strong central government.

Chart 1 can be interpreted in two ways, however. One is that inflation rates are indeed converging within the euro area. Alternatively, it could merely be a

---

3   The catching-up process implies that wages and prices, typically lower in poorer countries, rise when evaluated in foreign currencies. This Balassa-Samuelson effect implies higher than average inflation. Another exception is Germany during the post-war period, with negative inflation in 1950 (-6.2%) and in 1953 (-1.9%).

Table I Sixty years of inflation: ten-year annual averages						
	1949-58	1959-68	1969-78	1979-88	1989-98	1999-08
Austria	8.9	3.1	6.0	4.0	2.6	1.9
Belgium	1.4	2.4	7.1	5.0	2.3	2.0
Finland	6.1	5.0	9.9	7.4	2.7	1.7
France	6.2	3.8	8.4	8.1	2.2	1.7
Germany	1.1	2.3	4.7	3.0	2.7	1.6
Greece	7.7	1.9	10.7	20.0	12.2	3.2
Ireland	4.0	3.3	12.2	10.3	2.6	3.7
Italy	3.1	3.4	11.1	12.0	4.6	2.3
Luxemburg	2.6	2.0	6.3	4.8	2.5	2.4
Netherlands	4.1	3.5	7.4	3.2	2.3	2.2
Portugal	0.8	3.4	15.5	18.7	7.0	2.9
Spain	6.1	6.3	13.0	11.1	4.7	3.2
Denmark	4.0	5.2	8.7	7.4	2.3	2.1
Sweden	4.4	3.6	8.1	8.0	3.9	1.2
Switzerland	1.1	2.8	4.9	3.3	2.6	0.9
UK	3.8	3.1	11.8	8.0	4.3	2.7

Sources: 1949–2007: International Financial Statistics, IMF; 2008: Economic Outlook, OECD.
Note: West Germany only before 1992.

statistical artefact. Indeed, when inflation rates decline, absolute differences are bound to become smaller. A natural way to account for this possibility is to use a

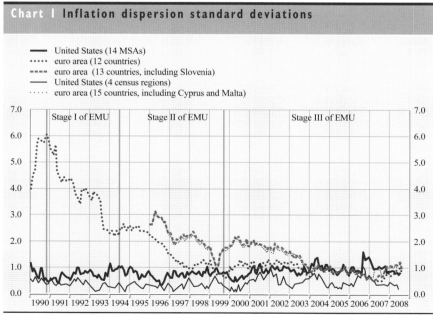

Chart I Inflation dispersion standard deviations

——— United States (14 MSAs)
····· euro area (12 countries)
‑ ‑ ‑ euro area (13 countries, including Slovenia)
——— United States (4 census regions)
····· euro area (15 countries, including Cyprus and Malta)

Source: Eurostat and US Bureau of Labor Statistics. Unweighted standard deviation in percent. 14 MSA are the main Metropolitan Statistical Areas in the US.

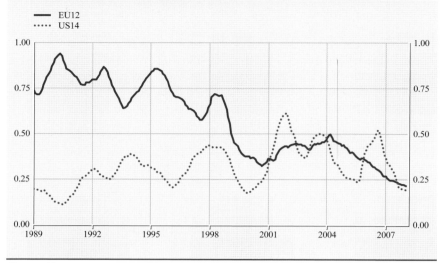

Chart 2 Inflation dispersion: coefficient of variation (July 1989 – August 2008)

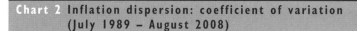

Source: Eurostat.
Note: 12-month moving average.

different measure of dispersion, the coefficient of variation, as in Chart 2. The chart shows that inflation rates have converged; in addition, they have also declined. The clear break after the adoption of the common currency confirms that, in the euro area, dispersion is as low as and even more stable than in the United States.

This is surprising, as a number of factors instead suggest that inflation dispersion should be higher in the euro area than in the United States.

a. One factor is divergent fiscal policies. While theory predicts that in a monetary union, divergent fiscal policies are unlikely to lead to sustained differences in inflation rates, their short-run effects can be sizeable. In Europe fiscal policy is almost exclusively a national prerogative, whereas US states face strict limits on their ability to run deficits, as explained in Bayoumi and Masson (1995). We discuss this further in Section 3.2.

b. An additional factor is the incidence of different idiosyncratic cost-push shocks, for example due to different wage pressures in decentralised national labour markets. Instead, we have seen generally lower wage pressure than in the past. The result suggests that wage claims were subdued to the same extent throughout the euro area during its first ten years.

c. Another possible factor is that the conversion rates adopted in 1998 might not have been close to their equilibrium exchange rates for all countries.[4] One would expect that US states have long made any correction, while possible

---

4   Angeloni and Ehrmann (2004) provide evidence to that effect.

discrepancies in the euro area would trigger relative price adjustments, hence greater inflation variability.

d. Finally, equilibrium exchange rates can change over time, in particular because of income catching up, a phenomenon often referred to as the Balassa-Samuelson effect. Levels of development are more diverse in the euro area than in the United States, and labour mobility is lower as well. Chart 3 takes a long-term look at a price indicator based on purchasing power parity (PPP) values of USD 1 in euro terms.[5] The PPP rates of euro area countries show that over almost two decades, the levels of purchasing power of countries with an initially lower level of GDP per capita have caught up substantially. This increase in purchasing power has broadly corresponded to an increase in real GDP per capita. Hence, the presumption is that there should be more variability in the euro area.

The achievement of low inflation during the first decade of EMU is reassuring, but a legitimate question is whether the credit goes entirely to the ECB. Most of the first decade of the euro coincided with the "Great Moderation", a long period

---

5   The hypothesis is that, ceteris paribus, persistence in inflation differentials for countries starting off at rather different price levels can reflect convergence towards a new equilibrium characterised by price convergence as differences in living standards are eliminated (i.e. those in the countries below the euro area average). PPPs are currency conversion rates that convert to a common currency (the US dollar in this case) and that equalise the purchasing power of different currencies. In other words, they eliminate the differences in price levels between countries by means of conversion.

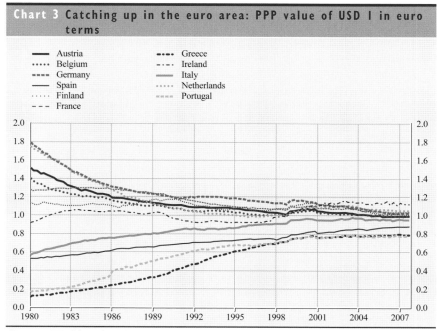

Chart 3 Catching up in the euro area: PPP value of USD 1 in euro terms

Sources: World Bank and ECB calculations.

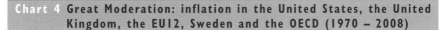

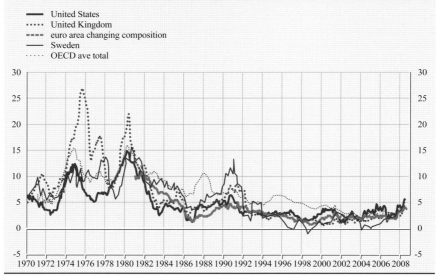

Chart 4 Great Moderation: inflation in the United States, the United Kingdom, the EUI2, Sweden and the OECD (1970 – 2008)

Sources: OECD, Eurostat and ECB calculations.

of low output volatility in many countries around the world. The achievement of low and stable inflation may therefore be due to the absence of large shocks. Chart 4 shows that euro area inflation performance is very much in line with what was observed elsewhere among developed countries. On the face of it, the ECB has performed as well as, but not better than other central banks. That, in itself, is a significant achievement, given the challenge of conducting policy for a large number of countries that had not been previously accustomed to sharing the same currency.

A growing literature has started to explore the reasons for the Great Moderation, focusing on output variability. The issue is whether the phenomenon is due to a decrease in the size of exogenous shocks or to an enhanced ability to absorb these shocks. This ability could well include better monetary policies. The literature is surveyed in Giannone et al. (2008), whose own evaluation of the US case supports the view that the economy's response is the main source of the Great Moderation.

To sum up, the evidence on inflation dispersion presented above may be reassuring, but it is also puzzling. It could be that these various effects all materialised and yet somehow compensated each other. We return to this issue later in the paper when we bring together various strands of discussion.

Whether shocks were milder or not over the last decade, there is little doubt that this period has now come to an abrupt end. The 2007-08 combination of rising commodity prices (that subsequently declined rapidly) and the financial crisis amounts to a massive shock and a serious challenge for the ECB (as well as other central banks).

2.2 GROWTH

Before the launch of the euro, there were widespread fears that the ECB would want to establish its reputation as a determined inflation fighter at the expense of economic growth and employment. These fears were partly based on the Maastricht Treaty, which identifies price stability as the ECB's primary objective and "the economy" as a secondary one "without prejudice to the objective of price stability". The fears were further stoked by the ECB's own vocabulary, which was carefully chosen to emphasise the Deutsche Bundesbank's legacy.

It rapidly turned out instead, that the ECB was conducting its policy in a pragmatic manner. The first period of the euro's existence was marked by a sizeable depreciation, which could have led a hawkish ECB to drive up interest rates. In fact, the euro depreciated less as a result of ECB policy than as a result of US dollar appreciation. In addition, inflation was low because all member countries had to pass the convergence criteria to be admitted to EMU.

Table 2 shows the growth performance of the euro area and other major economies. It varies from country to country, which is an indication that monetary policy, in and by itself, has not had any particular effect, as theory would predict. Those countries where the outcome was disappointing relative to the previous decade – Austria, Germany, Italy, Portugal, and to some extent also France – obviously need to carry out structural reforms to revive their supply side (see Duval and Elmeskov (2006)).

Table 2 GDP growth rates: ten-year annual averages

	1971-78	1979-88	1989-98	1999-2008
Austria	3.6	2.2	2.6	2.3
Belgium	3.4	2.0	2.1	2.3
Finland	3.0	3.7	1.7	3.4
France	3.5	2.4	2.0	2.1
Germany	2.9	2.0	2.5	1.6
Greece	5.4	0.7	1.9	4.2
Ireland	5.2	2.8	6.6	6.1
Italy	3.4	2.8	1.6	1.4
Luxemburg	2.9	3.8	4.9	5.2
Netherlands	3.3	1.7	3.2	2.3
Portugal	4.7	3.3	3.2	1.7
Spain	4.3	2.2	2.7	3.6
Denmark	2.4	2.2	2.2	2.0
Sweden	1.7	2.4	1.5	3.1
Switzerland	0.7	2.1	1.4	1.9
United Kingdom	2.4	2.4	2.1	2.7
United States	3.7	3.0	3.0	2.7
OECD	**3.8**	**3.0**	**2.7**	**4.5**

Source: OECD.

2.3 ECONOMIC AND FINANCIAL INTEGRATION

Sharing the euro was expected, ceteris paribus, to stimulate among other things intra-euro area trade, financial flows and cross-border portfolio investment activity by eliminating exchange rate volatility, thereby removing uncertainty about returns and profits due to exchange rate fluctuations. In addition to the elimination of exchange rate volatility, the so-called "Rose effect" could possibly provide an additional boost to intra-euro area trade.[6] It was also expected that directly comparable prices would enhance competition both for goods and services, including financial services. What can we say ten years later?

A. TRADE EVIDENCE

Since 1998, trade among euro area countries has risen strongly. The most comprehensive study to date (Baldwin et al. (2008)) concludes that, so far, the euro has probably increased trade by some 5%.[7] These results are substantial, considering that trade among European countries has risen uninterrupted for about five decades. The value of imports and exports of goods within the euro area increased from about 26% of GDP in 1998, the year before the euro was introduced, to 33% of GDP in 2007. In the same period, intra-euro area services trade also went up, rising from 5% to 7% of GDP. Since 1998, the year-on-year growth of euro area exports of goods to the three EU15 countries that have not adopted the euro has been 3% lower on average than the year-on-year growth of exports within the euro area. Extra-euro area trade has grown more than intra-euro area trade, an indication that the euro has not had a trade-diversion effect, as was sometimes feared. Hence, there is no "fortress Europe".

B. REAL EFFECTS OF FINANCIAL INTEGRATION

The financial openness of the euro area has risen by about 60% of euro area GDP over the past ten years. Between 2000 and 2005, the euro area countries – either as recipients or as sources of investment – accounted for as much as 57% of world foreign direct investment (FDI) flows. EMU seems to have been a magnet for FDI activities particularly in the manufacturing sector, while an increasing share of FDI flows is taking place between euro area countries. A positive trend can also be observed when looking at FDI stocks, given that intra-euro area FDI stocks as a proportion of total euro area FDI stocks increased from almost 43% in 1999 to 45% in 2006. Overall, it seems that the positive average effect of the euro on aggregate FDI flows within the euro area is about 15%, while the impact of the euro on FDI flows from outside the euro area to the euro area countries is about 7% (see Petroulas (2007), Schiavo (2007), Ottaviano et al. (2007) and Flam and Nordström (2007)).

---

6   Rose (2000) initially predicted that trade would nearly triple. Similar results emerged from the "border effect" literature (Engel and Rogers, 1996). In the meantime, the most recent empirical literature has reassessed these results (see de Grauwe and Mongelli (2005)).

7   These figures must be seen in perspective. Mongelli et al. (2007) show that, over the past 50 years, trade in goods among the six founding members of the European Union has risen in volume by over 1,200%. Hence, any further trade deepening would be remarkable.

By eliminating exchange rate risk, the euro has also boosted cross-border portfolio investment activity between euro area countries. Empirical estimates by De Santis and Gerard (2006) suggest that the adoption of the euro played a key role in the reallocation of portfolios among euro area members as well as countries worldwide. The total impact of the euro on bilateral transactions between individual euro area countries has been estimated to amount to 3.5% of equity securities and 4.2% of bonds and notes of the respective total international holdings (see De Santis and Gerard (2006)). Moreover, non-euro area countries have on average increased their relative investment in euro area bonds.

2.4 INTERNATIONAL ROLE OF THE EURO

When it was launched, the euro was "international" simply because it replaced 11 existing currencies. It was immediately used to replace the Deutsche Mark, the French franc as well as other legacy currencies as a reserve currency (and as an anchor for the exchange rate policy of some countries).[8] Although the ECB has adopted a neutral stance on the international use of the euro (which is determined by market forces), the euro's role has grown beyond this legacy, as documented in Chart 5.

A distinctive feature of the international role of the euro is still its regional character. Borrowers outside the euro area are increasingly issuing bonds in euro, more than half of which are purchased by euro area investors. Countries close to the euro area naturally choose the euro as a financing currency. For example,

---

8   See various issues of the ECB's Review of the international role of the euro.

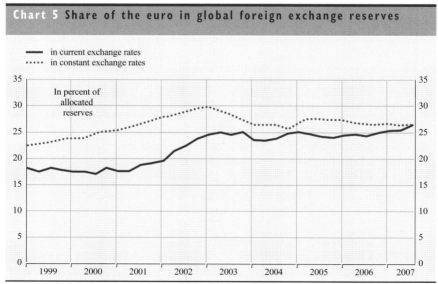

Chart 5 Share of the euro in global foreign exchange reserves

Source: IMF's COFER database.
Note: The shares in constant exchange rates are reported in exchange rates of the third quarter of 2007.

Table 3 Outstanding volume of international bonds and notes by region

(percentages; second quarter of 2007)

	Euro area	Denmark, Sweden, United Kingdom	New Member States	Non-EU Europe	North America	Asia & Pacific	Latin America	Off-shore centres	International organisations	Other
EUR		44.7	3.1	3.8	23.6	5.5	2.0	10.0	6.3	1.0
USD	23.7	19.0	0.3	2.4	4.9	10.8	6.6	23.1	5.0	4.2
JPY	30.0	12.7	1.2	2.9	18.6	4.9	0.6	21.1	7.6	0.5

Sources: BIS and ECB calculations.

issuers resident in Denmark, Sweden and the United Kingdom account for a significant part of euro-denominated debt issuance by non-residents (Table 3), and the City of London, as a major international financial centre, has developed its transactions in euro along with those in US dollars. Likewise, all countries running a euro-related exchange rate policy are in close geographic proximity to the euro area. Finally, the degree of currency substitution is highest in the new non-euro area EU Member States, as well as in EU candidate and potential candidate countries in south-eastern Europe.

2.5 WELFARE EFFECTS OF THE EURO

All in all, consumers and corporations have benefited from price stability, including low interest rates at all maturities, which in turn have lowered the cost of servicing high public debts, and they have benefited from trade integration. Financial integration has also progressed, although to a limited extent only, largely because of many surviving barriers. Crucially, the risk of possible speculative attacks on national currencies has been removed. For example, prior to the launch of the euro, the impact of movements by the Deutsche Mark against the US dollar was often aggravated by similar movements between the currencies that have now merged to form the euro. This can no longer happen.

Obviously, adopting a common currency also entails costs, the key cost being the loss of direct control of monetary policy and the exchange rate. The costs depend largely on each country's ability to enhance its adjustment capacities. Countries with slow dynamic adjustment mechanisms and responsiveness – in the wake of shocks and new developments – are at a competitive disadvantage. At least, this enhances the incentives to undertake structural reforms in goods, services and labour markets (see European Commission (2006)).

3 UNFULFILLED THREATS

Prior to the launch of the euro, a number of concerns were voiced. We consider three of them: the challenge of establishing the ECB's credibility (Section 3.1), the risk of pro-cyclical fiscal policies (Section 3.2), and the risk of asymmetric transmission through diverging real interest rates, i.e. the Walters critique (Section 3.3). These three threats matter, because the benefits listed above greatly depend on maintaining the ECB's credibility, securing fiscal discipline, and addressing over time sustained current account imbalances.

3.1 CENTRAL BANK CREDIBILITY AT BIRTH

When the ECB's strategy was designed in 1998, there was concern that the new institution would have to earn credibility the hard way and possibly very slowly. This would lead to inflation expectations that were higher than actual inflation and thus to inefficiently high real interest rates. Efforts were therefore directed at "borrowing the Deutsche Bundesbank's credibility". The main tool was monetary policy strategy, which adopted a two-pillar approach with a prominent role assigned to monetary growth. Throughout much of its first decade, the ECB also followed the Bundesbank's model of talking tough and acting pragmatically, an issue to which we return in Section 4.1. Here, we merely study the outcome. There are various measures of credibility based on expectations. Do people expect the ECB to deliver price stability? We look here at two complementary approaches.

THE ECB'S SURVEY OF PROFESSIONAL FORECASTERS
Inflation expectations can be observed directly thanks to the quarterly survey of professional forecasters (SPF). For each term since the launch of the euro, Chart 6 reports the actual inflation rate and the two-year ahead forecast. Several observations about inflation expectations may be made:

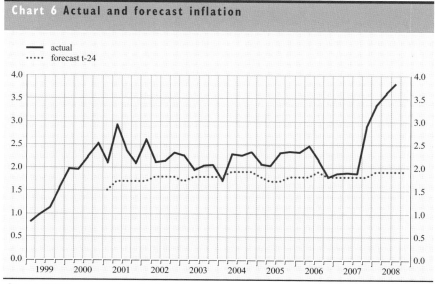

Chart 6 Actual and forecast inflation

— actual
····· forecast t-24

Source: ECB's survey of professional forecasters.
Note: The chart displays actual HICP inflation and the corresponding two-year ahead forecast collected 24 months previously.

- First, professional forecasters have systematically underestimated inflation at the two-year horizon. The same is true for all other horizons surveyed. The ECB argues that, because they are affected by shocks, expectations at the two-year horizon may be an imperfect measure of credibility. The ECB prefers to measure credibility at the five-year horizon.[9] On the other hand, a two-year horizon corresponds best to commonly accepted estimates of the lag of monetary policy effects:

- Second, until the third quarter of 2008, inflation had always been expected to be at or below 2%. This is not exactly the Eurosystem's definition of price stability of "close to, but below, 2%", but it is close enough;

- Third, inflation expectations according to this measure were very low at the outset and slowly edged upwards; and

- Fourth, these measures of credibility might also be affected by the perceived likelihood of shocks.

These observations suggest that the ECB in fact started with a very high degree of credibility. The ECB, it appears, inherited the Deutsche Bundesbank's credibility from the outset. Indeed, until mid-2008, inflation expectations were anchored at or below 2%. Quite remarkably, this happened even though inflation has almost never fallen below 2% since mid-2000. In addition, the euro initially depreciated sharply against the US dollar. Even though this was a dollar issue, many commentators saw euro depreciation as proof that "the euro wasn't working". Throughout this period of euro weakness, as further confirmed by the evolution of long-term interest rates, markets nevertheless remained confident that inflation would stay low. Credibility exists when people believe less what they see – inflation above 2%, an initially weak euro – than what they are promised. This suggests that the ECB achieved credibility at birth. Yet the SPF survey indicated that forecasters had gradually come to recognise that the ECB was facing a real challenge in meeting its own definition of price stability. We pursue this issue further in Section 4.1.

INFLATION EXPECTATIONS BASED ON CONSENSUS ECONOMICS

A different perspective is provided by international forecast surveys conducted by Consensus Economics.[10] Chart 7 compares long (6 to 10 years ahead) forecasts for inflation for the euro area, the United Kingdom and the United States from 1999 onwards. This comparison is useful, given the fact that the period from 1999 to 2007 was dominated by the Great Moderation, as discussed above, and that the euro area's inflation performance is not significantly different from that of other countries. The chart fully confirms this impression. From early 1999, inflation forecasts have been lower for the euro area than for the United Kingdom and the United States , thus supporting the view that the ECB

---

9   See the article entitled "The outcome of the ECB's evaluation of its monetary policy strategy" in the June 2003 issue of the ECB's Monthly Bulletin.

10 The SPF and Consensus Economics forecasts are generally very consistent with each other. However, the SPF offers greater detail.

Chart 7 An international comparison of inflation expectations

(6 to 10 years ahead)

- euro area
- United States
- United Kingdom

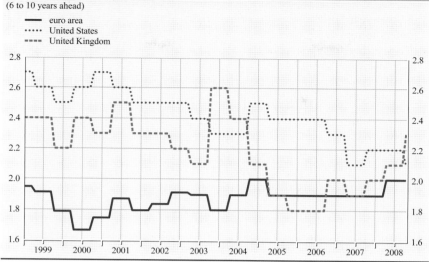

Source: Consensus Economics. Latest data October 2008.

achieved credibility at birth. The observation that forecasts converge over time (upward for the euro area and mostly downward for the United Kingdom and the United States) further amplifies the previous impression that credibility has been gradually eroded in the euro area.

3.2 NATIONAL FISCAL POLICIES

How to deal with fiscal policy has been a controversial issue from the start. Having surrendered monetary policy autonomy, euro area member states can rely only on fiscal policy for demand management. At the same time, the Maastricht Treaty has identified national fiscal policies as a matter of common concern, which has led to the adoption of the Stability and Growth Pact. Its intention is to enforce discipline, which had been lacking in several member countries in the previous decades. The precise theoretical reasons for "common concern" have long been debated (see e.g. Wyplosz (2006)). Policymakers refer only to the history of big inflations, all of which can be linked to fiscal profligacy, as the ultimate justification for the Pact, but critics note that the ECB's independence and the EU's no-bailout clause should also be taken into account.

Another reason for the Pact is that two of the criteria for admission to the euro area concern fiscal policy. The Pact can be seen as a way to avoid a post-entry relaxation of discipline. Indeed, as Chart 8 illustrates, the run-up to EMU coincided with a tight fiscal stance for most countries. Directly after the introduction of the euro, fiscal policy was loosened in some countries and, on average, in the euro area as a whole. This loosening was not justified by prevailing economic conditions. The following downturn brought a general worsening of budgetary balances, and during the 2003 to 2005 period, some

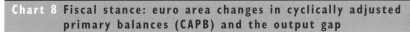

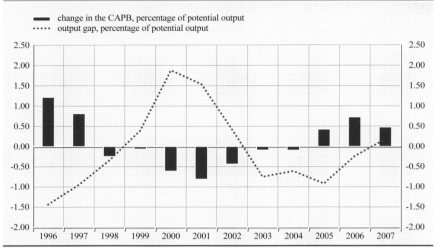

— change in the CAPB, percentage of potential output
····· output gap, percentage of potential output

Source: AMECO.

countries even ran excessive deficits. Thus, the post-entry fiscal policy relaxation can be seen both as a justification of the Stability and Growth Pact and as an indication that its effectiveness has not been established so far.

The Pact faces serious analytical issues. Its aim is to encourage fiscal discipline. Its central requirement that deficits not exceed 3% of GDP in normal circumstances runs the risk of leading to pro-cyclical policies because the Pact is likely to be binding during periods of a slowdown in growth. To deal with this undesirable property, emphasis has shifted to the preventive arm – the requirement that adjustments be pursued during the upside of the cycle – so that the Pact never binds during the downside. A stricter version would want member countries to forgo discretionary actions, relying on the automatic stabilisers to deal with cyclical fluctuations.

This issue is important because available evidence indicates that, even before the adoption of the euro, fiscal policies were often pro-cyclical in Europe. The situation has changed somewhat since then. The report European Commission (2006) provides evidence that the fiscal stance has been pro-cyclical in good times and broadly neutral in bad times. Von Hagen and Wyplosz (2008) argue that national fiscal policies have become less pro-cyclical during these ten years than they were previously.[11] This is broadly confirmed by Chart 9, which displays the euro area's overall budget balance along with the maximum and minimum national balances achieved in each year. The chart shows the powerful effect of the entry criterion in the run-up to the introduction of the euro. It confirms a relapse during the cyclical downturn in 2001-03, but even then there is no

---

11 Fatas and Mihov (2008) show instead that pro-cyclicality is found less frequently among non-euro area developed countries.

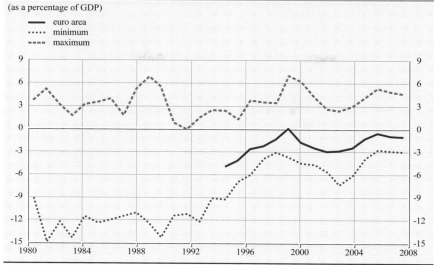

Chart 9 Budget balances in the euro area (12 countries)

(as a percentage of GDP)

——— euro area
····· minimum
---- maximum

Source: AMECO.

return to the pre-1995 levels, and the slippage was corrected as soon as cyclical conditions had improved.

On the institutional side, the Stability and Growth Pact had a rough ride. When by late 2003 the two largest countries, France and Germany, had fallen foul of the 3% limit, the excessive deficit procedure was held in abeyance for these two countries. This episode confirmed the view that the Pact was too rigid. The reform ultimately adopted in 2005 introduced some flexibility. In particular, it gave a broader definition of the exceptional circumstances under which the Pact would be suspended. The same will happen again in 2009. As a result, in practice, the Pact has never been binding. Even so, there has not been a widespread lack of discipline. If anything, Charts 8 and 9 suggest that fiscal discipline has improved.

3.3 THE WALTERS CRITIQUE

Another early concern centred on real interest rates in EMU. With a unified bond market, nominal interest rates are equalised, at least as long as all countries remain on the common currency in line with expectations. Mechanically, therefore, real interest rates are lower when inflation is higher, and are expected to remain so. This observation is encapsulated in the Walters critique that is named after Sir Richard Walter, a counsellor to Margaret Thatcher in the 1980s. The critique holds that the effects of the common monetary policy are more expansionary in countries with high inflation rates and more contractionary in countries with low ones. As a result, growing disequilibria may occur, with inflation rising where it started higher and declining where it started lower.

(percentages)

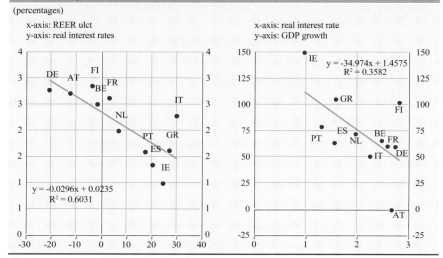

Sources: Eurostat, OECD and ECB calculations.
Note: REER stands for real effective exchange rates.

Euro area experience has clearly borne out several steps of the above reasoning. At fixed exchange rates, higher inflation translates into real appreciation, so we can use both measures interchangeably. Chart 10 plots the total change in the real exchange rate – a measure of the cumulated inflation differential[12] – against the average real interest rate in euro area member countries over the period 1999-2008. The link is quite close and is as expected. The next step in the Walters critique is that lower real interest rates generate faster growth. This too is confirmed, as Chart 10 shows.

Yet, overall, the evidence thus far shows that the key implication of the Walters critique has not materialised: as noted in Section 2.1, inflation rates have actually converged over the past decade. Some countries have long had higher or lower inflation rates than the euro area average; however, there is no evidence of the growing divergence predicted by the Walters critique. Why is this so? An interesting question is what, in the logic of the Walters critique, may be wrong. As previously noted by Angeloni and Ehrmann (2004), the most obvious answer is that international competition is overlooked.

With a fixed exchange rate, higher inflation means an appreciating exchange rate, which causes competitiveness to deteriorate and reduces demand. Thus the expansionary effect of low real interest rates stands to be compensated by the contractionary effect of an appreciating real exchange rate. Which effect dominates and, therefore, whether the process is inherently unstable, as predicted by the Walters critique, is partly an empirical issue. The evidence is that inflation

---

12 Since real effective exchange rates based on unit labour costs have been used, the correspondence is only approximate.

rates did not diverge – quite the opposite. From a theoretical viewpoint, it also seems likely that continuing real appreciation is impossible unless justified by higher productivity gains, so that ultimately the process has to be stable. We return to this issue in Section 4.

4   UNEXPECTED CHALLENGES

In this section, we look at some of the issues that emerged after the adoption of the euro but were not prominent in the analysis preceding the start of EMU. These new challenges concern the communication strategy of the ECB (Section 4.1) – central bank communication has emerged as an important issue over the past decade – as well as the emergence of large current account deficits in some member countries (Section 4.2).

4.1   COMMUNICATION [13]

We argued in Section 3.1 that measures of inflation expectations suggest that the ECB was born with inherent credibility. A more detailed analysis can be carried out using the same survey but looking at the distribution of forecasts. Geraats et al. (2008) argue that the proportion of forecasters who predict inflation at the two-year horizon to be below 2% (and still be positive) is a better measure of credibility than the average forecast of inflation depicted in Charts 6 and 7. Indeed, one can argue that the ECB is credible if it manages to convince forecasters that, irrespective of the prevailing inflation rate, it will bring inflation back in line with the definition of price stability over the policy horizon, which can be approximated by a two-year medium term.

To that effect, we turn to Chart 11, which displays the proportion of forecasters included in the SPF that expect HICP inflation to be below 2% – the ECB's definition of price stability. The chart shows that, early on, forecasters were highly confident inflation would indeed fall to within the range defined as price stability. Over the years, that confidence gradually declined as realised inflation systematically exceeded forecasts (Charts 6 and 7).

It is true that, historically, large increases in energy and commodity prices starting in early 2006 were bound to have an inflationary impact. However, unless forecasters had expected these prices to increase continuously, they would have expected the ECB to return inflation to the range desirable within five years. It is therefore impossible to avoid concluding that some difficulty has arisen.

One reason for this evolution, suggested by Geraats (2009), is that the problem lies with the ECB's communication strategy. The euro was launched at a time when the inflation targeting strategy was slowly being adopted by a number of developed and emerging economies. As explained before, the ECB chose instead to follow the Deutsche Bundesbank's two-pillar strategy, which has become

13 This section reflects only the views of Charles Wyplosz.

Chart 11 Proportion of ICP inflation forecasts between 0% and 2%

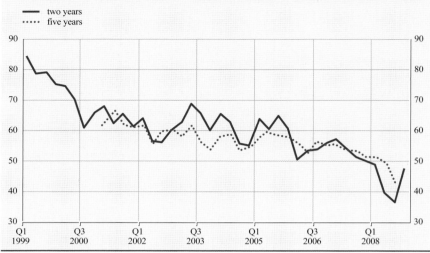

Source: ECB's survey of professional forecasters.
Notes: The chart shows the probability reported by SPF respondents of inflation being between 0% and 2% at the two-year and five-year forecast horizon. It does not refer to their point forecasts. In the latest (Q4 2008) round, 80% of respondents reported that their longer-term (five years ahead) inflation expectations were between 1.7% and 2.0%.

increasingly controversial. That strategy has been criticised repeatedly from the start (see e.g. Begg et al. (1998), Svensson (1999, 2003), Alesina et al. (2001) and Gali (2003)).

While it gradually emerged that, like the Bundesbank before it, the ECB was actually quite flexible in making policy decisions, the ECB's communication has remained firmly based on the two-pillar strategy. This is most visible in its Monthly Bulletin and in the President's monthly press conferences. The result has been the impression of a disconnect between policy decisions and their justification. The disconnect has become very visible because many other leading central banks have gradually developed a great degree of transparency in the way they prepare and explain their decisions. The evolution of the Federal Reserve System, for instance, has been quite spectacular.

In 2003 the ECB responded to its critics by conducting an in-house review summarised in a report (Issing (2003)). The result of this review was that a change in the order of presentation of the two pillars and a clarification of how they combine and are used to inform the Governing Council. Thus, the economic analysis now aims to flag short-run risks to price stability, whereas monetary analysis permits the identification of medium and long-term risks. However, this has not reduced the controversy. Continuing criticism of the ECB's strategy is presented in Gali et al. (2004) and Woodford (2007), for example, while a defence of the ECB's strategy is provided by Beck and Wieland (2007) and Sauer (2007).

Table 4 Central bank transparency rankings

	Crowe and Meade	Dincer and Eichengreen	Eijffinger and Geraats
Year	2006	2005	2002
No. of countries	28	100	9
ECB ranking	17	6	4

Sources: Crowe and Meade (2008), Dincer and Eichengreen (2007) and Eijffinger and Geraats (2006).

Although the debate on the strategy is unlikely to abate any time soon, the transparency aspects are of particular interest. One key advantage of the inflation-targeting strategy is that it lends itself naturally to a communication strategy: the inflation forecast is a summary statistic that is transparently comparable to the inflation target. While a flexible inflation-targeting strategy still leaves much freedom to the central bank, and therefore does not automatically deliver full transparency, the two-pillar strategy inevitably injects considerably more arbitrariness, which significantly complicates communication. Other leading central banks, such as the Federal Reserve System and the Bank of Japan, have not adopted an inflation-targeting strategy, but they have taken important steps to enhance transparency. For instance, both promptly release the minutes of their decision-making meetings, and the Federal Reserve System now releases many details of individual Open Market Committee members' inflation forecasts.

This may matter for credibility and therefore for policy effectiveness. A growing literature has been examining the characteristics and effects of transparency, and some international estimates have been produced. Table 4 presents the ECB's ranking in the three most recent studies. Not surprisingly, different methodologies lead to different results. The ECB's performance is good in one case and somewhat disappointing in the two other reported cases. Other findings of these studies are that the ECB's transparency has improved over the years, but that is a general trend. In some studies, the ECB has slipped a bit in the ranking.[14]

An important result of this literature is that, ceteris paribus, inflation and output variability are inversely related to central bank transparency. This helps to explain why this issue, which is related to the description of the strategy, has become important in policy debates. Another reason why this issue matters is political. As emphasised by Feldstein (1997), sharing a currency may be a source of tension among member countries. It is therefore crucially important that the ECB be perceived as a trusted institution by the population at large.

According to Eurobarometer survey results, the percentage of citizens who consider the common currency as "advantageous overall" declined from 59% in September 2002 to 48% in September 2006 (Flash Eurobarometer, November 2006). The Eurobarometer of spring 2008 shows instead that, during the surveys spanning spring 2006 and spring 2007, between 61% and 63% of

14 Blinder et al. (2008) provide extensive discussions of the limits of transparency indices.

Table 5	Percentage of citizens who consider inflation the most important issue facing their country							
Belgium	Bulgaria	Czech Rep.	Denmark	Germany	Estonia	Greece	Spain	France
48	51	38	18	44	54	33	26	51
Ireland	Italy	Cyprus	Latvia	Lithuania	Luxembourg	Hungary	Malta	Netherlands
22	44	28	71	63	43	35	40	16
Austria	Poland	Portugal	Romania	Slovenia	Slovakia	Finland	Sweden	UK
54	33	42	48	71	43	33	9	19

Source: Eurobarometer 69, June 2008.

respondents looked favourably on EMU, up from 59% to 60% in the previous three surveys. The share of respondents expressing negative opinions on monetary union declined steadily from 35% in the spring of 2003 to 31% in the most recent survey.[15]

Unsurprisingly, in 2008 37% of all respondents in the EU as a whole indicated that inflation had become the "most important issue facing the country".[16] The detailed country results shown in Table 5 indicate that percentages are high in all euro area countries except Greece, Spain, Ireland, the Netherlands and Finland. The unweighted average for the euro area is 39.7%, almost the same as that for the non-euro area member countries (40.2%). It is also interesting to note that concern for inflation was low in Sweden and the United Kingdom, two countries whose central banks are usually considered highly transparent.

Not too much should be made of these public opinion polls, but they do remind us of the widespread perception that inflation has increased since the adoption of the euro. They also suggest that the general public supports the ECB's focus on maintaining price stability, which should help it in dealing with political pressures of the kind that have repeatedly arisen since 1999. The ECB's formal independence is unassailable – it would require a new Treaty to change its status – but its room for manoeuvre could be reduced through constraints on the exchange rate or by setting up a powerful political body designed to deal with the euro area economy.

4.2 CURRENT ACCOUNT IMBALANCES

There is no reason for current accounts to balance at either the euro area level or the national level. Yet, Chart 12 documents a striking and unexpected feature of the recent experience: some national current account imbalances have become large in

15 See spring 2008 surveys in: http://ec.europa.eu/public_opinion/archives/eb/eb69/eb69_ en.htm, and http://ec.europa.eu/public_opinion/archives/eb/eb68/eb_68_en.pdf.
16 This share went up by 11% with respect to the autumn 2007 survey. Concerns about unemployment, crime and the economic situation stood at 24%, 20% and 20% respectively.

Chart 12 Current account balances

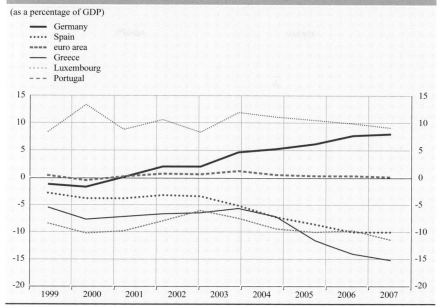

(as a percentage of GDP)

— Germany
····· Spain
■■■■ euro area
— Greece
······ Luxembourg
--- Portugal

Sources: OECD Economic Outlook.

both directions, while the euro area current account has remained nearly balanced. Does this challenge the "one size fits all" requirement for monetary policy?

Current account deficits may be benign if they correspond to productive investments. Alternatively, they may be unsustainable if they reflect excessive spending by either the private or the public sector. Market-imposed limits on extensive borrowing formerly limited the size and duration of external imbalances to the point that this was called the Feldstein-Horioka paradox. There is mounting evidence (Blanchard and Giavazzi (2003), Lane and Milesi-Feretti (2004), Caballero et al. (2008)) that the paradox is vanishing, as financial globalization makes it possible to borrow and lend internationally on a large scale. Within the euro area, the absence of any currency risk and increased financial integration imply that the new phenomenon should be even more pronounced than elsewhere. The fact that the euro area's current account has remained approximately balanced indicates that some countries lend to others, quite possibly indirectly. The question is why and, importantly, whether this is a disequilibrating or re-equilibrating mechanism. The question is reminiscent of the Walters critique. We now argue that the current account divergences are in fact an unexpected manifestation of that phenomenon.

A. CURRENT ACCOUNT IMBALANCES AND THE WALTERS CRITIQUE

We have noted that, as initially stated, the Walters critique has not been fully borne out by the facts. It remains that countries with higher inflation face a lower real interest rate, a situation that should ceteris paribus be expansionary. Chart 12 readily confirms this. The association between inflation and growth

Chart 13 The real exchange rate and the current account, 1998-2008

(in percentages)

x-axis: REER ulct
y-axis: CA ratio

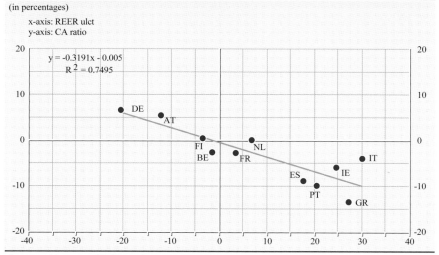

Sources: Eurostat, OECD and ECB calculations.

is quite strong, but it says nothing about causality, not even about the cause. It may well be that inflation fuelled growth via the real interest rate, but it can also be that growth fuelled inflation along the traditional Phillips curve link. Most likely, both effects reinforced each other, hence the potential source of growing divergences within the euro area.

At the same time, as noted by Angeloni and Ehrmann (2004), real exchange rate appreciation is likely to reduce demand. The strong link between the cumulated real exchange change rate change and the cumulated current account deficit-to-GDP ratio displayed in Chart 13 supports this assumption. Pressure from international competition may explain why inflation rates did not diverge.

B. AN ILLUSTRATIVE MODEL
It may be that the Walters critique has materialised in the form of current account divergences in the euro area and that this is what prevented inflation from diverging. While it may be reassuring that inflation did not converge, replacing inflation divergence with current account divergence is not particularly reassuring. To explore this issue, we look at a small illustrative model.

The Walters critique can be described as follows. Let π be the inflation rate in the EMU country of interest and let λ be the log of its real exchange rate, defined such that an increase is a real depreciation. EMU membership implies that the log of the real exchange rate is equal to $p - p^*$, where p and p^* are, respectively, the log price levels in the country and in EMU as a whole. It follows that the cumulated change in the real exchange rate is:

(1) $$\dot{\lambda} = \pi^* - \pi .$$

Thus a higher rate of inflation leads to a real appreciation.

The real interest rate is $r = i - \pi$, where i is the euro area-wide nominal interest rate. Without loss of generality, we assume that the EMU inflation rate is zero, i.e. $\pi^* = 0$. Alternatively, we define π as the inflation differential.

In line with New Keynesian models, the Walters critique assumes that the real interest rate affects demand (the IS curve) and that inflation is driven by its past value, its expected future value and by demand (the Phillips curve). Setting aside the role of expectations that lead to considerations irrelevant to the present case, we specify the Phillips curve with only a backward component. Therefore we express it as the change in the inflation rate:

$$\dot{\pi} = ay$$

where a is a parameter, y is the deviation of real demand for domestic goods from trend GDP and a dot represents the time derivative. The output gap is defined as:

$$y = d + x$$

where d is the deviation of total domestic demand from trend GDP and x represents net exports or the current account. This specification implicitly assumes that, in the long run, the current account is balanced, an important assumption.[17] Both components of demand are specified as:

(2) $$d = -b(r - \bar{r})$$

(3) $$x = x_0 t + x_1 \lambda$$

In (2), $\bar{r}$ is the neutral real interest rate. Note that we allow for time t to appear in (3), a shorthand for the Balassa-Samuelson effect. This implies that the real equilibrium exchange rate $\bar{\lambda}$, which corresponds to external equilibrium $x=0$, appreciates continuously:

(4) $$\bar{\lambda} = -\frac{x_0}{x_1} t$$

Bringing together these terms, we have:

(5) $$\dot{\pi} = -\alpha(r - \bar{r}) + \beta(\lambda - \bar{\lambda}),$$

where $\alpha = ab$ and $\beta = ax_1$.

The Walters critique is a statement about the stability of the system when the central bank sets the interest rate at a level optimal for EMU as a whole, ignoring country-specific conditions. We capture this situation by assuming that the central bank sets the nominal interest rate i at its neutral level. Assuming that the neutral real interest rate is the same in the home country and EMU, given that $\pi^* = 0$,

---

17 Removing this assumption is an interesting and challenging issue left for further work.

this means that $i = \bar{r}$ and the home country real interest rate is $r = \bar{r}$. As a result, (5) becomes:

(6)
$$\dot{\pi} = \alpha\pi + \beta(\lambda - \bar{\lambda}).$$

Together with (1), which can be rewritten as:

(1')
$$\dot{\lambda} = -\pi,$$

(6) fully describes the economy. The first term in (6) captures the Walters critique: the real interest rate in the home country is lower than in EMU, the difference being equal to the inflation differential. This term is a clear source of instability. The second term seems to be a source of stability, since (1') indicates that a positive inflation differential leads to a real appreciation, which reduces demand and inflation.

The question is therefore one of model stability. If the model is unstable, we should observe growing divergences in both inflation and the current account. In fact, the model made up of (1') and (6) is always unstable as long as $\alpha > 0$.[18] Merely recognising that competitiveness works against the Walters critique is not enough, in this model, to restore stability. We need to allow for other channels that reverse the sign of $\alpha = ab$. One possibility is to allow for FDI, driven by the real interest differential $r - \bar{r} = -\pi$. In that case, (2) is changed to:

(2')
$$d = -b(r - \bar{r}) + h(r - \bar{r}),$$

where the second term captures FDI. The system remains described by (1') and (6), with one difference: the crucial term α is now $\alpha = a(b - h)$. If the interest rate effect on consumption is dominated by the effect on foreign investment, $\alpha < 0$ and the model is stable. If the absolute value of α is small relative to β, the model is oscillatory: the home economy, and its current account, will exhibit cycles of decreasing amplitude.[19]

There are many other ways of extending the model that may make it stable. The important theoretical point is that the Walters critique is not a fatality. If the model is stable, the current account may well diverge for a while but any imbalance must eventually be corrected by the evolution of inflation and the real exchange rate. In that case the process is self-equilibrating and current account divergences are no cause for concern.

C. OTHER SOURCES OF DIVERGENCE

The model ignores other potential sources of divergence. One prominent case is the possibility of persistent and unabated excessive domestic spending. Easy

---

18 The eigenvalues of the system's determinant are $s = (\alpha \pm \sqrt{\alpha^2 - \Delta})/2$, with $\Delta = \alpha^2 - 4\beta$. When β is large, the determinant is negative and the solution is oscillatory but still unstable. In that case, the current account is alternatively negative and positive, but the amplitude grows over time (as $\exp(\alpha t/2)$).

19 If $b = h$, $\alpha = 0$, and the economy keeps oscillating between current surpluses and deficits of equal magnitude.

(as a percentage of GDP)

x-axis: CA ratio
y-axis: deficit to GDP ratio

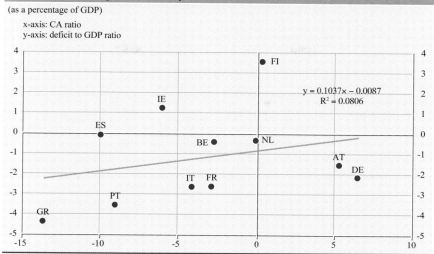

$y = 0.1037x - 0.0087$
$R^2 = 0.0806$

Sources: Budget balances: European Commission, AMECO database; current accounts: OECD Economic Outlook.

external financing, allowed by financial integration and the absence of any exchange rate risk, could make it possible for a country to sustain large current account deficits for a significant amount of time, making the eventual correction all the more painful.[20] In the absence of a nominal exchange rate adjustment, the correction would require a significant fall in demand, which could be imposed by serious financial stress.

It may be impossible to disentangle the two alternative interpretations of the current account imbalance phenomenon. Both start with excessive demand and work through inflation and current account deficits. In the Walters critique, the proximate cause of excessive demand is inherited inflation; in the alternative case, excessive demand is driven by other factors. But these factors may well be the consequence of real interest rates that are too low and that push up asset and housing prices.

The only possibly exogenous factor that is not part of the Walters critique is excessive public spending that leads to budget deficits. This is examined in Chart 14, which plots the average budget and current account balances of the first ten years for each of the 12 original members of the euro area. There is a very low positive correlation between the two variables (the correlation coefficient is just 0.10 and the explained share of the variance is minuscule). Hence, there is at least a weak link between excessive spending and current account deficits to budget deficits, and with large current account surpluses linked to large budget surpluses.

In fact, even if they move in the same direction as budget imbalances, current account imbalances are much larger. This indicates that net private savings should

20 This is reminiscent of the global imbalances resulting from excessive spending in the United States that lie at the root of the financial crisis.

be highly and positively correlated with the budget balances, as predicted by the Ricardian equivalence. Thus the evidence does not rule out the simultaneous presence of current account effects of the Walters critique.

D. THE BALASSA-SAMUELSON EFFECT

Taken together, Charts 10 in Section 3.3 establish a clear link between the real exchange rate and growth. Note that we measure GDP to calculate relative per capita growth vis-à-vis the euro area average. While we have interpreted these figures in terms of the Walters critique, an alternative interpretation is possible: the Balassa-Samuelson effect predicts that catching-up countries exhibit real appreciation.

This could be an alternative interpretation of Charts 10, but not of the growing current account divergence. In fact, the Balassa-Samuelson effect rests on the combination of real exchange rate appreciation and stable current accounts, not on the increasing current account deficits that we observe. This interpretation is contradicted by Chart 13. In addition, we note that the appreciating countries did most of their catching up prior to the adoption of the euro.

5   CONCLUDING REMARKS

The first ten years of the euro have been far better than many had hoped. The success is testimony to the institutional robustness of the ECB, which inherited the credibility of the Bundesbank and succeeded in generally displaying an adequate mixture of commitment to price stability and recognition that central banks are also concerned about general economic conditions and, more recently, financial stability.

EMU has also led to significant advances in economic and financial integration, which have provided euro area citizens and firms with important welfare and efficiency gains. The euro area now provides a more secure and stable economic and financial environment to safeguard the gains from trade integration and, as recently demonstrated, to prevent periodical financial crisis and disruptions from tearing apart member countries. Monetary integration also secures a level playing-field and permits cross-border investment, such as more M&As and significant cross-border FDI.

Interestingly, a number of initial fears have not materialised, but new issues have arisen. Some apparent, albeit modest, erosion of credibility, if confirmed, could be related to the difficulty of keeping inflation close to, but below, 2%. Concerns about the use of fiscal policies at the national level could also be relevant. However, if we look at the first ten years of the euro, we have not seen fiscal policies diverging in responses to idiosyncratic shocks, and fiscal policies have been broadly neutral. At the same time, it is impossible to determine how much of the improvement is to be assigned to the existence of the Stability and Growth Pact and how much simply to the growing recognition that fiscal discipline must be achieved after years of rising public debts.

National inflation rates have converged to a degree similar to that observed in the United States. This important result conceals a significant degree of persistence in national outcomes and could be linked to the Walters critique, meaning that national real interest rates could diverge sizeably and lead to an asymmetric transmission channel. Rather, we have not observed permanently increasing inflation differentials and have advanced the hypothesis that the Walter critique may have instead led to widening current account imbalances – in both directions – in several euro area countries, while the euro area has remained nearly balanced. Financial globalization has rendered it possible to borrow and lend internationally on a large scale: providing evidence of the vanishing of the Feldstein-Horioka paradox. Within the euro area, the absence of any currency risk and increased financial integration has rendered this new phenomenon more pronounced than elsewhere. Hence, we might be witnessing a transmutation of the Walters critique. Importantly, this is in part a self-equilibrating mechanism since real appreciation reduces demand for domestic goods, which exerts downward pressure on domestic inflation. Yet this phenomenon still needs to be better understood and would need to be addressed over time.

REFERENCES

Adjaute, K., and J.P. Danthine. 2003. "European Financial Integration and Equity Returns: A Theory Based Assessment". In *The Transformation of the European Financial System*, ed. V. Gaspar, P. Hartmann and O. Sleijpen , 185-246. Frankfurt am Main: European Central Bank.

Alesina, A., O. Blanchard, J. Gali, F. Giavazzi, and H. Uhlig. 2001. *Monitoring the European Central Bank*. Vol. 3, *Defining a Macroeconomic Framework for the Euro Area*. London: Centre for Economic Policy Research.

Allsopp, C., and D. Vines. 1998. "The Assessment: Macroeconomic Policy after EMU." *Oxford Review of Economic Policy*, 14(3):1-23.

Angeloni, I., and M. Ehrmann. 2004. "Euro Area Inflation Differentials." European Central Bank Working Paper 388.

Asdrubali, P., B. Sorensen, and O. Yosha. 1996. "Challenge of Interstate Risk Sharing: United States 1963-1990." *Quarterly Journal of Economics*, 111(4): 1081-1110.

Baele, L., A. Ferrando, P. Hördahl, E. Krylova, and C. Monnet. 2004. "Measuring Financial Integration in the Euro Area." European Central Bank Occasional Paper 14.

Baldwin, R, V. Di Nino, L. Fontagné, R.A. De Santis, and D. Taglioni. 2008. *European Economy: Economic Papers*. Vol. 321 *"Study on the Impact of the Euro on Trade and Foreign Direct Investment."* Brussels: European Commission.

Baldwin, R.G. 2006. "The euro's trade effects." European Central Bank Working Paper 594.

Baldwin, R. 2006. *In or Out: Does it Matter? An Evidence-Based Analysis of the Euro's Trade Effects*. London: Centre for Economic Policy Research.

Baldwin, R., F. Skudelny, and D. Taglioni. 2005. "Trade Effects of the Euro – Evidence from Sectoral Data." European Central Bank Working Paper 446.

Balvers, R. J., and J. H. Bergstrand. 2002. "Government Expenditure and Equilibrium Real Exchange Rates." *Journal of International Money and Finance*, 21(5): 667-692.

Begg, D., P. De Grauwe, F. Giavazzi, H. Uhlig, and C. Wyplosz. 1998. *Monitoring the European Central Bank*. Vol. 1, *The ECB: Safe at Any Speed?* London: Centre for Economic Policy Research.

Bergstrand, J.H. 1991. "Structural Determinants of Real Exchange Rates and National Price Levels: Some Empirical Evidence." *American Economic Review*, 81(1): 325-334.

Blinder, A. S., M. Ehrmann, M. Fratscher, J. De Haan, and D.J. Jansen. 2008. "Central Bank Communication and Monetary Policy: a Survey of Theory and Evidence." *Journal of Economic Literature*, 46(4): 910-45.

Bun, M., and F. Klaassen. 2007. "The Euro Effect on Trade is not as Large as Commonly Thought." *Oxford Bulletin of Economics and Statistics*, 69(4): 473-496.

Berg, J., M. Grande, and F.P. Mongelli, ed. 2005. *Elements of the euro area: integrating financial markets*. Aldershot, Hampshire, England: Ashgate Publishing Ltd.

Bertola, G. 2000. "Labor Markets in the European Union." *Ifo-Studien*, 46(1): 99-122.

Blanchard, O., and F. Giavazzi. 2003. "Macroeconomic Effects of Regulation and Deregulation in Goods and Labor Markets." *Quarterly Journal of Economics*, 118(3): 879-907.

Blanchard, O., and J. Wolfers. 2000. "The Role of Shocks and Institutions in the rise of European Unemployment: The Aggregate Evidence." *The Economic Journal*, 110(462): C1-C33.

Bayoumi, T., and P.R. Masson. 1995. "Fiscal Flows in the United States and Canada: Lessons for Monetary Union in Europe." *European Economic Review*, 39(2): 253-274.

Cappiello, L., P. Hördahl, A. Kadareja, and S. Manganelli. 2006. "The Impact of the Euro on Financial Markets." European Central Bank Working Paper 556.

Cappiello, L., R.F. Engle, and K. Shephard. 2006. "Asymmetric Dynamics in the Correlations of Global Equity and Bond Returns." *Journal of Financial Econometrics*, 4(4): 537-572.

Coeurdacier, N., R. De Santis, and A. Aviat. 2009. "Cross-Border Mergers and Acquisitions: Financial and Institutional Forces." European Central Bank Working Paper 1018.

Coeurdacier, N. and P. Martin. 2007. "The Geography of Asset Trade and the Euro: Insiders and Outsiders." Centre for Economic Policy Research Discussion Paper 6032.

Crowe, C.W., and E.E. Meade. 2008. "Central Bank Independence and Transparency: Evolution and Effectiveness." International Monetary Fund Working Paper 119.

Danthine, J. P., F. Giavazzi, L. von Thadden, and X. Vives. 1999. *Monitoring European Integration*. Vol. 9, *The Future of European Banking*. London: Centre for Economic Policy Research.

De Grauwe, P. and F.P. Mongelli. 2005. "Endogeneities of Optimum Currency Areas: What Brings Countries Sharing a Single Currency Closer Together?" European Central Bank Working Paper 468.

De Santis, R.A., and B. Gérard. 2006. "Financial Integration, International Portfolio Choice and the European Monetary Union." European Central Bank Working Paper 626.

De Santis, R.A. 2006. "The Geography of International Portfolio Flows, International CAPM and the Role of Monetary Policy Frameworks." European Central Bank Working Paper 678.

De Sousa, J., and J. Lochard. 2009. "Does the Single Currency Affect Foreign Direct Investment? A Gravity-Like Approach." University of Paris 1. http://jdesousa.univ.free.fr/recherche/travaux/deSousa_Lochard_FDI_jan09.pdf

Decressin, J., H. Fauqee and W. Fonteyne, ed. 2007. *Integrating Europe's Financial Markets*. Washington D.C.: International Monetary Fund.

Di Mauro, F., and R. Anderton, ed. 2007. *The External Dimension of the Euro Area: Assessing the Linkages*. New York: Cambridge University Press.

Dincer, N., and B. Eichengreen. 2007. "Central Bank Transparency: Where, Why, and with What Effects?" National Bureau of Economic Research Working Paper 13003.

Dornbusch, R. 1980. *Open Economy Macroeconomics*. New York: Basic Books.

Duval, R., and J. Elmeskov. 2006. "The Efects of EMU on Structural Reforms in Labour and Product Markets." European Central Bank Working Paper 596.

Eijffinger, S.C.W., and P.M. Geraats. 2006. "How Transparent Are Central Banks?" *European Journal of Political Economy*, 22(1): 1-21.

Emerson, M., D. Gros, A. Italianer, J. Pisani-Ferry, and H. Reichenbach. 1992. *One Market, One Money: An Evaluation of the Potential Benefits and Costs of Forming an Economic and Monetary Union*. New York: Oxford University Press.

Engel, C., and J.H. Rogers. 1996. "How Wide is the Border?" *American Economic Review*, 86(5): 1112–1125.

Engel, C., and J. Rogers. 2004. "European Product Market Integration After the Euro." *Economic Policy*, 39(19): 347-384.

European Central Bank. 2005 "Monetary Policy and Inflation Differentials in a Heterogeneous Currency Area." *Monthly Bulletin*, 7(5): 61-78.

European Central Bank. 2005. *Review of the International Role of the Euro.* Vol. 4. Frankfurt am Main, Germany: European Central Bank.

European Central Bank. 2007. "Output Growth Differentials in the Euro Area: Sources and Implications." *Monthly Bulletin*, 9(4): 73-86.

European Central Bank. 2007. *Financial Integration in Europe.* Vol. 1. Frankfurt am Main, Germany: European Central Bank.

European Central Bank. 2008. "Globalisation, Trade and the Euro Area Macroeconomy." *Monthly Bulletin*, 10(1): 75-88.

European Central Bank. 2008. "European Central Bank – The First Ten Years." *Special Edition of the Monthly Bulletin*, 10(5): 1-158.

European Commission. 1990. European Economy. Vol. 44, *One market, One money. An evaluation of the Potential Benefits and Costs of Forming an Economic and Monetary Union.* Luxembourg: Office for Official Publications of the European Commission.

European Commission. 2004. *European Economy Special Report.* Vol. 1, *EMU after five years.* Brussels: Office for Official Publications of the European Commission.

European Commission. 2006. European Economy. Vol. 6, *The EU Economy 2006 Review: Adjustment Dynamics in the Euro area, Experiences and Challenges.* Luxembourg: Office for Official Publications of the European Commission.

European Commission. 2008. *European Economy.* Vol. 2, *EMU@10: Successes and Challenges after 10 Years of Economic and Monetary Union.* Brussels: The European Commission.

Fatás, A., and I. Mihov. 2001. "Fiscal Policy and Business Cycles: An Empirical Investigation." *Monéda y Credito*, 212:167-212.

Feldstein, M. 1997. "The Political Economy of the European Economic and Monetary Union: Political Sources of an Economic Liability." *Journal of Economic Perspectives*, 11(4): 23-42.

Ferreira, A.L., and M.A. Leon-Ledesma. 2007. "Does the Real Interest Rate Parity Hold? Evidence for Developed and Emerging Markets." *Journal of International Money and Finance*, 26(3): 364-382.

Fischer, B., M. Lenza, H. Pill, and L. Reichlin. 2006. "Money and Monetary Policy: The ECB Experience 1999-2006."http://www.ecb.int/events/pdf/conferences/cbc4/ReichlinPillLenzaFisher.pdf.

Flam, H., and H. Nordström. 2007. "The Euro and Single Market Impact on Trade and FDI", Institute for International Economic Studies, Stockholm University. http://www-2.iies.su.se/~flamh/EuroeffectsontradeandFDI.pdf

Gali, J. 2003. "Monetary Policy in the Early Years of EMU". In *EMU and Economic Policy in Europe: Challenges of the Early Years*, ed. M. Buti and A. Sapir. Northampton, MA: Edward Elgar Publishing.

Gali, J., and R. Perotti. 2003. "Fiscal Policy and Monetary Integration in Europe." *Economic Policy*, 18(37): 533-572.

Gali, J., S. Gerlach, J. Rotenberg, H. Uhlog, and M. Wooford. 2004. *Monitoring the European Central Bank*. Vol. 5, *The Monetary Policy Strategy of the ECB Reconsidered*. London: Centre for Economic Policy Research.

Geraats, P. 2009. "Trends in Monetary Policy Transparency." University of Cambridge. http://www.econ.cam.ac.uk/faculty/geraats/tptrends.pdf

Geraats, P. M., F. Giavazzi and C. Wyplosz. 2008. *Monitoring the European Central Bank*. Vol. 6, *Transparency and Governance*. London: Centre for Economic Policy Research.

Gérard, M. 2006. "Reforming the Taxation of Multijurisdictional Enterprises in Europe, a Tentative Appraisal. " Centre for Economic Studies and Ifo Institute for Economic Research 1795.

Giannone, D., M. Lenza, and L. Reichlin. 2008. "Explaining the Great Moderation: It Is Not the Shocks." European Central Bank Working Paper 865.

Giannone, D., and L. Reichlin. 2006. "Trends and Cycles in the Euro Area: How Much Heterogeneity and Should We Worry about It?" European Central Bank Working Paper 595.

Ishiyama, I. 1975. "The Theory of Optimum Currency Areas: A Survey. " *International Monetary Fund Staff Papers*, 22: 344-383.

Issing, O. 2003. "Overview of the Background Studies for the Reflections on the ECB's Monetary Policy Strategy." In *Background Studies for the Reflections on the ECB's Monetary Policy Strategy*, 2-31. Frankfurt am Main, Germany: European Central Bank.

Kalemli-Ozcan, S., B. E. Sørensen, and O. Yosha. 2003. "Economic Integration, Industrial Specialization, and the Asymmetry of Macroeconomic Fluctuations." *Journal of International Economics*, 55(1): 107-137.

Maes, I. 2007. *Half a Century of European Financial Integration: From the Rome Treaties to the 21st Century*. Brussels: Mercatorfonds.

Manganelli, S., and G. Wolswijk. 2006. "Market Discipline, Financial Integration and Fiscal Rules: What Drives Spreads in the Euro Area Government Bond Market?" European Central Bank Working Paper 745.

Melitz, J. 2004. "Risk Sharing and EMU." *Journal of Common Market Studies*, 42(4): 815-840.

Micco, A., E. Stein, and G. Ordoñez. 2003. "The Currency Union Effect on Trade: Early Evidence from EMU." *Economic Policy*, 18(37): 315–356.

Mongelli, F.P. 2005. "What Is European Economic and Monetary Union (EMU) Telling us about the Optimum Currency Area Properties?" *Journal of Common Market Studies*, 43(3): 607-635.

Mongelli, F.P. 2008. "European Economic and Monetary Integration, and the Optimum Currency Area Theory." DG ECFIN European Economy Economic Paper 302.

Mongelli, F.P., E. Dorrucci, and I. Agur. 2007. "What Does European Institutional Integration Tell Us about Trade Integration?" *Integration and Trade*, 11(26): 151-200.

Organisation for Economic Co-operation and Development. 2005. *Economic Policy Reforms*. Vol. 1, *Going for Growth*. Paris: OECD.

Ottaviano, G., D. Taglioni, and F. Di Mauro. 2007. "Deeper, Wider and More Competitive? Monetary Integration, Eastern Enlargement and Competitiveness in the European Union." European Central Bank Working Paper 847.

Paredes, J., and J.J. Pérez. 2008. "A Quarterly Fiscal Database for the Euro Area (1970-2007), Based on Intra-Annual Fiscal Information." European Central Bank and Bank of Spain. Unpublished.

Pedregal, D.J., and J.J. Pérez. 2008. "Should quarterly government finance statistics be used for fiscal surveillance in Europe?" European Central Bank Working Paper 937.

Pesaran, M.H., S. Yongcheol, and R.P. Smith. 1999. "Pooled Mean Group Estimation of Dynamic Heterogeneous Panels." *Journal of the American Statistical Association*, 94(446): 621-634.

Petroulas, P. 2007. "The Effect of the Euro on Foreign Direct Investment." *European Economic Review*, 51(6): 1468-1491.

Pisani-Ferry, J., P. Aghion, A. Ahearne, M. Belka, J. von Hagen, L. Heikensten, and A. Sapir. 2008. *Coming of Age: Report on the euro area*. Vol. 4. Brussels: Bruegel Blueprint Series.

Rose, A. 2000. "One money, One Market: the Effect of Common Currencies on Trade." *Economic Policy*, 15(30): 7-46.

Rose, A. 2004. "A Meta-Analysis of the Effects of Common Currencies on International Trade." National Bureau of Economic Research Working Paper 10373.

Rose, A., and E. van Wincoop. 2001. "National Money as a Barrier to International Trade, The Real Case for Currency Union." *American Economic Review*, 91(2): 386-390.

Nouriel, R., E. Parisi-Capone, and C. Menegatti. 2007. "Growth Differentials in the EMU: Facts and considerations." http://www.aei-ecsa.de/dokumente/ tagung_eurozone_roubini.pdf

Sachs, J., and X. Sala-i-Martin. 1991. "Fiscal Federalism and Optimum Currency Areas: Evidence for Europe from the United States." National Bureau of Economic Research Working Paper 3855.

Saint-Paul, G., and S. Bentolila. 2000. "Will EMU Increase Eurosclerosis?" Centre for Economic Policy Research Discussion Paper 2423.

Sauer, S. 2007. "Discretion Rather than Rules? When is Discretionary Policy-Making Better than the Timeless Perspective?" European Central Bank Working Paper 717.

Schiavo, S. 2007. "Common Currencies and Foreign Direct Investment Flows." *Oxford Economic Papers*, 59(3): 536-560.

Smets, F. 2008. "Monetary Policy in the Euro area: A Comment on Geraats and Neumann." Unpublished.

Svensson, L.E.O. 1999. "Monetary Policy Issues for the Eurosystem." *Carnegie-Rochester Conference Series on Public Policy*, 51(1): 79-136.

Svensson, L.E.O. 2003. "How Should the Eurosystem Reform Its Monetary Strategy?" Briefing Note. Brussels: European Parliament.

Sørensen, B.E., and O. Yosha. 2000. "Is Risk Sharing in the United States a Regional Phenomenon?", *Federal Reserve Bank of Kansas City Economic Review*, 85:33-47.

Van der Cruijsen, C., and M. Demertzis. 2007. "The Impact of Central Bank Transparency on Inflation Expectations." *European Journal of Political Economy*, 23(1): 51-66.

Von Hagen, J., and C. Wyplosz. 2008. "EMU's Decentralized System of Fiscal Policy." European Commission's European Economy Economic Paper 306.

Woodford, M. 2007. "Does a 'Two-Pillar Phillips Curve' Justify a Two-Pillar Monetary Policy Strategy?" Centre for Economic Policy Research Discussion Paper 6447.

Wyplosz, C. 2006. "European Monetary Union: the Dark Sides of a Major Success." *Economic Policy*, 46(46): 207-261.

COMMENT

BY FRANCESCO CASELLI, LONDON SCHOOL OF ECONOMICS

This very interesting paper presents a rich, indeed almost encyclopedic, overview of the many issues emerging from the first ten years of the adventure called EMU. I will not try to offer a blow-by-blow response to all the points made in the paper, particularly because I agree with much of what the authors say. Instead, I will focus my remarks on two main themes, where my perspective diverges somewhat from the one set out by the authors. Before I do that, however, I want to reiterate my admiration for the authors for the rich canvas of data and observations they have mobilized to give us as complete a picture of the economic evolution of the Euro area in the last ten years as I know of.

The two themes I will focus my remarks on are interrelated. The first is the question of success. Mongelli and Wyplosz are clear enthusiasts, and the overall message of the paper, in tone if not in substance, is that the Euro has been a great success. In my comments I will begin by arguing that this assessment is likely to depend on how we define success. Furthermore, if one measures success in terms of improvement in welfare-relevant measures relative to likely outcomes had EMU not happened – which I argue to be the most reasonable definition of success – it is very hard to qualify EMU as a success.

The second theme I want to revisit is the theme of surprise. Mongelli and Wyplosz stress many aspects of the *economic* experience with EMU that have been surprising. While I agree that some of the specific points they make are valid, I also think it is important to recognize that overall things have gone roughly the way most economists would have predicted ten years ago. In particular, I believe that a "representative economist" would have predicted EMU to be a fairly minor economic event, with some small microeconomic benefits roughly balanced out by some equally small macroeconomic costs. On average, I think one can argue that this is roughly what has happened. On the other hand, I do believe there have been very surprising *political* developments. In particular, the process of European political unification has stalled. In my concluding paragraphs I will advance the conjecture that EMU may unwittingly have contributed to the creation of a political climate inimical to political union.

I   IS EMU A SUCCESS?

It is very easy to argue that EMU (or for that matter any policy) has been a huge success. All one has to do is to choose a very undemanding definition of success. If all one asks of EMU is not to have been a disaster, then EMU was a rousing success: inflation has been stable, interest rates have been low, countries have not run wildly pro-cyclical fiscal policies out of fear of running foul of the stability and growth path (though that may have something to do with the intrinsic lack of credibility of the pact, which may be an issue for EMU enthusiasts), and more generally the macroeconomic environment has been fairly stable. Not even the most rabid critic can argue that the EMU has been a disaster.

However, we can't possibly be content with setting the bar for success so low. After all, we would never have embarked upon the EMU adventure had the economic case for it been that the outcome was unlikely to be disastrous. Rather, a clear case was made that EMU would be *welfare improving*. What that meant was that living standards in the EMU would increase more under EMU over the subsequent ten years, than they would without EMU. And indeed that was the only basis on which an *economic* argument for EMU could have been made. By the same token, the correct way to think about success is to ask whether we are better off than we would have been without EMU.

Unfortunately, confidently assessing success by this more demanding criterion is exceedingly difficult – which, incidentally, may explain why so often we give into the temptation of using less demanding, but easier to measure, yardsticks. Obviously we will never know what would have happened in the EMU area had EMU not happened, so we can't make the comparison that we really want to make. The best we can do is to compare the experience of EMU members with the experience of non-EMU members, i.e. to use the non-EMU members as "stand ins" for EMU members under the alternative scenario in which EMU did not happen. Clearly such an exercise is fully convincing only if EMU participation is the only systematic source of difference in outcomes between EMU and non-EMU countries. Since there is no reason to believe this to be the case, and plenty of scope for arguing that the opposite is likely to be true, it is fair to say that the extent to which EMU was a success or a failure will always be a matter of speculation.[1] With that very important caveat firmly in mind, let me indulge in some speculation.

An important preliminary question is what the outcomes are by which we should judge EMU. There is a thriving literature trying to assess the effects of the euro on a number of economic outcomes that are thought to be important: bilateral trade, capital flows, interest rates, etc. Ultimately, though, we care about these things not in their own right, but because we expect them to affect our overall level of welfare. EMU should thus be evaluated for its ability to lift *welfare-relevant* indicators.

The most obvious choice of welfare-relevant indicator is *GDP per capita*. An economy's output of good and services per person remains, despite all the appropriate caveats, the best available proxy for its capacity to satisfy human wants. In Chart 1 I plotted EMU GDP per capita as well as GDP per capita in

---

1 Of course a partial solution to the problem discussed above is to try to control for as many other determinants of country performance as possible. Indeed, there is a growing literature of multi-variable regressions of various outcomes on an EMU dummy and controls. The solution is only partial, however, because some of the determinants of differences in outcomes may be unmeasurable, and therefore omitted by definition from the list of controls. Furthermore, the multivariable-regression approach brings its own problems, particularly if some of the control variables are themselves endogenous.

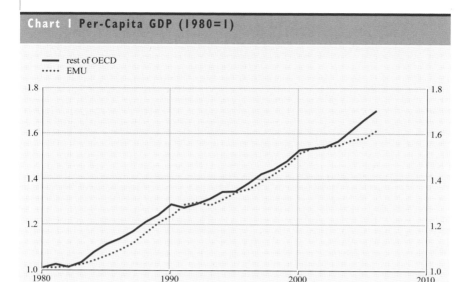

Chart I Per-Capita GDP (1980=1)

— rest of OECD
····· EMU

the rest of the OECD against time. I am choosing the rest of the OECD as my control group because it is a natural subset of countries that are "similar" to the countries that formed EMU, so I suspect it is the group whose experience is most likely to be informative about what would have happened to the Emu countries without EMU. By GDP per capita I literally mean the aggregate GDP of the EMU (non-EMU) countries divided by their aggregate population (in other words I am weighting national GDPs by population). To facilitate comparison, I have normalized both GDPs in 1980 to 1 – in other words I am comparing growth experiences. The source for the data in this and all subsequent Charts is the OECD database.

Chart 1 shows that in the 1980s and 1990s the growth performance of OECD countries that would later go on to form EMU was essentially undistinguishable from the growth performance of the rest of the OECD. In other words, so-called "pre-trends" are similar, and this to some (admittedly very limited) extent is good news for the validity of the rest of the OECD as a control group for EMU. After EMU, a gap opens up in favor of the Rest of the OECD. As I already emphasized before, there are likely other factors driving the relatively poorer performance of the EMU area in the EMU era. What is certain is that the *prima facie* evidence is hardly supportive of a beneficial role of EMU in fostering improved living standards in the countries that adopted the euro.

When thinking about welfare, economists do not only focus on average levels, but also on *volatility*. In particular, one could argue that policies that lead to more stable consumption patterns are welfare improving even if they do not imply a higher average consumption level. This is because consumers are deemed to prefer a smooth pattern of consumption over a volatile one. Accordingly, in Chart 2 I plot a measure of consumption volatility inside and outside EMU. Specifically, for each country I first compute a rolling standard deviation of the

CASELLI

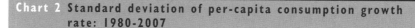

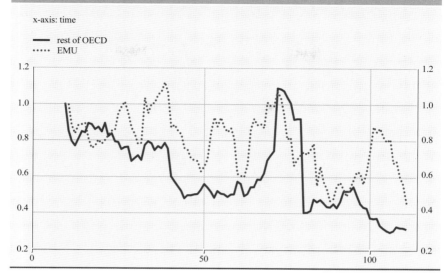

Chart 2 Standard deviation of per-capita consumption growth rate: 1980-2007

x-axis: time

— rest of OECD
····· EMU

per-capita consumption growth rate, using quarterly data and a two-year window. I then take the period average of the standard deviations across the countries inside and outside EMU.

Chart 2 indicates that both EMU and non-EMU countries have experienced a substantial decline in macroeconomic volatility since the 1970s. There is of course nothing new in this finding: this is the era of the Great Moderation – a topic I return to briefly below. Overall, however, the trend towards lower volatility seems somewhat more marked outside than inside EMU. Also after EMU (quarter 76) volatility seems to have fallen a bit more outside EMU. The Chart makes it even harder than before to hazard any statements on causality, particularly because pre-trend seem to differ in this case. But at a minimum it does not encourage us to conjecture that EMU reduced macro volatility relative to what would have been the case without EMU.

While many economists assume that inflation affects welfare indirectly, some economists attach welfare significance to the inflation rate *per se*. Without taking a stand on this issue, in Chart 3 I plot the average inflation rate in my "treatment" and "control" group. Clearly by a naïve standard the rest of the OECD did better since EMU, as it experienced declining inflation while the EMU area did not, and by the end of the sample period the inflation rate was the same inside and out. But this would be too unfair to EMU: the pre-trends are very different, and in particular by the beginning of EMU monetary policy in the euro area was already so good that inflation had nowhere lower to fall. In this respect, EMU represents a curious example of wholesale removal of power from a set of institutions (the national central banks) that had been doing a remarkably good job – and may

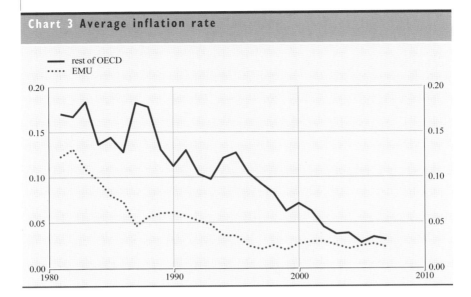

Chart 3 Average inflation rate

rest of OECD
EMU

well have continued to do so had they been allowed to continue, as the experience of the non-EMU countries suggest.

In sum, a very simple comparisons of the experiences of the EMU area and the Rest of the OECD is not consistent with the view that EMU has brought its citizens higher or more stable living standards than they would have enjoyed had EMU not been introduced. If anything, the *prima facie* evidence points in the opposite direction. But perhaps the best way to think about the evidence in Charts 1-3 is the following. Given the similarity of performance between EMU and the control group under EMU, *arguing that the EMU has brought welfare gains means arguing that EMU countries would have severely under-performed the rest of the OECD had EMU not been introduced.* It is very hard for me to think of compelling reasons why that would have been true.

2   HOW SURPRISING HAVE THE LAST 10 YEARS BEEN?

Mongelli and Wyplosz focus on a number of economic developments since EMU that have been somewhat surprising. Without dissenting from their analysis of these issues, I would argue that the overall *economic* picture has been remarkably unsurprising.

Asked in the late 1990s to list pros and cons of joining EMU I suspect most economists would have come up with very similar lists, as well as similar assessments of their magnitudes. On the positive side of the list he/she would have listed some gains from lower transaction costs on existing trade (small positive), some increase in within-EMU trade (small positive), some efficiency gain from greater transparence in price differences (very small positive), some efficiency gain from greater capital mobility (small positive), some increased seigniorage, as acquisition of world reserve status may more than compensate for loss of seigniorage at national level (small positive). On the negative side there would of course have been the inability of conducting monetary policies appropriate to each country's needs. It is probably fair to say that opinions would have differed more substantially among economists about the magnitude of this cost, ranging from small to sizable, than about the benefits of the items in the "pros" list. But my very rough guess is that on balance most economists would have been inclined to think that, by and large, cost and benefits would cancel each other out, resulting in either a small net benefit, or a small net cost.[2]

For reasons we already discussed, it is very difficult to say whether the various specific predictions on costs and benefits were accurate, but I don't think there is anything in the data, or in casual observation, that would lead us to conclude in the negative. Furthermore, the coarse exercises I have presented in the previous section are clearly in keeping with what I described as the representative ex-ante view of the net overall effect: whether positive or negative, it was likely quite small, as expected. In sum, in terms of economics, the last 10 years have not been surprising at all.

One important qualification to this conclusion is that 10 years may not be long enough for the effects of the euro, whether positive or negative, to fully reveal themselves. On the positive side, one could potentially argue that some of the microeconomic gains come from gradual investments and structural changes that take a long time to come to fruition. For example, the point has been made that we have not yet seen the full effect of the Euro on trade. While this is possible, I suspect that, if there are surprises lurking in the future, they are more likely to be on the cost side of the ledger.

The main concern is that the last 10 years have been characterized, as already noted, by an unprecedented climate of macroeconomic stability. Thanks to the Great Moderation, virtually any monetary arrangement would have worked well for EMU countries. In this sense the ECB has been very lucky: it got 10 years of very calm waters to learn the ropes. But this also means that EMU is still somewhat untested. In particular, we still don't know how the system will cope with big asymmetric shocks, or even from a sequence of large aggregate shocks – particularly in the face of mounting political pressures from national governments. In this sense, we may end up learning more about the costs and benefits of EMU in the next 10 months than we did in the last 10 years.

While, subject to the caveat above, the economic effects of EMU have been rather unsurprising, one could potentially argue that the euro has had some surprising, and unintended, *political* consequences. The starting point for this argument is to acknowledge that, in fact, the main point of the euro was never

2   Mongelli and Wyplosz tend to give the impression that the balance of opinion in the economic profession was much more negative than this. But my impression is that they are over-sampling from the tail of the distribution. It also goes without saying that I am not only averaging across economists, but also across countries: any economist worth her salt knows that these costs and benefits will vary, sometimes dramatically, depending on a country's circumstances.

economic. The main reason why we have EMU is that it was a central element in the strategy, long pursued by certain European governments largely with the cooperation of the European Commission, to bring about political unification by stealth. In this strategy, economic unification would create the momentum to bring about political unification, and European economic institutions would form the blueprint for the future political institutions of the United States of Europe.

The "unification by stealth" project seemed hard to stop or reverse in the late 1990s. In my view the big surprise of the last ten years has been that, contrary to expectation, the process has stalled. There have undoubtedly been many reasons for the unification process to hit the rocks. For example, enlargement diluted the political weight of some of the countries at the core of the unification drive (while at the same time making these countries less keen on unification). But the difficulties encountered by the various treaties and constitutions that European leaders have submitted to their citizens' approval stem, at least in some part, from popular disillusion with things European.

As Mongelli and Wyplosz point out, the euro has suffered a substantial decline in popularity over its lifetime. As anyone who has regular conversations with individuals who are not particularly literate in economics knows, part of this loss in popularity comes from the fact that many in the general population suspect the euro of being responsible for the fairly lackluster rates of economic growth experienced by many EMU countries in the last few years (see Chart 1). This view is, of course, probably unfair: as my discussion in the previous section suggests, while we can't credit the euro for lifting living standards (relative to the no-euro alternative), we also probably can't blame it for the slow growth of the last several years. Fair or unfair, however, it is out there, and it shapes political orientations.[3]

If (some) voters blame the euro for slow growth in their country, it will not take them a huge leap to extend their dislike to other European institutions and policies. Disappointment with the euro may therefore feed into political opposition to further steps towards European integration, including, if not primarily, political unification. Since the euro was actually originally introduced to facilitate that project, this would be a textbook example of the law of unintended consequences.

CONCLUSION

It is nearly impossible to say with any high degree of confidence whether the euro has been a success or a failure, when success and failure are sensibly defined. But

---

3   Mongelli and Wyplosz suggest a different explanation for the decline in popularity of the euro. They hint that it has to do with the ECB's lack of transparency. There are many arguments in favor of greater ECB transparency that one could very plausibly, indeed conclusively, make, but this is not one of them. It is very far fetched that the publication of ECB minutes would make the Euro popular. As mentioned, it is much more likely that consumers are responding to the lack of tangible benefits from Euro adoption (particularly in the face of inflated pre-Euro hype) and to national politicians' encouragement to blame the ECB (which would likely become even easier to do with transparency).

it is possible to make a fairly plausible educated guess that, if it was a success, it was a small success, and if it was a failure, the failure was also small. In other words, the most plausible thing one can say is that it has had very little impact on the welfare of EMU-area citizens. This is exactly as one should have expected. There were no compelling reasons ex-ante to expect EMU to have a large net impact on living standards, so we should not be surprised that we detect little effect ex-post.

What has been surprising is that political unification in Europe has stalled. Even more startling, given that EMU was expected to have exactly the opposite effect, is that one can potentially build an argument that EMU has contributed to slowing down the unification drive.

COMMENT

BY VÍTOR CONSTÂNCIO, GOVERNOR OF BANCO DE PORTUGAL

The euro area is a milestone in the realm of monetary economics. A decade past, it is a pleasure to take an evaluative look back at our experience of sharing a single currency. The paper by Mongelli and Wyplosz is a good starting point to spark this reflection and discussion.

I would like to start with a note of caution. Any evaluation of the impact of monetary unification has to tackle the overriding issue of the absence of a consensual counterfactual. The problem here is that the equilibrium outcomes that we observe in the data result from the combination of the myriad of shocks, structures and policies in the euro area, and only a subset of these are directly or indirectly related to the introduction of the euro. The absence of such a counterfactual poses serious challenges in any assessment of the role of the euro area in driving the data.

Nonetheless, there are several transmission channels and adjustment mechanisms in the context of EMU that can be well identified and that are broadly discussed by Mongelli and Wyplosz. The authors are particularly careful in surveying the literature and cautious in drawing conclusions, even though some of the instruments used seem not robust and are ultimately unconvincing (most prominently the bivariate relations presented in Charts 13 and 20). With this in mind, I would subscribe to most of them. In particular it seems important to underline three of those conclusions. First, a commonly encountered misperception in popular circles states that there is a high level of heterogeneity among euro area countries. However, in reality, the degree of dispersion of GDP growth, output gaps and inflation among euro area countries has been broadly stable in the last decade, and at levels that are relatively low by historical standards (see Charts 1, 2 and 3 below and Chart 1

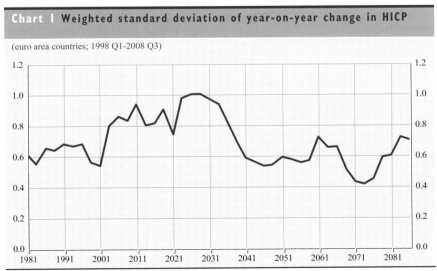

Chart I Weighted standard deviation of year-on-year change in HICP

(euro area countries; 1998 Q1-2008 Q3)

Sources: Eurostat and Banco de Portugal.

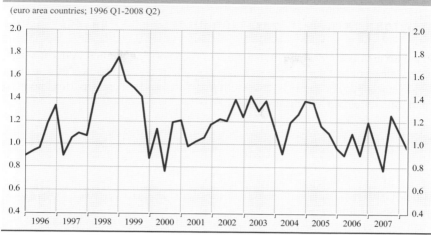

Chart 2 Weighted standard deviation of year-on-year change in GDP

(euro area countries; 1996 Q1-2008 Q2)

Sources: Eurostat and Banco de Portugal.

in Mongelli and Wyplosz's paper). Second, the conduct of fiscal policy in a monetary union is very important. This can be illustrated by the role played by the Stability and Growth Pact (in particular in its recently revised form) in setting the right incentives aimed at fiscal sustainability. This medium to long run goal is particularly pertinent in the current context of financial crisis. The third conclusion of the authors worth highlighting is that adjustment mechanisms work in the euro area. This is particularly the case of the equilibrating mechanism through external competitiveness (which the authors inaccurately link to Hume's description of the stability of a metallic system through monetary flows) as well as the supposedly destabilising effect of real interest rate movements (which the authors dub "Walters Critique").

Chart 3 Weighted standard deviation of the business cycle in euro area countries

(percentage points)

Source: AMECO; HP filter with lambda=30.

In the remainder of this discussion, I would like to build on the authors' analysis and evaluate the euro area experience through the lens of the Portuguese economy. The Portuguese adjustment experience is particularly interesting given that many of the incentive structures and adjustment mechanisms underlying the functioning of a monetary union can be vividly observed since 1995. In fact, the behaviour of the Portuguese economy in the past decade can be described as a story of adjustment to the new rules of the game in a monetary union.

To start with, it is useful to distinguish between the transition of the economy to the new monetary regime and the subsequent adjustment of the economy within the rules and incentives established in the euro area. I will deal with each in turn.

THE TRANSITION TO THE EURO AREA

The introduction of the euro represented a true regime change in Portugal (see Mongelli and Vega (2006) and Fagan and Gaspar (2007)). As in other converging countries, the transition to a regime of low and stable inflation and interest rates, without exchange rate risk and with easier access to external financing by domestic agents, led in equilibrium to a boom in consumption and investment (see Charts 4 and 5), a decline in the private sector's savings rate and an appreciation of the real exchange rate. The indebtedness of the private sector also increased significantly, in line with the new regime of permanently lower and more stable interest rates.

In normal circumstances, this boom phase would be followed by a gradual deceleration towards the new steady state growth path (arguably slightly higher than the one prevailing before the monetary unification), as agents adapted to the new solvency conditions resulting from their intertemporal budget constraints.

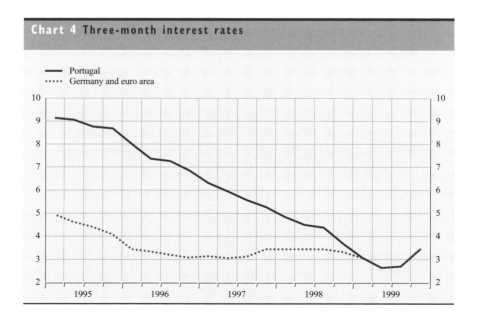

Chart 4 Three-month interest rates

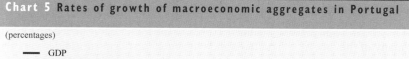

Chart 5 Rates of growth of macroeconomic aggregates in Portugal

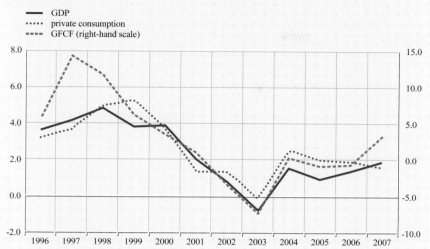

(percentages)

— GDP
••••• private consumption
==== GFCF (right-hand scale)

However, in the Portuguese case, the transition to the euro area was followed, at the beginning of the 00s, by a sharp adjustment to a protracted period of very low growth. It should be noted that given the brevity of the boom, and in contrast to other euro area economies, no house price bubble emerged in the property market.

This sharp deceleration of the economy was related, as usual, to the interplay between the shocks – of differing persistence – hitting the economy, the structural characteristics influencing the incentives of the agents and the set of policies followed during this period. Four of these elements are worth highlighting. First, the early 2000s decade were characterised by a deceleration of the Portuguese main trading partners and significant oil price shocks, which had a sizeable impact on the Portuguese economy. Second, the prospects of monetary unification triggered a rational intertemporal response of bringing forward consumption and investment decisions, also magnified by enhanced growth expectations; the subsequent sharp revision of these expectations led to a related revision of investment decisions (see Christiano et al. (2008) for a description of the main mechanisms). Fiscal policy also contributed to a reversal of these expectations. Third, the Portuguese economy did not seize up fully the global technological improvements observed since the 90s, given its relatively low level of human capital. Finally, the intensification of the globalization process led to significant changes in the revealed comparative advantage of the Portuguese economy, with the increasing participation in world trade of countries with relatively similar specialization patterns compared to the Portuguese economy but much lower unit labour costs. The transition to these new comparative advantages was also hampered by the existence of several rigidity factors in the economy. These four factors are good illustrations of the difficulty in singling out the role of the introduction of the euro to explain the behaviour of the observed macroeconomic data in any country of the monetary union (other structural developments, namely the increased worldwide financial integration could also be mentioned in this respect).

THE ADJUSTMENT IN THE EURO AREA

Despite the identification issues mentioned in the previous section, I will now contend that shortly after the introduction of the euro the Portuguese economy started an adjustment process, fostered *inter alia* by the incentives set in place by the "rules of the game" in the monetary union and by the structure of the Portuguese economy. I will focus on four elements: the role of fiscal policy, the real interest rate channel, the competitiveness channel and the role of risk-sharing.

During the run-up to the euro area and until 2005, fiscal policy in Portugal was mostly procyclical and characterized by an unsustainable increase in primary expenditure (including in the pension system) and by successive revisions in budgetary plans and targets (see Charts 6 and 7). This behaviour of the fiscal authorities (i) exacerbated growth expectations in the late 90s and contributed to the sharp reversion of expectations in the early 00s; (ii) increased the uncertainty surrounding the decisions of economic agents – namely given the uncertainty concerning the measures that would be implemented to correct the fiscal imbalance – and thus failed to deliver a macroeconomic stability framework that would enhance intertemporal investment decisions; (iii) delayed the decisions towards ensuring a sustainable fiscal framework in the long-run. This Portuguese experience underlines the importance of attaining a sustainable fiscal position before joining the monetary union and maintaining it afterwards.

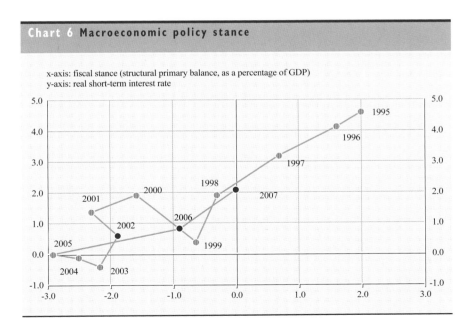

Chart 6 Macroeconomic policy stance

x-axis: fiscal stance (structural primary balance, as a percentage of GDP)
y-axis: real short-term interest rate

CONSTÂNCIO

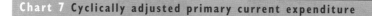

Chart 7 Cyclically adjusted primary current expenditure

(as a percentage of GDP)

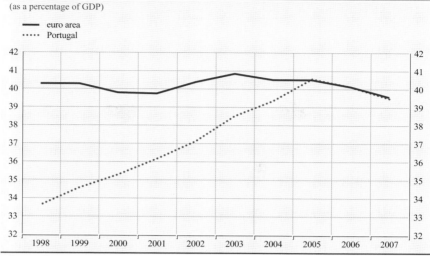

Sources: European Commission and Banco de Portugal.

In 2005, with the budget deficit reaching over 6 per cent of GDP, the newly-elected government supported by a single-party majority in the Parliament took measures to reverse the situation, in a context of broad public support for budgetary action. Furthermore, the revised Stability and Growth Pact (SGP) offered an agreed multilateral framework to support the consolidation effort and to rationalize fiscal measures aimed at sustainability. After 2005 fiscal policy accomplished a decline of the deficit (adjusted for temporary measures) below the 3 per cent threshold, a fall in the cyclically-adjusted primary current expenditure as a percentage of GDP, the fulfilment (and surpassing) of the targets set in the Stability Programmes and the implementation of an important reform of the pension system, which allowed Portugal to move from a high to a medium-risk group in terms of ageing related expenditures. In the Portuguese case, it is clear that the revised SGP was a crucial tool to communicate the rationale of the need for fiscal consolidation and also to enforce a higher degree of control of public expenditures.

In a monetary union, there are mechanisms which endogenously amplify or mitigate the propagation of shocks to the economies (see European Commission (2008)). The real interest rate channel is typically interpreted as a destabilizing factor, given that countries with higher growth and inflation face lower real rates which foster higher demand and growth, and subsequent higher inflation (this is what Mongelli and Wyplosz call "the Walters critique"). A high degree of inflation persistence tends to exacerbate this real interest rate channel. In the specific case of the Portuguese economy inflation expectations were anchored at levels slightly above the euro area throughout the last decade (see Chart 8). Ex-ante and ex-post real interest rates were thus lower in Portugal relative to the euro area. However, and in contrast with the "Walters critique" the gap vis-à-vis the euro area did not grow throughout this period (actually, inflation was below the euro area levels in 2008).

Chart 8 Short-term real interest rates

(computed with 1-year ahead inflation expectations; percentages)

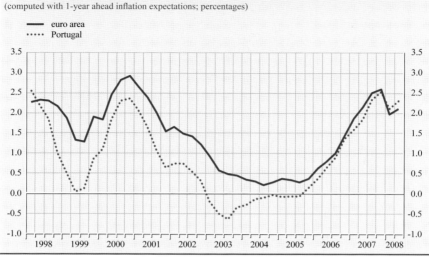

Source: Consensus Economics.

It is also interesting to note that movements in the short term interest rates have a stronger real impact in Portugal vis-à-vis the euro area, due to the relatively higher indebtedness levels of the private sector and the relatively higher share of loans with variable interest rates indexed to money market rates. This implied that the low level of nominal and real interest rates throughout the last decade contributed to foster growth in Portugal vis-à-vis the euro area. Given that the Portuguese economy lagged behind the euro area in terms of growth during the last decade, the behaviour of the real interest rate thus acted as a stabilizing channel.

In contrast with the real interest rate channel, the competitiveness channel is typically interpreted as an equilibrating mechanism in a monetary union. Countries with higher inflation (usually countries with strong domestic demand) become less competitive, which reduces external demand for home produced goods and increases import penetration by foreign suppliers, thus reducing the initial growth differential. General-equilibrium simulations suggest that the competitiveness channel tends to build up slowly but is dominant in the long run. In particular, if the responsiveness of inflation to the buoyancy/weakness of economic activity and the responsiveness of output to changes in competitiveness are weak, the adjustment may be very lengthy. In the case of the Portuguese economy, most indicators suggest that during the last decade there was an overall loss in competitiveness vis-à-vis the rest of the euro area, using the typical relative real exchange rate indicators based on inflation or unit labour costs.[1] However, a closer look at the data suggests that the dynamics of both inflation

1 A note of caution is nevertheless required in this context: the interpretation of these competitiveness indicators is very challenging, in particular in the context of the intensification of the globalization process and given the lack of reliable series for sectoral unit labour costs in the Portuguese economy.

Chart 9 Unit labor costs – total economy

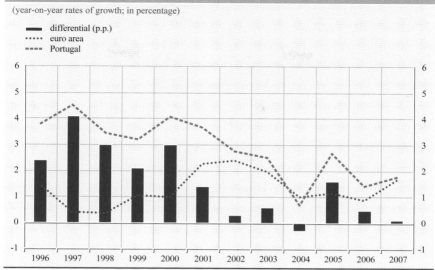

(year-on-year rates of growth; in percentage)

Sources: Eurostat, INE and Banco de Portugal.

and unit labour costs broadly converged to the euro area levels already in the early 2000s decade (Charts 9 and 10). More recently, the Portuguese inflation rate actually declined below the euro area average.

In the context of a relatively low rate of growth of the economy, the magnitude of adjustment of prices and unit labour costs was arguably moderate. This may have

Chart 10 Inflation (HICP)

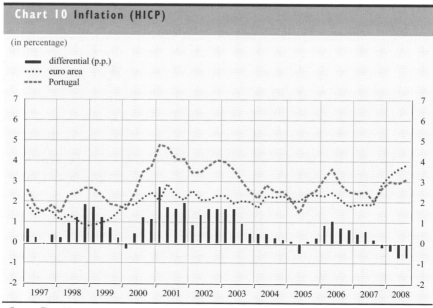

(in percentage)

Source: Eurostat.

Chart II Borrowing requirements of the private sector

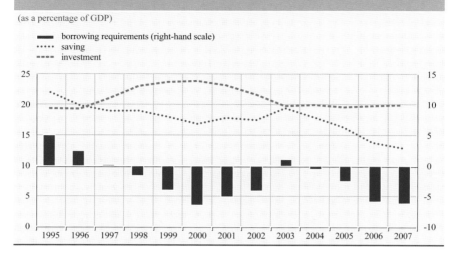

(as a percentage of GDP)

■ borrowing requirements (right-hand scale)
⋯⋯ saving
▬▬ investment

been related to the high degree of downward nominal wage rigidity in the context of a protracted period of low inflation and low productivity growth, which may have limited the responsiveness of wages to the unemployment rate. It may also have been due to the increased financial integration of the Portuguese economy, which allowed a greater sharing of risk within the euro area and the smoothing of temporary and idiosyncratic shocks to the agents' income and wealth.

This increased sharing of risk is a general feature across euro area countries since the 1990s (see Giannone and Reichlin (2006)). The behaviour of the Portuguese economy after 2003 illustrates particularly well this pattern, with the maintenance of a downward trend in the private sector's saving rate and a broad stabilization of the investment rate (Chart 11). The ensuing current account

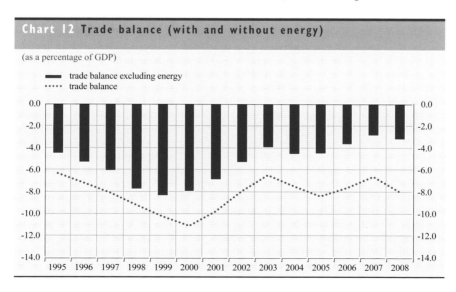

Chart 12 Trade balance (with and without energy)

(as a percentage of GDP)

■ trade balance excluding energy
⋯⋯ trade balance

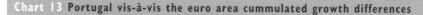

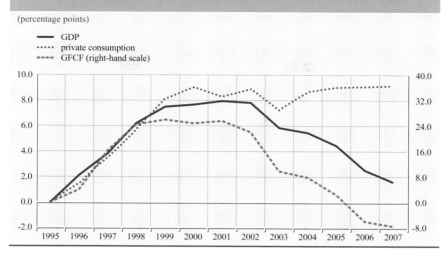

(percentage points)

— GDP
····· private consumption
---- GFCF (right-hand scale)

deficit was accommodated by particularly favourable conditions in international financial markets until mid-2007. These conditions were reflected in favourable financing conditions of the private sector. In fact, over these years, Portuguese banks ensured the channelling of funds from international investors to finance consumption and investment of the non-financial private sector. This allowed the smoothing of expenditures even in the face of the unprecedented oil price shocks observed in the 2000s decade (Chart 12). Moreover, relative to the euro area, there was a significant smoothing of consumption expenditures by households in recent years, in contrast with the behaviour of investment (Chart 13). The favourable financing conditions translated into an increase in the indebtedness of households and firms (Chart 14). However, interest payments are estimated to have been broadly stable as a percentage of GDP.

Chart 14 Indebtedness of the non-financial private sector

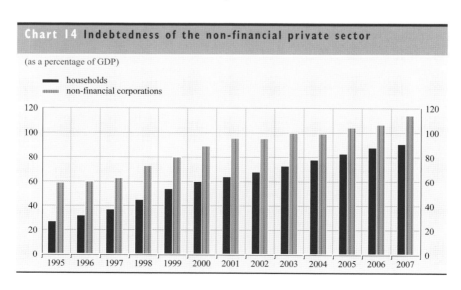

(as a percentage of GDP)

— households
▬▬ non-financial corporations

The banking sector also adjusted fast to the changing economic environments during this period. One example is the increase in the capital adequacy ratio since 2000. Another prominent example is that the supply conditions in the credit market changed in recent years, mitigating the effect of rising interest rates on the debt service and improving the ability of households and firms to service debt and sustain the demand for credit. The lengthening of loan maturities was among those changes.

Increased risk-sharing tends to prolong the reallocation of resources. On the one hand, increased access to financing "buys time" for temporarily insolvent agents to improve their intertemporal financial position. On the other hand, it sustains the maintenance of significant mismatches between domestic supply and demand and delays the decision of insolvent companies to leave the market. Participation in a monetary union thus implies that the equilibrium adjustment of an economy will be smoothened and more prolonged over time.

CONCLUDING REMARKS

The developments in the Portuguese economy during the last decade illustrate several of the main features of the incentive structure and the adjustment mechanisms working in the euro area. Four main insights from the Portuguese experience are worth highlighting.

First, it is important to learn the rules of the game well in advance. When Portugal entered the euro area, the functioning of the new regime was not broadly understood. This was clear, for example, in the fact that fiscal authorities continued to respond to short-term incentives instead of focusing on long-run sustainability or that structural reforms implemented during this period were not ambitious enough to significantly facilitate domestic adjustment in the face of common or idiosyncratic shocks.[2] The long period to learn the rules of the game in Portugal may have mitigated the welfare gains associated with the participation in the euro area. Second, the real interest rate and the competitiveness channels seem to have favoured a gradual adjustment of the economy and have worked in a stabilizing way in the Portuguese case. This evaluation is obviously conditional on the interplay between the (temporary and structural) shocks hitting the economy, the economic structures and the policies in place.

Third, increased financial integration, in part fostered by the participation in the euro area, allowed an increased risk sharing of the economy – enlarging the choice-set faced by economic agents – but prolonged the necessary adjustment process of the economy to the changing international landscape. Fourth, the participation in the euro area accentuated the importance of focusing on the long-run sustainability of fiscal positions. In particular, the revised SGP represented a framework that eventually allowed the right incentives to be delivered to the public authorities in Portugal.

2   For an analysis of the absence of reforms in the euro area, see Leiner-Killinger et al. (2007).

To conclude, the Portuguese experience adds to the evidence on the appropriate functioning of adjustment mechanisms in the euro area. However, it should be clear that these mechanisms can never be expected to be substitutes for reforms aimed at facilitating economic adjustment in the face of shocks or ultimately increasing productivity in the long run.

REFERENCES

Christiano, L., C. Illut, R. Motto and M. Rostagno. 2008. "Signals: Implications for Business Cycles and Monetary Policy." Unpublished.

European Commission. 2008. European Economy. Vol. 2, *EMU@10: Successes and challenges after 10 years of Economic and Monetary Union*. Brussels: The European Commission.

Fagan, G. and V. Gaspar. 2007. "Adjusting to the Euro." Banco de Portugal Working Paper 3.

Giannone, D. and L. Reichlin 2006. "Trends and Cycles in the Euro Area/How Much Heterogeneity and Should We Worry About It?" European Central Bank Working Paper 595.

Leiner-Killinger, N., Pérez, V., Stiegert, R. and Vital, G. 2007. "Structural Reforms in EMU and the Role of Monetary Policy – A Survey of the Literature." European Central Bank Occasional Papers Series 66.

Mongelli, F. and Vega J. 2006. "What Effects is EMU Having on the Euro Area and its Member Countries." European Central Bank Working Paper 599.

GENERAL DISCUSSION

Assaf Razin pointed out that one can currently observe current account imbalances in many counties outside the euro area, for example in the United Kingdom and in the United States. This suggests that the cause of the current account imbalances within the euro area may have nothing to do with EMU. **Philip Lane** observed that the euro seems to have had a large impact on small countries in EMU and a small impact on large countries in EMU. Furthermore, people in small countries, such as Ireland, seem to be happy with the euro. **Lucas Papademos** said that, while the inflation rates have broadly converged within the euro area, the ECB will continue to watch any persistent inflation differentials. Furthermore, he expressed scepticism concerning the view that the ECB has been lucky during the first decade of the EMU, for example, because wage growth has been moderate. In fact, monetary policy of the ECB has contributed to the wage growth moderation. **Lucrezia Reichlin** found it important to distinguish between the effects of the euro on long-term phenomena, such as the effects on trade, and the effects of the euro on short-term phenomena, such as the effects on the synchronization of business cycles within the euro area. Reichlin's research shows that there has been no significant change in the business cycle synchronization within the euro area since the launch of the euro. In this sense, there is no evidence that the abandonment of national monetary policy has been harmful. According to **Alex Cukierman**, the ECB is credible and it has inherited credibility from the Bundesbank. As a consequence, after the launch of the euro real interest rates fell in the euro area countries other than Germany, uncertainty decreased, and economic outcomes improved. **Francesco Giavazzi** expressed surprise at the view that assessing the economic consequences of the euro is impossible due to the absence of a counterfactual. In fact, careful identification can provide a counterfactual. Furthermore, Giavazzi found the transmutation of the Walters critique outlined in the Mongelli-Wyplosz paper to be a red herring. According to Giavazzi, an increase in financial integration between the euro area countries has naturally allowed greater persistence of current account deficits and surpluses. **Seppo Honkapohja** noted that Finland and Sweden have both done well in the last decade, although one country is in EMU and the other country is not. It is difficult to see a difference in economic outcomes between Finland and Sweden in the last decade. The only difference seems to be that travelling to Sweden is a nuisance, because one needs to change money. In comparing the experiences of Finland and Sweden, it is important to keep in mind that Sweden has followed good economic policies, including good monetary policy. Hence, one can say that it is possible for a European country to do well without the euro, provided that the country follows good policies. According to **Sebnem Kalemli-Ozcan**, the euro has clearly benefited people in the euro area. Kalemli-Ozcan's research shows that small countries have gained substantially from the euro in terms of international risk sharing.

Elias Papaioannou, Sebnem Kalemli-Ozcan, Simone Manganelli, Marco Pagano,
Axel A. Weber, José Manuel González Páramo, José Luis Peydró-Alcalde,
Philip Lane (from left to right)

SESSION 2

EUROPEAN MONETARY UNION
AFTER TEN YEARS – WHAT HAS EMU BROUGHT
TO CONSUMERS AND THE CORPORATE SECTOR?
THE EVOLUTION AND THE ROLE
OF FINANCIAL MARKETS

EMU AND FINANCIAL INTEGRATION [1]

BY PHILIP R. LANE, IIIS, TRINITY COLLEGE DUBLIN AND CEPR

ABSTRACT

We assess the impact of the euro on financial integration. We document how the single currency has re-shaped financial markets and international investment patterns. We address the macroeconomic implications of enhanced financial integration, with a particular focus on the shift in net capital flows and the extent of international risk sharing. Finally, we outline the challenges posed by increased financial integration for the ECB and other European policymakers.

I   INTRODUCTION

The financial system provides the central link between the issuers of currency and the real economy. Accordingly, an evaluation of the response of the financial system to the introduction of the euro is centrally important in assessing the economic impact of monetary union. To this end, this paper seeks to provide an overview of the financial impact of the euro, with a particular focus on the macroeconomic implications of enhanced financial integration.

To the extent that the euro has contributed to financial integration, this plays a dual role in the economics of monetary union. First, the efficiency gains from financial development contributes positively to the net welfare gains that accrue from the formation of the monetary union. Second, to the extent that financial integration improves the macroeconomic coherence of the monetary union, it endogenously helps the euro area to fulfill the criteria for an optimal currency area. In what follows, we consider both aspects of the inter-relation between monetary union and financial integration.

It is important to appreciate that it is not straightforward to establish the impact of the euro on financial integration. In particular, the last decade has also been a period in which the pace of global financial integration has accelerated, such that the impact of the euro cannot be considered in isolation. Moreover, there has been considerable progress in promoting financial integration across the European Union, not just within the euro area. Finally, within countries, there have been policy moves to attack historic barriers to regional financial integration. In each of these cases, the introduction of the euro has been a central motivating factor in driving reform. However, at the same time, it would be excessive to attribute the full impact of these innovations to the euro. For instance, the improvements in telecommunications technology have been an important driving force behind

---

1   I thank the discussants Marco Pagano and Axel Weber for their comments. I am also indebted to Patrick Honohan and Richard Portes for helpful conversations and to ECB and BIS staff for help with data. I thank Agustin Benetrix, Barbara Pels and Martin Schmitz for helpful research assistance.

international financial integration, while non-euro member countries (most notably, the United Kingdom) have also been key actors in the promotion of a single market in financial services across the European Union.

Beyond the direct impact of monetary union on financial systems, it is important to assess how financial integration has affected macroeconomic behaviour in the euro area. At the aggregate level, enhanced financial development may have boosted the level of area-wide potential output, in view of the well-established connection between financial development and economic growth. In addition, financial development may also contribute to a lower level of macroeconomic volatility, through a range of mechanisms. To the extent that the euro has fostered enhanced global financial integration, it may also have increased the interdependence between the euro area economy and the rest of the world. From the perspective of an individual member country, monetary union may have altered the economics of net capital flows, the relation between domestic activity and domestic asset prices and the scope for international risk sharing.

Finally, the structural economic changes associated with the transformation of the financial system has posed challenges for the European Central Bank and other European policymakers. In relation to the execution of monetary policy, the transmission mechanism has been altered by financial integration. Moreover, as has been vividly illustrated by the events of the last year, European and global financial integration also poses challenges in terms of the management of financial turmoil and the maintenance of financial stability.

The structure of the rest of the paper is as follows. Section 2 lays out a conceptual framework for thinking about the impact of monetary union on financial integration. We turn to the empirical evidence on the extent of financial integration in Section 3. The macroeconomic impact of financial integration is analysed in Section 4, while Section 5 discusses the outstanding policy issues and offers some concluding remarks.

2 ONE MONEY, ONE FINANCIAL SYSTEM

As was widely discussed in the ex-ante debate on monetary union, the replacement of independent, national currencies by a common, single currency was expected to re-shape financial markets, financial institutions and the behaviour of investors and asset creators.

Most directly, a single currency should promote deeper and more liquid markets for monetary assets. Portes and Rey (1998) emphasise the network characteristic of financial markets – a greater take-up of a currency improves liquidity and thereby increases the attractiveness of that currency for financial transactions, which in turn increases usage of that currency and further propels a virtuous circle of greater liquidity and declining transactions costs. Furthermore, the creation of deep and liquid markets also makes a monetary union a more attractive destination for external investors. In similar fashion, it makes the single currency a potentially attractive vehicle currency for international asset trade even between buyers and sellers that are not resident in the monetary union, permitting a further expansion in the size and scope of financial markets (Papaioannou and Portes 2008a, 2008b). In turn, the scaling up of financial markets increases the payoff to financial innovation and asset creation (Martin and Rey 2001). A wider range of financial products can be supported by a larger-scale financial system and the incentive to capitalise off-market income streams is enhanced.

Another useful framework is provided by Coeurdacier and Martin (2007) who propose that the adoption of a single currency combines aspects of preferential and unilateral financial liberalisations. In particular, within the monetary union, a single currency reduces transactions costs but also increases the elasticity of substitution between assets issued by member countries. Accordingly, the net effect is ambiguous: a decline in transaction costs should increase cross-border holdings, while the increase in the elasticity of substitution reduces the scope for diversification. For non-members, the creation of a monetary union reduces the transaction cost of investing in the monetary union, relative to the cost of transacting in multiple legacy currencies.

Moreover, by eliminating intra-area exchange rate risk, monetary union may also promote integration in equity-type markets and in foreign direct investment. Especially for the smaller, peripheral member countries, the interest rate environment of a monetary union should be more stable relative to a small, open economy that may be vulnerable to the vicissitudes of international capital flows and the episodic risk of currency crises. In addition, the currency markets of small economies may suffer from illiquidity, resulting in higher average interest rates relative to more liquid markets.

For investors, the expanded menu of assets and the impact of a single currency on the matrix of returns will plausibly reduce the degree of home bias. At one level, the elimination of exchange rate risk and the decline in intra-area transaction costs should promote crossborder investment within the monetary union. However, there will also be an increased incentive to invest in destinations outside the monetary union, in view of the limited scope for diversification within a monetary union.

The creation of a monetary union will also alter the organisational structure of the financial system. For banks, monetary union increases the range of potential counterparties in a unified inter-bank market, while also creating a new regime in terms of access to the resources of the monetary authority. While potentially raising the level of competition within the monetary union, there is also an incentive for entry by externally-resident banks that may have a competitive advantage in realising the opportunities provided by a larger market. Financial integration should also expand the menu of financial options for nonbanks. At least for larger firms, a deeper and more liquid bond market enables these firms to reduce reliance on bank finance by having the option to issue corporate bonds. For all firms, increased competition in the banking sector should reduce the cost of capital and improve the quality of financial services.

Monetary union will also affect both sides of the balance sheet of households. By reducing home bias, households should be able to hold a more diversified portfolio of assets, with a greater proportion taken by cross-border holdings. On the liability side, all else equal, we may expect to see an increase in the gross indebtedness of households to the extent that the removal of liquidity premia in interest rates, more intense competition between banks and greater direct or indirect access to cross-border funds relaxes credit constraints. Finally, monetary union also affects the financial environment of national governments, since a deeper area-wide bond market reduces risk premia and improves opportunities to issue debt in home currency.

In the next section, we turn to a quantitative assessment of the degree to which EMU indeed delivered on the promise of greater financial integration.

3   THE IMPACT OF EMU ON FINANCIAL INTEGRATION

In this section, we provide an overview of the evidence concerning the impact of EMU on the financial integration of the euro area. Since the extent of financial integration may be expected to vary across the different sectors of the European financial system, we organise the analysis into a sector-by-sector tour of the evidence.

3.1   DEBT MARKETS

Between 1999 and 2007, Chart 1 shows that the unsecured money market was highly integrated, with the creation of the euro leading to a near-complete convergence in key indicators such as the overnight lending rate. Similarly, the rates on longer-maturity inter-bank unsecured lending also rapidly converged across the euro area. Differences in national legal systems in the treatment of collateral remain a barrier to full integration in the secured money markets but Table 1 shows that the share of cross-border counterparties in the secured markets has largely converged with the share in the unsecured markets (European Central Bank (2008a)). In turn, the integration of swaps and future markets is significantly higher than the cash-based markets, reflecting the greater concentration in the derivatives markets among larger, more sophisticated institutions. However, the short-term securities markets are the least-integrated component of the money markets: a basic obstacle to a unified short-term securities market has been the diversity in norms and definitions in the design of short-term securities contracts.[2]

However, as documented by Cassola et al. (2008), the 2007/2008 turmoil has led to increased segmentation in the euro area money market. Asymmetric

---

2   To this end, the Short-Term European Paper (STEP) initiative has been launched by the Financial Markets Association (ACI) and the European Banking Federation (EBF) and is heavily backed by the Eurosystem. The STEP Market Convention grants the STEP label to securities that meet its criteria for information disclosure, documentation, settlement and statistical information and STEP-labelled securities have gained in popularity over the last two years; the outstanding stock of STEP-labelled securities stood at €342 billion by August 2008.

Chart I Cross-country dispersion in money market rates

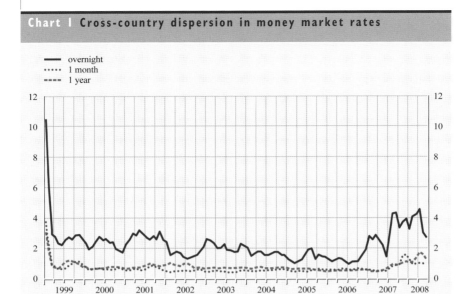

Note: Cross-country standard deviation in unsecured lending rates.

information problems have been a central feature of the malfunctioning of the money markets. This has led to a two-tier market structure, with the larger banks possessing the highest credit standing active in the cross-border money markets whereas smaller banks are confined to trading with domestic counter-parties. The segmentation is reflected in pricing data, with interest rates on cross-border inter-bank lending lower than on domestic inter-bank lending. As the money markets return to more normal conditions, we may expect the degree of segmentation to decline even if it does not fully return to pre-turmoil levels.

As with the money markets, the level of general integration in the longer-term debt securities markets has been impressive. For sovereign debt, spreads across

Table I Share of domestic counter-parties in money market business

(percentage of euro money market business done with domestic counterparties)

	2002	2003	2004	2005	2006	2007
Unsecured money market	28.2	32.9	34.5	31.5	25.3	28.2
Repo money market	42.9	35.8	37.7	36.6	28.1	40.0
Short-term securities	32.2	54.9	39.7	46.8	37.9	47.8
Forward Rate Agreements		12.3	18.0	18.0	21.4	24.4
Foreign exchange swaps	19.2	22.9	20.9	19.2	27.1	25.0
Interest rate swaps	26.6	20.2	22.1	20.3	21.3	24.4
Overnight interest rate swaps	16.9	14.6	21.5	22.7	22.08	24.5
Cross-currency swaps	22.9	11.8	24.5	19.7	17.4	13.2

Source: ECB Money Market Survey (ECB Statistical Data Warehouse).

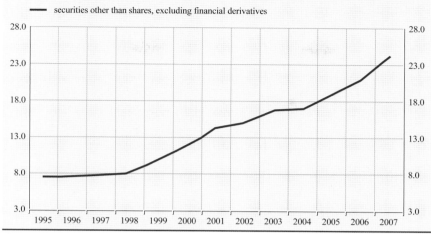

Chart 2 Outstanding securities issued by non-MFI corporations

—— securities other than shares, excluding financial derivatives

Source: Author's calculations based on ECB data.

member governments are small relative to pre-EMU patterns and can be related to differences in liquidity properties and credit risk. Although spreads are reasonably low in the government bond market, the efficiency and liquidity of that market is constrained by differences in the issuance practices of the member countries (Dunne et al. (2006), European Commission (2008)). For corporate debt, spreads can be related to sectoral and firm-level characteristics, with no important role for country-level factors (Baele et al. (2004)).[3] In relation to liquidity, Biais et al. (2006) show that the liquidity of euro-denominated bonds is superior to Sterling- or dollar-denominated bonds, which can be attributed to an open and competitive area-wide market in which a large number of banks offer dealership services to a wide array of prospective buyers. Moreover, these authors find that bid-ask spreads on euro-denominated corporate bonds increase with maturity and default risk and decrease with trade size.

The deeper market has in turn stimulated a remarkable increase in the scale of bond issuance by corporations. Chart 2 shows a steep increase in the volume of securities issued by non-MFI corporations, with the timing clearly associated with the beginning of EMU. As is emphasised by Pagano and von Thadden (2004), the growth in the volume of corporate bond issues can be in part attributed to the euro, in relation to the contribution of the single currency to the increase in competition among underwriters, which led to a substantial reduction in issuance costs and improved access for smaller and higher-risk firms. That bonds from across the euro area are viewed as increasingly close substitutes is evident from the composition of cross-border bond portfolios. Chart 3 shows that the share of

---

3   The current financial crisis shows that the bonds issued by banks represent an important exception, in view of the role of national governments in resolving solvency and liquidity problems in relation to the liabilities of banks.

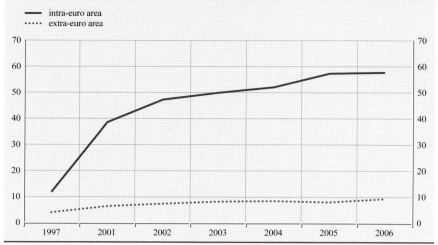

Chart 3 Cross-border ownersvhip of euro long-term debt

— intra-euro area
····· extra-euro area

Source: European Central Bank's *Financial Integration Indicators* database.

bond issues held by investors in other euro areas has grown from 10 percent in 1997 to nearly 60 percent in 2006.

The development of the bond market has benefited from the growing international role of the euro. Many non-resident entities have issued euro-denominated securities, adding to the depth and liquidity of the euro market. Table 2 shows the share of the euro in the total international debt securities outstanding for a selection of major non-EMU economies at the end of 2007 relative to the share of the euro's legacy currencies in total debt outstanding at the end of 1997. The increase in the share of the euro has been quite striking for most of the countries in Table 2. Bobba et al. (2007) confirm this pattern in an econometric study of the determinants of currency choice in the denomination of international securities and find that the euro gained market share relative to the legacy currencies upon the formation of EMU.

At the aggregate level, Lane (2006b) investigates whether the pattern of cross-border bond investment has been influenced by the introduction of the euro. Following the specification developed by Lane and Milesi-Ferretti (2008a), the pattern of bilateral bond positions is modeled as

$$\log(B_{ij}) = \alpha_i + \alpha_j + \beta EMU_{ij} + \sigma Z_{ij} + \varepsilon_{ij}$$

where B_{ij} is the stock of country j's bonds held by country i, (α_i, α_j) control for source and host-country fixed effects and EMU_{ij} is a 0-1 dummy that takes the value 1 if both i and j are members of the euro area and 0 otherwise. The set of control variables Z_{ij} include a host of bilateral characteristics such as EU membership, bilateral exchange rate volatility, bilateral trade, distance and other gravity-type variables that are plausibly correlated with joint EMU membership.

Table 2 Issuance of euro securities by non-euro countries

	1998	2007
United States	9.9	15.9
United Kingdom	11.1	33.5
Japan	6.0	15.6
Switzerland	18.4	50.9
Denmark	38.3	73.4
Sweden	25.6	58.9
Norway	15.7	41.4
Iceland	30.3	52.0
Canada	9.3	13.4
Australia	4.5	26.3
South Africa	14.9	40.8
Brazil	9.5	8.8
Russia	15.3	15.7
India	3.6[*]	4.7
China	3.9	7.5
Korea	5.6	12.9
Mexico	13.3	16.5

Source: Author's calculations based on data from Bank of International Settlements. Share of Euro-denominated securities in total outstanding securities.
[*] 1996.

Even controlling for these factors, this study finds that common membership of the euro area doubles the level of pairwise cross-border bond holdings relative to other country pairs in a levels specification for the year 2004 and by (85,125) percent in a first-differences specification that examines changes in portfolios between 1997 and 2004. In an extension of this approach, Pels (2008) estimates repeated cross-sections for each year 2001 through 2006 and finds that the estimated β is quite stable across these years, with the interpretation that the adjustment of bond portfolios to the creation of the euro was essentially complete by 2001.

Cœurdacier and Martin (2007) explore a slightly-altered specification

$$\log(B_{ij}) = \alpha_i + \beta_1 \text{EMU}_{ij} + \beta_2 EMU_j + \sigma_1 Z_{ij} + \sigma_2 Z_j + \varepsilon_{ij}$$

where the host-country fixed effects (the α_j vector) are dropped and a host of country-j characteristics are included. In particular, these authors include the 0-1 dummy $EMUj$ which takes the value 1 if the destination country is a member of the euro area and 0 otherwise. While the exclusion of host-country fixed effects runs the risk of conflating an EMU effect with other general characteristics of euro area countries, this alternative specification has the virtue of enabling an estimation of the impact of the euro on the bond portfolios of non-member countries. Indeed, these authors find that both β_1 and β_2 are significantly positive: while EMU has the greatest positive impact on the level of bond holdings between two members of the euro area, it also raises the level of euro area bond holdings by non-member countries. As postulated by Coeurdacier and Martin, a reasonable interpretation is that EMU works as a combination of a preferential financial liberalization (being disproportionately beneficial to the members of the monetary union) and a unilateral financial liberalization (increasing the attractiveness of euro area assets to all investors, regardless of origin).

3.2   PORTFOLIO EQUITY

To the extent that a single currency reduces transaction costs and ameliorates risk, it is also possible that EMU may facilitate the integration of equity markets. Regarding risk, it is not so clear that nominal exchange rate uncertainty should be a major factor in the determination of optimal equity portfolios, in view of the low covariance between exchange rate movements and the excess return on home equity versus foreign equity, relative to the variance of excess returns (Adler and Dumas (1983), Van Wincoop and Warnock (2007)). However, there may be regulatory and institutional factors that increase the importance of the currency regime for equity decisions. For instance, many investment funds operate under guidelines that limit the extent of foreign-currency risk that may be taken on. Moreover, even if the covariance between the exchange rate and equity return differentials is low during normal periods, it is plausible that this covariance increases during periods of sharp economic dislocation, such that a long-term investor that seeks to limit exposure to catastrophic events may have a preference for domestic-currency holdings.

At the aggregate level, Lane and Milesi-Ferretti (2007a) find that common membership of the euro area substantially increases the level of pairwise cross-border portfolio equity holdings by about 67 percent, even controlling for a host of other determinants of bilateral investment positions. A similar result for equities is also obtained by Coeurdacier and Martin (2007), who also find evidence that the level of equity investment by non-members into the euro area has also increased. Related evidence is provided by De Santis and Gerard (2006) who compute the shift in portfolio weights between 1997 and 2001 and find a substantial euro effect, especially for those countries with very limited levels of cross-border exposure in the pre-EMU period. Similar to her results for bond holdings, Pels (2008) finds that the estimated effect is stable across the years 2001 through 2006. Again, the interpretation is that the adjustment of equity portfolios to the euro was essentially complete by 2001.

The euro has also altered the dynamic structure of equity returns. Financial globalisation has led to an increasing role for a global factor in determining national equity returns. Baele and Inghelbrecht (2008) show that the introduction of the euro has increased the role of the global factor in determining European equity returns - in effect, the single currency has facilitated the globalisation of the investor base for European equity returns. Baele and Inghelbrecht (2008) also show that the volatility of the country-specific element in equity returns has declined. In related fashion, Fratzscher and Stracca (2008) show that the response of national equity indices to national shocks (such as electoral surprises or major disasters) has declined for members of the euro area. The muted response of national equity returns can be related to the elimination of a major historical source of return volatility – that is, country-specific monetary innovations – and the absorptive capacity of an international investor base in coping with idiosyncratic shocks. Rather, market sentiment is now largely determined at a European level, with a lesser role for national factors.

3.3 FOREIGN DIRECT INVESTMENT

Direct investment represents a key channel for cross-border financial integration, through cross-border mergers and acquisitions and greenfield investments. Moreover, once a direct investment is established, all subsequent financial transactions between parent and affiliate (whether equity or debt) are classified as direct investment. In principle, this category also includes cross-border investments in residential and commercial property, which anecdotal evidence suggests has grown strongly in recent years. Finally, in examining the geographical distribution of FDI, it is important to bear in mind the prevalence of 'transhipment' FDI flows in which financial centres are intensively used as locations for holding companies, corporate headquarters and special purpose entities for reasons of organisational and tax efficiency (Taylor (2007)).

Several studies have found a significantly positive euro effect in the determinants of the bilateral pattern of FDI. Petroulas (2007) studies FDI flows over 1992- 2001 in a gravity-type framework and finds that common membership of the euro area raises bilateral flows by 16 percent. In addition, FDI from member countries to non-members is boosted by 11 percent and from non-members to members by 8 percent. He finds that the effect is strongest for FDI flows between two members of the euro area but there is also evidence of an increase in FDI into the euro area from non-members. De Sousa and Lochard (2009) study the impact of EMU on the geographical distribution of FDI stocks over 1982-2004 and estimate that the euro has increased FDI stocks between member countries by 26 percent.

Aviat et al. (2009) emphasise the contribution of the euro to the expansion in M&A activity is confined to the manufacturing sector, while these authors do not find a significant euro effect for M&A in the services sector. As argued by the authors, this may be related to the greater progress in achieving a single market in goods than in services, demonstrating the complementarity between trade integration and financial integration. In a model in which first-time cross-border direct investment involves a sunk cost, Russ (2007) shows theoretically and, using bank-level data, empirically that exchange rate volatility deters FDI. Baldwin et al. (2008) highlight that the Russ results apply in particular to the introduction of the euro: the positive effect of the single currency on cross-border M&A is primarily due to novice firms undertaking cross-border investment for the first time, rather than an expansion in the scale of investment by existing multinational corporations. An expansion along the extensive margin of investment parallels the role of the extensive margin in trade dynamics, since much of the boost provided by the euro to trade takes the form of new firms exporting and an expansion in the range of export destinations.

3.4   BANKING

The retail banking market remains quite fragmented, with non-trivial differences in lending and deposit rates for households and firms across the euro area.[4] Chart 4 shows the cross-sectional standard deviation in interest rates to small businesses and households over 2002-2007, with the spreads showing relatively little convergence. Moreover, ECB data show that the extent of cross-border lending to non-bank entities is quite small, constituting only 5 percent of total loans to non-banks. While this share has grown from an average of about 3 percent in the early years of EMU, the rate of increase is very slow. At one level, this fragmentation is not too surprising, in view of the importance of local information in assessing small-business and consumer loans and differences in national legal systems in the enforcement of repayment and foreclosure procedures. In relation to retail payments, ongoing high charges for cross-border payments have limited the tangible benefits of a single currency for bank customers. However, the 2008 launch of the Single Euro Payments Area (SEPA) should help in providing a low-cost unified payments system that does not discriminated between intra-national and cross-national payments within the euro area.

Even if retail banking remains fragmented, the banking sector has been a central driver of financial integration, through cross-border inter-bank loans and deposits and the areawide market in which banks are major cross-border purchasers of securities issued by other banks. The scale of cross-border inter-bank lending and borrowing within the euro area far exceeds the levels vis-a-vis nonbanks. This has transformed the balance sheets of banks in the euro area. Cross-border

---

4   The EU Banking Structures report (European Central Bank, (2008b)) provides comprehensive data on the European banking system.

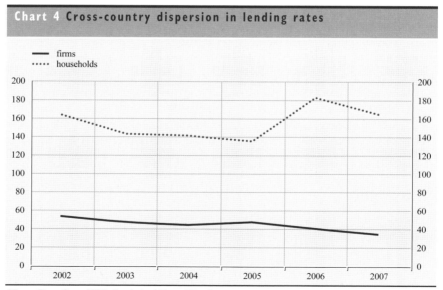

Chart 4 Cross-country dispersion in lending rates

Note: Data from ECB Statistical Data Warehouse.

interbank loans between euro area banks have grown from 15.5 percent of total inter-bank loans in 1997 to 23.5 percent in 2008, while the holdings by euro area banks of the debt securities issued by banks in other euro area countries grew from a 12.1 percent share in 1997 to 31.3 percent in 2008. The expansion of cross-border activity has also included other EU countries, with the shares of inter-bank loans and debt securities between the euro area and the rest of the EU growing from 10.3 percent and 1.4 percent respectively in 1997 to 18.6 percent and 11 percent in 2008.

In terms of econometric studies, Blank and Buch (2007) estimate a gravity model for cross-border bank assets and liabilities. These authors find a significantly positive euro effect on the distribution of bank assets, with a weaker estimate obtained for bank liabilities.[5] Spiegel (2008a) shows that the sources of external financing for Portuguese and Greek banks radically shifted with the advent of EMU, with these banks traditionally reliant on dollar debt but now able to raise funds from counterparts elsewhere in the euro area. More generally, Spiegel (2008b) shows that the relative increase in bilateral bank claims involving euro area members can be attributed to three different channels: (a) a "borrower" effect, by which EMU membership increases creditworthiness such that EMU members increase borrowing from all sources; (b) a "creditor" effect that increases the attractiveness of a member country's banks as financial intermediaries, with EMU members increasing lending to all destinations; and (c) a "pairwise" effect such that joint membership of EMU increases the quality of intermediation when both lender and borrower are in the monetary union, such that the increase in cross-border bank transactions is focused on pairs of countries that are both members of EMU. He finds that the pairwise effect is the dominant factor in the data. Moreover, there is some evidence of an interaction effect, by which the pairwise effect is strongest for those country pairs that also have high levels of bilateral trade, such that the single currency reinforces bilateral links in which information flows are high.

Some of the benefits of financial integration may be obtained through foreign direct investment in the banking sector, with large banks exploiting scale economies by operating in multiple national markets. Goldberg (2007) and De Blas and Russ (2008) provide evidence that FDI in the financial sector reduces lending rates through an increase in competition and an improvement in cost efficiencies. Indeed, the relative importance of large international banks has grown in recent years. As reported by the European Commission (2008) and the European Central Bank (2007), there are 46 EU banking groups (out of a total of 8,000 banks) that hold 68 percent of total EU banking assets. Of these, 16 major banks hold at least 25 percent of their assets in other EU countries and are present in at least 25 percent of other EU countries. These major banks have been important drivers of enhanced financial integration at the EU level.

---

5   Coeurdacier and Martin (2007) also find that a positive euro effect on bilateral bank lending among the member countries, in addition to increased lending by banks from outside the euro area to entities in the member countries.

However, consistent with the evidence provided by Aviat et al. (2009), there is no evidence of a euro effect in cross-border merger and acquisitions in the banking sector. Rather, cross-border banking consolidation can be explained by regional factors and global strategies followed by some of the largest banking groups. This also lines up with the data reported by the European Central Bank (2008b) which show that cross-border mergers and acquisitions that involve euro area banks are evenly split between intra-union and extra-union deals. This study also finds that the propensity to engage in cross-border deals is increasing in the ownership share of foreign institutional investors, such that there is an interesting complementarity between portfolio integration and integration in the banking sector. Looking to the future, cross-border consolidation in the European banking sector is likely to be a key agent of credit market integration. Accordingly, understanding the barriers to such consolidation is a major research priority.

3.5   TRADE IN FINANCIAL SERVICES

In an integrated financial system, we may expect an increase in the cross-border provision of financial services. Table 5 shows the export and import data for financial services in 1998 and 2006. For most countries, Table 5 shows that trade in financial services has remained quite stable as a share of GDP, with the major exception of the rise of Ireland as an international financial centre. Consistent with the evidence for the banking sector, the generally low level of financial trade reflects the lack of progress in promoting services trade in Europe.

Table 3 Trade in financial services

	1998		2006	
	Exports	**Imports**	**Exports**	**Imports**
Austria	0.7	0.8	0.6	0.5
Belgium			1.1	1.0
France	0.2	0.2	0.1	0.3
Germany	0.2	0.2	0.4	0.3
Italy	0.2	0.3	0.2	0.2
Luxembourg			84.3	44.3
Netherlands	0.2	0.3	0.3	0.4
Finland	0.0	0.1	0.1	0.2
Greece	0.2	0.1	0.1	0.4
Ireland	0.3	1.1	8.6	6.2
Portugal	0.2	0.2	0.2	0.3
Spain	0.3	0.3	0.4	0.5
Switzerland	3.1	0.2	4.4	0.4
United Kingdom	1.6	0.3	2.4	0.5

Source: Author's calculations based on data from OECD Services Trade database. Data are expressed as ratios to GDP.

3.6   SUMMARY ON FINANCIAL INTEGRATION

The evidence reviewed in this section shows that EMU has been associated with a substantial increase in cross-border financial integration across the euro area, with both price-based and volume-based measures pointing in this direction. In turn, greater financial integration has stimulated financial development across the euro area, through the lowering of transactions costs and the expansion in the volumes of financial assets.

That said, it is also clear that the process of financial integration is far from complete, with a range of real frictions and institutional factors slowing down the rate of progress especially in relation to banking. Moreover, the current financial crisis has led to some degree of national segmentation of financial systems. In part, the re-emergence of country-specific factors reflects differential exposures to country-specific macroeconomic vulnerabilities. However, the dominant source of this segmentation surely relates to cross-country differences in the design of government intervention in the financial sector in response to the international financial crisis, including some asymmetries in the treatment of domestic-versus foreign-owned financial institutions. We return to the design of the financial stability framework in Section 5. In the next section, we turn to the analysis of the macroeconomic impact of financial integration.

4   MACROECONOMIC IMPACT

In analysing the macroeconomic impact of financial integration, three major issues arise. First, we may expect financial integration to contribute to the financial development of euro area countries. Second, financial integration has the potential to improve cross-border risk sharing. Third, financial integration may ease barriers to net capital flows, leading to increased dispersion in current account balances and net foreign asset positions. In this section, we investigate each of these three predictions.

4.1   FINANCIAL DEVELOPMENT

An extensive literature has shown that financial development boosts income levels (see Levine (2005) for a comprehensive survey of this literature, while Guiso et al. (2004), Papaioannou (2007), and Jappelli and Pagano (2008) provide European-focused reviews of the links between financial development and growth). In particular, the evidence from aggregate and micro-level studies is that financial development boosts total factor productivity among the advanced economies, while it additionally promotes growth through lowering the cost of capital in emerging and developing economies.[6] Accordingly, if cross-border financial integration positively contributes to financial development, there is the

---

6   There are many mechanisms by which financial development may promote productivity growth and there is an extensive literature that investigates each channel. For instance, Hartmann et al. (2007) emphasise the role of financial development in facilitating the reallocation of capital to faster-growing industries and find evidence in support of that channel.

potential for a substantial long-term economic payoff via the benefits conferred by greater financial development.

Financial integration may promote financial development through several mechanisms. Deeper and more liquid financial markets should lower the cost of capital through the improved risk diversification opportunities for investors and a decline in transactions costs through greater volumes and greater specialisation in the provision of financial services. Moreover, the expansion of financial markets improves the financing choices faced by firms, with a greater proportion no longer solely reliant on bank-based funding. In addition, the evidence shows that greater financial development improves the inter-sectoral allocation of capital, with faster-growing sectors receiving more investment funding (Hartmann et al. (2007)). The greater scope for risk diversification also facilitates the funding of riskier projects which may offer the scope for higher long-term returns, as in the analysis of Obstfeld (1994).

The impact of financial integration on the banking sector is critically important. Again, the scope for a more diversified loan book should improve the funding opportunities of riskier and smaller firms. On the funding side, the potential depositor base is expanded, while the development of integrated inter-bank and securities markets provides additional channels of funding for banks. Financial integration should also increase the level of competition in national banking systems. In addition to the positive contribution to contestability provided by cross-border lending (both directly for larger firms and indirectly via the improved access to funding for smaller banks), the expansion of the most efficient banks through cross-border FDI (whether through the formation of new entities or via mergers and acquisitions) offers the scope for reduced costs and lower lending rates.

In summary, through the transformation of financial markets and banking systems in the direction of greater openness, financial integration should improve the allocation of capital, leading to improved productivity and innovation. Moreover, as is emphasised by Guiso et al. (2004), the potential benefits should be greatest for those member countries that entered monetary union with relatively under-developed financial systems and those sectors most reliant on external finance. However, the member countries with advanced financial systems should also benefit by permitting domestic financial firms to succeed in the newly-expanded markets created by financial integration.

In terms of evidence, the literature primarily relies on longer-term studies of the relation between financial development and economic performance, while maintaining the assumption that financial integration promotes financial development. As pointed out by Jappelli and Pagano (2008), it is difficult to capture the full impact of financial integration and financial development, since financial integration may promote financial development by either allowing the domestic financial system to expand or by allowing domestic firms and households to bypass domestic intermediaries in favour of external partners.

However, there are several studies that have specifically examined the impact of the euro on different dimensions of financial integration. Papaioannou and Portes (2008b) estimate a difference-in-difference model of the impact of the euro on the growth rates of a set of financial development indicators. These authors find that the ratio of liquid liabilities to GDP and narrow and broad measures of private sector credit grew significantly more quickly for member countries relative to non-members after the formation of EMU. Moreover, these authors show that the medium-term impact has been stronger than the short-term impact, such that the major gains in terms of financial development took a few years to materialise. In terms of convergence of financial systems across the euro area, Jappelli and Pagano (2008) note that bond market capitalisation has converged across the euro area but there is less evidence that the euro has contributed to convergence in equity market capitalisation or the ratio of private credit to GDP.

Bris et al. (2009) show that EMU has boosted corporate valuations for firms in the euro area. In particular, these authors show that Tobin's Q increased by an average of 9 percent over 1998-2004 for firms in the euro area relative to other firms. Moreover, the effect was strongest for firms from "weak currency" countries (that is, those member countries that devalued during the 1992-1993 currency crisis), with Tobin's Q increasing by 15.3 percent for this group. Their results also show that the effect was relatively stronger for firms whose stock returns were historically negatively correlated with the exchange rate. In terms of the underlying components, the increase in Tobin's Q can be attributed in part to a reduction in the risk-free rate (due to a more credible monetary environment), a reduction in market risk premia (due to the elimination of bilateral currency risk within the euro area and improved risk sharing due to the expansion of the investor base) and an increase in expected cash flows (for instance, due to expanded trade opportunities).

In turn, there is evidence that firms have responded by increasing the level of investment. Using industry-level data, Dvorak (2006) shows that the introduction of the euro boosted the level of investment in member countries relative to non-members over 1998 to 2003. Moreover, in line with a priori expectations, Dvorak finds that the effect is strongest for those sectors most dependent on external finance and resident in the least financially-developed member countries.

Finally, the literature on financial development in emerging market economies and developing countries has emphasised that episodes of major financial liberalisation frequently involve a crisis phase in which excess debt levels lead to banking and currency crises. The evidence of Ranciere et al. (2008) is that liberalisation still raises long-term growth even accounting for such "bumpiness". In similar fashion, the current financial crisis may be in part attributed to the radical shift in the financial environment associated with the major increase in financial integration over the last decade. Of course, it remains too early to tell whether this crisis will overshadow the putative long-term gains from increased financial development in Europe. Relative to the country experience in other episodes, a major difference is that debt liabilities are predominantly denominated in euro, such that the banking crisis is not being accompanied by a currency crisis.

4.2 INTERNATIONAL RISK SHARING

A key hope is that financial integration improves the extent of cross-border risk sharing. In principle, international risk diversification can serve as an alternative stabilisation mechanism, since domestic wealth and consumption may be insulated from domestic production and asset shocks. Moreover, if consumption dynamics are similar across the euro area, the coherence of a single monetary policy is improved. Increased risk sharing may also improve the long-run growth rate of the economy, since expanded hedging opportunities should encourage entrepreneurs to pursue riskier projects that may offer higher payoffs (Obstfeld 1994).

Holding other factors constant, the increase in cross-border investment positions should have increased risk sharing within the euro area. At the microeconomic level, it is surely the case that the personal financial portfolios and pension fund assets of households are more internationally diversified than in the pre-EMU era.[7] For the corporate sector, the increase in foreign direct investment means that earnings are more geographically diversified. For banks, cross-border assets now consitute a greater fraction of total assets. Moreover, the increase in financial development also increases the scope for risk sharing. A greater share of wealth is now tradable, due to the capitalisation of income streams that is facilitated by financial development. Accordingly, the capacity of individuals to share risks within borders and across borders is positively related to the extent of financial development.

7   See Jappelli and Pistaferri (2008) for an analysis of the impact of the euro on the portfolios of Italian households.

Chart 5 Dispersion of consumption growth rates, 1970-2007

Source: Author's calculations based on United Nations data.
Note: Cross-country standard deviation of consumption growth rates.

It is difficult to empirically measure the macroeconomic extent of risk sharing, especially in the context of less than ten years of data for the euro area. Under certain conditions, the correlation in consumption growth rates provides an indicator of international risk sharing. Chart 5 plots the cross-country standard deviation of consumption growth across the Euro 12 group of countries. While the dispersion in consumption growth rates is certainly lower in the post-1999 period relative to the 1970s, it is difficult to discern any clear shift in the pattern relative to the 1980s and 1990s, despite the massive increase in cross-border financial integration over the last decade.

Of course, there is a limit to what can be learned from simple unconditional correlations. A popular approach has been to investigate the conditional dependence of domestic consumption on domestic output fluctuations. In an endowment economy under financial autarky, consumption is perfectly correlated with domestic output. International risk sharing provides one mechanism that can break the link between domestic consumption and domestic output and an active line of research measures the covariance between domestic consumption and domestic output as a rough proxy of the extent of international risk sharing. More precisely, this approach typically runs a regression of the form

$$\Delta \log c_{it} - \Delta \log c_t = \alpha + \beta_t \left(\Delta \log GDP_{it} - \Delta \log GDP_t \right) + \varepsilon_{it}$$

where c_{it} is country i's level of consumption in year t and c_t is the aggregate level of consumption for the group of countries in the sample and β_t measures the average comovement of the idiosyncratic component of consumption with the idiosyncratic component of GDP growth. Accordingly, the degree of

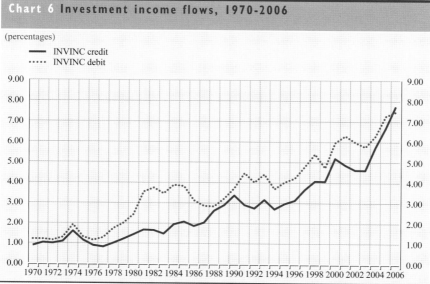

Chart 6 Investment income flows, 1970-2006

(percentages)

— INVINC credit
····· INVINC debit

Source: Author's calculations, based on data from the IMF's *Balance of Payments* Statistics database.
Note: Ratios to GDP, median of Euro 12 group of countries.

consumption insurance is measured by $(1-\hat{\beta}_t)$. Demyanyk et al. (2008) provide an extensive review of this literature and test whether EMU has altered the β coefficient for members of the euro area. Their results indicate no improvement in consumption risk sharing among the EMU member countries during the post-1999 period. However, these authors do find that "income risk sharing" has improved among this group after 1999: the pass-through from gross domestic product shocks to gross national income has declined. This is consistent with increasing financial integration since gross investment income flows are increasing in the scale of cross-border investment positions and are a component of gross national income but not of gross domestic product (Chart 6 shows the rapid increase in gross investment income flows for the Euro 12 group in recent years). However, their analysis finds little direct support for a role for measures of financial integration in explaining the patterns of consumption or income risk sharing during this period.

Gerlach and Hoffmann (2008) pursue an alternative empirical strategy by examining bilateral comovements in consumption among pairs of advanced economies. Their empirical specification is

$$\Delta \log c_{it} - \Delta \log c_{jt} = \varnothing_{ij} + \delta_t + \beta\,(\Delta \log GDP_{it} - \Delta \log GDP_{jt}) + \varepsilon_{ijt}$$

with

$$\beta = \beta_0 + \beta_1 EXTRA_{ij} + \beta_2 INTRA_{ij}$$

where $EXTRA_{ij}$ is 0-1 dummy which scores 1 if only one country is a member of the euro area, $INTRA_{ij}$ is a 0-1 dummy which scores 1 if countries i and j are both members of the euro area. A decrease in β is consistent with an improvement in bilateral risk sharing, with a decrease in β_1 suggesting improved risk sharing between EMU members and outside countries and a decline in β_2 showing the extent of improved risk sharing among pairs of EMU member countries. Using consumption and GDP data from the Penn World Tables over 1990 to 2004, these

Table 4 Bilateral consumption co-movements

	PWT		Hybrid	UN	
	1990-98	1999-04	1999-06	1990-98	1999-06
β_0	0.83	0.95	0.96	0.72	0.77
	[0.02]***	[0.06]***	[0.05]***	[0.02]***	[0.04]***
β_1	-0.16	-0.21	-0.15	-0.11	0.04
	[0.03]***	[0.06]***	[0.05]***	[0.03]***	[0.04]
β_2	-0.24	-0.28	-0.23	-0.16	0.02
	[0.03]***	[0.06]***	[0.05]***	[0.03]***	[0.05]
Observations	2277	1518	2024	2277	2024

Notes: See equation (4) in the text.
*** denotes significance at the 1 percent level.
PWT: Penn World Tables.

authors find that β_1 and β_2 declined during 1999-2004 relative to 1990-1998. We confirm their finding at a qualitative level in column (1) of Table 6, even if the changes are not statistically significant. Moreover, this pattern continues to hold when we extend the time period to 2006 by extending the Penn World Tables data with data from the United Nations in column (2). However, if the United Nations data are used for the whole sample in columns (3) and (4), the β_1 and β_2 coefficients are not significant for the 1999-2006 period.

Jappelli and Pistaferri (2008) pursue an alternative empirical approach by examining consumption smoothing across Italian households. These authors investigate whether the capacity to smooth consumption in the face of income shocks has improved after the introduction of the euro but reject that the euro has decreased the sensitivity of consumption to income shocks.

The mixed nature of the results from these studies serves to highlight that establishing the impact of EMU on risk sharing faces several complications. First, even aside from the data quality issues in measuring consumption, it is difficult to properly derive a measure of international financial integration that is relevant for tests of risk sharing. For instance, gross levels of foreign assets and liabilities (and/or gross flows of investment income credits and debits) face the linkage problem that many types of international financial positions generate an intimate connection between returns on foreign assets and returns on foreign liabilities. For instance, a bank in country i may have an affiliate in country j and obtain FDI earnings in line with the profits of the affiliate. However, in turn, the shares of the bank in country i may be predominantly owned by foreign portfolio investors, such that an increase in FDI earnings is offset by some combination of an increase in portfolio equity investment income debits (if the bank raises its dividend to shareholders) or an increase in foreign liabilities (if the increase in profits is embedded in the market value of the bank). Even more mechanically, a significant proportion of cross-border investment positions represent trades by financial intermediaries. For instance, foreign investors may own shares in a mutual fund that is resident in country j, where the mutual fund exclusively holds foreign portfolio assets. In this case, an increase in the value of the mutual fund represents a symmetric increase in foreign assets (the foreign assets held by the mutual fund) and foreign liabilities (the ownership shares in the mutual fund that are held by foreign investors).

Second, as was argued above, the introduction of the euro was an important stimulus to financial liberalisation in several member countries, with a sharp reduction in real interest rates and a relaxation of credit constraints. In these countries, it was rational for the level of consumption to increase in response to the change in the credit environment. In some cases, the scale of the adjustment in consumption was amplified by a local asset price boom, especially in residential and commercial property sectors. Since these assets were predominantly owned by domestic residents, these national asset price booms primarily raised domestic wealth and, together with the relaxation in borrowing constraints, have been a factor contributing to a divergence in wealth and consumption dynamics across the euro area.

Chart 7 Cumulative house price increases, 1997-2007

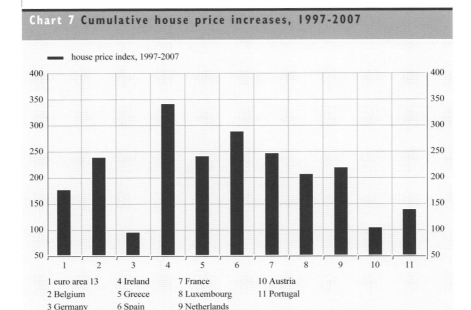

■ house price index, 1997-2007

1 euro area 13   4 Ireland   7 France   10 Austria
2 Belgium   5 Greece   8 Luxembourg   11 Portugal
3 Germany   6 Spain   9 Netherlands

Source: Author's calculations based on ECB data.

Chart 7 shows the dispersion in house price dynamics across the euro area over 1997-2007. Peripheral member countries such as Ireland, Spain and Greece experienced cumulative house price increases of 342 percent, 289 percent and 241 percent respectively. In contrast, housing price growth in Germany and Austria was much more modest at 95 percent and 105 percent respectively. In view of such dispersion in housing wealth growth during this period, it is hardly surprising that national consumption growth rates have not converged.

More generally, the relaxation of credit constraints means greater scope for the delinking of consumption and income through international borrowing and lending. This mechanism does not constitute risk sharing but just involves the intertemporal redistribution of consumption. While it can improve welfare by promoting consumption smoothing, the capacity to borrow and lend internationally can also lead to over-borrowing scenarios if other frictions mean that consumption decisions are distorted. Moreover, even if international risk sharing is promoted by geographical diversification, an increased capacity to engage in cross-border borrowing may increase sectoral risk to the extent that domestic firms in given sectors increase leverage to expand overseas and domestic property investors build on domestic capital gains to acquire debt-financed international property portfolios.[8]

---

8   A good example is provided by the Irish situation. Many domestic households used a combination of equity release from the large capital gains earned on owner-occupied housing to buy overseas holiday homes and buy-to-let properties across Europe, the United States and further afield. In similar fashion, commercial property developers leveraged domestic profits to aggressively invest in commercial property, especially in the United Kingdom.

Furthermore, the largest increase in cross-border investment positions within the euro area has been in debt assets that are very close substitutes for domestic debt assets. Accordingly, the extent of diversification provided by these investments is quite limited. Indeed, the elimination of nominal assets that provide payoffs in national currencies may actually have reduced the scope of diversification, to the extent that historical payoffs on domestically-denominated debt instruments systematically co-moved with domestic macroeconomic conditions (Neumeyer (1998)).

Member countries have also increased the scale of international investments in nonmember countries. While this in itself may contribute to global risk sharing, heterogeneity across the member countries in the geographical and sectoral patterns of international investment means that these external investments may reduce the similarity of wealth dynamics within the euro area. Indeed, this mechanism has been emphasised an important factor in the decision of the United Kingdom not to join EMU (HM Treasury (2003)). Examples include the importance of Central and Eastern Europe as a direct investment destination for Austrian banks and Latin America for Spanish and Portuguese firms, while the scale of Ireland's direct investment liabilities vis-a-vis the United States is especially striking.

Table 3 shows that the growth in international investment positions has been quite heterogeneous across the euro area, even ignoring the outsized statistics for the major financial-processing centres of Ireland and Luxembourg. Moreover, Table 4 also shows that the relative importance of the euro area as a destination for portfolio investment shows considerable variation across the member countries. Accordingly, member countries are asymmetrically exposed to

Table 5 International financial integration

(foreign assets and foreign liabilities as ratios to GDP)

	1997		2001		2006	
	FA	FL	FA	FL	FA	FL
Austria	78.5	95.2	137.0	163.0	258.4	283.7
Belgium	241.6	211.6	331.8	281.6	488.2	453.6
Finland	56.7	97.0	128.2	209.1	213.3	226.5
France	117.3	108.1	180.1	167.4	287.0	281.5
Germany	81.2	77.5	140.6	133.6	197.8	175.0
Greece	36.8	51.3	39.3	79.6	62.0	139.8
Ireland	313.8	299.7	724.0	734.3	1,187.7	1,194.4
Italy	67.4	73.8	94.5	101.4	128.8	145.2
Luxembourg	5,118.4	5,013.4	7,705.9	7,636.1	11,984.5	11,840.0
Netherlands	162.8	186.3	307.0	322.2	443.8	445.0
Portugal	84.4	100.8	133.4	184.7	179.6	266.3
Spain	55.4	71.6	99.8	127.1	140.7	200.8

Source: Updated version of External Wealth of Nations database reported by Lane and Milesi-Ferretti (2007).

	Debt			Equity		
	1997	2001	2006	1997	2001	2006
Austria	46.7	62.0	65.5	50.2	53.5	55.6
Belgium	59.8	74.9	77.4	84.1	78.9	79.7
Finland	28.7	75.1	74.6	34.9	31.1	38.8
France	45.2	58.9	66.8	39.3	51.1	50.5
Germany	46.9	65.0	66.6	39.2	59.7	69.6
Greece		33.5	30.7		50.1	43.0
Ireland	42.6	43.8	48.4	13.9	18.5	26.8
Italy	19.7	49.5	64.9	55.6	64.3	79.2
Luxembourg		60.4	57.4		37.0	33.6
Netherlands	68.5	66.7	69.3	22.7	26.5	25.6
Portugal	43.2	57.1	60.6	54.0	65.5	67.3
Spain	27.6	67.0	56.8	45.8	54.2	77.0

Note: Author's calculations based on data from the IMF's Coordinated Portfolio Investment Survey and the Bundesbank.

international financial shocks, such that the variation in international financial integration can act as a source of disharmony under some scenarios.

Fourth, a host of real frictions limit the true scope for international risk sharing. At a general level, the literature on limited enforceability and contract incompleteness provides strong theoretical reasons as to why production risk cannot be completely diversified. Moreover, financial transaction costs are non-trivial. For instance, in relation to the issuance of securities, scale factors are important, such that smaller firms are not proportionately represented on public markets. For private financing, informational asymmetries and contract enforcement issues mean that local financiers have a comparative advantage over external investors. More generally, the non-tradability of claims on labour income limits the extent of domestic and international risk sharing, such that even perfectly-diversified financial portfolios would not necessarily hedge macroeconomic risks. Finally, as is emphasised by a growing literature, the importance of non-tradables and domestically-produced tradable goods in consumption means that domestic and foreign households may choose quite different portfolios, since consumption risks differ across countries (Obstfeld and Rogoff (2001), Obstfeld (2007), Cœurdacier (2008)).

Finally, it is possible that the risk sharing gains from increased financial integration may not show up in data over a relatively short interval such as a decade. In particular, the main gain from international risk sharing may be in terms of diversification vis-a-vis large-scale rare disasters.[9] To the extent that such adverse rare events are country-specific in nature, the increase in cross-border asset positions provides useful insurance even if it is rarely called upon.

---

9   The literature on rare disasters and asset pricing is growing rapidly. See Barro (2006) amongst others.

4.3   NET CAPITAL MOVEMENTS

Along another dimension, financial integration may also alter the dynamics of net capital movements. Net flows have the potential to improve welfare through two main channels: (a) the allocation of capital to the most productive uses; and (b) the smoothing of consumption during the convergence process and in the event of temporary macroeconomic shocks. In relation to the capital allocation function, monetary union eliminates the national currency risk that historically posed a major risk to investment returns, especially in relation to the risk of episodic currency crises. At one level, greater efficiency in capital allocation should allow countries to converge more rapidly to steady-state output levels. At the cylical frequency, as was emphasised by the real business cycle literature, it should also increase the responsiveness to productivity shocks, possibly amplifying the local business cycle.

One form of consumption smoothing relates to the convergence process, since the prospect of higher future incomes stimulates an increase in current consumption. In relation to temporary shocks, the welfare cost of cyclical fluctuations is ameliorated by the capability to insulate consumption from excessive fluctuations. The impact of monetary union on cyclical consumption smoothing should be greatest for those countries that historically were characterized by a low level of domestic financial development and pro-cyclical access to credit (as is the standard pattern for emerging market economies).

In relation to consumption smoothing, the ability to borrow and lend in response to shocks has been particularly enhanced by participation in an integrated wholesale banking market and the growth in multi-country banks. Banks play a critical role since small firms and households primarily raise external finance through the banking system. Accordingly, a more developed banking system that is populated by diversified banks will be better able to provide stable financing in the event of shocks. As is emphasised by Demyanyk et al. (2007, 2008), the evidence from the United States is that the deregulation of the US banking system in relation to restrictions on cross-state banking activity has substantially improved the smoothing of personal incomes, especially for small business owners. At the international level, Cetorelli and Goldberg (2008) highlight the role of internal capital markets within global banks in smoothing national liquidity shocks. Moreover, such channels contribute to the stabilisation of output in addition to the smoothing of income by weakening the impact of the financial accelerator mechanism on the production and investment decisions of firms.

However, in the presence of other distortions, a more elastic supply of external capital may lead to over-borrowing. In relation to governments, political economy factors may generate a temptation to borrow more in order to increase public spending or cut taxation; however, the fiscal restraints built into the Maastricht Treaty and embodied in the Growth and Stability Pact curb that tendency. For banks and near-banks, poorly-designed regulations or inadequate supervision may encourage excessive lending on the back of funds raised through the wholesale market or securitisation.[10] For corporates, if the corporate governance environment is inadequate, international leveraging may tempt some executives to undertake excessive investment or make ill-advised acquisitions. Under these scenarios, capital flows magnify the impact of such distortions and may amplify cyclical shocks through a pro-cyclical pattern in capital flows.

Chart 8 shows the cross-sectional dispersion of current account balances for the EMU 12 group of countries over 1970 to 2007, while Chart 9 shows the dispersion in accumulated net international investment positions. While large current account imbalances were run in the late 1970s and early 1980s, these proved to be very temporary in nature, with large deficits typically closed through a crisis episode. In contrast, the increase in dispersion in current account balances over the last decade has been associated with highly-persistent net flows for certain countries. Table 7 shows that the persistence of current account balances has drifted upwards and that persistence within the euro area since 1999 is significantly higher than among non-member advanced countries.[11]

Moreover, as is shown by Blanchard and Giavazzi (2002), the link between net flows and income levels has strengthened under EMU, with the lower-income countries typically running large current account deficits. Fagan and

10 Historically, politically-connected non-banks may have also been tempted to over borrow, in the belief that the government would provide a rescue package in the event of trouble. However, EU restrictions on state aids sharply limit the scope for the bail out of non-financial firms.
11 The non-EMU group consist of Australia, Canada, Denmark, Iceland, Israel, Japan, New Zealand, Norway, Sweden, Switzerland, United Kingdom and the United States.

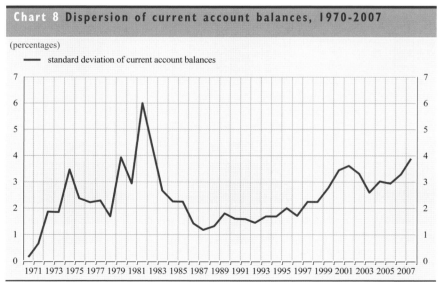

Chart 8 Dispersion of current account balances, 1970-2007

(percentages)

— standard deviation of current account balances

Source: Author's calculations, based on data from the World Bank's *World Development Indicators* database.
Note: Standard deviation of CA/GDP ratio for Euro 12 group of countries (excluding Luxembourg).

Chart 9 Dispersion of NFA positions, 1970 to 2006

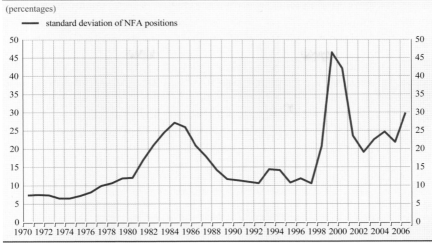

(percentages)

— standard deviation of NFA positions

Source: Author's calculations based on an extended version of the "External Wealth of Nations" dataset documented in Lane and Milesi-Ferretti (2007).
Note: Standard deviation of NFA/GDP ratios for Euro 12 group (excluding Luxembourg).

Gaspar (2007) provide a model of how EMU led to a major increase in the current account deficits of those member countries that may have been expected to grow relatively quickly for convergence reasons and that historically operated under credit constraints. For these countries, the advent of EMU was associated with a reduction in real interest rates and a major increase in cross-border borrowing. While such factors help to explain the emergence of persistent current account deficits, it is also possible that access to external capital contributed to excessive expansion in the property sector in some countries and to an unsustainable increase in local asset prices.

The emergence of large and persistent current account imbalances within the euro area also raises important adjustment issues, especially to the extent that deficits have been used to finance consumption or investment in low-productivity

Table 7 Current account persistence

	1980-1989	1990-1998	1999-2007
EMU			
δ	0.59	0.67	0.81
	[7.6]***	[8.5]***	[11.3]***
Observations	105	108	108
Non-EMU			
δ	0.43	0.64	0.59
	[4.7]***	[7.7]***	[8.1]***
Observations	108	108	108

sectors. While monetary union may insulate a member country from speculative attacks on a national currency, the real exchange rate depreciation that is a typical part of the adjustment to an increase in net external liabilities cannot be achieved through nominal depreciation. Moreover, there is increasing evidence that nominal depreciation offers a double benefit for the external balance sheet of a debtor economy. In addition to the presumed positive impact on the trade balance (albeit with a lag), nominal depreciation that is not fully offset by a differential in expected returns also generates a positive valuation effect to the extent that foreign assets are disproportionately in foreign currency and foreign liabilities in domestic currency. For instance, Gourinchas and Rey (2007) find a substantial role for the currency-based valuation channel in the adjustment dynamics of the United States (see also Tille (2003) and Lane and Milesi-Ferretti (2005)). The absence of independent national currencies means that this valuation channel does not play a role in the adjustment dynamics of the member countries of the euro area, at least in relation to intra-area imbalances.

Moreover, real depreciation vis-a-vis other member countries can only be achieved through a negative inflation differential. Accordingly, this requires wages to grow more slowly than in other member countries, which is difficult to achieve if the institutional environment governing the domestic labour market does not facilitate rapid corrections in wage levels. Moreover, a drawn-out period of anticipated real depreciation can amplify the negative impact on domestic activity, since the ex-ante real interest rate will be higher, depressing domestic spending. The slow pace of adjustment in Portugal in correcting its large current account deficit and loss of external competitiveness shows the difficulties involved in external adjustment under EMU (Blanchard (2007)). Moreover, there is evidence that the sensitivity of wages to the level of competitiveness is also weak in some other member countries (Honohan and Leddin (2006)).

We also note that the prominence of inter-bank lending as a source of finance for current account deficits within the euro area means that a version of the "sudden stop" mechanism is a potential risk. If banks in a given deficit country are unable to rollover short-term debt, the current account deficit may quickly close in a manner that is compounded by a domestic banking crisis. While the generalised nature of the 2007-2008 financial turmoil has permitted the European Central Bank to provide liquidity support to all banks in the euro area, a similar response would not necessarily apply in the context of a country-specific problem. While national governments have intervened to provide support to domestic banks during the current crisis, it is too early to tell whether this will be sufficient to avert a sharp reversal in capital flows to major deficit countries in the euro area.

Accordingly, the external adjustment process for member countries is potentially quite challenging. However, it is important to keep in mind the appropriate counterfactual. In particular, it is not so obvious that a floating exchange rate is automatically helpful in facilitating adjustment. As the current international financial crisis reminds us, a deficit country may also be vulnerable to a currency attack especially during a period of international turmoil, with currency and financial crises feeding on each other. Moreover, the beggar-thy-neighbour characteristics of independent monetary responses to crisis situations were an important motivation for the formation of EMU, since free trade and cooperation on other economic and political issues is difficult to sustain if nominal exchange rates are subject to manipulation (Eichengreen (1993)).

5   CONCLUSIONS

The evidence is that the first ten years of EMU has generated a remarkable increase in financial integration, even if it the extent of convergence varies across different sectors within the overall financial system. However, it is also clear that there remain many outstanding barriers to full integration. In relation to technical frictions, initiatives such as SEPA, Target-2, the proposed integration of securities settlement with the payments system(T2S) and the new version 2 of the Correspondent Central Banking System(CCBS2) should improve the support infrastructure to enable greater progress in achieving deeper and broader financial integration.[12]

Further financial integration is also dependent on the success of moves to improve the European financial stability framework and the system for the supervision of large multi-country banks. The tension between the internationalisation of banking activity and national responsibility for financial stability was evident from the outset of EMU (see, amongst others, Begg et al. (1999) and Portes (2001)). Indeed, considerable efforts have been made to promote cooperation and coordination between the different national systems in order to make this approach operate in an effective manner but the 2007-2008 international financial crisis has illustrated the limits to voluntary cooperation and the potential for "beggar-thy-neighbour" interventions. Accordingly, the current crisis clearly signals the imperative of establishing a truly pan-European mechanism to cope with stresses in the financial system. However, the viability of an area-wide regime faces the limitation that the provision of financial stability ultimately requires a fiscal backstop and the political acceptability of pooling fiscal resources is open to question. The current crisis has also vividly highlighted the global interdependence of financial systems, such that the internationalisation of the financial stability function requires improved coordination mechanisms at the global level, in addition to making progress in respect of the intra-European dimension.

A major focus of this paper has been to analyse the impact of increased financial integration on the macroeconomic behaviour of the member countries. There is a presumption that financial integration promotes financial development and thereby contributes to a higher long-run level of productivity and the initial evidence provides encouraging support for this channel. However, a decade of data is not long enough to establish conclusive evidence on contribution of the euro to financial development, such that this area requires ongoing research attention. Moreover, the current crisis is sure to complicate the analysis of the contribution

---

12 See European Central Bank (2008) for a comprehensive description of the ESCB's role in fostering further financial integration.

of expanded capital markets to long-term macroeconomic performance, since the full impact cannot be assessed until recovery is fully established.

In relation to international diversification, we have highlighted that there is little evidence to support that EMU has generated a substantial increase in the cross-border sharing of macroeconomic risks. This should not be interpreted as a surprising outcome, in view of the mechanisms that give rise to wealth divergence during the transition phase in which peripheral member countries have enjoyed a sustained decline in risk premia and large credit booms. However, over the longer term, the contribution of increased cross-border investment positions to risk sharing may well show up more strongly in the data. The third macroeconomic dimension that we covered was to argue that EMU has allowed some member countries to run persistent current account deficits. While this may well accelerate convergence in income levels, the improved access to external credit may also have contributed to over-investment in property and unsustainable increases in domestic asset prices in some membership countries. Moreover, membership of a monetary union also alters the external adjustment process such that the transition from trade deficits to trade surpluses may be more prolonged than under a floating exchange rate.

Finally, EMU over the next decade is set to undergo further transformation over the next decade, with the entry of increasing numbers of the new EU member states.[13] The analysis in this paper suggests that the euro has the greatest financial impact on those member countries with initially less-developed financial systems. Accordingly, as is projected by Masten et al. (2008), joining the euro area should accelerate the financial development of the new member states. In addition, conditional on possessing a high degree of macroeconomic and fiscal stability upon entry to EMU, the euro area should be a safe haven for the new member states relative to the difficulties involved in managing an floating exchange rate in a world of high capital mobility. Finally, the enlargement of the euro area further reinforces the urgency to improve the European financial stability framework, in view of the risks posed by the increased heterogeneity in banking systems across the euro area.

13 See Darvas and Szapary (2008) for an analysis of euro adoption strategies by this group of countries.

REFERENCES

Adler, M., and B. Dumas. 1983. "International Portfolio Choice and Corporation Finance: A Synthesis." *Journal of Finance*, 38(3): 925-984.

Aviat, A., N. Coeurdacier and R. De Santis. 2009. "Cross-Border Mergers and Acquisitions and European Integration." *Economic Policy*, 24(57): 55-106.

Baele, L., and K. Inghelbrecht. 2008. "Time-Varying Integration, the Euro and International Diversification Strategies." European Economy Economic Paper 333.

Baldwin, R., V. DiNino, L. Fontagné, R. A. De Santis and D. Taglioni. 2008. "Study on the Impact of the Euro on Trade and Foreign Direct Investment." European Economy Economic Paper 321.

Barro, R. 2007. "Rare Disasters, Asset Prices, and Welfare Costs." National Bureau of Economic Research Working Paper 13690.

Barros, P., E. Berglof, P. Fulghieri, J. Gual, C. Mayer and X. Vives. 2005. *Monitoring European Deregulation.* Vol. 3, *Integration of European Banking: The Way Forward.* London: Centre for Economic Policy Research.

Begg, D., P. De Grauwe, F. Giavazzi, H. Uhlig and C. Wyplosz. 1999. *Monitoring the European Central Bank*. Vol. 1, *The ECB: Safe at Any Speed?* London: Centre for Economic Policy Research.

Benetrix, A. and S. Walti. 2008. "Indicators of Regional Financial Integration." Institute for International Integration Studies Discussion Paper 243.

Biais, B., J. Dow, R. Portes and E. L. Von Thadden. 2006. "European Corporate Bond Markets: Transparency, Liquidity, Efficiency." Centre for Economic Policy Research Report.

Blanchard, O. 2007. "Adjustment within the Euro: The Difficult Case of Portugal." *Portuguese Economic Journal*, 6(1): 1-22.

Blanchard, O. and F. Giavazzi. 2002. "Current Account Deficits in the Euro Area. The End of the Feldstein Horioka Puzzle?" *Brookings Papers on Economic Activity*, 2: 147-209.

Blank, S. and C. Buch. 2007. "The Euro and Cross-Border Banking: Evidence from Bilateral Data." *Comparative Economic Studies*, 49(3): 389-410.

Bobba, M., G. Della Corte and A. Powell. 2007. "On the Determinants of International Currency Choice: Will the Euro Dominate the World?" Inter-American Development Bank Research Department Working Paper 611.

Bris, A., Y. Koskinen and M. Nilsson. 2009. "The Euro and Corporate Valuations." *Review of Financial Studies*, 22(8): 3171-3209.

Cassola, N., C. Holthausen and M. Lo Duca. 2008. "The 2007/2008 Turmoil: A Challenge for the Integration of the Euro Area Money Market?" http://esst2006. com/download/vfz/konferenzen/2008_10_17_muenchen/paper_cassola_ holthausen_duca.pdf

Cetorelli, N. and L. S. Goldberg. 2008. "Banking Globalization, Monetary Transmission, and the Lending Channel." National Bureau of Economic Research Working Paper 14101.

Coeurdacier, N. 2008. "Do Trade Costs in Goods Market Lead to Home Bias in Equities?" Centre for Economic Policy Research Discussion Paper 6991.

Coeurdacier, N. and P. Martin. 2007. "The Geography of Asset Trade and the Euro: Insiders and Outsiders." Centre for Economic Policy Research Discussion Paper 6032.

Darvas, Z. and G. Szapary. 2008. "Euro Area Enlargement and Euro Adoption Strategies." European Economy Economic Paper 304.

Demyanyk, Y., C. Ostergaard and B. E. Sorensen. 2007. "US Banking Deregulation, Small Businesses, and the Interstate Insurance of Personal Income." *Journal of Finance*, 62: 2763-2801.

Demyanyk, Y., C. Ostergaard and B. E. Sorensen. 2008. "Risk Sharing and Portfolio Allocation in EMU." European Economy Economic Paper 334.

De Blas, B. and K. Russ. 2008. "FDI in the Banking Sector: Why Borrowing Costs Fall While Spread Proxies Increase." http://www.econ.ucdavis.edu/ faculty/knruss/deBlas_Russ_7_08.pdf

De Santis, R. and B. Gerard. 2006. "Financial Integration, International Portfolio Choice and the European Monetary Union." ECB Working Paper 626.

De Sousa, J., and J. Lochard. 2009. "Does the Single Currency Affect Foreign Direct Investment? A Gravity-Like Approach." University of Paris 1. http://jdesousa.univ.free.fr/recherche/travaux/deSousa_Lochard_FDI_jan09.pdf

Dunne, P., M. Moore and R. Portes. 2006. "European Government Bond Markets: Transparency, Liquidity, Efficiency." Centre for Economic Policy Research Report.

Dvorak, T. 2006. "The Impact of the Euro on Investment: Sectoral Evidence." In *Financial Development, Integration and Stability: Evidence from Central, Eastern and South-Eastern Europe*, ed. K. Liebscher, J. Christl, P. Mooslechner and D. Ritzberger-Grunwald. Northampton, MA: Edward Elgar Publishing.

Eichengreen, B. 1993. "European Monetary Unification." *Journal of Economic Literature*, 31(3): 1321-1357.

European Central Bank. 2007. *Review of the International Role of the Euro*. Frankfurt am Main, Germany: European Central Bank.

European Central Bank. 2008a. *Euro Money Market Survey*. Frankfurt am Main, Germany: European Central Bank.

European Central Bank. 2008b. *EU Banking Structures*. Frankfurt am Main, Germany: European Central Bank.

European Central Bank. 2008c. *Financial Integration in Europe*. Frankfurt am Main, Germany: European Central Bank.

European Central Bank. 2008d. "Cross-Border Bank Mergers & Acquisitions and Institutional Investors." *ECB Monthly Bulletin*, 10(10): 67-80.

Fagan, G. and V. Gaspar. 2007. "Adjusting to the Euro." European Central Bank Working Paper 716.

Ferguson, R., P. Hartmann, F. Panetta and R. Portes. 2007. "International Financial Stability." Ninth Geneva Report on the World Economy.

Francois, J. and F. Eschenbach. 2006. "Financial Integration and Growth with Imperfect Competition in Banking." Johannes Lunz University. Unpublished.

Fratzscher, M. and L. Stracca. 2008. "Political Economy of Monetary Union: Has EMU Made a Difference?" *Economic Policy*, 24(58): 307-348.

Goldberg, L. 2007. "Financial Sector FDI and Host Countries: New and Old Lessons." *Federal Reserve Bank of New York Economic Policy Review*, 13(1): 1-17.

Gourinchas, P. O. and H. Rey. 2007. "International Financial Adjustment," *Journal of Political Economy*, 115(4): 665-703.

Guiso, L., T. Jappelli, M. Padula and M. Pagano. 2004. "Financial Market Integration and Economic Growth in the EU." *Economic Policy*, 19(40): 523-577.

Hartmann, P., F. Heider, E. Papaionnou and M. Lo Duca. 2007. "The Role of Financial Markets and Innovation in Productivity and Growth in Europe." European Central Bank Occasional Paper 72.

Honohan, P. and A. J. Leddin. 2006. "Ireland in EMU: More Shocks, Less Insulation?" *Economic and Social Review*, 37(2): 263-294.

Jappelli, T. and L. Pistaferri. 2008. "Financial Integration and Consumption Smoothing." University of Naples. Centre for Studies in Economics and Finance Working Paper 200.

Jappelli, T. and M. Pagano. 2008. "Financial Market Integration under EMU." European Economy Economic Papers 312.

Lane, P. R. 2006a. "The Real Effects of European Monetary Union." *Journal of Economic Perspectives* 20(4): 47-66.

Lane, P. R. 2006b. "Global Bond Portfolios and EMU." *International Journal of Central Banking*, 2(2): 1-23.

Lane, P., R. and S. Walti. 2007. "The Euro and Financial Integration." in *The Travails of the Eurozone: Economic Policies, Economic Developments*, ed. D. Cobham. New York: Palgrave Macmillan.

Lane, P. R. and G. M. Milesi-Ferretti. 2007a. "The International Equity Holdings of Euro Area Investors," in *The Importance of the External Dimension for the Euro Area: Trade, Capital Flows, and International Macroeconomic Linkages*, ed. R. Anderton and F. di Mauro. New York: Cambridge University Press.

Lane, P. R. and G. M. Milesi-Ferretti. 2007b. "Capital Flows to Central and Eastern Europe." *Emerging Markets Review*, 8: 106-123.

Lane, P. R. and G. M. Milesi-Ferretti. 2008. "The Drivers of Financial Globalization." *American Economic Review*, 98(2): 327-332.

Lane, P. R. and J. C. Shambaugh. 2007. "Financial Exchange Rates and International Currency Exposures." National Bureau of Economic Research Working Paper 13433.

Levine, R. 2005. "Finance and Growth: Theory and Evidence." In *Handbook of Economic Growth*, ed. P. Aghion and S. Durlauf. The Netherlands: Elsevier Science.

Martin, P. and H. Rey. 2004. "Financial Super-Markets: Size Matters for Asset Trade." *Journal of International Economics*, 64: 335-361.

Masten, A., F. Coricelli and I. Masten. 2008. "Non-Linear Growth Effects of Financial Development: Does Financial Integration Matter?" *Journal of International Money and Finance*, 27(2): 295-313.

Neumeyer, P. A. 1998. "Currencies and the Allocation of Risk: The Welfare Effects of a Monetary Union." *American Economic Review*, 88: 246-259.

Obstfeld, M. 1994. "Risk-Taking, Global Diversification, and Growth." *American Economic Review*, 84(5): 1310-1329.

Obstfeld, M. 2007. "International Risk Sharing and the Costs of Trade." University of California at Berkeley. http://elsa.berkeley.edu/~obstfeld/Ohlin_show.pdf

Obstfeld, M. and K. Rogoff. 2001. "The Six Major Puzzles in International Macroeconomics: Is There a Common Cause?" *National Bureau of Economic Research Macroeconomics Annual*, 15(2000): 339-390.

Pagano, M. and E. L. Von Thadden. 2004. "The European Bond Market under EMU." *Oxford Review of Economic Policy*, 20: 531-554.

Papaionnou, E. and R. Portes. 2008a. "The International Role of the Euro: A Status Report." European Economy Economic Papers 317.

Papaionnou, E. and R. Portes. 2008b. "Costs and Benefits of Running an International Currency." *Draft Report for Directorate General-Economic and Financial Affairs of the European Commission*.

Pels, B. 2008. "The Euro Effect in International Asset Holdings." Trinity College Dublin. Unpublished.

Petroulas, P. 2007. "The Effect of the Euro on Foreign Direct Investment." *European Economic Review*, 51: 1468-1491.

Portes, R. and H. Rey. 1998. "The Emergence of the Euro as an International Currency," *Economic Policy*, 26: 305-343.

Portes, R. 2001. "Financial Stability and Banking Supervision in the Euro Area." http://www.europarl.europa.eu/comparl/econ/pdf/emu/speeches/20010528/20010528_portes.pdf

Ranciere, R., A. Tornell and F. Westermann. 2008. "Systemic Crises and Growth." *Quarterly Journal of Economics*, 123(1): 359-406.

Russ, K. 2007. "Exchange Rate Volatility and First-Time Entry by Multinational Firms." National Bureau of Economic Research Working Paper 13659.

Schmitz, M. Forthcoming. "Financial Markets and International Risk Sharing." *Open Economies Review*.

Spiegel, M. 2008a. "Monetary and Financial Integration: Evidence from the EMU." *Journal of the Japanese and International Economies*. 23(2): 114-130.

Spiegel, M. 2008b. "Monetary and Fiscal Integration in the EMU: Push or Pull?" *Review of International Economics*, 17(4): 751-776.

Taylor, C. 2008. "Foreign Direct Investment and the Euro: The First Five Years." *Cambridge Journal of Economics*, 32(1): 1-28.

United States Treasury. 2007. *Report on Foreign Portfolio Holdings of the United States Securities*. Washington, DC.: United States Treasury:

Van Wincoop, E. and F. Warnock. 2007. "Is Home Bias in Assets Related to Home Bias in Goods?" National Bureau Economic Research Working Paper 12728.

FINANCIAL INTEGRATION, MACROECONOMIC VOLATILITY AND RISK SHARING – THE ROLE OF THE MONETARY UNION[1]

BY SEBNEM KALEMLI-OZCAN, UNIVERSITY OF HOUSTON AND NBER
SIMONE MANGANELLI, ECB
ELIAS PAPAIOANNOU, DARTMOUTH COLLEGE AND CEPR
JOSÉ LUIS PEYDRÓ, ECB

ABSTRACT

This paper is composed of two parts. We first review the literature on the effects of the euro on financial integration. We discuss the measurement of financial integration and describe the main legislative and regulatory harmonization policies that the EU member states have implemented in financial markets. We then review empirical results showing a positive impact of these policies and of the single currency on financial integration. Second, we present new empirical evidence of the impact of cross-border financial integration on macroeconomic volatility and cross-country risk sharing for 20 industrialized countries (including EU-15) over 1978-2007. We find that higher cross-border banking integration leads to lower consumption volatility and higher output volatility. These results imply that banking integration spurs risk sharing. The quantification of the amount of consumption and income smoothing reveals an economically significant positive effect of integration on risk sharing. Our results, therefore, suggest that the increased financial integration has fostered ex-post the optimality of the currency union.

1   Essential parts of this paper were prepared while Sebnem Kalemli-Ozcan was visiting the
    European Central Bank as 2008 Duisenberg Fellow. She thanks the economists at the bank
    for providing a stimulating research environment. We thank Dimitrios Rakitzis for excellent
    research assistance, and Marco Lo Duca, Vladimir Lazarov, and Bernadette Lauro for help in
    obtaining part of the data used in this paper. Fabio Fiorello from the European Commission
    and Ana Margarida Monteiro from the Legal Department of the ECB helped us gather the data
    related to the implementation of EU Financial Acts. Ana Margarida Monteiro also provided
    us with very useful suggestions and feedback related to the EU Acts. We also thank Ignazio
    Angeloni, Luca Dedola, Charles Engel, Domenico Giannone, Philipp Hartmann, Michele
    Lenza, Roberto de Santis, Patrick Sandars, Bent Sorensen, Marc Spiegel, and Frank Smets,
    and especially the discussants Marco Pagano and Axel Weber, for helpful comments and
    suggestions.

I   INTRODUCTION

Financial systems play a key role in the functioning of modern economies. Capital markets, by efficiently allocating resources across space and time, are instrumental in ensuring long-term non-inflationary growth. In addition, financial integration may be welfare enhancing by enabling agents to smooth consumption and share idiosyncratic risk. From a central banking perspective, financial systems represent the primary channel through which monetary policy is conducted. A stable, integrated and efficient financial system enhances the smooth and effective transmission of monetary policy throughout the economy.

Barriers and obstacles to financial integration prevent the allocation of capital to the most valuable projects at the lowest possible cost. European capital markets had been shaped by decades of national policies and cultural norms. Although the various stages of the Economic and Monetary Union (EMU) project eliminated many obstacles and barriers, numerous domestic conventions and practices remained, mainly because strong network externalities made it costly for market participants to abandon them. Thus, while the introduction of the single currency has spurred financial integration across euro area member states, existing barriers implied an important loss of efficiency. As a consequence, promoting integration of European financial markets has been one of the priorities of European policy makers.

This paper is composed of two parts. First, we review the literature on the impact of the single currency on various forms of financial integration. Although the introduction of the euro has arguably been the single most important force behind the evolution of European financial markets over the past two decades, it has been preceded and followed by a series of policy initiatives aimed at creating a level playing field across the euro area. Most previous work do not distinguish the impact of monetary union from the accompanying policy reforms. We argue that, the importance of these reforms in the process of financial integration should not be understated: they are continuously shaping the legislative architecture and technical infrastructure on which financial markets operate. For these reasons, we discuss the main legislative actions taken at the European level, as well as the ongoing efforts aimed at integrating the infrastructure of the different market segments. Then, we review results from Kalemli-Ozcan, Papaioannou, and Peydró (2008b), who analyze the effect of the euro and the most important legislative and harmonization policies in the European financial sector – the Financial Sector Action Plan (FSAP) – on banking integration.

Second, we present new empirical evidence regarding the impact of financial integration on macroeconomic volatility and risk sharing. Our key innovation compared to previous research is distinguishing between external assets and cross-border liabilities. Using banking integration data for 20 industrial countries over the past 30 years, we find that a higher degree of external asset holdings is associated with a lower level of consumption volatility. We also find that a higher level of external bank liabilities tends to increase output fluctuations. Jointly these results suggest that banking integration may facilitate risk sharing. These results are supportive for the models in the spirit of Obstfeld (1994), who emphasize the welfare enhancing aspects of financial globalization. Yet our results differ from previous empirical studies, which fail to detect a significant effect of financial integration on macroeconomic volatility (e.g. Kose et al. 2006). We, also, following Demyanyk et al. (2008), quantify the degree of international diversification as a result of banking integration by estimating formal risk-sharing specifications. We find that the average consumption risk sharing among the 20 developed countries is 38%. This means that 38% of the country-specific risk is diversified away, on average, through cross-border bank investment and lending. In addition, we find that a country that doubles the holdings of its external assets (relative to population) is able to diversify away an additional 17%. External bank liabilities seem to have a dis-smoothing effect, but the estimated coefficient is not significant. We also estimate income (GNI) risk-sharing regressions. We estimate that the average income risk sharing over the last two decades has increased from zero to 12%. More importantly, a country that increases the holdings of external liabilities (relative to population) by 100% achieves 18% of additional income smoothing. To our knowledge these results are the first to reveal an economically significant positive effect of cross-border banking integration on risk sharing. The only other study that we are aware of is Demyanyk et al. (2008), who also investigated the effect of bank integration on risk sharing for Europe. Demyanyk et al. (2008), however, do not find a significant effect of banking integration on consumption risk sharing. Most likely this difference is due to our sample, which covers a larger number of countries and years.

Our findings have important implications for policy makers in the euro area. Asymmetric shocks in a currency union generate output and inflation differentials. The impact of such shocks can be considerably reduced if financial markets enable cross-country risk sharing. To the extent that risk-sharing allows for the hedging of consumption, it represents a key counteracting mechanism against output shocks among members of a currency union. This mechanism reduces the need for policy intervention in dealing with such asymmetries. Our results, therefore, suggest that the increased cross-border banking integration has improved ex-post the optimality of the currency union by improving consumption risk sharing.

The paper proceeds as follows. Section 1 reviews the vast and growing literature on the effect of the single currency on various forms of financial integration. We then describe the main regulatory and legislative policies that the EU member states have (are) implemented (implementing). We conclude this review part by summarizing the findings from Kalemli-Ozcan, Papaioannou, and Peydró (2008b), who isolate the effect of monetary union from that of the parallel financial sector reforms that took place under the Financial Service Action Plan (FSAP) on cross-border financial integration. Section 2 investigates the "real" effects of banking integration. We start by examining the impact of cross-border banking integration on GDP and consumption volatility. Besides using an aggregate index of banking integration that blends foreign assets and liabilities, we also distinguish between the two. We then quantify the degree of risk sharing that is explained by banking integration. Section 3 concludes.

2   THE IMPACT OF THE SINGLE CURRENCY ON THE EVOLUTION OF THE EURO AREA FINANCIAL SYSTEM

There is a vast and growing literature on measuring financial integration (e.g. Adam et al. (2002)). The literature tends to measure integration both from the "price" side and also from the "quantity" side. Most studies consider the financial markets to be integrated if all agents face the same set of rules, are treated equally and have equal access to financial products (e.g. Baele et al. (2004)). If these conditions are satisfied, any price difference between identical assets will be immediately arbitraged away. Given the variety of assets traded, the measurement of financial integration with "price-based" indicators is not straightforward. Hence the literature also looks at the volume of cross-border transactions in the various market segments.

By opening access to foreign markets, financial integration offers agents a wider range of financing sources and investment opportunities, and permits the creation of deeper and more liquid markets. This allows more information to be pooled and processed more effectively, and economies of scale to be exploited. Financial integration also increases competition, thereby putting pressure on the cost of production for financial services, and increases financial development.

Although increased financial integration and development are usually associated with better economic performance, the implications for financial stability are more ambiguous. A higher degree of financial integration and development can have a positive impact on financial stability, to the extent that both facilitate risk sharing among agents. On the other hand, as the recent turmoil clearly demonstrates, some new (ill-designed or badly implemented) financial instruments may magnify problems arising from asymmetric information, distort incentives and offer opportunities for extreme risk taking. As pointed out among others by Rajan (2006) and Ferguson et al. (2007), financial integration will improve stability most of the times, but may make rare and extreme events more severe.

A key summary statistic to gauge the development of a financial system is the capital market size.[2] Chart 1 reports the total size of capital markets, which aggregates the size of stock, bond and loan markets as a share of GDP. The Chart shows that the size of capital markets it has been growing steadily over the past fifteen years for all developed economies. Papaioannou and Portes (2009) provide formal econometric evidence that the euro has accelerated the growth of financial development among euro area member countries. Establishing larger and more liquid capital markets is key to financial development, which in turn has a positive effect on investment and total-factor-productivity (see Levine (2005) and Papaioannou (2007) for reviews).

---

2   One important caveat is the following: the data behind the indicators discussed in this survey stop in mid 2008. Therefore, they do not cover the very recent developments. Preliminary evidence from ECB (2009) shows signs of divergence on price-based indicators (for instance in the cross-country dispersion of money market lending rates). From a financial integration perspective, it is important to understand how much of this divergence reflects differences in credit risk among banks, or alternatively higher market segmentation.

Chart I Size of capital markets

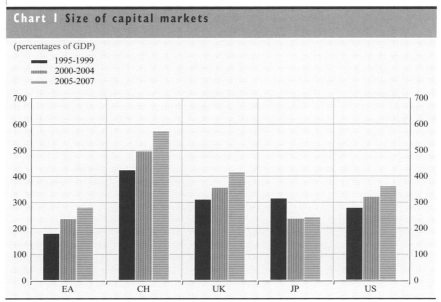

(percentages of GDP)
- 1995-1999
- 2000-2004
- 2005-2007

Source: WFE, IMF, ECB, Datastream, Eurostat.
Note: Sum of (i) stock market capitalisation, (ii) bank credit to the private sector and (iii) debt securities issued by the private sector divided by GDP.

The growing size of the euro area financial system shown in Chart 1, hides uneven developments of its individual segments. In the rest of this section we will review the literature that examines the impact of the single currency on the most important market segments, namely the money, bond, equity and banking market. Following the literature on financial integration, we will distinguish between price-based measures (based on asset pricing models) and quantity-based measures (based on cross-border asset allocations) (Obstfeld and Taylor (2004)).[3]

MONEY MARKETS

The euro area money market covers interbank short-term lending and borrowing and deposit taking.[4] The most important segment is the (unsecured and secured repo) markets. The unsecured deposit market is where credit institutions exchange short-term liquidity without posing collateral as guarantee. In the repo market, participants obtain liquidity against collateral, with the agreement to reverse the transaction at some pre-specified future date and price. The derivatives market includes interest rate futures, options and swaps, and has become increasingly important in recent years. The short-term securities market consists of commercial paper issued by corporations and certificates of deposit issued by banks with less than one year maturity.

---

3   For early surveys see Adam et al. (2002), Hartmann et al. (2003) and Baele et al. (2004). Recently, the European Commission and the ECB have been publishing comprehensive reports on financial integration (see EC (2008) and ECB (2008)).
4   See ECB (2008d) for a review of the recent developments in money markets.

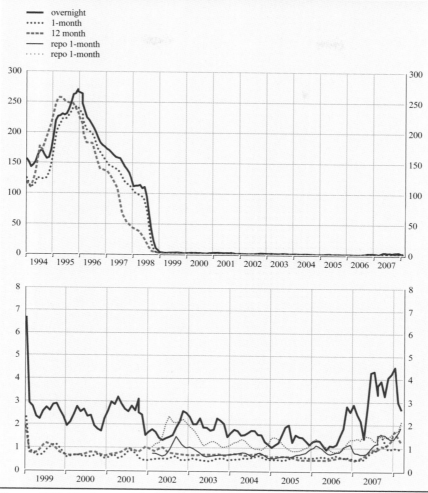

— overnight
···· 1-month
--- 12 month
— repo 1-month
···· repo 1-month

Source: ECB, http://www.ecb.int/stats/finint/html/index.en.html.
Note: Each indicator is constructed as the unweighted standard deviation of average daily interest rates (in basis points) prevailing in each euro area country. The bottom figure reports the indicators since the introduction of the euro.

Hartmann et al. (2003), Gaspar et al. (2001) and Perez-Quiros and Mendizabal (2006) analyze the evolution and integration of these markets in the early years of EMU. Financial integration in money markets is typically measured by the dispersion of average daily interest rates prevailing in each euro area country. Since transactions in these markets are characterized by similar cash flows and, given the very short term maturity contained very little credit risk (until the start of the turmoil), the law of one price suggests that in perfectly integrated markets any dispersion should converge to zero. The available evidence suggests that both the unsecured and secured segments of money markets have reached a high degree of integration (see Chart 2). The cross-sectional standard deviation of

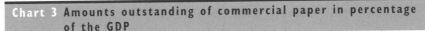

Chart 3 Amounts outstanding of commercial paper in percentage of the GDP

(percentages)

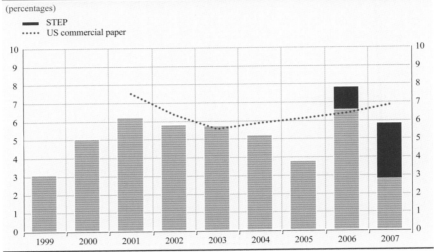

— STEP
····· US commercial paper

Sources: ECB, Euroclear, Banque De France, Dealogic and FED.
Note: The height of the bar for Europe is the sum of Euro Commercial Paper (ECP), and the commercial paper outstanding in the Belgian, German, Dutch, Spanish and French markets. Certificates of deposits and Asset Backed commercial paper are excluded. The blue area indicates the fraction of commercial paper that has the STEP, Short-Term European Paper, label. Since issuance in the ECP market is mainly undertaken by residents in the euro area and UK, the amounts outstanding of European commercial paper have been expressed in percentage of the sum of the Euro area and UK GDP.

the overnight lending rates across euro area countries fell sharply to almost zero following the introduction of the euro. Spreads between the policy rate and the inter-bank rates have been also small and have remained stable until the summer of 2007, the start of the financial turmoil. Similar results hold for the 1-month and 12-month EURIBOR and EUREPO rates.

Following the collapse of Bear Stearns and Lehman Brothers even very short term interbank loans are perceived as risky.[5] This in part explains the higher dispersion of money market rates observed over the last year, which must not necessarily be associated with an increased market segmentation. In the presence of asymmetric information – for instance with high uncertainty about the number of risky borrowers in the interbank market – the interest rate rises and safer borrowers may choose to drop out of the market. As counterparty risks increase even further, banks may prefer not to lend to other banks, thus reducing liquidity and increasing volatility in the interbank market (Heider, Hoerova and Holthausen (2008)).[6]

---

5   For systemic risk in banking see de Bandt, Hartmann, and Peydró (2009), and for interbank contagion see Iyer and Peydró (forthcoming).
6   Cassola, Lo Duca and Holthausen (2008) show that cross-border trades declined significantly after the start of the turmoil. At the same time the price for cross-border transactions has been significantly lower than that for domestic trades. According to the authors, these facts are consistent with a two-tier system of the money market: cross-border interbank trades are conducted by banks with a relatively high credit standing, while the other banks are mainly trading in domestic markets where interest rates are higher because the average credit risk is perceived to be higher.

The market for short-term securities, on the other hand, has shown little signs of integration, mainly because of differences in market practices and standards. Since commercial paper contracts vary across countries due to differences in legal systems and regulatory requirements, the market for short-term paper in Europe has remained largely of domestic nature.[7] Since June 2006, the STEP initiative (Short-Term European Paper) aims at fostering the integration of this market by promoting convergence of market standards.

Chart 3 illustrates the progress achieved so far. In 2007 more than half of the outstanding commercial paper in euros had been assigned the STEP label. As more issuers use a common STEP label, obstacles to cross-border transactions represented by different domestic practices are progressively eliminated. The commercial paper market has therefore the potential to become a truly integrated euro area market, whose dimension is comparable to that of the US.

BOND MARKETS

With the introduction of the euro and the removal of exchange rate risk, yields in the bond market have converged in all euro area member countries, and spreads tend to be increasingly driven by common factors. The extant literature and available indicators show that the euro had a substantial impact in these markets. Unlike for money markets, whose rates are directly comparable, naïve comparisons of bond yield differentials may give a misleading indication of the state of integration of bond markets. Besides exchange rate risk, bond returns differentials reflect differences in perceived credit risk, stemming for example from fiscal policies, a history of default, and current account positions. As such, bond spreads reflect the proper functioning of market discipline, rather than lack of integration. Most price-based measures of integration in bond markets are based on the intuition that in integrated markets bond yields should react to common, rather than local, factors. We review the evidence for government and corporate bond markets separately.

Government Bond Markets Examining the effect of monetary integration on government bonds is quite important, as even a small reduction of spreads may entail significant savings for the tax payer. A reduction in the cost of borrowing may free resources to invest in public works and social welfare programs. After the impressive convergence in the run up to EMU spreads have narrowed significantly in the initial post-euro period, although differences have not disappeared completely. Yet since the start of the financial market turmoil in summer 2007, spreads have increased significantly, specifically among countries with huge levels of debt, budget and trade deficits.

Although part of the remaining spread reflects cross-country differences in debt levels and budget deficits/surpluses, a common finding of the literature that clearly points to a higher degree of integration is that following the advent of the euro spreads tend to move together (see Pagano and Von Thadden (2004) for an early review of the literature). The empirical literature tries to identify

---

7   The London based Euro Commercial Paper (ECP) market is the only market where the short term paper is traded on a cross border basis.

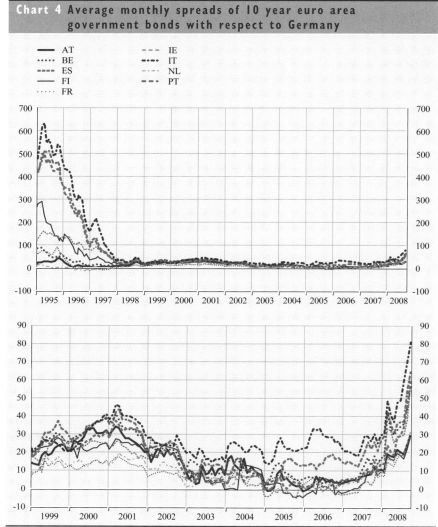

Chart 4 Average monthly spreads of 10 year euro area government bonds with respect to Germany

Legend:
- AT
- BE
- ES
- FI
- FR
- IE
- IT
- NL
- PT

Source: Datastream.
Note: Spreads are expressed in basis points. The small figure reports the behaviour of spreads since the introduction of the euro.

which common factors explain spread co-movement. Codogno et al. (2003) find that yield differentials between government bonds can be explained by variations in international risk factors, such as risk aversion proxied by the spread between the U.S. corporate and government bonds. The results are obtained with simple regressions, where spreads are regressed against countries' deviation of debt-to-GDP ratios with respect to Germany and their proxy for the international risk premium. Using alternative econometric techniques Geyer et al. (2004) and Bernoth et al. (2004) reach similar conclusions. Manganelli and Wolswijk (2008) show that the spreads of euro area government bonds are tightly related to the level of short-term interest rates set by the Eurosystem, which in turn may be related to time-varying risk aversion: an increase in interest rates is associated to a widening of spreads and conversely lower interest rates induce a reduction in spreads. Their finding is also consistent with an emerging line of empirical research, showing how tight monetary policy decreases the willingness of investors to bear risks.[8] Liquidity appears to be an important factor (e.g., Gomez-Puig (2006); Jankowitsch et al. (2006); Favero et al. (2007)). The general finding of this body of work is that the benchmark property appears to command a liquidity premium, although there may be relevant non-linear interactions between liquidity and credit risk.

Corporate Bond Market The introduction of the euro has been one of the driving forces behind the strong development of the euro area corporate bond market. Pagano and von Thadden (2004) provide a broad overview of the major structural developments. On the supply side, the introduction of the euro has offered companies the opportunity to access a larger pool of investors and diversify their liabilities away from traditional loans. Rajan and Zingales (2003), using panel data on domestic outstanding corporate debt in several countries till the early years of the single currency (2001, 2002), document that EMU had a positive and statistically significant effect on the amount of net debt issues.

Similarly, the market for corporate euro bond underwriting, after the introduction of the euro became a much more contestable business. Santos and Tsatsaronis (2003) show that the arrival of the euro had an important negative impact on the underwriting fees of international corporate bonds issued in the new currency. Biais et al. (2006) document how euro area corporate bonds have narrower bid-ask spreads than comparable bonds denominated in other currencies. According to the study this spread reduction is largely the outcome of the large pool of institutional investors, which was made possible by the integration of the European corporate bond market after the introduction of the euro. On the demand side, there has been a strong increase in the geographical diversification of euro area bond portfolios.

Chart 5 shows that the trend towards internationalization is ongoing. The Chart plots cross-border holdings among euro area member states of long-term debt securities. Overall, euro area residents have strongly increased their cross-border holdings of debt securities since the end of the 1990s, from about 10% to almost 60%. Given the very low starting point in 1997, this indicator suggests that investors have substantially diversified their portfolios across the euro area. One obtains similar results by looking at cross-border holdings of financial institutions. Cross-border holdings of long-term debt securities have continued to increase over the past ten years from about 15% in 1999 to about 40% in 2007 (see ECB 2008). The visual impression of Chart 5 is conformed by formal econometric studies. Lane (2006) and Cœurdacier and Martin (2007) regress the amount of cross-border bond holdings on an EMU dummy, controlling for several bilateral characteristics, among which EU membership and bilateral trade. They find that the introduction of the euro had a substantial impact on the amount of cross-border bond investments.

---

8   See, for instance, Rajan (2006), Bernanke and Kuttner (2005) and Jimenez et al. (2008).

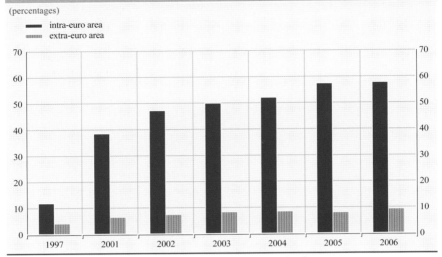

Chart 5 The degree of cross-border holdings of long-term debt securities issued by euro area residents.

(percentages)

- ▬ intra-euro area
- ▦ extra-euro area

Sources: ECB, http://www.ecb.int/stats/finint/html/index.en.html.
Note: "Intra-euro area" is defined as the share of long-term debt securities issued by euro area residents and held by residents (excluding central banks) in other euro area countries. "Extra-euro area" is defined as the share of long-term debt securities issued by euro area residents and held by non-residents (excluding central banks) of the euro area.

Researchers studying price-based measures also find a significant impact of the euro on integration in the corporate bond market. Baele et al. (2004) test whether risk-adjusted yields have a systematic country component. In an integrated market, the proportion of the total yield spread variance that is explained by country effects should be close to zero. The respective indicator shows that the euro area corporate bond market is quite integrated. Country effects explain only a very small proportion of the cross-sectional variance of corporate bond yield spreads (see ECB (2008)).

EQUITY MARKETS

Equity markets in Europe have developed substantially over the past two decades, in the midst of a wave of consolidation of stock exchanges. A higher volume of transactions lowers intermediation fees and increases market efficiency (see ECB (2007a)). Through network externalities and economies of scale the consolidation of stock exchanges can further spur integration. Market consolidation occurred initially at the national level. Consolidation continued then at the regional level (Euronext and OMX), and more recently outside the euro area (with the NYSE-Euronext and LSE-Borsa Italiana mergers). Schmiedel and Schönenberger (2005) report that securities exchanges (including stocks and derivatives) in the 12 euro area countries have decreased from 30 in 1999 to 22 in 2005.

It is much harder to assess the degree of integration of equity markets relative to money and bond markets, as equity returns are not directly comparable. In principle, in a perfectly integrated market only common risk factors are priced, while diversifiable country risks command no risk premia. In practice,

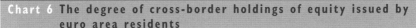

(percentages)

▬ intra-euro area
▦ extra-euro area

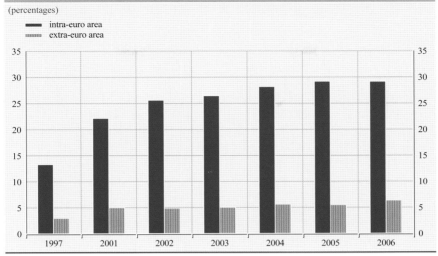

Source: ECB, http://www.ecb.int/stats/finint/html/index.en.html.
Note: "Intra-euro area" is defined as the share of equities issued by euro area residents and held by residents (excluding central banks) in other euro area countries. "Extra-euro area" is defined as the share of equities issued by euro area residents and held by non-residents (excluding central banks) of the euro area.

it is difficult to disentangle the impact on equity returns of changing economic fundamentals from changes in the pricing mechanism (see Adjaouté and Danthine (2004) for an in-depth discussion). A simple, direct attempt to quantify the impact of integration in equity markets is to look at the dynamics of investors' portfolios. In a truly integrated market, investors should not prefer national over foreign equities. Evidence of decreased home bias can therefore be consistent with the disappearance of psychological or physical barriers to cross border investments.

The available quantity-based measures indicate a rising degree of integration in equity markets. De Santis and Gerard (2006) investigate the determinants of international portfolio reallocation for 30 large economies between 1997 and 2001. They find an overall decrease in home bias that is more pronounced for euro area member states. Lane and Milesi-Ferretti (2007) and Cœurdacier and Martin (2007) reach similar results. Chart 6 shows that euro area residents increased their holdings of equity issued in another euro area country between 1997 and 2004. Over this period, the share of intra-euro area cross-border holdings of equity securities doubled to 28%, while the share of euro area equity assets held outside the euro area is much lower and increased only slightly.

Another strand of the literature studies integration in equity markets by looking at asset returns. A first group of papers uses asset pricing models, while a second group looks at changes in comovements at country and sectoral level. Hardouvelis et al. (2006) use a conditional asset pricing model where the risk premium of the stock market is decomposed into a euro area wide and country specific risk factors. The relative importance of these two factors is measured by a time-varying parameter that reflects the (conditional) level of integration of each market. The empirical findings show that the degree of integration has gradually increased to the point where individual euro area country stock markets appear to be fully integrated into the EU market. In a similar fashion, Cappiello, Lo Duca and Maddaloni (2008) use an intertemporal CAPM to study the dynamics of equity risk premia for the five largest euro area economies. They also find that euro area equity markets are well integrated. Fratzscher (2002), Baele et al. (2004) and Fratzscher and Stracca (2009) assess to what extent local equity returns react to news. The estimates are interpreted as a measure of the intensity with which euro area and world factors are transmitted to local equity markets. They find that greater economic and financial integration leads to a higher degree of co-movement across countries and therefore to an increase in sensitivities to euro area factors.

Asset pricing models depend on the particular methodology and empirical specification of the risk factors. Furthermore, any test of market integration based on an asset pricing model is at the same time a test of the asset pricing model itself. To address these limitations, the literature has developed measures of integration based on less-restrictive ("model free") approaches.[9] Following Heston and Rouwenhorst (1994) a common approach is to analyze the relative importance of country and industry factors in driving returns.[10] The idea of this body of work is that in segmented financial markets the benefits of cross-country diversification should be relatively higher than those of cross-sector diversification. An interesting finding of this line of research is that the dominance of country factors has decreased substantially and at certain points in time it has been overcome by industry factors in the euro area.

BANKING MARKETS

Banking markets encompass interbank (or wholesale) activities, capital market-related activities and retail banking activities. Since we have already analyzed interbank and capital market related activities, we focus here on the retail segment.[11] As banking is a multi-product business and banking services are quite heterogeneous it is hard to precisely assess the degree of integration. Retail customers typically buy packages of financial services that differ from bank to bank, let alone from country to country. Furthermore, because of limited access to "hard information" (such as publicly accessible account statements or an observed repayment track record), banks' loans to small customers have to rely on "soft information", such as personal interaction with the customer and knowledge of the local customs.

---

9   Ayuso and Blanco (2001) follow the approach proposed by Chen and Knez (1995). Although their application is limited to US, German and Spanish stock markets, their results point to an already substantial degree of integration during the nineties.

10 See Adjouté and Danthine (2004), Galati and Tsatsaronis (2003), Brooks and Del Negro (2004), Cappiello, Lo Duca and Maddaloni (2008), Cappiello, Kadareja and Manganelli (2008), Carrieri, Errunza and Sarkissian (2004), Bekaert, Hodrick and Zhang (2008), Eiling, Gérard and de Roon (2005).

11 Dermine (2006), Cabral, Dierick and Vesala (2002), and Goddard, Molyneux, Wilson and Tavakoli (2007) survey recent developments in European banking systems.

(as a share of total holdings, excluding the Eurosystem; percentages)

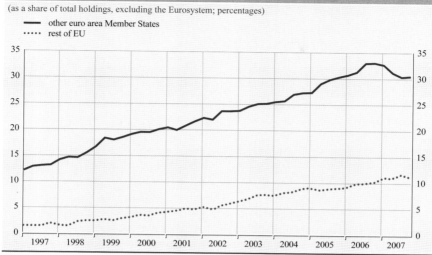

Source: ECB, http://www.ecb.int/stats/finint/html/index.en.html.
Notes: Geographical counterparty diversification of securities issued by euro area MFIs and held by MFIs in other euro area and non-euro area EU countries.

A simple way to describe the progress of integration in the banking market is to examine whether barriers to entry have been progressively removed. In principle, the absence of barriers to entry and the threat of new entries should deter incumbents from charging prices in excess of their marginal costs. In practice, such an ideal condition is rarely met. Several studies show that even in the U.S. the distance between borrower and lender is a highly significant determinant of lending conditions (e.g. Petersen and Rajan (2002)). Degryse and Ongena (2005) using a data set containing more than 17,000 firm loans of a large Belgian bank find that rates decrease in the distance between the firm and the lender. Similarly, loan rates increase in the distance between the firm and competing banks. Degryse and Ongena (2004) provide an extensive overview of empirical and theoretical literature suggesting that market segmentation may persist in retail banking for some time.

Notwithstanding these caveats, quantitative measures of integration in the retail bank market can be obtained directly by looking at the dispersion of interest rates on loans and deposits from banks to non-financial corporations and households. Euro area cross-country dispersion of bank interest rates has remained relatively high (at least when compared to the government bond market and interest rates on debt securities more generally, see ECB (2008)).[12]

---

12 An alternative way to gauge directly the degree of integration in banking market is to compare cross-country efficiency of European banks, as suggested for instance by Bos and Schmiedel (2007).

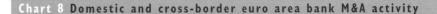

Chart 8 Domestic and cross-border euro area bank M&A activity

(percentages)

- ▬ target in the euro area; acquirer in the rest of the world
- ▦ acquirer in the euro area; target in the rest of the world
- ▤ acquirer and target in the euro area
- ▨ domestic

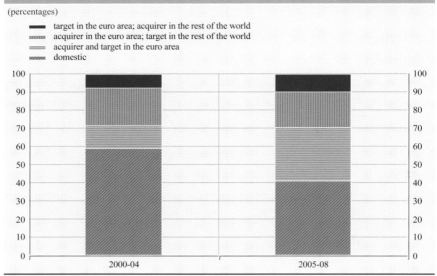

Source: ECB.
Notes: Domestic deals comprise M&A deals where the acquirer and the target bank are located in the same euro area country. All acquisition transactions are taken into account provided that the resulting stake is above 10% of the share capital. 2008 data is related to the first half of the year.

Quantity-based indicators of banking integration are based on measures of cross-border activities. Chart 7 reports the geographical holdings of securities issued by euro area financial institutions and held by other financial institutions resident in other euro area countries or in the rest of the European Union. The indicator shows substantial progress in the degree of euro area diversification. Other indicators, such as loans to other financial and non-financial institutions also reveal the existence of an increasing trend of cross-border activity (see ECB (2008)). The econometric analysis of Perez, Salas-Fumas and Saurina (2005) shows that this integration process has been boosted by the introduction of the euro.

The intrinsic nature of the banking system – characterized by strong information asymmetries – suggests that bank mergers and acquisitions (M&A) may be the best strategy to enter another market and provide truly pan-European cross-border services. Cross-border M&A in banking were low compared to related activities in the manufacturing sector. This reflected the existence of barriers, not only of geographical but also of regulatory and legal nature (see ECB (2007b), Berger (2007), Altunbas and Marqués-Ibáñez (2008)). The introduction of the euro has spurred cross-border bank M&A. Chart 8 reports average cross-border M&A activities of euro area banks, broken down by the geographical location of the deals. We notice that there has been a substantial reduction in the proportion of domestic deals which has been substituted by intra-euro area cross-border M&A activity. The extent to which banks are owned by foreign institutional investors appears to be an important determinant of cross-border M&A activity

(ECB (2008e)). If foreign institutional ownership and cross-border M&A help to reduce home bias and encourage foreign portfolio investments, they may represent important channels to foster financial integration.

2.1   POLICY INITIATIVES COMPLEMENTING MONETARY UNION

The degree of financial integration varies considerably across the various market segments. The more uniform the characteristics of the asset the more integrated that market. The unsecured money market, where banks lend to each other on such a very short term that the credit risk was essentially null (until the start of the turmoil), appeared to be the most integrated. Bond markets, where cash flows are directly comparable and credit risk can be reasonably estimated, also appear quite integrated. Equity and banking markets appear to be the least integrated.

Lack of integration reflects the existence of barriers to cross-border activities. We can classify the obstacles to financial integration in three main categories:

1. Cultural/informational

2. Regulatory/legal

3. Technical/infrastructure

CULTURAL/INFORMATIONAL
Recent work shows that there are non-negligible psychological and cultural barriers to financial integration (see for a review Guiso et al. (2006)). For example cultural differences and mistrust explains a significant portion of bilateral financial (and trade) flows (see Kalemli-Ozcan et al. (2008) and Guiso et al. (2008) for evidence). Giannetti and Yafeh (2008) show that cultural similarities correlate significantly with rates and the loan structure in the international syndicated bank loan market. Besides cultural and psychological reasons, information frictions seem to have a significant effect on financial integration. Research by Portes and Rey (2005) shows that variables reflecting information asymmetries among countries (such as telephone costs, trading time, foreign newspaper circulation) correlate significantly with cross-border equity flows. Subsequent work on other forms of financial integration reaches similar results (e.g. Aviat and Cœurdacier (2006); Papaioannou (2009)). Quite importantly in all studies, distance is negatively correlated with financial integration even if one accounts for cultural, regulatory, or informational differences. EU integration policies mainly focus on removing regulatory-legal barriers and building the necessary infrastructure for cheap and fast trading and settlement procedures. These measures can also serve to ease the informational frictions. We henceforth focus our analysis on these barriers.

REGULATORY/LEGAL OBSTACLES
A precondition for financial integration is the removal of any legislative or regulatory differences discriminating agents on the basis of their location. Many of the efforts at the European level have been directed at the removal of barriers to cross-border activities.

The legal and regulatory environment of the European banking industry has been radically changed over the past three decades (see Dermine (2003, 2006)). The transformation started in 1977, with the First Banking Directive establishing the principle of home country control: supervision of financial institutions operating in two or more member countries was shifted to the home country of the parent institution. It was followed in 1988 by the Second Banking Directive, under which all credit institutions authorized in a EU country were able to establish branches or supply cross-border financial services in other EU countries without further authorization ("single banking license"). In parallel with these EU-wide policies member states adopted additional policies that aimed at further strengthening the banking system (e.g. privatization policies).

After the introduction of the single currency, the European Commission launched in 1999 the Financial Services Action Plan (FSAP). The FSAP included a set of initiatives aiming at increasing financial integration along three strategic objectives (see Hartmann et al. 2003 for details):

- A single EU market for wholesale financial services,

- Open and secure retail markets,

- State of the art prudential rules and supervision.

While the FSAP constituted a major overhaul of the EU legislation for the entire financial sector, most of the initiatives related to securities markets. Major measures in this respect included, for example, the Markets in Financial Instruments Directive (MiFID), the Transparency Directive, the Market Abuse Directive, and the Prospectus Directive. Building on the achievements under the FSAP, the Commission adopted in December 2005 a White Paper on EU financial services policy for the years 2005-2010. The White Paper aimed at ensuring the effective and consistent implementation of the FSAP measures and at consolidating and simplifying the existing EU legislation.

Several EU initiatives have recently been adopted in the areas of banking regulation and supervision removing existing obstacles to cross-border banking. As already discussed in the banking section, cross-border banking groups are central for the integration process, as they enhance competition across jurisdictions. Against this background, the removal of policy-related obstacles to cross-border banking has become a policy priority in recent years. Partly as a result of a survey of the European Commission on barriers to cross-border banking consolidation, three main obstacles have been identified:

- Prudential – Differences in supervisory approval process and prudential rules.

- Legal – Incompatibilities in national company laws and insufficient legal harmonization.

- Fiscal – Differences in tax treatment of operations related to cross-border banks' M&A activities.

The European Commission has adopted several directives to address some of these issues. For instance, legal obstacles to cross-border M&A operations arising from differences in national company laws have been addressed to some extent with the Directive on take-over bids, adopted under the FSAP, and with the more recent Directive on cross-border mergers. Similarly, a Directive adopted in 2007 clarifies the procedural rules and the evaluation criteria for the prudential assessment of acquisitions and increases of holdings in the financial sector (see ECB (2007b) for details).[13] In Section 2 we investigate the effect of these policies on cross-border banking integration finding that the implementation of these policies did have a positive impact.

TECHNICAL OBSTACLES

Technical market infrastructures are also key for financial integration. Impediments to securities trading across national borders inhibit arbitrage forces and induce violations of the law of one price. European policy makers and the Eurosystem in particular have devoted great efforts to the establishment of a common infrastructure.

TARGET and TARGET2 There is unanimous agreement that the high degree of integration of the large value payment systems (mostly used for interbank payment transactions) has been instrumental to the integration of money markets and wholesale banking activities. Before 1999, the system was highly fragmented, with only domestic platforms operating in legacy currencies. Payments across national borders within the EU were typically made via correspondent banking, at higher costs and delays compared to national transactions.

The effective conduct of the single monetary policy required the elimination of any difference between intra euro-area and within country payments. With the introduction of TARGET (Trans-European Automated Real-time Gross settlement Express Transfer system) payments between credit institutions within the euro-area take place in real-time and at a harmonized transaction fee. At the same time the number of payment systems was reduced from seventeen to six in 1999.[14]

TARGET was based on the principle of minimum harmonization, linking the national settlement systems of the 15 EU Member States and the ECB payments

---

13 Many of these initiatives have been implemented in the context of the so-called "Lamfalussy framework", a legislative architecture introduced by the EU to increase the speed and flexibility of the regulatory process. The framework distinguishes four levels in the approach to financial legislation. Level 1 concerns the development of basic principles, which are adopted by the European Parliament and the Council. Level 2 involves the implementation of the technical details of level 1 directives and regulations, which is delegated to suitable committees. At level 3 the committees ensure the homogeneous implementation of community legislation at national level. At level 4 the European Commission is in charge of strengthening the enforcement of EU law at national level, co-operating with the relevant Member States parties. The practical functioning of the Lamfalussy framework – which since 2003 has also been implemented in the banking and insurance sectors – has been closely monitored and improved over the years.

14 Since the introduction of the euro, two of the remaining six systems were closed down. Amongst the remaining four systems, the TARGET system and the private net settlement system EURO1 process most of the traffic, with TARGET being the largest of the two.

mechanism into a single platform. In response to the growing demand from financial institutions, the Eurosystem launched TARGET2 on 19 November 2007, which is no longer based on a decentralized architecture of "system of systems", but on a single shared platform. TARGET2 has replaced the TARGET system in full since 19 May 2008.[15] TARGET2 is expected to further enhance the integration of wholesale payments by providing its participants with:

- a single pricing structure for both domestic and cross-border transactions,

- a harmonized set of cash settlement services in central bank money for ancillary systems,

- a single technical communication interface for multi-country users, to process the information from branches in different countries.

The centralization of payment business is expected to allow users to exploit benefits from economies of scale and efficiency gains in speed and quality.

TARGET2-Securities The integration of the infrastructure-underlying bond and equity markets is much less advanced, partly reflecting the greater complexities of these markets. Each country has developed it own system based on different practices, as well as different legal, regulatory and fiscal regimes. The resulting fragmentation implies higher post-trading costs for EU cross-border securities transactions and constitutes a significant barrier to a truly integrated European financial market. These problems have been under the radar screen of EU policy makers for quite some time, and a number of actions have already been taken, such as:

- Harmonization of market practices, law, regulation and taxation to remove the so-called "Giovannini barriers".[16]

- The development of a "Code of Conduct for clearing and settlement" to stimulate fair and open competition among all exchanges, central counterparties and central securities depositories.

- The development of standards for the securities settlement systems aimed at promoting convergence towards the highest standards of safety and efficiency.

To fully exploit the benefit of scale and competition from a truly pan-European securities market, the Eurosystem is working at the establishment of TARGET2-

---

15 We refer to ECB (2008c) for comprehensive information about the main recent developments.
16 The Giovannini Group identified a set of barriers to cross-border clearing and settlement, stemming from differences in market practices, legal, regulatory and fiscal provisions. For details, see http://ec.europa.eu/economy_finance/eu_economic_situation/integrating_markets300_en.htm. See Giovannini (2008) for an extensive overview of clearing and settlement systems in Europe.

Securities (T2S), a borderless and neutral platform for securities settlement.[17] The resulting system endeavors making cross border settlement as cheap and efficient as domestic settlement. At the same time, it will allow market participants to pool their liquidity and collateral, reducing costs. The use of a common settlement platform should increase transparency and facilitate investors' decision to hold securities in the issuing depository, in an investor depository or in a custodian bank. Once implemented, investors should be able to choose the provider on the basis of costs and services offered, rather than the location of the security. This, in turn, will reduce custodian services fees, which currently represent a significant fraction of the costs for end-users.

SEPA: Single Euro Payments Area The integration of retail banking markets has been hampered by, among other things, the high level of fragmentation of the retail payments infrastructure.

Prices for cross-border credit transfers were higher and the execution time substantially longer than for domestic transfers. Despite some initiatives by the banking industry, progress was slow and the pricing structure remained highly heterogeneous. The processing of credit transfers, direct debits and payment cards remained fragmented reflecting the underlying payment infrastructures.

European Parliament and the Council adopted a Regulation in December 2001, which enforced an equal pricing of cross-border and national euro payments for consumers. This was followed in early 2002 by the launch of the Single Euro Payments Area (SEPA) initiative for the banking industry. In SEPA all euro payments will be treated as domestic payments and remaining distinctions between national and cross-border payments will disappear. By creating a truly integrated infrastructure, SEPA should foster the integration and improve the efficiency of the euro area retail banking markets (see ECB (2007c) for details).[18]

STEP: Short-Term European Paper To promote integration in the short-term debt securities (i.e. commercial papers and certificates of deposit) the ECB called for market participants to improve the functioning of this market. In response, the Financial Market Association (ACI) launched the Short-Term European Paper (STEP) initiative to foster the integration of the European market segments for short-term securities. The STEP initiative aimed at (i) identifying a set of common market standards and practices suitable to promote market integration and (ii) fostering the voluntary compliance of market participants by granting a common label to compliant issuance programmes.

The project has been implemented in two main phases. The first phase – concluded in June 2006 with the STEP Market Convention – focused on identifying and codifying adequate market standards. The second phase aimed to raise public

---

17 The T2S project was official launched by the Governing Council of the ECB on 17 July 2008. See http://www.ecb.int/paym/t2s/html/index.en.html for more details.
18 Although the Eurosystem was not the main driver of SEPA, it had a catalyst role in fostering agreement and convergence towards common standards among market participants.

awareness. The campaign contributed to the rapid acceptance and the increasing relevance of the STEP market (see Chart 3).[19]

2.2 THE EFFECTS OF THE EURO AND EU-WIDE POLICIES ON FINANCIAL INTEGRATION

A fast growing body of research analyzes the effect of the euro on various forms of financial integration.[20] For example Lane (2006), Courdacier and Martin (2007), and De Santis and Gerard (2006) use bilateral cross-sectional bond and equity holding data (from IMF's Coordinated Portfolio Investment Survey) in advanced economies to examine the effect of the euro on cross-border bond and equity holdings. Likewise, Papageorgiou (2005), Petroulas (2007), and Flam and Nordstrom (2006) quantify the impact of the single currency on bilateral FDI flows. Bobba et al. (2008) document an increased role of the euro in international debt issuance, while Spiegel (2009) shows a sizable positive impact of the single currency on cross-border banking activities. While estimates differ across studies, the overall evidence shows that the euro has spurred financial integration in equity and bond markets among member states. For example in the context of banking integration Spiegel (2009) finds that cross-border bank lending more than doubled after the introduction of the euro in Portugal and Greece.

Yet little attention has been given to isolating the effects of harmonization policies from monetary union and other parallel developments. In this section we summarize the empirical strategy and results from Kalemli-Ozcan, Papaioannou and Peydró (2008b), who as far as we are aware, is the only study that disentangles the monetary union effect on financial integration from legislative harmonization policies in the financial sector.

Kalemli-Ozcan, Papaioannou and Peydró (2008b) exploit a confidential data-set from the Bank of International Settlements (International Locational Banking Statistics Database) which contains information on bilateral bank holdings and flows among developed countries. This dataset reports asset and liability holdings of banks located in the main industrial countries and some financial centers in roughly 150 countries since 1977. The analysis is carried over a group of 20 advanced economies over the 1977-2007 period. To assess the effect of legislative-regulatory harmonization policies the authors use information from the European Commission on the implementation of the 21 Directives of the FSAP.[21] To measure the impact of the single currency on exchange rate volatility, the authors use the Reinhart and Rogoff (2004) classification.

---

19 Like SEPA, STEP is a market led initiative. The ECB played a key catalyst role by providing assistance in the formulation and promotion of the project (see ECB 2008b for further details).

20 This work follows an earlier literature on the effects of free-trade-agreements and currency unions on international trade (e.g. Rose (2000); Micco et al. (2003); Flam and Nordstrom (2006); see Baldwin (2006) for a review).

21 The Commission has created league tables to put pressure on the countries to quickly adopt the directives. The data is available at: http://ec.europa.eu/internal_market/finances/index_en.htm. They also analyzed the other Directives that entered after 2003 finding similar results.

In contrast to previous work that mainly used cross-sectional approaches,[22] their three dimensional panel structure allows them to control for year fixed effects and country-pair fixed-effects. Year fixed-effects account for global trends on banking integration. This is important as, for example, cross-border bank flows have increased considerably among the past twenty years (e.g. Lane and Milessi-Feretti (2007)). Country-pair fixed-effects enables them to control for all sources of (to a first-approximation) time-invariant bilateral characteristics that affect financial integration. Country-pair fixed-effects control for distance, adjacency, and other (gravity-like) factors that correlate with banking integration (e.g. Portes and Rey (2005); Aviat and Cœurdacier (2006); Papaioannou (2009)). In addition, country-pair fixed-effects account for other unobserved or hard-to-account-for factors, such as cultural proximity, political ties, legal system similarities, etc. that affect financial and international banking in particular linkages (Guiso et al. (2009); Giannetti and Yafeh (2008)).

Kalemli-Ozcan, Papaioannou and Peydró (2008b) first estimate difference-in-difference specification where euro area member countries constitute the "treatment" group, while the three EU and the five non-EU countries serve as the "control" group. The estimates suggest that cross-border banking activities between euro area countries increased by 40% – 45% , compared to the general evolution of international financial integration in the control group of countries. The difference-in-difference specifications further show that it was the adoption of the single currency rather than EU membership that spurred banking integration.

Second, the authors augment the model with the bilateral measure of the rigidity of the exchange rate regime and the index that quantifies the implementation of financial sector reforms in the context of the FSAP. The panel estimates show that international banking activities is significantly higher among pair of countries with a fixed exchange rate regime.[23] Thus a primary reason behind the positive impact of the euro on financial integration was the elimination of exchange rate volatility. Legislative harmonization in financial sector tends also to have a significant effect on cross-border banking integration. Roughly one third of the overall positive impact of the euro in the unconditional estimates is explained by these reforms.

Third, the authors also investigate whether the positive effect of the single currency on financial integration is driven by a similarly positive impact on goods trade. Although trade in goods and assets is positively correlated the estimates imply that monetary unification and financial legislation harmonization are the key drivers of cross-border banking integration.[24]

---

22 This is because previous work mainly relies on IMF's CPIS data that started becoming available at 1997. Since the initial surveys covered a small number of countries and the data was questionable, most studies use CPIS data after 2001.

23 This finding is interesting in light of the so-called "fear of floating" literature (e.g. Calvo and Reinhart (2003); Klein and Shambaugh (2007)). Yet while this literature focuses on developing economies, these results reveal a similar pattern across developed countries.

24 See Kalemli-Ozcan, Papaioannou and Peydró (2008b) for the robustness of the results reviewed here and also for further results.

3 THE REAL EFFECTS OF FINANCIAL INTEGRATION

In the second part of the paper, we analyze the "real effects" of financial integration. First, we evaluate the effect of banking integration on macroeconomic volatility. Second, we investigate the effect of banking integration on the amount of consumption and income risk sharing.

In this section we use data from BIS's Banking Statistics on cross-border bank holdings and flows at the country level over the 1978-2007 period and examine the effect of banking integration on output and consumption growth volatility, and on consumption and income risk sharing. Our sample includes the initial 12 euro area member countries, the three non euro area EU15 countries (namely the UK, Sweden, and Denmark) and five other industrial countries (the US, Japan, Australia, Canada, and Switzerland).

3.1 THE EFFECTS OF BANKING INTEGRATION ON MACROECONOMIC VOLATILITY

Standard theory predicts that financial integration should lead to lower consumption volatility, as agents will be able to smooth idiosyncratic fluctuations. In contrast income volatility may increase as financial integration may magnify productivity differences. Yet the empirical literature fails to find such effects in the data (see for example Kose et al. 2008)). For example cross-country studies find an insignificant effect of international financial integration on output and consumption volatility.[25]

EMPIRICAL SPECIFICATION
We investigate the question of volatility in a panel framework and run the following regression:

$$FLUCT_{i,t}^{Y,C} = \alpha_t + \alpha_i + \beta FININT_{i,t-1} + \gamma TRADE_{i,t-1} + X'_{i,t-1}\delta + \varepsilon_{i,t} \qquad (1)$$

where dependent variable $FLUCT_{i,t}^{Y,C}$ is a proxy of the fluctuations of output (Y) and consumption (C) growth for country i in year t,. We construct the two meaures using the analogous study of Morgan, Rime, and Strahan (2004), who quantify the effect of banking integration on GSP fluctuations across US states. The index is constructed in two steps. First, we regress real p.c. GDP growth

---

25 Besides volatility the literature on the "real" effects of financial integration focuses on the correlation between integration and business cycle synchronization (see for example Flood, et al. (2008)). The standard international real business cycle model implies that a positive productivity shock will yield low cross-country output correlations, as capital will flow to the country where the marginal product of labor is high and workers there will substitute leisure for labor (e.g. Backus, Kehoe, and Kydland (1992), Baxter and Crucini (1995), Heathcote and Perri (2002)). (Kalemli-Ozcan, Reshef, Sorensen, and Yosha (2008)). Yet Kalemli-Ozcan et al reference after Heatcote and Perri reference cross-sectional cross-country works find that financial integration makes business cycles more rather than less alike (Imbs (2004, 2006); see Rose (2008) for a review). Yet Kalemli-Ozcan, Papaioannou, and Peydró (2008a), however, utilize a unique panel dataset of bilateral financial flows and show robust evidence that a higher degree of banking integration leads to less synchronized output patterns.

for each country i on country fixed-effects and time fixed-effects. The residuals of these models ($v_{i,t}^Y$) reflect how much GDP growth differs in each country and year compared to average growth in this year (across countries) and the average growth of this country over the estimation period. The absolute value of these residuals reflects GDP fluctuations with respect to the cross-country and the across-year mean growth

$$(FLUCT_{i,t}^Y \equiv \left| v_{i,t}^Y \right| \text{ growth:}$$

We do the same for consumption growth (C) and we obtain

$$FLUCT_{i,t}^C \equiv \left| v_{i,t}^C \right|.$$

For robustness, we also estimate the model using non-overlapping windows of five-year averaged data, where we measure volatility with the standard deviation of output and consumption growth over each of the six five-year periods.

Our focus is on the coefficient of country-level financial integration with respect to the rest of the world. We use the publicly available version of BIS's Locational Banking Statistics database and we construct for robustness three measures of integration: First measure is the growth of total bank external assets and liabilities in country i, in year t. Following Morgan et al. (2004) we also distinguish between assets and liabilities. This is important as international finance theories suggest that they can have different effects on business cycle patterns. Hence our second measure is the growth of bank external liabilities in country i in year t; and last but not least we use the growth of bank external assets in country i in year t, as our third measure.

Given the emphasis of previous work on international trade and production similarities as determinants of volatility, we also construct proxy measures of trade and specialization patterns. Following Frankel and Rose (1998), we measure $TRADE_{i,t}$ with the log of real (deflated with US price deflator) exports and imports as a share of GDP. For specialization we follow Kalemli-Ozcan, Sorensen, and Yosha (2003) and Imbs (2006), among others, and measure differences in the production structure (specialization) with the following index:

$$SPEC_{i,t} = \sum_{n=1}^{N} \left(s_{i,t}^n - \frac{1}{J-1} \sum_{j\neq i}^{N} \sum_n s_{j,t}^n \right)^2,$$

where $s_{i,t}^n$ denote the GDP share of manufacturing industry n in year t in country i (data are retrieved from UNIDO). $SPEC_{i,t}$ therefore measures the distance between the vector of sector shares in country i, and the vector of average sector shares in the other countries, where the total number of countries $J = 20$. Thus, a higher number in $SPEC_{i,t}$ indicates that the country has less similar production structures to the other 19 countries.

Table 1 reports summary statistics for the country level variables.

Table 1 Descriptive statistics

	Obs.	Mean	St. dev.	Min.	Max.
FLUCT GDP	600	1.00	1.00	0.00	8.00
FLUCT Cons	575	1.00	1.00	0.00	7.00
BI Assets	594	13.00	14.00	-29.00	175.00
BI Liabilities	594	13.00	20.00	-32.00	298.00
BI Total	594	12.00	14.00	-27.00	218.00

Notes: FLUCT GDP and FLUCT Cons is the volatility of real p.c GDP growth and consumption growth respectively. Volatility is calculated as the absolute residual of these respective growth rates after accounting for country fixed-effects and year fixed-effects. FLUCT measures are reported as percent. BI Assets the growth of external bank assets adjusted for valuation effects and exchange rate movements at the country level. BI Liabilities is the growth of external bank liabilities is adjusted for same effects at the country level. BI Total is the growth of sum of external assets and liabilities, also adjusted for the valuation eects. The growth rates are calculated as change in stocks of assets from $t-1$ to t (or liabilities or total) divided by stocks of assets (or liabilities or total) in $t-1$. They reported as percent.

Table 2 Fluctuations of GDP growth

	Btwn (1)	Wthn (2)	Btwn (3)	Wthn (4)	Btwn (5)	Wthn (6)	Btwn (7)	Wthn (8)
BI total	0.09	0.01			0.05	0.01		
	3.57	1.71			1.99	1.22		
BI assets			0.05	0.00			0.00	-0.01
			1.55	-0.51			0.15	-0.76
BI liabilities			0.04	0.01			0.04	0.01
			1.82	2.51			1.60	2.26
Trade					0.00	-0.01	0.00	-0.02
					-0.28	-1.21	-0.37	-1.36
Specialization					0.32	-0.14	0.30	-0.14
					2.24	-0.95	1.98	-0.92
Year FE	No	Yes	No	Yes	No	Yes	No	Yes
Country FE	No	Yes	No	Yes	No	Yes	No	Yes
R^2	0.41	0.25	0.43	0.25	0.54	0.32	0.55	0.33
Observations	574	574	574	574	375	375	375	375
Countries	20	20	20	20	20	20	20	20

Notes: t-statistics are reported underneath the estimated coefficients. Fluctuations of GDP growth is a volatility measure and calculated as the absolute residual of growth rates after accounting for country fixed-effects and year fixed-effects. BI Assets the growth of external bank assets adjusted for valuation effects and exchange rate movements at the country level. BI Liabilities is the growth of external bank liabilities is adjusted for same effects at the country level. BI Total is the growth of sum of external assets and liabilities, also adjusted for the valuation effects. The growth rates are calculated as change in stocks of assets from $t-1$ to t (or liabilities or total) divided by stocks of assets (or liabilities or total) in $t-1$. Trade is the logarithm of exports plus imports as a share of GDP. Specialization is an index that reflects the dis-similarities in industrial production between the two countries.

We now examine the effect of aggregate (country-level) financial (banking integration) on business cycle volatility. We first examine the effect of financial integration on output fluctuations. Second, we study the effect of integration on consumption fluctuations.

OUTPUT FLUCTUATIONS

Tables 2 and 3 report the estimates on the effect of financial integration on GDP volatility. In Table 2 we employ annual data using as the dependent variable the fluctuation index $(FLUCT_{i,t}^{Y})$ of Morgan et al. (2004). Table 3 reports otherwise identical specifications but now the dependent variable is the standard deviation of real GDP p.c. growth over each of the six non-overlapping 5-year periods. For comparability with previous work, besides the panel fixed-effect estimates, we also report the "between" results. We report unconditional correlation coefficients and models that also control for trade and specialization.

The coefficient on the financial (banking) integration measure is positive and significant in the cross-sectional models in columns (1) and (5). This shows that a higher degree of external assets and liabilities is associated with more volatile GDP growth. Yet this correlation could be driven by numerous country-factors.

Table 3 Fluctuations of GDP growth: 5 year of panel

	Btwn (1)	Wthn (2)	Btwn (3)	Wthn (4)	Btwn (5)	Wthn (6)	Btwn (7)	Wthn (8)
BI total	0.06	0.00			0.04	0.01		
	2.76	0.66			1.47	0.70		
BI assets			0.04	-0.01			0.02	-0.02
			0.03	-1.24			0.77	-1.57
BI liabilities			0.03	0.02			0.02	0.02
			0.02	2.27			0.68	2.83
Trade					0.00	-0.05	0.00	-0.08
					0.58	-0.26	0.56	-0.38
Specialization					0.18	-0.00	0.18	-0.01
					1.29	-0.59	1.23	-0.77
Year FE	No	Yes	No	Yes	No	Yes	No	Yes
Country FE	No	Yes	No	Yes	No	Yes	No	Yes
R^2	0.30	0.44	0.32	0.46	0.38	0.43	0.39	0.47
Observations	119	119	119	119	102	102	102	102
Countries	20	20	20	20	20	20	20	20

Notes: t-statistics are reported underneath the estimated coefficients. Fluctuations of GDP growth is a volatility measure and calculated as the standard deviation over a 5-year window of growth rates. BI Assets the growth of external bank assets adjusted for valuation effects and exchange rate movements at the country level. BI Liabilities is the growth of external effects bank liabilities is adjusted for same effects at the country level. BI Total is the growth of sum of external assets and liabilities, also adjusted for the valuation effects. The growth rates are calculated as change in stocks of assets from $t-1$ to t (or liabilities or total) divided by stocks of assets (or liabilities or total) in $t-1$. Trade is the logarithm of exports plus imports as a share of GDP. Specialization is an index that reflects the dis-similarities in industrial production between the two countries.

Table 4 Fluctuations of consumption growth

	Btwn (1)	Wthn (2)	Btwn (3)	Wthn (4)	Btwn (5)	Wthn (6)	Btwn (7)	Wthn (8)
BI total	0.05	0.00			0.02	-0.01		
	1.81	-1.92			1.99	1.22		
BI assets			0.04	-0.01			0.00	-0.01
			1.12	-2.08			-0.10	-1.59
BI liabilities			0.01	0.00			0.02	0.00
			0.50	0.95			0.68	-0.17
Trade					0.00	-0.01	0.00	-0.01
					-0.27	-1.20	-0.29	-1.26
Specialization					0.20	-0.20	0.20	-0.20
					1.39	-1.39	1.28	-1.36
Year FE	No	Yes	No	Yes	No	Yes	No	Yes
Country FE	No	Yes	No	Yes	No	Yes	No	Yes
R^2	0.15	0.23	0.15	0.23	0.25	0.27	0.25	0.27
Observations	574	574	574	574	374	374	374	374
Countries	20	20	20	20	20	20	20	20

Notes: t-statistics are reported underneath the estimated coefficients. Fluctuations of Consumption growth is a volatility measure and calculated as the absolute residual of growth rates after accounting for country fixed-effects and year fixed-effects. BI Assets the growth of external bank assets adjusted for valuation effects and exchange rate movements at the country level. BI Liabilities is the growth of external bank liabilities is adjusted for same effects at the country level. BI Total is the growth of sum of external assets and liabilities, also adjusted for the valuation effects. The growth rates are calculated as change in stocks of assets from $t-1$ to t (or liabilities or total) divided by stocks of assets (or liabilities or total) in $t-1$. Trade is the logarithm of exports plus imports as a share of GDP. Specialization is an index that reflects the dis-similarities in industrial production between the two countries.

In columns (2) and (6) we add a vector of country fixed-effects and period fixed-effects to account for time-invariant country characteristics and global trends. The estimate drops considerably both in the annual and the five-year averaged models and is statistically insignificant. This result is in line with previous work that using broader measures of financial openness and larger samples also show weak correlations between financial integration and macroeconomic volatility.

Theory, however, suggests that external assets and liabilities can have differential effects on macroeconomic performance. A high degree of external assets may lower volatility through international diversification (e.g. Obstfeld (1994)); yet large amounts of external liabilities can magnify fluctuations as foreign investors might leave the country in recession times (e.g. Kaminsky, Reinhart and Vegh (2004)). In models (3), (4), (7), and (8) we thus split the composite measure of financial integration into an assets and liabilities based measure. The "within" estimates clearly show that the two types of financial openness have opposing effects. The coefficient on external liabilities is positive and significant in all model permutations. This suggests that countries that experience a fast

Table 5 Fluctuations of consumption growth: 5 year panel

	Btwn (1)	Wthn (2)	Btwn (3)	Wthn (4)	Btwn (5)	Wthn (6)	Btwn (7)	Wthn (8)
BI total	0.04	-0.01			0.02	0.01		
	1.57	-1.24			0.72	-1.12		
BI assets			0.03	-0.02			0.01	-0.02
			0.82	-2.93			0.44	-2.69
BI liabilities			0.01	0.01			0.00	0.01
			0.45	1.19			0.13	1.57
Trade					0.09	0.00	0.00	-0.01
					0.62	-0.61	0.44	-0.79
Specialization					0.00	-0.10	-0.11	-0.12
					0.39	-0.59	0.70	-0.69
Year FE	No	Yes	No	Yes	No	Yes	No	Yes
Country FE	No	Yes	No	Yes	No	Yes	No	Yes
R^2	0.12	0.47	0.10	0.48	0.13	0.45	0.13	0.48
Observations	119	119	119	119	102	102	102	102
Countries	20	20	20	20	20	20	20	20

Notes: Fluctuations of GDP growth is a volatility measure and calculated as the standard deviation over a 5-year window of growth rates. BI Assets the growth of external bank assets adjusted for valuation effects and exchange rate movements at the country level. BI Liabilities is the growth of external bank liabilities adjusted for same effects at the country level. BI Total is the growth of sum of external assets and liabilities, also adjusted for the valuation effects. The growth rates are calculated as change in stocks of assets from $t-1$ to t (or liabilities or total) divided by stocks of assets (or liabilities or total) in $t-1$. Trade is the logarithm of exports plus imports as a share of GDP. Specialization is an index that reflects the dis-similarities in industrial production between the two countries. See table 1 for detailed description of variables.

accumulation of foreign external liabilities tend to have more volatile GDP fluctuations.[26] In contrast, the estimate on the growth of external foreign assets is negative and insignificant at standard confidence levels.

CONSUMPTION FLUCTUATIONS

Theoretical work emphasizes the welfare effects of financial openness. The standard argument is that through international diversification, financial integration enhances welfare by lowering consumption fluctuations. In Tables 4 and 5 we thus report analogous to the GDP fluctuations estimates, quantifying the effect of banking integration on consumption volatility. Table 4 reports results in the annual dataset using the Morgan et al. (2004) index of consumption fluctuations ($FLUCT_{i,t}^C$) and Table 5 gives analogous estimates using the standard deviation of real consumption growth over 6 non-overlapping five year periods.

---

26 This result is consistent with Kalemli-Ozcan, Sorensen, and Volosovcyh (2009), who shows a positive effect of foreign ownership on regional level volatility within Europe.

In line with the previous evidence on output volatility there seems to be no effect of financial integration on consumption fluctuations, when we use the composite measure of banking integration that blends assets and liabilities. When we split the results between external asset growth and liability growth, we still do not find significant results in the cross-sectional models. However, once we exploit the time variation, controlling for country fixed-effects, we find that a higher degree of external bank asset growth reduces consumption volatility. This applies both when we use the annual fluctuation index (in Table 4) and when we use the standard deviation of real consumption growth (in Table 5) in the LHS of the specification. This new result offers direct support to theories in international finance that international investment enables agents to smooth consumption and diversify idiosyncratic country-specific risk. In the next section we quantify the effects of banking integration on risk sharing.

3.2 BANKING INTEGRATION AND RISK SHARING

If consumption growth rates in all countries are identical, then there is perfect risk sharing. As shown by Arrow and Debreu this is an equilibrium outcome assuming consumers have identical CRRA utility functions and access to a complete set of Arrow-Debreu securities.[27] The empirical implication is that consumption in each country is a constant share of aggregate consumption. Starting with Mace (1991) the literature generally tests whether or not the growth rates are identical, where a rejection implies no perfect risk sharing.[28]

The literature constructed standard measures of the degree of consumption risk sharing among groups of countries as follows. Denote country i's year t (per capita real, government plus private) final consumption, C_{it}, and denote aggregate consumption in year t, C_t. Similarly, denote country i's year t (real per capita) output, GDP_{it}, and aggregate output in year t, GDP_t. This measure build on the observation that the correlation of country-specific consumption, with country-specific output shocks is zero under perfect risk sharing. One must consider country-specific growth rates, because aggregate shocks cannot be eliminated by the sharing of risk, and the aggregate component is, therefore, deducted from the individual countries' growth rates.

$$\Delta logC_{it} - \Delta logC_t = \mu_i + \kappa \left(\Delta logGDP_{it} - \Delta logGDP_t\right) + \epsilon_{it} \qquad (2)$$

In the above panel specification, suggested by Asdrubali, Sorensen, and Yosha (1996), $1-\kappa$ is the measure of average amount of risk sharing over the period.[29] κ measures the average co movement of the countries idiosyncratic consumption

---

27 See Obstfeld and Rogoff (1996).
28 Mace (1991) uses individual level data and Obstfeld (1994) uses country level data to test the same prediction.
29 Note that the above equation is equivalent to using a time fixed effect to remove the aggregate shock as shown by Ravallion and Chaudhuri, (1997). So we can also run,

$$\Delta log\, C_{it} = \mu_i + \lambda_t + \kappa \Delta logGDP_{it} + \epsilon_{it} \qquad (3)$$

growth with their idiosyncratic GDP growth. The inclusion of country fixed effects is equivalent to subtracting the country average over the period for each variable and running the regression with no constant. Hence, since the country averages over time are removed, risk sharing over longer horizons will not be captured here. This regression with country fixed effects will only capture risk sharing at the business cycle frequency, which is our aim here.

Our purpose is to evaluate how much risk sharing is driven by banking integration. Following Melitz and Zumer (1999), Sorensen et al. (2007), and most importantly Demyanyk et al. (2008), we modify the basic regression as follows:

$$\Delta log\, C_{it} - \Delta log\, C_t = \mu_i + \kappa_{it} + (\Delta logGDP_{it} - \Delta logGDP_t) + \epsilon_{it} \qquad (4)$$

where

$$\kappa_{it} = \kappa_0 + \kappa_1.(t-\bar{t}) + \kappa_2.(BANKINT_{it-1} - BANKINT_{t-1}) \qquad (5)$$

$\bar{t}$ is the middle year of the sample period, and $BANKINT_{t-1}$ is the (un-weighted) average across countries of $BANKINT_{it-1}$ at time t−1. Demeaning the interaction terms is equivalent to removing permanent differences between countries in banking integration and hence the regressions captures the effect of time variation in banking integration on risk sharing.

The estimated value of $1-\kappa_0$ corresponds to the average amount of consumption risk sharing over time and within the group of countries. $1-\kappa_0-\kappa_1.(t-\bar{t})-\kappa_2.$ $(BANKINT_{it-1} - BANKINT_{t-1})$ then measures the amount of risk sharing obtained in period t by country i with bank integration level $BANKINT_{it-1}$. We include a time trend in order to guard against the upward trending bank integration measures spuriously capturing trend changes in risk sharing that may be caused by other developments in international markets. The parameter $-\kappa_1$ captures the average year-by-year increase in risk sharing. Hence here the amount of risk sharing is allowed to change over time with the trend and with bank integration. The parameter $-\kappa_2$ measures how much higher than average banking integration lowers the co-movement and hence increases the risk sharing.

One can think of other interaction effects. At the same time, the choice of the interaction effect should not violate the fact that risk sharing is about buffering shocks via large gross holdings of assets within a group of countries such as OECD or EU. Hence, primarily, one should account for this direct effect. For example, the euro is not suitable to use as an interaction effect, since as we have shown in section 2.1, the euro has spurred banking integration in the euro area. This implies the effect of the euro on risk sharing works via financial integration. In addition, the euro might be capturing issues such as trade increases, decreases in transaction costs, all of which may or may not have an indirect effect on risk sharing through financial integration. Hence, given the fact that we have a good proxy for financial integration itself, there is no reason for us to consider the euro as a proxy for integration as done in some previous works.

Table 6 Risk sharing

	Dependent Variable: Idiosyncratic Growth of:			
	Cons.	Cons.	HH Cons.	GNI
Sample:	All	No LUX	All	All
	(1)	(2)	(3)	(4)
Idiosyncratic GDP Growth	0.62	0.66	0.66	0.88
	21.51	21.95	21.30	2.76
Idiosyncratic GDP Growth*	-0.17	-0.13	-0.14	0.08
log (assets/pop)	-3.00	-1.93	-2.00	1.10
Idiosyncratic GDP Growth*	0.08	0.09	0.07	-0.18
log(liab/pop)	1.61	1.82	1.52	-3.52
Idiosyncratic GDP Growth*	-0.01	-0.01	-0.01	-0.02
Trend	-2.74	-2.34	-3.05	-1.91
Country FE	Yes	Yes	Yes	Yes

Note: All bank integration variables are lagged 1 period. Log (assets/pop) and log (liab./pop) are also included but they are not signicant so not reported. All RHS variables are demeaned by period by period country means. t-stats are reported in the table.

Since external assets and liabilities might have asymmetric effects on risk sharing, we specify the risk sharing equation as follows:

$$\kappa_{it} = \kappa_0 + \kappa_1.(t-\bar{t}) + \kappa_2.(BANKINT_{it-1}^{Assets} - BANKINT_{t-1}^{Assets})$$
$$+ \kappa_3.(BANKINT_{it-1}^{Liab} - BANKINT_{t-1}^{Liab}) \qquad (6)$$

Table 6 reports the estimated coefficients. On average consumption risk sharing is 38% (=1−0.62) across the 20 countries over 1978-2007. This number is similar to what has been found in other studies (see Demyanyk et al. (2008)). The effect of banking integration is also economically and statistically significant. The interpretation of these coefficients in the interaction term of idiosyncratic growth with the banking integration measures (κ_2 and κ_3) are as follows: A country that increases the holdings of external assets (relative to population) by 100% achieves 17% of additional consumption smoothing, i.e. an additional 17% of the idiosyncratic shocks to GDP will be smoothed out. The liabilities seem to have a dis-smoothing effect but the coefficient is not significant at the standard levels.

Column (2) drops Luxembourg. This country is an outlier and, hence, this is a necessary robustness test. The average level of risk sharing (κ_0) and the risk sharing through assets (κ_2) slightly decrease, but the results remain qualitatively similar. The dis-smoothing role of liabilities is now significant at 10%. One should note that asset and liability banking integration measures are highly correlated and, hence, dropping observations will lead to an increase in the signal-to-noise ratio. Nevertheless, it is important to show the results with and without Luxembourg. In both cases we confirm the presence of significant amounts of risk sharing on average and through foreign bank assets. Finally, in column (3) we look at household consumption. The results are similar. The coefficients are slightly lower, possibly due to the smoothing role of governments. Overall our results indicate much higher levels of risk sharing across our sample in the last 30 years, compared to what has been found in the literature. The main reason for this is likely the fact that we have longer time series, which increase the precision of our estimates.

Finally, as shown in the last column, we estimate a similar regression on income (instead of consumption) data.[30] We find that income risk sharing has increased over the years. Specifically, the average income risk sharing over the last two decades has increased and must be fluctuated around 12%. More importantly, a country that increases the holdings of external liabilities (relative to population) by 100% achieves 18% of additional income (GNI) smoothing. If we estimate income risk sharing only for the EU sample, we find 15% additional income smoothing. These results lead us to conclude that banking integration, facilitated both by the harmonization policies and the single currency, has improved ex-post the optimality of the currency union by improving risk sharing.

4   CONCLUSIONS

The introduction of the euro and the implementation of financial harmonization policies have transformed European capital markets. Transaction costs in equity and corporate bond markets have fallen considerably, whereas spreads in the government bond markets have narrowed and tend to move together. While retail banking activities remain fragmented, the interbank markets have shown considerable integration. The degree of integration differs across market segments, but nevertheless the overall evidence suggests that the euro has accelerated financial integration during the 10 years since its introduction. In addition the recent episodes of strong financial problems of European countries outside the euro area, especially in the smaller countries, suggest that being a member of the euro during a crisis may protect against extreme volatility as compared to not being a member of the euro area.

This paper comprised two parts. In the first part, we reviewed the vast and growing literature on the effects of the European monetary union on money, bond and equity markets, and on the banking sector. We then discussed the key financial policy initiatives that accompanied and strengthened the monetary union. We also reviewed empirical evidence from Kalemli-Ozcan, Papaioannou and Peydró (2008b) that shows that these policies (in particular, the FSAP) and also the single currency increased cross-border banking integration.

In the second part, we presented empirical evidence regarding the impact of financial integration on macroeconomic volatility and risk sharing.[31] Using banking integration data in a sample of 20 industrial countries over the past 30 years, we find that a higher degree of external asset holdings is associated with a lower level of consumption volatility. We also find that a higher level of

---

30   We thank our discussant Axel Weber to suggest this exercise.
31   For the results on the other effects of financial integration, see Kalemli-Ozcan, Papaioannou, and Peydró (2008a).

cross-border bank liabilities tends to increase output fluctuations. Jointly these results suggest that banking integration may facilitate risk-sharing. We find that a country that increases the holdings of external assets (relative to population) by 100% achieves 17% of additional consumption smoothing, i.e. an additional 17% of the idiosyncratic shocks to GDP will be smoothed out. We also estimate income (GNI) risk-sharing regressions. A country that increases the holdings of external liabilities (relative to population) by 100% achieves 18% of additional income smoothing.

Our findings have important policy implications. Asymmetric shocks in a currency union generate output and inflation differentials. The impact of such shocks is considerably reduced if risk sharing is significant. To the extent that risk-sharing allows hedging of consumption, it represents a key counteracting mechanism against asymmetric output shocks among members of a currency union. This mechanism reduces the need for policy intervention in dealing with such asymmetries. Our results, therefore, suggest that the increased cross-border banking integration due to the harmonization policies and the single currency has improved ex-post the optimality of the currency union by improving consumption and income risk sharing. The right criterion for an optimum currency area, then, is not the output fluctuations asymmetry but rather consumption fluctuations asymmetry given the fact that risk sharing via financial integration will imply a reduction in the latter, but not necessarily in the former.

REFERENCES

Adam, K., T. Jappelli, A.M. Menichini, M. Padula and M. Pagano. 2002. "Analyse, Compare, and Apply Alternative Indicators and Monitoring Methodologies to Measure the Evolution of Capital Market Integration in the European Union." Report to the European Commission.

Adjaouté, K. and J-P. Danthine. 2004. "Equity Returns and Integration: Is Europe Changing?" *Oxford Review of Economic Policy*, 20(4): 555-570.

Altunbas, Y. and D. Marqués-Ibáñez. 2008. "Mergers and Acquisitions and Bank Performance in Europe: the Role of Strategic Similarities." *Journal of Business and Economics*, 60(3): 179-290.

Asdrubali, P., B. E. Sørensen, and O. Yosha. 1996. "Channels of Interstate Risk Sharing: United States 1963-90." *Quarterly Journal of Economics* 111: 1081-1110.

Ayuso, J. and R. Blanco. 2001. "Has Financial Market Integration Increased during the Nineties?" *Journal of International Financial Markets, Institutions and Money*, 11: 265-287.

Aviat, A. and N. Coeurdacier. 2007. "The Geography of Trade in Goods and Assets." *Journal of International Economics*, 71(1): 22-51.

Backus, D.P. Kehoe, and F. Kydland. 1992. "International Real Business Cycles." *Journal of Political Economy*, 100: 745-775.

Baele, L. A. Ferrando, P. Hoerdahl, E. Krylova, C. Monnet. 2004. "Measuring Financial Integration in the Euro area." European Central Bank Occasional Paper 14.

Baldwin, R.A. 2006. "The Euro's Trade Effects." European Central Bank Working Paper 594.

Bank of International Settlements, Monetary and Economic Department. 2003a. "Guide to International Financial Statistic." Bank of International Settlements Paper 14.

Bank of International Settlements, Monetary and Economic Department. 2003b. "Guide to International Banking Statistics." Bank of International Settlements Paper 16.

Bekaert, G., R.J. Hodrick and X. Zhang. 2008. "International Stock Return Co-movements." European Central Bank Working Paper 931.

Berger, A.N. 2007. "Obstacles to a Global Banking System: 'Old Europe' versus 'New Europe'." *Journal of Banking and Finance*, 31: 1955-1973.

Bernanke S., and K. Kuttner. 2005. "What Explains the Stock Market's Reaction to Federal Reserve Policy?" *Journal of Finance*, 60(3): 1221-1257.

Bernoth, K., J. von Hagen and L. Schuknecht. 2004. "Sovereign Risk Premia in the European Government Bond Market." European Central Bank Working Paper 369.

Bertrand, M.E. Duflo, and S. Mullainathan. 2004. "How Much Should We Trust Difference in Differences Estimates?" *Quarterly Journal of Economics*, 119(1): 249-275.

Biais, B., F. Declerck, J. Dow, R. Portes and E.-L. von Thadden. 2006. "European Corporate Bond Markets: Transparency, Liquidity, Efficiency." Centre of Economic Policy Research Report.

Bos, J.W.B. and H. Schmiedel. 2007. "Is There a Single Frontier in a Single European Banking Market?" *Journal of Banking and Finance*, 31: 2081-2102.

Brooks, R. and M. Del Negro. 2004. "The Rise in Co-movements across National Stock Markets: Market Integration or IT bubble?" *Journal of Empirical Finance*, 11: 649-680.

Cabral, I., F. Dierick, and J. Vesala. 2002. "European banking integration." European Central Bank Occasional Paper 6.

Campbell, J.Y. and A. Deaton. 1989. "Why Is Consumption So Smooth?" *Review of Economic Studies*, 56(3): 357-73.

Cappiello, L., A. Kadareja and S. Manganelli .2008. "The Impact of the Euro on Equity Markets." Forthcoming. *Journal of Financial and Quantitative Analysis*.

Cappiello, L., M. Lo Duca and A. Maddaloni. 2008. "Equity Risk Premia in the Euro Area: an Intertemporal Approach." European Central Bank Working Paper 913.

Carrieri, F., V. Errunza and S. Sarkissian. 2004. "Industry Risk and Market Integration." *Management Science*, 50: 207-221.

Cassola, N., C. Holthausen and M. Lo Duca. 2008. "The 2007/2008 Turmoil: a Challenge for the Integration of the Euro Area Money Market?" http://esst2006. com/download/vfz/konferenzen/2008_10_17_muenchen/paper_cassola_ holthausen_duca.pdf

Chen, Z. and P.J. Knez. 1995. "Measurement of Market Integration and Arbitrage." *Review of Financial Studies*, 8(2): 287-325.

Codogno, L., C. Favero and A. Missale. 2003. "Yield Spreads on EMU Government Bonds." *Economic Policy*, Vol. 18(37): 505-532.

Coeurdacier, N. and P. Martin. 2007. "The Geography of Asset Trade and the Euro: Insiders and Outsiders." Centre for Economic Policy Research Discussion Paper 6032.

De Bandt, O., P. Hartmann, and J.-L. Peydró. 2009. "Systemic Fisk in Banking: An Update." In the *Oxford Handbook of Banking*, ed. A. Berger, P. Molyneux and J. Wilson. Oxford: The Oxford University Press.

De Santis, R. and B. Gerard. 2006. "Financial Integration, International Portfolio Choice and the European Monetary Union." European Central Bank Working Paper 626.

Degryse, H. and S. Ongena. 2004. "The Impact of Technology and Regulation on the Geographical Scope of Banking." *Oxford Review of Economic Policy*, 20(4): 571-590.

Degryse, H. and S. Ongena. 2005. "Distance, Lending Relationships, and Competition." *Journal of Finance*, 60(1): 231-266.

Demyanyk, Y., C. Ostergaard, and B. Sorensen. 2008. "Risk Sharing and Portfolio Allocation in EMU." European Union Commission Working Paper 334.

Dermine, J. 2003. "Banking in Europe: Past, Present and Future." In *The Transformation of the European Financial System*, ed. Gaspar, Hartmann and Sleijpen. Frankfurt am Main, Germany: European Central Bank.

Dermine, J. 2006. "European Banking Integration: Don't Put the Cart Before the Horse." Journal of Financial Markets. *Institutions and Instruments*, 15(2): 57-106.

European Commission. 2008. *European Financial Integration Report*. Brussels: European Commission.

European Central Bank. 2007a. "The Stock Market's Changing Structure and Its Consolidation: Implications for the Efficiency of the Financial System and Monetary Policy." *Monthly Bulletin*, 9(11): 61-74.

European Central Bank. 2007b. "Strengthening the EU Framework for Cross-Border Banks." Special Feature B of the European Central Bank Report on the Financial Integration in Europe.

European Central Bank. 2007c. "The SEPA Initiative and Its Implications for Financial Integration." Special Feature C of the European Central Bank Report on the Financial Integration in Europe.

European Central Bank. 2008. *Financial Integration in Europe*. Frankfurt am Main, Germany: European Central Bank.

European Central Bank. 2008a. "Financial Development: Concepts and Measures." Special Feature A of the European Central Bank Report on the Financial Integration in Europe.

European Central Bank. 2008b. "The Step Initiative." Special Feature B of the European Central Bank Report on the Financial Integration in Europe.

European Central Bank. 2008c. "Integration of Large-Value Payment and Securities Transactions: TARGET2, TARGET2-Securities and CCBM2." Special Feature C of the European Central Bank Report on the Financial Integration in Europe.

European Central Bank. 2008d. "The analysis of the euro money market from a monetary policy perspective." *Monthly Bulletin*, 10(2): 65-79.

European Central Bank. 2008e. "Cross-Border Bank Mergers and Acquisitions and Institutional Ownership." *Monthly Bulletin*, 10(10): 67-80.

European Central Bank. 2009. *Financial Integration in Europe*. Frankfurt am Main, Germany: European Central Bank.

Eiling, E., B. Gérard and F. de Roon. 2005. "International Diversification in the Euro Zone: Currency, Industry and Country Effects Revisited" Tilburg University Centre of Economic Research Discussion Paper 2005-02.

Favero, C., M. Pagano, and E-L von Thadden. 2007. "How Does Liquidity Affect Government Bond Yields?" Forthcoming. *Journal of Financial and Quantitative Analysis*.

Ferguson, R.W., P. Hartmann, F. Panetta and R. Portes. 2007. "International Financial Stability." Geneva Reports on the World Economy.

Flam, H. and H. Nordström. 2006. "Euro Effects on the Intensive and Extensive Margins of Trade." Institute for International Economic Studies Seminar Paper 750.

Flood, R., A. Matsumoto, and N. Marion. 2008. International Risk Sharing During the Globalization Era." Dartmouth College. https://editorialexpress.com/cgi-bin/conference/download.cgi?db_name= MWM2008&paper_id=199

Fratzscher, M. 2002. "Financial Market Integration In Europe: On The Effects Of EMU On Stock Markets." *Journal of International Money and Finance*, 7: 165-193.

Fratzscher, M. and L. Stracca. 2009. "The Political Economy Under Monetary Union: Has The Euro Made A Difference?" *Economic Policy*, 24(4): 307-348.

Galati, G. and K. Tsatsaronis. 2003. "The Impact of the Euro on Europe's Financial Markets." *Financial Markets, Institutions and Instruments*, 12(2): 165-221.

Gaspar, V., G. Perez Quiros and J. Sicilia. 2001. "The ECB Monetary Policy Strategy and The Money Market." *International Journal of Finance and Economics*, 6: 325-342.

Geyer, A., S. Kossmeier, and S. Pichler. 2004. "Measuring Systematic Risk In EMU Government Yield Spreads." *Review of Finance*, 8: 171-197.

Giannetti, M. and Y. Yafeh. 2008. "Do Cultural Differences Between Contracting Parties Matter? Evidence From Syndicated Bank Loans." European Corporate Governance Institute Finance Working Paper 224.

Giovannini, A. 2008. "The Integration Of European Financial Markets: Why Has It Not Happened Yet?" Unpublished.

Goddard, J., P. Molyneux, J.O.S. Wilson and M. Tavakoli. 2007. "European Banking: An Overview." *Journal of Banking and Finance*, 31: 1911-1935.

Gómez-Puig, M. 2006. "Size Matters For Liquidity: Evidence From EMU Sovereign Yield Spreads." *Economics Letters*, 90: 156-162.

Guiso, L., P. Sapienza, and L. Zingales. 2006. "Does Culture Affect Economic Outcomes?" *Journal of Economic Perspectives*, 20(2): 23-48.

Guiso, L., P. Sapienza, and L. Zingales. 2008. "Cultural Biases in Economic Exchange?" *The Quarterly Journal of Economics*, 124(3): 1095–1131.

Hardouvelis, G.A., D. Malliaropulos, and R. Priestley. 2006. "EMU And European Stock Market Integration." *Journal of Business*, 79: 365-392.

Hartmann, P., A. Maddaloni, S. Manganelli. 2003. "The Euro-Area Financial System: Structure, Integration And Policy Initiatives." *Oxford Review of Economic Policy*, 19(1): 280-313.

Hartmann, P., F. Heider, E. Papaioannou and M. Lo Duca. 2007. "The Role Of Financial Markets And Innovation In Productivity And Growth In Europe." European Central Bank Occasional Paper 72.

Heider, F., M. Hoerova and C. Holthausen. 2008. "Information Asymmetries In The Interbank Market: Theory And Policy Responses." European Central Bank. Unpublished.

Heston, S. and K. Rouwenhorst. 1994. "Does Industrial Structure Explain The Benefits Of Industrial Diversification?" *Journal of Financial Economics*, 36(1): 3-27.

Imbs, J. 2006. "The Real Effects of Financial Integration." *Journal of International Economics*, 68(2): 296-324.

Iyer, R. and J. L. Peydró. 2006. "Interbank Contagion At Work: Evidence From A Natural Experiment." EFA 2006 Zurich Meetings. http://ssrn.com/abstract=895061

Jankowitsch, R., H. Mösenbacher and S. Pichler. 2006. "Measuring The Liquidity Impact On EMU Government Bond Prices." *The European Journal of Finance*, 12(2): 153-169.

Jimenez, G., Ongena, S., Peydró, J.L. and Saurina, J. 2008. "Hazardous Times For Monetary Policy: What Do Twenty-Three Million Bank Loans Say About The Effects Of Monetary Policy On Credit Risk-Taking?" Centre for Economic Policy Research Discussion Paper 6514.

Kalemli-Ozcan, S., B.E. Sorensen, and O. Yosha. 2001. "Regional Integration, Industrial Specialization and the Asymmetry of Shocks across Regions." *Journal of International Economics*, 55: 107-137.

Kalemli-Ozcan, S., B.E. Sorensen, and O. Yosha. 2003. "Risk Sharing and Industrial Specialization: Regional and International Evidence," *American Economic Review*, 93(3): 903-918.

Kalemli-Ozcan, B.E. Sorensen and Volosovcyh. 2009. "Deep Financial Integration and Volatility." Unpublished.

Kalemli-Ozcan, S., E. Papaioannou, and J.L. Peydró. 2008a. "Financial Integration and Business Cycle Synchronization." National Bureau of Economic Research Working Paper 14887.

Kalemli-Ozcan, S., E. Papaioannou, and J.L. Peydró. 2008b. "How Does the Euro Affect Financial Integration? The Role of Currency Risk, Regulation, and Trade." Unpublished.

Kose, M.A., E. Prasad, K. Rogoff and S.-J. Wei. 2006. "Financial Globalization: A Reappraisal." International Monetary Fund Working Paper 189.

Lane, P.R. 2006. "Global Bond Portfolios And EMU." *International Journal of Central Banking*, 2: 1-23.

Lane, P.R. and G.M. Milesi-Ferretti. 2007. "The International Equity Holdings of Euro Area Investors." In *The Importance of the External Dimension for the Euro Area*, ed. Robert Anderton and Filippo Di Mauro. New York: Cambridge University Press.

Mace, B.J. 1991. "Full Insurance in the Presence of Aggregate Uncertainty." *Journal of Political Economy*, 99(5): 928-956.

Manganelli, S. and G. Wolswijk. 2008. "What Drives Spreads in the Euro Area Government Bond Market?" European Central Bank Working Paper 745.

Micco, A., Stein, E., Ordonez, O. 2003. "The Currency Union Effect on Trade: Early Evidence from EMU." *Economic Policy*, 18(37): 315-356.

Morgan, D., B. Rime and P. E. Strahan. 2004. "Bank Integration and State Business Cycles." *Quarterly Journal of Economics*, 119(4): 1555-1585.

Obstfeld, M. and K. Rogoff. 1996. *Foundations of International Macroeconomics*. Cambridge, MA: The MIT Press.

Obstfeld, M. and A.M. Taylor. 2004. *Global Capital Markets: Integration, Crisis, and Growth*. New York: Cambridge University Press.

Pagano, M. and E.-L. Von Thadden. 2004. "The European Bond Markets under EMU." *Oxford Review of Economic Policy*, 20(4): 531-554.

Papageorgiou, T. 2005. "Estimating the Impact of Common Currencies on Foreign Direct Investment: Evidence from the EMU." Yale University. Unpublished.

Papaioannou, E. 2007. "Finance And Growth: A Macroeconomic Assessment Of The Evidence From A European Angle." In *The Handbook of European Financial Markets and Institutions*, ed. X. Freixas, P. Hartmann, and C. Mayer. Oxford, UK: Oxford University Press.

Papaioannou, E. 2009. "What Drives International Bank Flows? Politics, Institutions and Other Determinants." *Journal of Development Economics*, 88(2): 269-281.

Papaioannou E. and R. Portes. 2009. "Costs and Benefits of Running an International Currency." European Commission Special Report on the European Economy.

Perez, D. V. Salas-Fumas and J. Saurina. 2005. "Banking integration in Europe." Bank of Spain Working Paper 519.

Perez Quiros, G. and H.R. Mendizábal. 2006. "The Market for Funds In Europe: What Has Changed With The EMU?" *Journal of Money, Credit and Banking*, 38(1): 91-118.

Petersen, M. and R. Rajan. 2002. "Does Distance Still Matter? The Information Revolution And Small Business Lending." *Journal of Finance*, 57: 2533-2570.

Petroulas, P. 2007. "The Effect of the Euro on Foreign Direct Investment." *European Economic Review*, 51 (6): 1468-1491.

Portes, R. and H. Rey. 2005. "The Determinants of Cross-Border Equity Flows.," *Journal of International Economics*, 65(2): 269-296.

Rajan, R. 2006. "Has Financial Development Made The World Riskier?" *European Financial Management*, 12(4): 499-533.

Rajan, R. and L. Zingales. 2003. "Banks and Markets. The Changing Character of European Finance." In *The Transformation of the European Financial System*, ed. Gaspar, Hartmann and Sleijpen. Frankfurt am Main, Germany: European Central Bank.

Ravallion, M. and S. Chaudhuri. 1997. "Risk and Insurance in Village India: A Comment." *Econometrica*, 65(1): 171-184.

Rose, A. 2000. "One Market, One Money: Estimating the Effect of Common Currencies on Trade." *Economic Policy*, 30: 7-45.

Rose, A. 2001. "Currency Unions and Trade: the Effect Is Large." *Economic Policy*, 33: 449-461.

Rose, A., and M.M. Spiegel. 2004. "A Gravity Model of Sovereign Lending: Trade, Default, and Credit." *International Monetary Fund Staff Papers*, 51(1): 50-63.

Santos, J. and K. Tsatsaronis .2003. "The Cost of Barriers to Entry: Evidence From The Market For Corporate Euro Bond Underwriting." Bank of International Settlements Working Paper 134.

Schmiedel, H. and A. Schönenberger. 2005. "Integration of Securities Market Infrastructures In The Euro Area." European Central Bank Occasional Paper 33.

Sørensen, B.E., Y.T. Wu, O. Yosha, and Y. Zhu. 2007. "Home Bias and International Risk Sharing: Twin Puzzles Separated at Birth." *Journal of International Money and Finance*, 26(4):587-605.

Spiegel, M. 2008. "Monetary and Financial Integration: Evidence From The EMU". *Journal of the Japanese and International Economies*, 23(2): 114-130.

Spiegel, M. 2009. "Monetary and Financial Integration in the EMU: Push or Pull." *Review of International Economics*, 17(4): 751-776.

Wooldridge, P.D. 2002. "Uses of the BIS Statistics: An Introduction." *Bank for International Settlements Quarterly Review*, 39(1): 75-92.

COMMENT

BY MARCO PAGANO, UNIVERSITÀ DI NAPOLI FEDERICO II

Both of these papers provide a complete and up-to-date assessment of the literature on the effects of financial integration, with special reference to the Economic and Monetary Union (EMU). Each of the two papers is composed of two parts. First, it describes the evolution of various markets upon the inception of EMU and concomitant reforms (FSAP, TARGET, etc.), drawing extensively on the recent body of empirical work that has analyzed them. Second, it produces some novel results on the effects of EMU on financial integration, and of both of them on the real economy of the euro area. In these comments I will focus on the latter.

The first novel result – in the study by Kalemli-Ozcan et al. – concerns the relationship between EMU and the integration of the credit market. Previous work has documented that EMU has been associated with greater integration in money, bond and stock markets, though to different extents. But we know much less about the integration of banks, largely because the inherent heterogeneity of bank loans makes it hard to assess international integration of the credit market. Kalemli-Ozcan et al. overcome this problem by measuring integration of banks via BIS data on banks' bilateral cross-border holdings, and exploit the panel structure of these data to control for fixed country and country-pair effects. Interestingly, they find that this measure of bank integration is positively and significantly correlated not only with EMU, but also with the financial reforms associated with EMU. To my knowledge, this is the first study that documents a distinct effect of these reforms on financial integration, controlling for the effect of EMU itself.

The second set of novel results concerns the effect of EMU on risk sharing. Here we enter realm of the "real effects" of EMU and financial integration, with the latter being treated as an explanatory variable and no longer as the dependent variable. Most of the existing studies in this area have focused on "growth dividend" of EMU via financial integration and financial development. Much less effort has been directed to explore if EMU is also associated improved risk sharing, as the theory would predict. But both Lane and Kalemli-Ozcan et al. probe further into the macroeconomic evidence on this score.

They do so by using two variants of the same approach, based on the idea that in a financially integrated area the differences in consumption growth among pairs of countries should not be related to the respective difference in income growth. That is, if one estimates the regression

$$\Delta \log c_{it} - \Delta \log c_{jt} = \phi_{ij} + \delta_t + \beta(\Delta \log y_{it} - \Delta \log y_{jt})$$

for financially integrated countries, the coefficient β should not be significantly different from zero. Previous studies, which are replicated in Lane's paper, report that indeed the estimate of β has decreased over time, and more so for EMU country pairs than for non-EMU ones. However, Lane also documents that this result is not stable over time, since it does not hold if the sample is extended to 2006. Kalemli-Ozcan et al. instead investigate the relationship between β and their measure of banking integration, rather than EMU *per se*, and find that the estimate of β has decreased more for country pairs with more cross-border bank assets. However, they find the opposite for liabilities ("desmoothing").

A possible reading of this evidence is that indeed there is no detectable effect of EMU on risk sharing in macroeconomic data, which is consistent with the findings obtained by Jappelli and Pistaferri (2008) on microeconomic data for Italy. This is not contradicted by Kalemli-Ozcan et al.'s evidence of an effect of financial integration on risk sharing in a larger set of 20 countries, because this effect is not specifically connected with EMU. The "desmoothing effect" of cross-border liabilities may reflect episodes of "binge borrowing" arising from financial liberalization (including low interest rates upon entry in EMU: Spain, Ireland, etc.). Probably it is too early to expect detectable EMU-induced increases in risk sharing: the time series available since the inception of EMU are still quite short, and the short-term effects of such a large regime change are likely to cloud steady-state regularities.

Moreover, if indeed the greater financial integration induced by EMU truly increased international risk-sharing, it is likely to have done so not just among Euro-area countries but also between the Euro area as a whole and other countries, chiefly the United States. If so, perhaps the current financial crisis can be read as an instance of massive risk sharing, with Europe sharing the burden of the large negative shock arising in the United States. Of course, this is not a shock as normally defined in our models (that is, "news" about productivity or tastes), but a shock arising from a massive malfunctioning of markets. This suggests that better risk sharing may also mean sharing more in such malfunctioning. This point is emphasized by Lane, who points out that by facilitating financial integration, EMU may have strengthened "contagion": perhaps, had they been less internationally integrated, European banks would have bought fewer toxic asset-backed securities. But quite rightly Lane also highlights that EMU may also have had a powerful stabilizing influence once the financial crisis erupted and propagated to Europe, insofar as it prevented it from turning into a currency crisis as well.

This stabilizing role that EMU has played on the monetary front in the current crisis must however not make us oblivious to the fact that the crisis has also painfully exposed the unfinished state of the institutions of EU financial markets. This has been evident, for instance, in the uncoordinated policy response to bank solvency problems. Indeed, the crisis has tarnished two of the main "success stories" of European financial integration: a vibrant euro-area corporate bond market, and the emergence of a few large pan-European banks. The corporate bond market has been dramatically hit in terms of trading volumes, liquidity and issuance, while concerns have arisen about the solvency of the large pan-European banks that have played an important role in integrating euro-area financial markets. This suggests that in the current uneasy "middle station" the gains made by Europe on the front of greater financial integration are still at risk. In particular, monetary union badly needs to be complemented by coordinated supervision and crisis management of large pan-European banks. While this raises politically thorny regulatory and fiscal issues, it is a need that can no longer be neglected if financial integration is to be put on a firmer footing for the future. Hopefully the severity of the current crisis has convinced European policy-makers to face up to this challenge as soon as possible.

COMMENT

BY AXEL A. WEBER, PRESIDENT OF THE DEUTSCHE BUNDESBANK

I   INTRODUCTION

The euro at ten can justifiably be called a success story, and increasing financial integration in the euro area is a striking example of this. I am therefore pleased to comment on the two very interesting and insightful papers presented by Philip Lane and by Sebnem Kalemli-Ozcan, Simone Manganelli, Elias Papaioannou and José Luis Peydró.

Professor Pagano has already given some helpful and meaningful comments on the papers. In my comments, I shall first concentrate on Philip's reflections on EMU and financial integration and add to them some findings for Germany. Second, I shall discuss some issues raised by Sebnem Kalemli-Ozcan et al. in their paper on the role of the monetary union for financial integration and risk sharing.

2   PHILIP LANE

Philip Lane's paper builds on his extensive research on EMU and financial integration, and presents us with a comprehensive and well structured overview of recent research and market developments. The paper provides broadly based evidence that the first ten years of EMU have seen a remarkable increase in financial integration, even if the extent of convergence varies across different sectors. Philip notes that there are still many barriers to full integration, but that initiatives, such as SEPA, Target 2 and T2S should remove some of these obstacles. This is why the Eurosystem is actively supporting these projects. Philip then challenges a number of general predictions about the macroeconomic impact of financial integration on the financial development of euro-area countries, international risk sharing and net capital movements.

3   HOME BIAS

To complement Philip's findings on financial integration in bond and equity markets, I would like to focus on one issue of great importance: To what extent has investors' home bias changed over the past decade? Using German data it can be shown nicely, first, that home bias has declined and second, that EMU plays a prominent role in how the portfolios of German investors are diversified internationally.

To start with some theory, Solnik's (1974) international Capital Asset Pricing Model predicts – given there are no transaction costs – that the regional diversification of a securities portfolio should be the same in all countries worldwide and it should copy the structure of the global portfolio.

In reality, the portfolios in all countries show divergences from this "benchmark portfolio" in favour of domestic securities; this "home bias" can be explained by transaction costs and imperfect information, in particular, concerning foreign securities.

In the euro area, transaction costs should have declined significantly with the abolition of exchange rate movements within the European Monetary Union and further initiatives for harmonising the financial market institutions by the Financial Services Action Plan (FSAP). At the same time, information on foreign investments can be expected to have improved within EMU. To see whether these predictions are true, I shall now investigate the regional structure of the German international investment position. German investors' preference for domestic securities is calculated by comparing the share of actual foreign assets held by German investors with the percentage of foreign assets in the global benchmark portfolio.[1]

Against this backdrop, home bias on the assets side indicates whether foreign securities are less intensively (and domestic securities are more strongly) represented in the national portfolio compared with the benchmark. A home bias would reach the value 100 if investors were to take exclusively domestic securities into their portfolios. If the benchmark portfolio is perfectly copied, the home bias would carry the value 0. A negative number of the home bias indicates that domestic investors invest more heavily in the securities of a particular country or group of countries than is indicated by the global benchmark portfolio.

The calculations yield some interesting results: First, since the start of EMU, the home bias of German investors in equities has been tending to decline. While, in 1998, German investors invested 76% of their stock in domestic equities, this share had diminished to 58% at the end of 2007. By comparison, the percentage of German equities in the global benchmark portfolio was 6% in both years. In our calculations, this yields a decline in the home bias from 75% to 55% of the benchmark.

Second, German investors have developed a strong liking for stocks of EMU partner countries – as the corresponding negative home bias demonstrates. In the beginning, the German "EMU bias" was only small but it has grown to a notable amount during the past decade. At the end of 2007, the share of EMU equity securities in German investors' portfolio was 51% higher than the corresponding portion in the global benchmark portfolio.

Third, with regard to extra-EMU investment, German home bias was also reduced, albeit slightly.

---

1   The calculations are similar to those carried out by De Santis, R. A. and Gérard, B. (2006).

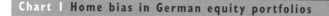

Chart 1 Home bias in German equity portfolios

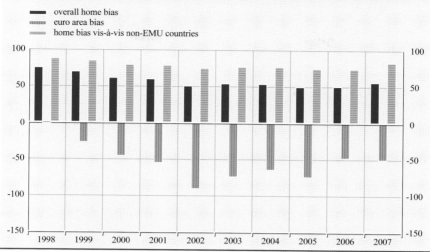

■ overall home bias
▦ euro area bias
▬ home bias vis-à-vis non-EMU countries

Source: Bundesbank calculations.
Note: Equity portfolios include investment certificates. The number indicates the underrepresentation of foreign securities in German portfolios as a percentage of their share in the benchmark portfolio. A negative number indicates an overrepresentation.

These results are not specific to German portfolios. Investors from other EMU countries also display a bias in favour of German bonds. This is reflected in the disproportionately large representation of German bonds in the portfolios of the other EMU member states.

Chart 2 Home bias in German bond portfolios

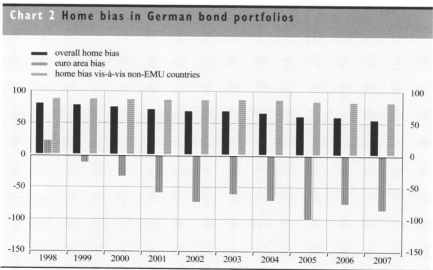

■ overall home bias
▦ euro area bias
▬ home bias vis-à-vis non-EMU countries

Source: Bundesbank calculations.
Note: Bond portfolios include medium to long-term debt securities. The number indicates the underrepresentation of foreign securities in German portfolios as a percentage of their share in the benchmark portfolio. A negative number indicates an overrepresentation.

To put it in a nutshell, the data on home bias and "EMU bias" with regard to German cross-border investment in securities give an idea of how EMU has influenced cross-border financial integration. The home bias is also an important issue when it comes to investigating international risk sharing. This brings me to the paper by Sebnem Kalemli-Ozcan, Simone Manganelli, Elias Papaioannou and José Luis Peydró.

4   SEBNEM KALEMLI-OZCAN ET AL.

Part I of their interesting and topical paper gives an overview of financial integration in EMU and describes the main legislative and regulatory policies that EU member states have implemented in financial markets. Part II provides empirical evidence for the impact of the single currency and European harmonisation policies on financial integration. Furthermore, it analyses the implications for consumption risk sharing in the euro area. The main findings are that the single currency and the harmonisation policies of EU have both fostered financial integration and that cross-border banking integration increases consumption risk sharing.

4.1   EMU AND CROSS-BORDER BANKING INTEGRATION

An important contribution made by Kalemli-Ozcan et al. is that they try to disentangle the impact of the single currency and harmonisation policies on financial integration. This distinction is of major relevance with respect to the further process of integration.

The authors' focus on banking integration is appropriate with regard to the subsequent analysis of consumption risk sharing, where bank lending is deemed to be a prominent transmission channel. However, it should be kept in mind that there are more financial market segments of interest and that the euro and harmonisation policies might affect them to a different degree. As I have already noted, there is strong evidence that monetary union has fostered integration of markets for equity and long-term debt securities.

4.2   BANKING INTEGRATION AND RISK SHARING

As for the authors' concept of consumption risk sharing, let me make two remarks. First, consumption smoothing is measured relative to a panel of 20 European and non-European countries. This reflects the fact that the paper concentrates on differences in consumption growth across countries and, therefore, analyses international consumption smoothing. Domestic smoothing is thereby ignored. Furthermore, the estimates do not make a distinction between whether consumption smoothing of EMU countries takes place within the euro area or vis-à-vis the rest of the world. It is true that, from a welfare point of view, a distinction between intra- and extra-euro-area risk sharing does not make sense. However, the authors conclude that "the increased cross-banking integration due to the euro has improved ex-post the optimality of the currency union by improving risk sharing". This implies that risk sharing of euro area countries takes place mainly among each other.

My second comment concerns the way the authors measure consumption smoothing. The paper regresses international differences in consumption growth on international differences in GDP growth, multiplied by a term including banking integration. A perfect consumption smoothing would imply that asymmetric GDP shocks do not transmit into diverging consumption paths at all.

Following Asdrubali, Sørensen and Yosha (1996) and the modification of Mélitz (2004), it might be helpful not to stop here but to have a further look at the individual components of GDP and the respective channels of risk sharing.

Expressed in logarithms and first differences, GDP growth can be decomposed into[2]

$$\Delta \ln GDP = \Delta \ln C \qquad \text{(growth of private consumption)}$$
$$+ \Delta \ln GDP - \Delta \ln C \qquad \text{(consumption smoothing)}$$

or, in more detail,

$$\Delta \ln GDP = \Delta \ln C \qquad \text{(growth of private consumption)}$$
$$+ \Delta \ln GDP - \Delta \ln GNP \qquad \text{(smoothing by net foreign income)}$$
$$+ \Delta \ln GDP - \Delta \ln A \qquad \text{(smoothing by external saving)}$$
$$+ \Delta \ln A - \Delta \ln C \qquad \text{(smoothing by domestic saving)}$$

In this disaggregation, we would expect the term $\Delta \ln GDP - \Delta \ln A$ to be the main channel through which consumption smoothing by cross-border banking integration should work.

In the following table, calculated for Germany, the coefficients β^E and β^H indicate the absorption of additional GDP growth by net foreign income and external saving, respectively.[3] A positive sign stands for a positive effect on consumption smoothing. The coefficients suggest that international consumption risk sharing in Germany is primarily achieved by countercyclical net foreign income, whereas external saving tends to go along with business cycles. This outcome holds for both overall consumption smoothing and consumption smoothing vis-à-vis other euro-area countries only.

---

2   Where GDP = Gross Domestic Product, GNP = Gross National Product, A = domestic absorption, C = private consumption.

3   The estimates result from the regressions

$$\Delta \ln GDP - \Delta \ln GNP = \alpha_E + \beta_E \Delta \ln GDP + \varepsilon_E$$
$$\Delta \ln GNP - \Delta \ln A = \alpha_H + \beta_H \Delta \ln GDP + \varepsilon_H.$$

The sum of β_E and β_H corresponds to $1-\kappa$ in the paper of Kalemli-Ozcan et al. However, the coefficients are calculated by simple OLS and do not account for endogeneity and other factors like – for example – serial correlation. Therefore, significance levels are not indicated and the values should be interpreted with caution.

Table	International consumption smoothing in Germany			

(absorption of additional GDP growth by net foreign income (β_E) and external saving (β_H))

	Overall		vis-à-vis EMU	
	β_E	β_H	β_E^{EWU}	β_H^{EWU}
1991-1998	0.01	-0.03	0.13	-0.23
1999-2007	0.22	-0.17	0.08	-0.16

Obviously, your paper goes beyond these simple correlations. It clearly identifies the impact of cross border banking integration and uses more sophisticated econometric techniques. I highly appreciate your work and consider it a valuable contribution to the current debate. Nevertheless, I would like to stress that this interesting topic leaves much room for further research.

5   CONCLUDING REMARKS

To conclude, both papers are very instructive in terms of learning more about details of the ongoing process of financial integration in the European Monetary Union. They have both shown that cross-border risk-sharing has improved during the past decade and that EMU has given a major stimulus to this. Our own calculations on the German home bias point in the same direction. These approaches, therefore, allow us to conclude that EMU has welfare-enhancing effects.

The Eurosystem will do its best to make them come to the fore with full force in the years to come.

REFERENCES

Asdrubali, P., B. Sørensen, and O. Yosha. 1996. "Channels of Inter-state Risk-sharing: United States 1963-1990." *Quarterly Journal of Economics*, 111: 1081-1110.

De Santis, R. A., and B. Gerard. 2006. "Financial Integration, International Portfolio Choice and the European Monetary Union." European Central Bank Working Paper 626.

Mélitz, J. 2004. "Risk-sharing and EMU." *Journal of Common Market Studies*, 42: 815-840.

Solnik, B. H. 1974. "An Equilibrium Model of the International Capital Market." *Journal of Economic Theory*, 8(4): 500-524.

GENERAL DISCUSSION

Charles Engel expressed the view that both papers in this session focused excessively on international risk sharing. He wondered whether there is evidence that greater financial market integration has improved capital allocation within the euro area. **Philip Lane** responded that cross-country capital flows have increased with the EMU. However, the market for venture capital remains little developed in Europe. **Sebnem Kalemli-Ozcan** thought that a study with firm-level data would be required to answer Engel's question concerning capital allocation. **Elias Papaioannou** added that research based on sector-level data shows a positive effect of financial integration on capital allocation.

Mark Spiegel observed that the empirical findings of Kalemli-Ozcan et al. concerning international risk sharing are about cross-country averages. However, there seems to be significant heterogeneity across countries which the authors fail to explore. **Alex Cukierman** thought that one way to summarize the papers in this session was to observe that small countries have benefited significantly from financial market integration in the euro area, while large countries have benefited by a lesser extent. This is exactly what trade theory would have predicted.

President Jean-Claude Trichet giving the keynote address

KEYNOTE ADDRESS

KEYNOTE ADDRESS[1]

BY JEAN-CLAUDE TRICHET, PRESIDENT OF THE ECB

I   INTRODUCTION

I am very pleased to welcome you to what we consider to be the ECB's flagship conference and to this dinner in these beautiful surroundings. The focus of this conference is on the lessons and challenges facing the euro, as it reaches its tenth anniversary. In recent months there has been no shortage of challenges, far from it. As for the lessons, I shall come to those towards the end of my address.

This evening, I would like to share with you some thoughts about the main factors bringing about the financial market turmoil that has shaken the global economy for more than a year now, and raise some of the possible long-term solutions.

2   THE CALM AND THE STORM

Until early 2007 we were living in a period often described as the "Great Moderation". The world economy was growing vigorously, macroeconomic indicators were significantly less volatile and, most importantly, inflation was low. Financial markets were performing strongly. Many asset prices were rising, while volatilities and risk premia were exceptionally low. Profitability in the financial sector was high, and banks seemed liquid and well capitalised.

However, there were warning signs, even back in 2006, that global markets were "priced for perfection" and that even a small change in conditions could severely disrupt financial markets.[2] Several policy makers had indicated to market participants that they needed to prepare for a significant correction. As chairman of the Global Economy Meetings of central bank governors, I myself reported my colleagues' sentiments on this matter.[3] At the same time, several financial stability reports – including from the ECB, the Bank for International Settlements (BIS), the Financial Stability Forum (FSF) and other organisations – analysed vulnerabilities and warned of emerging weaknesses.[4]

---

1   I would like to thank A. Maddaloni and P. Hartmann for their valuable input.
2   See, among others, IMF (2006a), IMF (2006b) and Gieve (2006).
3   Financial Times, "Prepare for asset repricing, warns Trichet", 29 January 2007.
4   The ECB noted signs of risks in several subsequent issues of the Financial Stability Review (FSR) in 2006 and 2007; see also Trichet (2007). Research by ECB staff also suggested increases in systemic risks among large and complex banking groups (LCBGs), particularly in the US and less so in Europe; see P. Hartmann, S. Straetmans and C. G. de Vries (2005a,b).

We knew that a storm was brewing but, admittedly, we did not know exactly where. Neither did we know what would trigger it, or when it would come.

As we all know today, the turmoil erupted in August 2007 when investors around the world suddenly faced a dramatic change in liquidity conditions, and it became increasingly difficult for banks to refinance themselves in the wholesale money market.[5] For many months, we have been facing a financial turmoil that was triggered by a liquidity shortage, countered by rapid and resolute action from central banks. The storm intensified very significantly in mid-September 2008, when some large failures of financial institutions led to a general loss of confidence and to a very severe reaction in financial markets. This transformed the turmoil into a crisis, and the liquidity shortage became a massive threat to solvency for many financial institutions in a large set of countries.

How can we conceptualise the sudden emergence of this turn of events in the terminology of risk assessment? A useful analogy is to think about the series of events during the development of the crisis as so-called "black swan" events. As many of you probably know, the analogy draws from the observation that for centuries people, including scientist, thought all swans to be white. Nobody considered that this assessment could ever change. In the discovery of the Australian continent, however, swans with black feathers were found there. A single observation invalided a general belief based on centuries of observations. Therefore, a "black swan" has been used to characterise an entirely unexpected event – an outlier – that has a major impact, and whose occurrence only becomes predictable with hindsight. It may reflect some of the limitations of human nature that we tend to concentrate on things that we already know and sometimes fail to consider the things that we do not know.[6]

3   UNDERVALUED RISKS, A PRIORI ASSUMPTIONS AND OPACITY

Coming back to the current financial situation, the root cause of the crisis was the, overall and massive undervaluation of risk across markets, financial institutions and countries. This derived from two main factors. First, the probability of certain events was misjudged. This means that these events were considered highly improbable, if not "impossible". Second, the impact of an increase in fundamental uncertainty at the systemic level on the distribution of returns across asset classes was largely neglected. Such a fundamental increase of uncertainty is what we observed with the massive shock to global confidence in mid-September.

With this in mind, a useful – albeit not the only – way to characterise recent events is to employ the concept of non-measurable risk, or "Knightian" uncertainty.[7,8]

5   For a detailed analysis of the sequence of events which led to the financial turmoil see N. Cassola, M. Drehmann, P. Hartmann, M. Lo Duca and M. Scheicher (2008) and ECB (2008a).
6   See Taleb (2007) and Taylor and Williams (2009).
7   See Knight (1921).
8   For other characterisations of systemic risk see Bandt and Hartman (2002).

The economist Frank Knight originally developed the distinction between risks, to which probabilities can be assigned; and uncertainty, for which even these probabilities are unknown. In the last two decades this distinction has been used again in formalising economic choices under so-called "uncertainty" aversion.[9]

Many episodes of financial instability over the last decades were characterised by a sharp increase in general "uncertainty". The reaction of investors is to suddenly assign very high probabilities to events they deemed very unlikely before. They concentrate on "bad" outcomes and worst-case scenarios and show a strong preference for safety and liquidity. This may be an important explanation for the very pronounced "flight to quality", which we often observe during episodes of financial turbulences.[10]

Both the underpricing of the unit of risk and the underestimation of the quantity of risk contributed to the emergence of the crisis. Inadequate assumptions were made about the distribution of returns to highly complex, new financial securities. This implied that the unit of risk was generally underpriced. Moreover, some large financial institutions showed a massive concentration of risk, suggesting that risk management systems failed to identify the quantity of risk that financial institutions were accumulating. These same systems also failed to assess the systemic consequences arising from a global loss of confidence.

UNDERPRICING OF A UNIT OF RISK
The structure of global markets is changing fast, and we need to model future default and risk profiles of new products with a short history. Statistical models using the recent past to estimate the parameters of the probability distributions turned out to be little helpful. Market participants used evaluation models that did not account properly for an additional dimension to risk. The distribution of returns depends on which "state of nature" prevails, for example if we are in normal market times or in crisis times. Very small changes in beliefs can translate into large changes in behaviour, which in turns have large effects on markets.[11]

One of the most important elements contributing to the underpricing of risk was the sheer complexity of structured financial products, which even sophisticated investors were not able to assess properly. Hence prices reflected only in part fundamentals, while the credibility of the issuer and the "willingness to purchase" of the buyer played an equally important role in the pricing of these products.

The general compression of spreads and risk premia in global financial markets also suggests that investors' preferences were characterised by comparatively low levels of risk aversion. This, in turn, further inflated flawed valuations based on very favourable expectations of future returns.

There are two additional elements that played a role in the underpricing of risk: first, the large ex ante excess of savings over investment, which was one of the

9   See Gilboa and Schmeidler (1989).
10 See in particular Caballero and Krishnamurthy (2008).
11 See O'Hara (2004).

consequences of the bursting of the internet bubble and of the Asian crisis. The phenomenon became even more important due to the oil and commodity price shocks, which triggered an additional ex ante excess of forced savings in the global economy. A second factor, closely correlated to the innovation in financial markets, has been the very powerful process of leveraging that has characterised global financial institutions in all different constituencies. This has included regulated and listed commercial and investment banks, private equity firms, hedge funds and all types of highly leveraged entities.

UNDER APPRECIATION OF THE QUANTITY OF RISK

In addition to the underpricing of the unit of risk, also the sheer quantitative accumulation of risk was underestimated, at the level of institutions as well as at the level of the system.

It is still debated to which degree the "Great Moderation" that had started in the mid-1980s and was observed until the middle of last year, and that consisted of a remarkable reduction of volatilities in the real economy, has influenced the overall assessment of the quantity of risk in a large array of asset markets during this period. The correlation between the reduction of volatilities and the magnitude of risk taking is there, but the direction and even the existence of a possible causality, remains an open question.[12]

Amongst other factors there was also a considerable lack of transparency about the allocation of risks across financial intermediaries, in particular in new and often highly leveraged, players. The nature of the business of certain financial intermediaries relied almost exclusively on the roll-over of short-term debt to finance longer-term assets. The ability of these players to stand the consequences of a significant market correction turned out to be greatly overstated. To make things worse, these consequences were intensified by the high leverage and the parcelling of risk. When the crisis occurred, the general loss of confidence and the large number of linkages among financial institutions resulted in a quick and powerful transmission of "fears".[13]

4   MAIN FACTORS TO BE ADDRESSED

Let me now look ahead to long-term solutions, which in my view need to start by addressing three important factors.

First, there has been considerable short-termism, i.e. an excessive focus on near-term returns. Modern financial systems have favoured instruments and intermediaries that promise large returns in the short-term. Such short-termism can naturally lead to a misjudgement of the underlying risk, as investors are less attentive to low probability outcomes. Short-termism can also result in a higher accumulation of risks since high risk-taking typically boosts short-term returns on relatively thin levels of capital. Finally, it can exacerbate the impact

12 See Trichet (2008).
13 See Borio (2008).

of conflicts of interest and perverse incentives that exist both at the top and at lower management levels.[14]

This environment creates the conditions for the widely observed herding behaviour, in which risk controls easily become a secondary issue. Banks that are achieving high returns put considerable pressure on their peers to do the same: "As long as the music is playing, you have got to get up and dance", has become a famous quote in the crisis.[15] But when the music stops, it's impossible for everybody to carry on dancing.

It is interesting to note that some of these problems had already surfaced in the aftermath of the corporate scandals of 2003. In particular, the presence of conflicts of interest and perverse incentives related to flawed compensation practices and to the provision of services with conflicting aims (especially by rating agencies).[16] Thus, the existence of these problems was well-known, and policy responses were put in place to address them. Hence, one question that remains open is: did we underestimate the consequences of not acting more forcefully and more quickly?

The second main factor concerns transparency. It is striking that despite all the regulatory advances and progress in information technology, the financial system that has emerged over the last decade has been characterised by a lack of transparency in certain securities markets and intermediaries. Regulated markets, characterised by standardised products, and a broad base of investors, with access to information and legal protection, generally offer better-quality information. However, the markets for structured products work largely over the counter, and a large part of the financial sector is unregulated. This implies that a fair evaluation of the instruments and of the counterparty risk is extremely difficult, not only for supervisors and institutions concerned with financial stability but also for the market participants themselves.

More standardised securities exchanged on regulated markets would make it easier to price these instruments, as investors could rely on public information and on the observations of traded prices. At the same time, it would help policy makers and regulators to understand where the risks are located and thus monitor the accumulation of imbalances.

Finally, the third factor I want to mention is the excessive pro-cyclicality of the financial system. We need to introduce a framework to dampen this phenomenon. There seems to be an inherent tendency for financial systems to cause periods of booms, by building up imbalances, and then to go through busts – the rapid and disorderly unwinding of these same imbalances. The challenge is to preserve an efficient financial system as an engine for economic growth and at the same time to ensure its stability.[17] Despite centuries of experience and observations

---

14 See Kashyap, Rajan and Stein (2008).
15 See *Financial Times*, 10 July 2007, quote by C. Prince, former CEO of Citigroup.
16 See Maddaloni and Pain (2004).
17 See Hartmann, Heider, Papaioannou and Duca (2007) and ECB (2008b).

of financial crises, it seems to be very difficult to strike the right balance and address this pro-cyclicality.

In this context, it seems to me that central banks have a "franchise" in assuming this role. They do not have vested interests and can provide for "stability" in the long term.

5   CONCLUSION

Let me bring this address to a close with some suggested elements for actions to improve significantly the resilience of financial systems to adverse shocks. Resilience is a key word and concept to guide us in the future.

First, we need to counter mechanisms leading to herding behaviour and establish the right incentives for achieving a balance between short-term and long-term investors and intermediaries. Second, we need to address the lack of transparency. Financial regulators need to tighten up requirements in certain segments of the markets and strengthen reporting requirements for formerly unregulated institutions. Third, in order to address the "excessive" procyclicality of the financial systems, we need to address the mechanisms that intensify fluctuations. For example, capital regulations and provisioning rules as developed by the Basel Committee of Banking Supervision need to restrain excessive risk-taking households is most needed.

What is the role of various authorities in this context? As we have seen, central banks were the very first among the authorities to react when in August 2007 the threat to liquidity in the financial system emerged. The resolute action of central banks constituted a "first line of defence" against the systemic liquidity threat. Almost the entire set of advanced economies and their financial systems were affected from the very beginning of the turmoil. In this context, there is one message that is particularly important for me in my reflections on the past 15 months. This is my wholehearted appreciation of the very intimate cooperation that we have been able to set up among central banks worldwide. We have been working virtually as a "global system of central banks", corresponding to the virtually global nature of today's financial system. Not only have we maintained the continuous flow of information and exchange of assessments of developments, but we have also established a set of common actions that would have been unthinkable even one year ago. As one example amongst many, I would like to mention the fact that the ECB has been providing with euro-denominated collateral US dollar liquidity to the European counterparties through swap arrangements with the Federal Reserve that have no precedent. This action reflects, as much as all the other common actions, the intimate level of trust and cooperation within the community of central banks and, in particular with the Federal Reserve, whose value has been priceless.

I have mentioned the exceptional liquidity support by central banks as the "first line of defence". A necessary "second line of defence" against the systemic solvency threat had to be set up by governments on both sides of the Atlantic.

It would have been unthinkable a year ago that in a number of advanced countries, governments would earmark double-digit percentages of their annual GDP to guarantee exposures and recapitalise their banking sectors. Here, too, we have seen indispensable and resolute action.

After having set up the previous two lines of defence, a third step is now needed in order to improve very significantly medium and long-term confidence. In this context, the credibility of the reforms to improve resilience of the global financial system as well as the stability of the global economy is of the essence. We will see the benefits of the reforms not only in a long-term perspective, but already today, because confidence today, and therefore the success of the decisions already taken by central banks and governments, depends on the quality and credibility of the ambitious reform exercise that has started a few months ago and that is presently deepening with the recent and future meetings of the G20.

In my remarks I have concentrated on the financial aspects of the turmoil, which are very much in the domain of the Financial Stability Forum. The Financial Stability Forum, whose task is to elaborate international supervisory and regulatory policies and standards, has drawn the first set of lessons from the turmoil along the lines I have described above. Deepening its work and implementing it is now of the essence to establish an appropriate and effective reform of the global financial system. The IMF participates in this work and provides relevant inputs as a member of the FSF.

There is also a very important role for the IMF itself in its assessment of macro-financial risks and systemic vulnerabilities, and in its surveillance of macroeconomic policies. Credible stability in the long run requires macroeconomic policies that have a medium-term orientation and are stability-oriented. Procyclicality can stem not only from unsatisfactory regulatory policies in the financial sphere, but also from macroeconomic policies, where it is equally undesirable. In a global context, there is hence a need to significantly strengthen IMF surveillance over economies that are systemically relevant. The IMF's multilateral consultation with key partners is a process that can be built upon in this context. In a long-term perspective, greater discipline in the global economy is needed to foster stability and help balance short-term and long-term prosperity more appropriately.

REFERENCES

Bandt, O. De and P. Hartmann. 2002. "Systemic Risk: A Survey." In *Financial Crisis, Contagion and the Lender of Last Resort: A Book of Readings*, ed. C.A.E. Goodhart and G. Illing, 249-298. London: Oxford University Press.

Borio, C. 2008. "The financial turmoil of 2007?: A Preliminary Assessment and Some Policy Considerations." Bank for International Settlements Working Paper 251.

Caballero, R. J. and A. Krishnamurthy. 2008. "Collective Risk Management in a Flight to Quality Episode." *Journal of Finance*, 63(5): 2195-2230.

Cassola, N., M. Drehmann, P. Hartmann, M. Lo Duca and M. Scheicher. 2008a. "A Research Perspective on the Propagation of the Credit Market." *European Central Bank Research Bulletin*, 7:2-5.

European Central Bank. 2008a. *Financial Stability Review*. Vol. 2. Frankfurt am Main, Germany: European Central Bank.

European Central Bank. 2008b. "Financial development: concepts and measures." *Financial Integration in Europe*, 2:21-36.

Gieve, J. 2006. "Pricing for perfection." Speech delivered at the Bank of England, London, United Kingdom.

Gilboa, I. and D. Schmeidler. 1989. "Maxmin Expected Utility Theory with Non-Unique Prior." *Journal of Mathematical Economics*, 18:141-153.

Hartmann, P., F. Heider, E. Papaioannou and M. Lo Duca. 2007. "The Role of Rinancial Markets and Innovation in Productivity and Growth in Europe." European Central Bank Occasional Paper 7.

Hartmann, P., S. Straetmans and C. G. de Vries. 2005a. "Banking System Stability: a Cross-Atlantic Perspective." European Central Bank Working Paper 527.

Hartmann, P., S. Straetmans and C. G. de Vries.b2005b. "Banking System Stability: a Cross-Atlantic Perspective." National Bureau of Economic Research Working Paper 11698.

International Monetary Fund. 2006a. *Global Financial Stability Report*. Vol. 1. Washington, DC: International Monetary Fund.

International Monetary Fund. 2006b. *Global Financial Stability Report*. Vol. 2. Washington, DC: International Monetary Fund.

Kashyap, A. K., R. G. Rajan and J. C. Stein. 2008 "Rethinking Capital Regulation." Paper presented at the Federal Reserve Bank of Kansas City Symposium, Jackson Hole, WY.

Knight, F. H. 1921. *Risk, uncertainty and profit*. Boston : Houghton-Mifflin.

Maddaloni, A. and D. Pain. 2004. "Corporate 'Excesses' and Financial Market Dynamics." European Central Bank Occasional Paper 17.

O'Hara, M. 2004. "Liquidity and Financial Market Stability." National Bank of Belgium Working Paper 55.

Taleb, N. N. 2007. *The Black Swan: The Impact of the Highly Improbable*. New York: The Random House.

Taylor, J. B. and J. C. Williams. 2009. "A Black Swan in the Money Market." *American Economic Journal*, 1(1): 58-83.

Trichet, J.C. 2007. "Some Reflections on the Development of Credit Derivatives." Speech delivered at the Twenty-Second Annual General Meeting of the International Swaps and Derivatives Association, Boston.

Trichet, J. C. 2008. "Risks and the Macro-Economy." Keynote address presented at the conference *The ECB and Its Watchers*, Frankfurt am Main, Germany.

Stephen G. Cecchetti, Seppo Honkapohja, Lorenzo Bini Smaghi, Raghuram G. Rajan (from left to right)

SESSION 3

CHALLENGES FOR MONETARY POLICY
AND FINANCIAL STABILITY FROM GLOBALISATION

THE GLOBAL ROOTS OF THE CURRENT FINANCIAL CRISIS AND ITS IMPLICATIONS FOR REGULATION

BY ANIL KASHYAP, UNIVERSITY OF CHICAGO
RAGHURAM RAJAN, UNIVERSITY OF CHICAGO
JEREMY STEIN, HARVARD UNIVERSITY

ABSTRACT

Where did the current financial crisis come from? Who or what is to blame? How will it be resolved? How do we undertake reforms for the future? These are the questions this paper will seek to answer. The analysis will have three parts. The first is a rough and ready sketch of the global roots of this crisis. Second, we will focus in a more detailed way on why it hit the financial sector, especially banks. Finally, we will end with some suggestions for future regulation, especially capital regulation.

I   A ROUGH SKETCH

It is always useful to start with the macroeconomic environment. In a sense, this is a crisis borne out of previous crises. An important difference between the recent period of sustained growth and previous periods is the low level of long term real interest rates over the last 5 years, certainly relative to the last two decades.

Long rates fell following the collapse in investment in both emerging markets and developed countries after the crises in 1998 and the ICT bubble in 2001. Emerging market governments became more circumspect and increased budgetary surpluses, even while cutting back on public investment. For instance, in Philippines, investment fell from 24% of GDP in 1996 to 17% in 2006, while its savings rose from 14% to 20%. From borrowing 10% of its GDP, it now pumps out 2.5 percent as a current account surplus.

Moreover, as industrial economies recovered, corporate investment did not pick up, at least not to the extent warranted by the growth. As a result, the worldwide excess of desired savings over actual investment – the so-called savings glut (Bernanke (2005)) – pushed its way into the main markets that were open to investment, housing in industrial countries, lifting house prices and raising residential construction.

The US was not by any means the highest in terms of price growth. Housing prices have reached higher values relative to rent or incomes in Ireland, Spain, the Netherlands, the United Kingdom, and New Zealand for example, though not in Germany or Japan. Then why did the crisis first manifest itself in the US?

Probably because the US went further on financial innovation, thus drawing marginal buyers into the market.

Essentially, the U.S. financial system managed to transform sub-prime mortgages that were local risks, historically handled by local bankers, into mortgage backed securities with AAA ratings, acceptable to pension funds, insurance companies, and banks around the world. The original mortgage was bundled into a pool, and then securities of different seniority sold against it, with the equity tranche bearing the first loss. However, the financial engineers were not content to stop here. They created more complicated pools, bundling the securities sold by the mortgage pools into securities pools, and selling tranched claims against them. So $ 100 of mortgages were converted into $ 80 of AAA bonds, $ 5 of A rated bonds and $ 10 of BBB bonds (see Benmelech and Dlugosz (2009)) . Then those BBB bonds were pooled and further securities issued against them to get more AAA bonds. Thus were born the CDO, the CDO squared and so on. Rating agencies went along certifying senior tranches of these as of the highest credit rating. Risk was sliced and diced but no one knew exactly what was in what. And because nearly everyone was paying, it did not matter.

Why were these assets created? Go back to the savings glut. Financial institutions in countries with excess savings like Germany and Japan were looking to invest their foreign exchange. Many of these institutions were constrained to invest in high quality debt instruments. The highly rated tranches of mortgage backed securities or of CDOs was exactly what they wanted, especially if the AAA tranche of the CDO paid 60 basis points above corporate AAAs. They did not investigate the details of the underlying collateral, even if they could get the information or knew how to, for the rating was guarantee enough.

It was not just the foreigners. Low interest rates made even usually staid domestic institutions like pension funds and insurance companies hungry for yield. So long as the rating companies were willing to certify these securities, and ensure they fit the rating thresholds of the institutions, they were willing to buy them for the extra yield. Of course, there is an old adage in finance – there is no return without risk – but this was forgotten in the frenzied search for yield.

As liquidity drained from the housing market, everything changed. Securitized mortgage pools were easy to understand and undifferentiated when the housing market was liquid – they all had low risk. But as liquidity started drying up and defaults increased, pools became differentiated based on how careful the originator had been, how well documented the loans were, who they were to, etc. Information about the quality of underlying pools started mattering more and much of it was hard to get at. Ratings became suspect.

This immediately created a problem for those who owned claims on the mortgage pools, and wanted to borrow against, or sell them. In the same way as a used car salesman has to sell a car at a significant discount because the buyer suspects the car may be a lemon, once the mortgage pool has become differentiated and information asymmetries have arisen, arm's length buyers like foreigners or pension funds are reluctant to buy, and lenders are unwilling to lend, without knowing much more.

But if mortgage pools became harder to value, the securities issued by CDOs and CDO squared became doubly hard to value, because not only were they subject to the same underlying information asymmetries besetting the underlying mortgages, but also because they were leveraged claims on these assets, which were really complicated to value when defaults rose. Thus illiquidity in the housing market created information risk, which coupled with complexity risk, destroyed liquidity for asset backed securities in the financial market.

Moreover, for a number of complex securities, default risk was actually much higher than foreseen because there was far less diversification in assets than originally thought. Put another way, if house prices fall 20%, losses on portfolios of mortgage backed securities will be substantial– say at the very least 15% on the most recent mortgages. But the BBB securities issued by these portfolios will be completely wiped out, so the CDOs that think they have diversified by buying BBB securities across the country will also be wiped out, as will all the securities issued by the CDOs, including those rated AAA in the past.

As liquidity for these complex securities evaporated, banks found they could no longer pledge these assets as collateral against borrowing. A little bit of arithmetic helps illustrate the consequences. Say an investment bank, levered about 24 to 1, had 96 dollars of debt and 4 dollars of equity capital funding 100 dollars of assets, before the crisis. And suppose 90 dollars of those assets were liquid securities and 10 dollars were mortgage backed securities. As mortgage backed securities plunged in value, say to 70 cents on the dollar, and nobody was willing to lend against them, the bank had two problems.

One was an immediate liquidity problem. It had to find a way to finance the 10 dollars of mortgage backed securities that were previously financed with debt. Four of those could be financed with the book capital it had, but it had to find six more dollars somewhere.

The second was a capital problem. Because the market value of its assets was now down to 97 dollars as a result of the fall in the market value of mortgage backed securities, it was very thinly capitalized on a market value basis. But this problem could be handled later.

This is a sense was the Bear Sterns situation– illiquidity rather than insolvency. Central banks reacted by expanding the range of entities they would lend to and the range of assets they would accept as collateral. The Fed was willing to take the 10 dollars of mortgage backed securities as collateral and lend up to 6 dollars against it. This immediately alleviated the liquidity problem, as banks borrowed pledging illiquid assets at the central bank.

But having solved the liquidity problem, banks did little to bolster their capital. Indeed, the capital problem has been getting worse. The mortgage backed securities have now fallen to 40 cents on the dollar, the assets of the bank are now worth 94 dollars, and it has 96 dollars of debt (including the loan from the central bank) outstanding. Unsecured lenders to the bank (and the inter-bank market is unsecured) are now unwilling to lend, knowing that their claims will be hit when the bank defaults. And unless the central bank is willing to substitute for the entire unsecured loan market, the bank will have to default. What was a liquidity problem is now a solvency problem, which cannot be solved by further small increases in liquidity infusion.

Why have the banks not been more pro-active in raising capital? Clearly they felt they had time, in large part because the assistance from the central banks alleviated the liquidity problem. Rather than selling equity when asset prices were moderately depressed, they thought they could wait the crisis out. And central banks have been at fault in not pressing the issue harder when it was easier to raise capital, especially given that their liquidity assistance was helping banks postpone capital raising.

As of the writing of this paper, we are in the midst of a global financial crisis, and the Paulson plan has been voted down. Some of the questions this preliminary account raises include the role of monetary policy (was it too lax, did it account insufficiently for the effects of low interest rates on asset prices, credit growth, and credit quality), the role of prudential supervision (could more have been done to monitor the "originate to distribute" model, was enough attention paid to institutional incentives and compensation structures, was enough attention paid to the rise of new markets such as the credit default swap market), and the role of global interdependence (were emerging markets too reliant on industrial country demand, were there ways to encourage public investment in the U.S. rather than private consumption, did foreign investors have too much faith in U.S. securities)?

This crisis does put paid to the notion that we had entered a new era of stability, where emerging markets could run current account surpluses and the U.S. would act both as consumer of last resort, as well as the world's banker. The truth is excess demand is difficult for any country, even one with as sophisticated institutions as the United States, to generate without succumbing to excesses. The notion that global capital flows can help smooth real sector imbalances for a sustained period of time will have to be reexamined. For all those who warned about unsustainable global imbalances, the biggest surprise has been that the weakest link has proved to be one that many thought the strongest– the U.S. financial system. Moreover, an industrial country crisis is likely to be far more damaging than emerging market crises to world growth– for the former has so much larger and widespread effects.

We have listed important questions, many of which this paper will not seek to answer. Instead, we will focus on much narrower questions. Why were banks so vulnerable to problems in the mortgage market? What does this vulnerability say about the effectiveness of current regulation?

2   WHY WERE BANKS SO EXPOSED?

Our brief answers are as follows. The proximate cause of the credit crisis (as distinct from the housing crisis) was the interplay between two choices made by banks. First, substantial amounts of mortgage-backed securities with exposure to subprime risk were kept on bank balance sheets even though the "originate and distribute" model of securitization that many banks ostensibly followed was supposed to transfer risk to those institutions better able to bear it, such as unleveraged pension funds.[1] Second, across the board, banks financed these and other risky assets with short-term market borrowing.

This combination proved problematic for the system. As the housing market deteriorated, the perceived risk of mortgage-backed securities increased, and it became difficult to roll over short-term loans against these securities. Banks were thus forced to sell the assets they could no longer finance, and the value of these assets plummeted, perhaps even below their fundamental values – i.e., funding problems led to fire sales and depressed prices. And as valuation losses eroded bank capital, banks found it even harder to obtain the necessary short-term financing – i.e., fire sales created further funding problems, a feedback loop that spawned a downward spiral.[2] Bank funding difficulties spilled over to bank borrowers, as banks cut back on loans to conserve liquidity, thereby slowing the whole economy.

Let us elaborate on this sketch. We begin our analysis by asking why so many mortgage-related securities ended up on bank balance sheets, and why banks funded these assets with so much short-term borrowing.

2.1   AGENCY PROBLEMS AND THE DEMAND FOR LOW-QUALITY ASSETS

Our preferred explanation for why bank balance sheets contained problematic assets, ranging from exotic mortgage-backed securities to covenant-light loans, is that there was a breakdown of incentives and risk control systems within banks.[3] A key factor contributing to this breakdown is that, over short periods of time, it is very hard, especially in the case of new products, to tell whether a financial manager is generating true excess returns adjusting for risk, or whether the current returns are simply compensation for a risk that has not yet shown itself but that will eventually materialize. Consider the following specific manifestations of the problem.

INCENTIVES AT THE TOP

The performance of CEOs is evaluated based in part on the earnings they generate relative to their peers. To the extent that some leading banks can

---

1   Throughout this paper, we use the word "bank" to refer to both commercial and investment banks. We say "commercial bank" when we refer to only the former

2   See Brunnermeier and Pedersen (2009) for a detailed analysis of these kinds of spirals and Adrian and Shin (2008b) for empirical evidence on the spillovers.

3   See Hoenig (2008) and Rajan (2005) for a similar diagnosis.

generate legitimately high returns, this puts pressure on other banks to keep up. Follower-bank bosses may end up taking excessive risks in order to boost various observable measures of performance. Indeed, even if managers recognize that this type of strategy is not truly value-creating, a desire to pump up their stock prices and their personal reputations may nevertheless make it the most attractive option for them (Stein (1989), Rajan (1994)).

There is anecdotal evidence of such pressure on top management. Perhaps most famously, Citigroup Chairman Chuck Prince, describing why his bank continued financing buyouts despite mounting risks, said:

"When the music stops, in terms of liquidity, things will be complicated. But as long as the music is playing, you've got to get up and dance. We're still dancing."[4]

FLAWED INTERNAL COMPENSATION AND CONTROL

Even if top management wants to maximize long-term bank value, it may find it difficult to create incentives and control systems that steer subordinates in this direction. Retaining top traders, given the competition for talent, requires that they be paid generously based on performance. But high-powered pay-for-performance schemes create an incentive to exploit deficiencies in internal measurement systems. For instance, at UBS, AAA-rated mortgage-backed securities were apparently charged a very low internal cost of capital. Traders holding these securities were allowed to count any spread in excess of this low hurdle rate as income, which then presumably fed into their bonuses.[5] No wonder that UBS loaded up on mortgage-backed securities.

More generally, traders have an incentive to take risks that are not recognized by the system, so they can generate income that appears to stem from their superior abilities, even though it is in fact only a market risk premium.[6] The classic case of such behavior is to write insurance on infrequent events, taking on what is termed "tail" risk. If a trader is allowed to boost her bonus by treating the entire insurance premium as income, instead of setting aside a significant fraction as a reserve for an eventual payout, she will have an excessive incentive to engage in this sort of trade.

This is not to say that risk managers in a bank are unaware of such incentives. However, they may be unable to fully control them, because tail risks are by their nature rare, and therefore hard to quantify with precision before they

---

4   Financial Times, July 9, 2007.
5   *Shareholder Report on UBS Writedowns*, April 18th 2008, http://www.ubs.com/1/e/investors/agm.html.
6   Another example of the effects of uncharged risk is described in the *Shareholder Report on UBS Writedowns* on page 13: "The CDO desk received structuring fees on the notional value of the deal, and focused on Mezzanine ("Mezz") CDOs, which generated fees of approximately 125 to 150 bp (compared with high-grade CDOs, which generated fees of approximately 30 to 50 bp)." The greater fee income from originating riskier, lower quality mortgages fed directly to the originating unit's bottom line, even though this fee income was, in part, compensation for the greater risk that UBS would be stuck with unsold securities in the event that market conditions turned.

occur. Absent an agreed-on model of the underlying probability distribution, risk managers will be forced to impose crude and subjective-looking limits on the activities of those traders who are seemingly the bank's most profitable employees. This is something that is unlikely to sit well with a top management that is being pressured for profits.[7] As a run of good luck continues, risk managers are likely to become increasingly powerless, and indeed may wind up being most ineffective at the point of maximum danger to the bank.

2.2   AGENCY PROBLEMS AND THE (PRIVATE) APPEAL OF SHORT-TERM BORROWING

We have described specific manifestations of what are broadly known in the finance literature as managerial agency problems. The poor investment decisions that result from these agency problems would not be so systemically threatening if banks were not also highly levered, and if such a large fraction of their borrowing was not short-term in nature.

Why is short-term debt such an important source of finance for banks? One answer is that shortterm debt is an equilibrium response to the agency problems described above.[8] If instead banks were largely equity financed, this would leave management with a great deal of unchecked discretion, and shareholders with little ability to either restrain value-destroying behavior, or to ensure a return on their investment. Thus banks find it expensive to raise equity financing, while debt is generally seen as cheaper.[9] This is particularly true if the debt can be collateralized against a specific asset, since collateral gives the investor powerful protection against managerial misbehavior.

The idea that collateralized borrowing is a response to agency problems is a common theme in corporate finance (see, e.g., Hart and Moore (1998)), and of course this is how many assets – from real estate to plant and equipment – are

---

7   As the Wall Street Journal (April 16, 2008) reports, "Risk controls at [Merrill Lynch], then run by CEO Stan O'Neal, were beginning to loosen. A senior risk manager, John Breit, was ignored when he objected to certain risks...Merrill lowered the status of Mr. Breit's job... Some managers seen as impediments to the mortgage-securities strategy were pushed out. An example, some former Merrill executives say, is Jeffrey Kronthal, who had imposed informal limits on the amount of CDO exposure the firm could keep on its books ($3 billion to $4 billion) and on its risk of possible CDO losses (about $75 million a day). Merrill dismissed him and two other bond managers in mid- 2006, a time when housing was still strong but was peaking. To oversee the job of taking CDOs onto Merrill's own books, the firm tapped a senior trader but one without much experience in mortgage securities. CDO holdings on Merrill's books were soon piling up at a rate of $5 billion to $6 billion per quarter." Bloomberg (July 22, 2008, "Lehman Fault-Finding Points to Last Man Fuld as Shares Languish") reports a similar pattern at Lehman Brothers whereby "at least two executives who urged caution were pushed aside." The story quotes Walter Gerasimowicz, who worked at Lehman from 1995 to 2003, as saying "Lehman at one time had very good risk management in place. They strayed in search of incremental profit and market share."

8   The insight that agency problems lead banks to be highly levered goes back to Diamond's (1984) classic paper.

9   By analogy, it appears that the equity market penalizes too much financial slack in operating firms with poor governance. For example, Dittmar and Mahrt-Smith (2007) estimate that $1.00 of cash holdings in a poorlygoverned firm is only valued by the market at between $0.42 and $0.88.

financed in operating firms. What distinguishes collateralized borrowing in the banking context is that it tends to be very short-term in nature. This is likely due to the highly liquid and transformable nature of banking firms' assets, a characteristic emphasized by Myers and Rajan (1998). For example, unlike with a plot of land, it would not give a lender much comfort to have a long-term secured interest in a bank's overall trading book, given that the assets making up this book can be completely reshuffled overnight. Rather, any secured interest will have to be in the individual components of the trading book, and given the easy resale of these securities, will tend to short-term in nature.

This line of argument helps to explain why short-term, often secured, borrowing is seen as significantly cheaper by banks than either equity or longer-term (generally unsecured) debt. Of course, short-term borrowing has the potential to create more fragility as well, so there is a tradeoff. However, the costs of this fragility may in large part be borne systemically, during crisis episodes, and hence not fully internalized by individual banks when they pick an optimal capital structure.[10] It is to these externalities that we turn next.

2.3 EXTERNALITIES DURING A CRISIS EPISODE

When banks suffer large losses, they are faced with a basic choice: either they can shrink their (risk-weighted) asset holdings, so that they continue to satisfy their capital requirements with their nowdepleted equity bases, or they can raise fresh equity. For a couple of reasons, equity-raising is likely to be sluggish, leaving a considerable fraction of the near-term adjustment to be taken up by asset liquidations. One friction comes from what is known as the debt overhang problem (Myers (1977)): by bolstering the value of existing risky debt, a new equity issue results in a transfer of value from existing shareholders. A second difficulty is that equity issuance may send a negative signal, suggesting to the market that there are more losses to come (Myers and Majluf (1984)). Thus banks may be reluctant to raise new equity when under stress. It may also be difficult for them to cut dividends to stem the outflow of capital, for such cuts may signal management's lack of confidence in the firm's future. And a loss of confidence is the last thing a bank needs in the midst of a crisis.

Chart 1 plots both cumulative disclosed losses and new capital raised by global financial institutions (these include banks and brokerage firms) over the last four quarters. As can be seen, while there has been substantial capital raising, it has trailed far behind aggregate losses. The gap was most pronounced in the fourth quarter of 2007 and the first quarter of 2008, when cumulative capital raised was only a fraction of cumulative losses. For example, through 2008Q1, cumulative losses stood at \$394.7 billion, while cumulative capital raised was only \$149.1 billion, leaving a gap of \$245.6 billion. The situation improved in the

---

10 A more subtle argument is that the fragile nature of short-term debt financing is actually part of its appeal to banks: precisely because it amplifies the negative consequences of mismanagement, short-term debt acts as a valuable ex ante commitment mechanism for banks. See Calomiris and Kahn (1991). However, when thinking about capital regulation, the critical issue is whether short-term debt has some social costs that are not fully internalized by individual banks.

Chart 1 Progress towards recapitalization by global financial firms

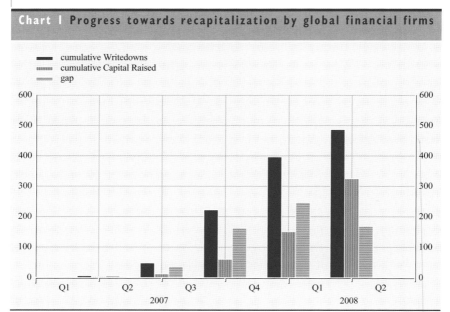

Source: Bloomberg, WDCI <GO> accessed August 6, 2008.

second quarter of 2008, when reported losses declined, while the pace of capital raising accelerated.

While banks may have good reasons to move slowly on the capital-raising front, this gradual recapitalization process imposes externalities on the rest of the economy.

THE FIRE SALE EXTERNALITY

If a bank does not want to raise capital, the obvious alternative will be to sell assets, particularly those that have become hard to finance on a short-term basis. [11] This creates what might be termed a firesale externality. Elements of this mechanism have been described in theoretical work by Allen and Gale (2005), Brunnermeier and Pedersen (2009), Kyle and Xiong (2001), Gromb and Vayanos (2002), Morris and Shin (2004), and Shleifer and Vishny (1992, 1997) among others, and it has occupied a central place in accounts of the demise of Long-Term Capital Management in 1998.

When bank A adjusts by liquidating assets – e.g., it may sell off some of its mortgage-backed securities – it imposes a cost on another bank B who holds the same assets: the mark-to-market price of B's assets will be pushed down, putting pressure on B's capital position and in turn forcing it to liquidate some of its

11 In a Basel II regime, the pressure to liquidate assets is intensified in crisis periods because measured risk levels – and hence risk-weighted capital requirements – go up. One can get a sense of magnitudes from investment banks, who disclose firm-wide "value at risk" (VaR) numbers. Greenlaw et al (2008) calculate a simple average of the reported VaR for Morgan Stanley, Goldman Sachs, Lehman Brothers and Bear Stearns, and find that it rose 34% between August 2007 and February 2008.

positions. Thus selling by one bank begets selling by others, and so on, creating a vicious circle.

This fire-sale problem is further exacerbated when, on top of capital constraints, banks also face short-term funding constraints. In the example above, even if bank B is relatively well-capitalized, it may be funding its mortgage-backed securities portfolio with short-term secured borrowing. When the mark-to-market value of the portfolio falls, bank B will effectively face a margin call, and may be unable to roll over its loans. This too can force B to unwind some of its holdings. Either way, the end result is that bank A's initial liquidation – through its effect on market prices and hence its impact on bank B's price-dependent financing constraints – forces bank B to engage in a second round of forced selling, and so on.

THE CREDIT CRUNCH EXTERNALITY

What else can banks do to adjust to a capital shortage? Clearly, other more liquid assets (e.g. Treasuries) can be sold, but this will not do much to ease the crunch since these assets do not require much capital in the first place. The weight of the residual adjustment will fall on other assets that use more capital, even those far from the source of the crisis. For instance, banks may cut back on new lending to small businesses. The externality here stems from the fact that a constrained bank does not internalize the lost profits from projects the small businesses terminate or forego, and the bank-dependent enterprises cannot obtain finance elsewhere (see, e.g., Diamond and Rajan (2005)). Adrian and Shin (2008b) provide direct evidence that these balance sheet fluctuations affect various measures of aggregate activity, even controlling for short-term interest rates and other financial market variables.

RECAPITALIZATION AS A PUBLIC GOOD

From a social planner's perspective, what is going wrong in both the fire-sale and credit-crunch cases is that bank A should be doing more of the adjustment to its initial shock by trying to replenish its capital base, and less by liquidating assets or curtailing lending. When bank A makes its privately-optimal decision to shrink, it fails to take into account the fact that were it to recapitalize instead, this would spare others in the chain the associated costs. It is presumably for this reason that Federal Reserve officials, among others, have been urging banks to take steps to boost their capital bases, either by issuing new equity or by cutting dividends.[12]

A similar market failure occurs when bank A chooses its initial capital structure up front and must decide how much, if any, "dry powder" to keep. In particular, one might hope that bank A would choose to hold excess capital well above the regulatory minimum, and not to have too much of its borrowing be short-term, so that when losses hit, it would not be forced to impose costs on others. Unfortunately,

---

12 For instance, Bernanke (2008) says: "I strongly urge financial institutions to remain proactive in their capitalraising efforts. Doing so not only helps the broader economy but positions firms to take advantage of new profit opportunities as conditions in the financial markets and the economy improve."

to the extent that a substantial portion of the costs are social, not private costs, any individual bank's incentives to keep dry powder may be too weak.

3   ALTERNATIVES FOR REGULATORY REFORM

Since the banking crisis (as distinct from the housing crisis) has roots in both bank governance and capital structure, reforms could be considered in both areas. Start first with governance. Regulators could play a coordinating role in cases where action by individual banks is difficult for competitive reasons – for example, in encouraging the restructuring of employee compensation so that some performance pay is held back until the full consequences of an investment strategy play out, thus reducing incentives to take on tail risk. More difficult, though equally worthwhile, would be to find ways to present a risk-adjusted picture of bank profits, so that CEOs do not have an undue incentive to take risk to boost reported profits.

But many of these problems are primarily for corporate governance, not regulation, to deal with, and given the nature of the modern financial system, impossible to fully resolve. For example, reducing highpowered incentives may curb excessive risk taking, but will also diminish the constant search for performance that allows the financial sector to allocate resources and risk. Difficult decisions on tradeoffs are involved, and these are best left to individual bank boards rather than centralized through regulation. At best, supervisors should have a role in monitoring the effectiveness of the decision-making process. This means that the bulk of regulatory efforts to reduce the probability and cost of a recurrence might have to be focused on modifying capital regulation.

To address this issue, we begin by describing the "traditional view" of capital regulation – the mindset that appears to inform the current regulatory approach, as in the Basel I and II frameworks. We then discuss what we see to be the main flaws in the traditional view. For reasons of space, our treatment has elements of caricature: it is admittedly simplistic, and probably somewhat unfair. Nevertheless, it serves to highlight what we believe to be the key limitations of the standard paradigm.

3.1   THE TRADITIONAL VIEW

In our reading, the traditional view of capital regulation rests largely on the following four premises.

PROTECT THE DEPOSIT INSURER (AND SOCIETY) FROM LOSSES DUE TO BANK FAILURES

Given the existence of deposit insurance, when a bank defaults on its obligations, losses are incurred that are not borne by either the bank's shareholders or any of its other financial claimholders. Thus bank management has no reason to internalize these losses. This observation yields a simple and powerful rationale for capital regulation: a bank should be made to hold a sufficient capital buffer such that, given realistic lags in supervisory intervention, etc., expected losses to the government insurer are minimized.

One can generalize this argument by noting that, beyond just losses imposed on the deposit insurer, there are other social costs that arise when a bank defaults – particularly when the bank in question is large in a systemic sense. For example, a default by a large bank can raise questions about the solvency of its counterparties, which in turn can lead to various forms of gridlock.

In either case, however, the reduced-form principle is this: bank failures are bad for society, and the overarching goal of capital regulation – and the associated principle of prompt corrective action – is to ensure that such failures are avoided.

ALIGN INCENTIVES

A second and related principle is that of incentive alignment. Simply put, by increasing the economic exposure of bank shareholders, capital regulation boosts their incentives to monitor management, and to ensure that the bank is not taking excessively risky or otherwise value-destroying actions. A corollary is that any policy action that reduces the losses of shareholders in a bad state is undesirable from an ex ante incentive perspective – this is the usual moral hazard problem.

HIGHER CAPITAL CHARGES FOR RISKIER ASSETS

To the extent that banks view equity capital as more expensive than other forms of financing, a regime with "flat" (non-risk-based) capital regulation inevitably brings with it the potential for distortion, because it imposes the same cost-of-capital markup on all types of assets. For example, relatively safe borrowers may be driven out of the banking sector and forced into the bond market, even in cases where a bank would be the economically more efficient provider of finance.

The response to this problem is to tie the capital requirement to some observable proxy for an asset's risk. Under the so-called IRB (internal-ratings-based) approach of the Basel II accord, the amount of capital that a bank must hold against a given exposure is based in part on an estimated probability of default, with the estimate coming from the bank's own internal models. These internal models are sometimes tied to those of the rating agencies. In such a case, risk-based capital regulation amounts to giving a bank with a given dollar amount of capital a "risk budget" that can be spent on either AAA-rated assets (at a low price), on A-rated assets (at a higher price), or on B-rated assets (at an even higher price).

Clearly, a system of risk-based capital works well only insofar as the model used by the bank (or its surrogate, the rating agency) yields an accurate and not-easily-manipulated estimate of the underlying economic risks. Conversely, problems are more likely to arise when dealing with innovative new instruments for which there exists little reliable historical data. Here the potential for mis-characterizing risks – either by accident, or on purpose, in a deliberate effort to subvert the capital regulations – is bound to be greater.

LICENSE TO DO BUSINESS

A final premise behind the traditional view of capital regulation is that it forces troubled banks to seek re-authorization from the capital market in order to continue operating. In other words, if a bank suffers an adverse shock to its capital, and it cannot convince the equity market to contribute new financing, a binding capital requirement will necessarily compel it to shrink. Thus capital requirements can be said to impose a type of market discipline on banks.

3.2 PROBLEMS WITH THE TRADITIONAL MINDSET

THE LIMITS OF INCENTIVE ALIGNMENT

Bear Stearns' CEO Jim Cayne sold his 5,612,992 shares in the company on March 25, 2008 at price of $10.84, meaning that the value of his personal equity stake fell by over $425 million during the prior month. Whatever the reasons for Bear's demise, it is hard to imagine that the story would have had a happier ending if only Cayne had had an *even bigger* stake in the firm, and hence higher-powered incentives to get things right. In other words, ex ante incentive alignment, while surely of some value, is far from a panacea – no matter how well incentives are aligned, disasters can still happen.

Our previous discussion highlights a couple of specific reasons why even very high-powered incentives at the top of a hierarchy may not solve all problems. First, in a complex environment with rapid innovation and short histories on some of the fastest-growing products, even the best-intentioned people are sometimes going to make major mistakes. And second, the entire hierarchy is riddled with agency conflicts that may be difficult for a CEO with limited information to control. A huge bet on a particular product that looks, in retrospect, like a mistake from the perspective of Jim Cayne may have represented a perfectly rational strategy from the perspective of the individual who actually put the bet on – perhaps he had a bonus plan that encouraged risk taking, or his prospects for advancement within the firm were dependent on a high volume of activity in that product.

FIRE SALES AND LARGE SOCIAL COSTS OUTSIDE OF DEFAULT

Perhaps the biggest problem with the traditional capital-regulation mindset is that it places too much emphasis on the narrow objective of averting defaults by individual banks, while paying too little attention to the fire-sale and credit-crunch externalities discussed earlier.[13] Consider a financial institution, which, when faced with large losses, immediately takes action to brings its capital ratio back into line, by liquidating a substantial fraction of its asset holdings.[14] On the one hand, this liquidationbased adjustment process can be seen as precisely the kind of "prompt corrective action" envisioned by fans of capital regulation with a traditional mindset. And there is no doubt that from the perspective of avoiding individual-bank defaults, it does the trick.

---

13 Kashyap and Stein (2004) point out that the Basel II approach can be thought of as reflecting the preferences of a social planner who cares only about avoiding bank defaults, and who attaches no weight to other considerations, such as the volume of credit creation.
14 See Adrian and Shin (2008a) for systematic evidence on this phenomenon.

Unfortunately, as we have described above, it also generates negative spillovers for the economy: not only is there a reduction in credit to customers of the troubled bank, there is also a fire-sale effect that depresses the value of other institutions' assets, thereby forcing them into a similarly contractionary adjustment. Thus liquidation-based adjustment may spare individual institutions from violating their capital requirements or going into default, but it creates a suboptimal outcome for the system as a whole.

REGULATORY ARBITRAGE AND THE VIRAL NATURE OF INNOVATION

Any command-and-control regime of regulation creates incentives for getting around the rules, i.e., for regulatory arbitrage. Compared to the first Basel accord, Basel II attempts to be more sophisticated in terms of making capital requirements contingent on fine measures of risk; this is an attempt to cut down on such regulatory arbitrage. Nevertheless, as recent experience suggests, this is a difficult task, no matter how elaborate a risk-measurement system one builds into the regulatory structure.

One complicating factor is the viral nature of financial innovation. For example, one might argue that AAA-rated CDOs were a successful product precisely because they filled a demand on the part of institutions for assets that yielded unusually high returns given their low regulatory capital requirements.[15] In other words, financial innovation created a set of securities that were highly effective at exploiting skewed incentives and regulatory loopholes. (See, e.g., Coval, Jurek and Stafford (2008a b), and Benmelech and Dlugosz (2009)).

INSUFFICIENT ATTENTION PAID TO COST OF EQUITY

A final limitation of the traditional capital-regulation mindset is that it simply takes as given that equity capital is more expensive than debt, but does not seek to understand the root causes of this wedge. However, if we had a better sense of *why* banks viewed equity capital as particularly costly, we might have more success in designing policies that moderated these costs. This is turn would reduce the drag on economic growth associated with capital regulation, as well as lower the incentives for regulatory arbitrage.

Our discussion above has emphasized the greater potential for governance problems in banks relative to non-financial firms. This logic suggests that equity or long-term debt financing may be much more expensive than short-term debt, not only because long-term debt or equity has little control over governance problems, it is also more exposed to the adverse consequences. If this diagnosis is correct, it suggests that rather than asking banks to carry expensive additional capital all the time, perhaps we should consider a *conditional capital arrangement*

---

15 Sub-prime mortgage originations seemed to take off to supply this market. For instance, Greenlaw et al show that subprime plus Alt-A loans combine represented fewer than 10% of all mortgage originations in 2001, 2002 and 2003, but then jumped to 24% in 2004 and further to 33% in 2005 and 2006; by the end of 2007 they were back to 9%. As Mian and Sufi (2008) and Keys et al. (2008) suggest, the quality of underlying mortgages deteriorated considerably with increased demand for mortgaged-backed securities. See European Central Bank (2008) for a detailed description of the role of structured finance products in propagating the initial sub-prime shock.

that only channels funds to the bank in those bad states of the world where capital is particularly scarce, where the market monitors bank management carefully, and hence where excess capital is least likely to be a concern. We will elaborate on one such idea shortly.

4   PRINCIPLES FOR REFORM

Having discussed what we see to be the limitations of the current regulatory framework for capital, we now move on to consider potential reforms. We do so in two parts. First, in this section, we articulate several broad principles for reform. Then, in Section V, we offer one specific, fleshed-out recommendation.

4.1   DON'T JUST FIGHT THE LAST WAR

In recent months, a variety of policy measures have been proposed that are motivated by specific aspects of the current crisis. For example, there have been calls to impose new regulations on the rating agencies, given the large role generally attributed to their perceived failures. Much scrutiny has also been given to the questionable incentives underlying the "originate to distribute" model of mortgage securitization (Keys et al. (2008)). And there have been suggestions for modifying aspects of the Basel II risk-weighting formulas, e.g., to increase the capital charges for highly-rated structured securities.

While there may well be important benefits to addressing these sorts of issues, such an approach is inherently limited in terms of its ability to prevent future crises. Even without any new regulation, the one thing we can be almost certain of is that when the next crisis comes, it won't involve AAA-rated subprime mortgage CDOs. Rather, it will most likely involve the interplay of some new investment vehicles and institutional arrangements that cannot be fully envisioned at this time. This is the most fundamental message that emerges from taking a viral view of the process of financial innovation – the problem one is trying to fight is always mutating. Indeed, a somewhat more ominous implication of this view is that the seeds of the next crisis may be unwittingly planted by the regulatory responses to the current one: whatever new rules are written in the coming months will spawn a new set of mutations whose properties are hard to anticipate.

4.2   RECOGNIZE THE COSTS OF EXCESSIVE RELIANCE ON EX ANTE CAPITAL

Another widely-discussed approach to reform is to simply raise the level of capital requirements. We see several possible limitations to this strategy. In addition to the fact that it would chill intermediation activity generally by increasing banks' cost of funding, it would also increase the incentives for regulatory arbitrage.

While any system of capital regulation inevitably creates some tendency towards regulatory arbitrage, basic economics suggests that the *volume* of this activity is likely to be responsive to incentives – the higher the payoff to getting around the rules, the more creative energy will be devoted to doing so. In the case of capital regulation, the payoff to getting around the rules is a function of two things: i) the level of the capital requirement; and ii) the wedge between the cost of equity capital (or whatever else is used to satisfy the requirement) and banks' otherwise preferred form of financing. Simply put, given the wedge, capital regulation will be seen as more cumbersome and will elicit a more intense evasive response when the required level of capital is raised.

A higher capital requirement also does not eliminate the fire-sale and credit-crunch externalities identified above. If a bank faces a binding capital requirement – with its assets being a fixed multiple of its capital base – then when a crisis depletes a large chunk of its capital, it must either liquidate a corresponding fraction of its assets, or raise new capital. This is true whether the initial capital requirement is 8% or 10%. [16]

A more sophisticated variant involves raising the ex-ante capital requirement, but at the same time pre-committing to relax it in a bad state of the world. [17] For example, the capital requirement might be raised to 10%, with a provision that it would be reduced to 8% conditional on some publicly observable crisis indicator. [18] Leaving aside details of implementation, this design has the appeal that it helps to mitigate the fire-sale and credit-crunch effects: because banks face a lower capital requirement in bad times, there is less pressure on them to shrink their balance sheets at such times (provided, of course, that the market does not hold them to a higher standard than regulators). In light of our analysis above, this is clearly a helpful feature.

At the same time, since crises are by definition rare, this approach has roughly the same impact on the expected cost of funding to banks as one of simply raising capital requirements in an un-contingent fashion. In particular, if a crisis only occurs once every ten years, then in the other nine years this looks indistinguishable from a regime with higher un-contingent capital requirements. Consequently, any adverse effects on the general level of intermediation activity, or on incentives for regulatory arbitrage, are likely to be similar.

Thus if one is interested in striking a balance between: i) improving outcomes in crisis states, and ii) fostering a vibrant and non-distortionary financial sector in normal times, then even time-varying capital requirements are an imperfect tool.

---

16 It should be noted, however, that higher ex ante capital requirements do have one potentially important benefit. If a bank starts out with a high level of capital, it will find it easier to recapitalize once a shock hits, because the lower is its post-shock leverage ratio, the less of a debt overhang problem it faces, and hence the easier it is issue more equity. Hence the bank will do more recapitalization, and less liquidation, which is a good thing.

17 See Tucker (2008) for further thoughts on this. For instance, capital standards could also be progressively increased during a boom to discourage risk-taking.

18 Starting in 2000 Spain has run a system based on "dynamic provisioning" whereby provisions are built up during times of low reported losses that are to be applied when losses rise. According to Fernández-Ordóñez (2008), Spanish banks "had sound loan loss provisions (1.3% of total assets at the end of 2007, and this despite bad loans being at historically low levels.)" In 2008 the Spanish economy has slowed, and loan losses are expected to rise, so time will tell whether this policy changes credit dynamics.

If one raises the requirement in good times high enough, this will lead to progress on the first objective, but only at the cost of doing worse on the second.

4.3 ANTICIPATE EX POST CLEANUPS; ENCOURAGE PRIVATE-SECTOR RECAPITALIZATION

Many of the considerations that we have been discussing throughout this paper lead to one fundamental conclusion: it is very difficult – probably impossible – to design a regulatory approach that reduces the probability of financial crises to zero without imposing intolerably large costs on the process of intermediation in normal times. First of all, the viral nature of financial innovation will tend to frustrate attempts to simply ban whatever "bad" activity was the proximate cause of the previous crisis. Second, given the complexity of both the instruments and the organizations involved, it is probably naïve to hope that governance reforms will be fully effective. And finally, while one could in principle force banks to hold very large buffer stocks of capital in good times, this has the potential to sharply curtail intermediation activity, as well as to lead to increased distortions in the form of regulatory arbitrage.

It follows that an optimal regulatory system will necessarily allow for some non-zero probability of major adverse events, and focus on reducing the costs of these events. At some level this is an obvious point. The more difficult question is what the policy response should then be, once an event hits. On the one hand, the presence of systemic externalities suggests a role for government intervention in crisis states. We have noted that, in a crisis, private actors do too much liquidation, and too little recapitalization, relative to what is socially desirable. Based on this observation, one might be tempted to argue that the government ought to help engineer a recapitalization of the banking system, or of individual large players. This could be done directly, through fiscal means, or more indirectly, e.g., via extremely accommodative monetary policy that effectively subsidizes the profits of the banking industry.

Of course, ad hoc government intervention of this sort is likely to leave many profoundly uncomfortable, and for good reason, even in the presence of a well-defined externality. Beyond the usual moral hazard objections, there are a variety of political-economy concerns. If, for example, there are to be meaningful fiscal transfers in an effort to recapitalize a banking system in crisis, there will inevitably be some level of discretion in the hands of government officials regarding how to allocate these transfers. And such discretion is, at a minimum, potentially problematic.

In our view, a better approach is to recognize up front that there will be a need for recapitalization during certain crisis states, and to "pre-wire" things so that the private sector – rather than the government – is forced to do the recapitalization. In other words, if the fundamental market failure is insufficiently aggressive recapitalization during crises, then regulation should seek to speed up the process of private-sector recapitalization. This is distinct from both: i) the government being directly involved in recapitalization via transfers; ii) requiring private firms to hold more capital ex ante.

5   A SPECIFIC PROPOSAL: CAPITAL INSURANCE

5.1   THE BASIC IDEA

As an illustration of some of our general principles, and building on the logic we have developed throughout the paper, we now offer a specific proposal. The basic idea is to have banks buy capital insurance policies that would pay off in states of the world when the overall banking sector is in sufficiently bad shape.[19] In other words, these policies would be set up so as to transfer more capital onto the balance sheets of banking firms in those states when aggregate bank capital is, from a social point of view, particularly scarce.

Before saying anything further about this proposal, we want to make it clear that it is only meant to be one element in what we anticipate will be a broader reform of capital regulation in the coming years. For example, the scope of capital regulation is likely to be expanded to include investment banks. And it may well make sense to control liquidity ratios more carefully going forward – i.e., to require, for example, banks' ratio of short-term borrowings to total liabilities not to exceed some target level (though clearly, any new rules of this sort will be subject to the kind of concerns we have raised about higher capital requirements). Our insurance proposal is in no way intended to be a substitute for these other reforms. Instead, we see it as a complement – as a way to give an extra degree of flexibility to the system, so that the overall costs of capital regulation are less burdensome.

More specifically, we envision that capital insurance would be implemented on an opt-in basis, in conjunction with other reforms, as follows. A bank with $500 billion in risk-weighted assets could be given the following choice by regulators: it could either accept an upfront capital requirement that is, say, 2% higher, meaning that the bank would have to raise $10 billion in new equity. Or it could acquire an insurance policy that pays off $10 billion upon the occurrence of a systemic "event" – defined perhaps as a situation in which the aggregate write-offs of major financial institutions in a given period exceed some trigger level.

To make the policy default-proof, the insurer (we have in mind a pension fund, or a sovereign wealth fund) would at inception put $10 billion in Treasuries into a custodial account, i.e., a "lock box". If there is no event over the life of the policy, the $10 billion would be returned to the insurer, who would also receive the insurance premium from the bank as well as the interest paid by the Treasuries. If there is an event, the $10 billion would transfer to the balance sheet of the insured bank. Thus from the perspective of the insurer, the policy would resemble an investment in a defaultable "catastrophe" bond.

---

19 Our proposal is similar in the spirit to Caballero's (2001) contingent insurance plan for emerging market economies.

5.2 THE ECONOMIC LOGIC

This proposal obviously raises a number of issues of design and implementation, and we will attempt to address some of these momentarily. Before doing so, however, let us describe the underlying economic logic.

One way to motivate our insurance idea is as a form of "recapitalization requirement". As discussed above, the central market failure is that, in a crisis, individual financial institutions are prone to do too much liquidation, and too little new capital raising, relative to the social optimum. In principle, this externality could be addressed by having the government inject capital into the banking sector, but this is clearly problematic along a number of dimensions. The insurance approach that we advocate can be thought of as a mechanism for committing the private sector to come up with the fresh capital injection on its own, without resorting to government transfers.

An important question is how this differs from simply imposing a higher capital requirement ex ante – albeit one that might be relaxed at the time of a crisis. In the context of the example above, one might ask: what is the difference between asking a pension fund to invest $10 billion in what amounts to a catastrophe bond, versus asking it to invest $10 billion in the bank's equity, so that the bank can satisfy an increased regulatory capital requirement? Either way, the pension fund has put $10 billion of its money at risk, and either way, the bank will have access to $10 billion more in the event of an adverse shock that triggers the insurance policy.

The key distinction has to do with the *state-contingent nature* of the insurance policy. In the case of the straight equity issue, the $10 billion goes directly onto the bank's balance sheet right away, giving the bank full access to these funds immediately, independent of how the financial sector subsequently performs. In a world where banks are prone to governance problems, the bank will have to pay a cost-of-capital premium for the unconditional discretion that additional capital brings.[20]

By contrast, with the insurance policy, the $10 billion goes into a custodial account. It is only taken out of the account, and made available to the bank, in a crisis state. And crucially, in such states, the bank's marginal investments are much more likely to be value-creating, especially when evaluated from a social

20 There may be a related cosmetic benefit of the insurance policy. Since the bank takes less equity onto its balance sheet, it has fewer shares outstanding, and various measures of performance, such as earnings per share, and return on equity, may be less adversely impacted than by an increase in the ex ante capital requirement. Of course, this will also depend on how the bank is allowed to amortize the cost of the policy.

perspective. In particular, a bank that has an extra $10 billion available in a crisis will be able to get by with less in the way of socially-costly asset liquidations.[21]

This line of argument is an application of a general principle of corporate risk management, developed in Froot, Scharfstein and Stein (1993). A firm can in principle always manage risk via a simple non-contingent "war chest" strategy of having a less leveraged capital structure and more cash on hand. But this is typically not as efficient as a state-contingent strategy that also uses insurance and/or derivatives to more precisely align resources with investment opportunities on a state-by-state basis, so that, to the extent possible, the firm never has "excess" capital at any point in time.

In emphasizing the importance of a state-contingent mechanism, we share a key common element with Flannery's (2005) proposal for banks to use reverse-convertible securities in their capital structure.[22] However, we differ substantially from Flannery on a number of specific design issues. We sketch some of the salient features of our proposal below, acknowledging that many details will have to be filled in after more analysis.

5.3   DESIGN

We first review some basic logistical issues and then offer an example to illustrate how capital insurance might work.

WHO PARTICIPATES?
Capital insurance is primarily intended for entities that are big enough to inflict systemic externalities during a crisis. It may, however, be unwise for regulatory authorities to identify ahead of time those whom they deem to be of systemic importance. Moreover, even smaller banks could contribute to the credit crunch and the fire-sale externalities. Thus we recommend that any entity facing capital requirements be given the option to satisfy some fraction of the requirement using insurance.

SUPPLIERS
Although the natural providers of capital insurance may include institutions such as pension funds and sovereign wealth funds, the securitized design we propose means that policies can be supplied by any investor who is willing to receive a

---

21 To illustrate, suppose a bank has 100 in book value of loans today; these will yield a payoff of either 90 or 110 next period, with a probability 1/2 of either outcome. One way for the bank to insure against default would be to finance itself with 90 of debt, and 10 of equity. But this approach leaves the bank with 20 of free cash in the good state. If investors worry that this cash in good times will lead to mismanagement and waste, they will discount the bank's stock. Now suppose instead that the bank seeks contingent capital. It could raise 105, with 100 of this in debt, and 5 in equity, and use the extra 5 to finance, in addition to the 100 of loans, the purchase of an insurance policy that pays off 10 only in the bad state. From a regulator's perspective, the bank should be viewed as just as well-capitalized as before, since it is still guaranteed not to default in either state. At the same time, the agency problem is attenuated, because after paying off its debt, the bank now has less cash to be squandered in the good state (10, rather than 20).
22 See also Stein (2004) for a discussion of state-contingent securities in a banking context.

higher than risk-free return in exchange for a small probability of a large loss. [23] The experience of the last several years suggests that such a risk profile can be attractive to a range of investors.

While the market should be allowed to develop freely, one category of investor should be excluded, namely those that are themselves subject to capital requirements. It makes no sense for banks to simultaneously purchase protection with capital insurance, only to suffer losses from writing similar policies. Of course, banks should be allowed to design and broker such insurance so long as they do not take positions.

TRIGGER

The trigger for capital insurance to start paying out should be based on losses that affect aggregate bank capital (where the term "bank" should be understood to mean any institution facing capital requirements). In this regard, a key question is the level of geographic aggregation. There are two concerns here. First, banks could suffer losses in one country and withdraw from another. [24] Second, international banks may have some leeway in transferring operations to unregulated territories. [25]

These considerations suggest two design features: First, each major country or region should have its own contingent capital regime, meeting uniform international standards, so that if, say, losses in the U.S. are severe, multinational banks with significant operations in the U.S. do not spread the pain to other countries. Second, multinational banks should satisfy their primary regulator that a significant proportion of their global operations (say 90 percent) are covered by capital insurance.

With these provisos, the trigger for capital insurance could be that the sum of losses of covered entities in the domestic economy (which would include domestic banks and local operations of foreign banks) exceeds some significant amount. To avoid concerns of manipulation, especially in the case of large banks, the insurance trigger for a specific bank should be based on losses of all other banks *except* the covered bank.

23 There may be some benefit to having the insurance provided by passive investors. Not only do they have pools of assets that are idle, and can profitably serve as collateral (in contrast to an insurance company that might be reluctant to see its assets tied up in a lock box), they also have the capacity to bear losses without attempting to hedge them (again, unlike a more active financial institution). Individual investors, pension funds, and sovereign wealth funds would be important providers. See Organization for Economic Cooperation and Development (2008) for a list of major investments, totaling over $40 billion, made by sovereign wealth funds in the financial sector from 2007 through early 2008.

24 Indeed, Peek and Rosengren (2000) document the withdrawal of Japanese banks from lending in California in response to severe losses in Japan.

25 The trigger might also be stated in terms of the size of the domestic market so that firms entering a market do not mechanically change the likelihood of a payment.

The trigger should be based on aggregate bank losses over a certain number of quarters.[26] This horizon needs to be long enough for substantial losses to emerge, but short enough to reflect a relatively sudden deterioration in performance, rather than a long, slow downturn. In our example below we consider a four-quarter benchmark, which means that if there were two periods of large losses that were separated by more than a year the insurance might not be triggered.

An alternative to basing the trigger on aggregate bank losses would be to base it on an index of bank stock prices, in which case the insurance policy would be no more than a put option on a basket of banking stocks. However, this alternative raises a number of further complications. For example, with so many global institutions, creating the appropriate country-level options would be difficult, since there are no share prices for many of their local subsidiaries. Perhaps more importantly, the endogenous nature of stock prices – the fact that stock prices would depend on insurance payouts and vice-versa – could create various problems with indeterminacy or multiple equilibria. For these reasons, it is better to link insurance payouts to a more exogenous measure of aggregate bank health.

PAYOUT PROFILE

A structure that offers large discrete payouts when a threshold level of losses is hit might create incentives for insured banks to artificially inflate their reported losses when they find themselves near the threshold. To deter such behavior, the payout on a policy should increase continuously in aggregate losses once the threshold is reached. Below, we give a concrete example of a policy with this kind of payout profile.

STAGGERED MATURITIES

An important question is how long a term the insurance policies would run for. Clearly, the longer the term, the harder it would be to price a policy, and the more unanticipated risk the insurer would be subject to, while the shorter the term the higher the transactions costs of repeated renewal. Perhaps a five-year term might be a reasonable compromise.

However, with any finite term length, there is the issue of renewal under stress: what if a policy is expiring at a time when large losses are anticipated, but have not yet been realized? In this case, the bank will find it difficult to renew the policy on attractive terms. To partially mitigate this problem, it may be helpful for each bank to have in place a set of policies with staggered maturities, so that each year only a fraction of the insurance needs to be replaced. Another point to note is that if renewal ever becomes prohibitively expensive, there is always the option to switch back to raising capital in a conventional manner, i.e., via equity issues.

26 Because this insurance pays off only in systemically bad states of nature, it will be expensive, but not relative to pure equity financing. For example, suppose that there are 100 different future states of the world for each bank, and that the trigger is breached only in 1 of the 100 scenarios. Because equity returns are low both in the trigger state and in many others (with either poor bank specific outcomes or bad but not disastrous aggregate outcomes), the cost of equity must be higher than the cost of the insurance.

AN EXAMPLE

To illustrate these ideas, Chart 2 provides a detailed example of how the proposal might work for a bank seeking $10 billion in capital insurance. We assume that protection is purchased via five policies of $2 billion each that expire at year end for each of the next five years. There are three factors that shape the payouts on the policies: the trigger points for both the initiation of payouts and the capping of payouts, the pattern of bank losses, and the function that governs how losses are translated into payouts.

In the example, the trigger for initiating payouts is hit once cumulative bank losses over the last four quarters reach $100 billion. And payouts are capped once cumulative losses reach $200 billion. In between, payouts are linear in cumulative losses. This helps to ensure that, aside from the time value of earlier payments, banks have no collective benefit to pulling forward large loss announcements.

The payout function also embeds a "high-water" test, so that – given the four-quarter rolling window for computing losses – only incremental losses in a given quarter lead to further payouts. In the example, this feature comes into play in the 3rd quarter of 2009, when current losses are zero. Because of the high-water feature, payouts in this quarter are zero also, even though cumulative losses over the prior four quarters continue to be high. Put simply, the high-water feature allows us to base payouts on a fourquarter window, while at the same time avoiding double-counting of losses.

These and other details of contract design are important, and we offer the example simply as a starting point for further discussion. However, given that the purpose of the insurance is to guarantee relatively rapid recapitalization of the banking sector, one property of the example that we believe should carry over to any real-world structure is that it be made to pay off promptly.

5.4   COMPARISONS WITH ALTERNATIVES

An important precursor to our proposal, and indeed the starting point for our thinking on this, is Flannery (2005). Flannery proposes that banks issue reverse convertible debentures, which convert to equity when a bank's share price falls below a threshold. Such an instrument can be thought of as a type of firm-specific capital insurance.

One benefit of a firm-specific trigger is that it provides the bank with additional capital in any state of the world when it is in trouble – unlike our proposal where a bank gets an insurance payout only when the system as a whole is severely stressed. In the spirit of the traditional approach to capital regulation, the firm-specific approach does a more complete job of reducing the probability of distress for each individual institution. The firm-specific trigger also should create monitoring incentives for the bond holders which could be useful. Finally, to the extent that one firm's failure could be systemically relevant, this proposal resolves that problem whereas ours does not.

However, a firm-specific trigger also has disadvantages. First, given that a reverse convertible effectively provides a bank with debt forgiveness if it performs poorly enough, it could exacerbate problems of governance and moral hazard. Moreover, the fact that the trigger is based on the bank's stock price may be particularly problematic here. One can imagine that once a bank begins to get into trouble, there may be the ingredients in place for a self-fulfilling downwards spiral: as existing shareholders anticipate having their stakes diluted via the conversion of the debentures, stock prices decline further, making the prospect of conversion even more likely, and so on. [27]

Our capital insurance structure arguably does better than reverse convertibles on bank-specific moral hazard, given that payouts are triggered by aggregate losses rather by poor individual performance. With capital insurance, not only is a bank not rewarded for doing badly, it gets a payout in precisely those states of the world when access to capital is most valuable – i.e., when assets are cheap and

---

27 Relatedly, such structures can create incentives for speculators to manipulate bank stock prices. For example, it may pay for a large trader to take a long position in reverse convertibles, then try to push down the price of the stock via short-selling, in order to force conversion and thereby acquire an equity stake on favorable terms.

Chart 2 Hypothetical Capital Insurance Payout Structure

In this example, Bank X purchases $10 billion in total coverage. It does so by buying five policies of $2 billion each, with expiration dates of 12/31/2009, 12/31/2010, 12/31/2011, 12/31/2012, and 12/31/2013. The payout on each policy is given by:

$$\text{Payout} = \frac{4 \text{ quarter loss} - \max(\text{high water}_{t-1}, \text{trigger})}{\text{Full payout} - \text{trigger}} * (\text{Policy face})$$

$$\text{if } 4 \text{ quarter loss} > \text{high water loss}_{t-1}$$
$$= 0 \quad \text{otherwise}$$

The trigger on each policy is $100 billion in aggregate losses for all banks other than X, and full payout is reached when losses by all banks other than X reach $200 billion.

Dollars

(billions)

	2008 Q4	2009 Q1	2009 Q2	2009 Q3	2009 Q4
Current quarter loss	50	40	20	0	140
Cumulative 4 quarter loss	80	120	140	110	200
High water mark on losses	80	120	140	140	200
Payout per policy	0	0.4	0.4	0	1.2
Payout total	0	2	2	0	6
Cumulative payout	0	2	4	4	10

profitable lending opportunities abound. Therefore, banks' incentives to preserve their own profits are unlikely to diminished by capital insurance.

Finally, ownership of the banking system brings with it important political-economy considerations. Regulators may be unwilling to allow certain investors to accumulate large control stakes in a banking firm. To the extent that holders of reverse convertibles get a significant equity stake upon conversion, regulators may want to restrict investment in these securities to those who are "fit and proper", or alternatively, remove their voting rights. Either choice would further limit the attractiveness of the reverse convertible. By contrast, our proposal does not raise any knotty ownership issues: when the trigger is hit, the insured bank simply gets a cash payout with no change in the existing structure of shareholdings.

The important common element of the Flannery (2005) proposal and ours is the contingent nature of the financing. There are other contingent schemes that could also be considered; Culp (2002) offers an introductory overview of these types of securities and a description of some that have been issued.

Security design could take care of a variety of concerns. For example, if investors do not like the possibility of losing everything on rare occasions, the insurance policies could be over-collateralized: the insurer would put $10 billion into the lock box, but only a maximum of $5 billion could be transferred to the insured policy in the event the trigger is breached. This is a transparent change that might get around problems arising because some buyers (such as pension funds or insurance companies) face restrictions on buying securities with low ratings.

A security that has some features of Flannery's proposal (it is tied to firm-specific events) and some of ours (it is tied to losses, not stock prices) is the hybrid security issued in 2000 by the Royal Bank of Canada (RBC). RBC sold a privately placed bond to Swiss RE that, upon a trigger event, converted into preferred shares with a given dividend yield. The conversion price was negotiated at date of the bond issue and the trigger for conversion was tied to a large drop in RBC's general reserves. The size of the issue (C$200 million) was set to deliver an equity infusion of roughly one percent of RBC's Tier capital requirement.

Of particular interest is the rationale RBC had for this transaction. Culp (2002, p. 51) quotes RBC executive David McKay as follows: "It costs the same to fund your reserves whether they're geared for the first amount of credit loss or the last amount of loss...What is different is the probability of using the first loss amounts versus the last loss amounts. Keeping capital on the balance sheet for a last loss amount is not very efficient."

The fact that this firm-specific security could be priced and sold suggests the industry-linked one that we are proposing need not present insurmountable practical difficulties.

Before concluding, let us turn to a final concern about our insurance proposal – that it might create the potential for a different kind of moral hazard. Even though banks do not get reimbursed for their own losses, the fact that they get a cash infusion in a crisis might reduce their incentives to hedge against the crisis, to the extent that they are concerned about not only expected returns, but also the overall variance of their portfolios. In other words, banks might negate some of the benefits of the insurance by taking on more systematic risk. To see the logic most transparently, consider a simple case where a bank sets a fixed target on the net amount of money it is willing to lose in the bad state (i.e., it implements a value-at-risk criterion). If it knows that it will receive a $10B payoff from an insurance policy in the crisis, it may be willing to tolerate $10B more of pre-insurance losses in the crisis. If all banks behave in this way, they may wind up with more highly correlated portfolios than they would absent capital insurance.

This concern is clearly an important one. However, there are a couple of potentially mitigating factors. First, what is relevant is not whether our insurance proposal creates any moral hazard, but whether it creates more or less than the alternative of raising capital requirements. One could equally well argue that, in an effort to attain a desired level of return on equity, banks target the amount of systematic risk borne by their stockholders, i.e. their equity betas. If so, when the capital requirement is raised, banks would offset this by simply raising the systematic risk of their asset portfolios, so as to keep constant the amount of systematic risk borne per unit of equity capital. In this sense, any form of capital regulation faces a similar problem.

Second, the magnitude of the moral hazard problem associated with capital insurance is likely to depend on how the trigger is set, i.e. on the likelihood that the policy will pay off. Suppose that the policy only pays off in an extremely bad state which occurs with very low probability – a true financial crisis. Then a bank that sets out to take advantage of the system by holding more highly correlated assets faces a tradeoff: this strategy makes sense to the extent that the crisis state occurs and the insurance is triggered, but will be regretted in the much more likely scenario that things go badly, but not sufficiently badly to trigger a payout. This logic suggests that with an intelligently designed trigger, the magnitude of the moral hazard problem need not be prohibitively large.

This latter point is reinforced by the observation that, because of the agency and performancemeasurement problems described above, bank managers likely underweight very low probability tail events when making portfolio decisions. On the one hand, this means that they do not take sufficient care to avoid assets that have disastrous returns with very low probability – hence the current crisis. At the same time, it also means that they do not go out of their way to target any specific pattern of cashflows in such crisis states. Rather, they effectively just ignore the potential for such states ex ante, and focus on optimizing their portfolios over the more "normal" parts of the distribution. If this is the case, insurance with a sufficiently low-probability trigger will not have as much of an adverse effect on behavior.

6   CONCLUSIONS

Our analysis of the current crisis suggests that governance problems in banks and excessive shortterm leverage were at its core. These two causes are related. Any attempt at preventing a recurrence should recognize that it is difficult to resolve governance problems, and, consequently, to wean banks from leverage. Direct regulatory interventions, such as mandating more capital, could simply exacerbate private sector attempts to get around them, as well as chill intermediation and economic growth. At the same time, it is extremely costly for society to either continue rescuing the banking system, or to leave the economy to be dragged into the messes that banking crises create.

If despite their best efforts, regulators cannot prevent systemic problems, they should focus on minimizing their costs to society, without dampening financial intermediation in the process. We have offered one specific proposal, capital insurance, which aims to reduce the adverse consequences of a crisis, while making sure the private sector picks up the bill. While we have sketched the broad outlines of how a capital insurance scheme might work, there is undoubtedly much more work to be done before it can be implemented. We hope that other academics, policymakers and practitioners will take up this challenge.

REFERENCES

Adrian, T. and H. S. Shin. 2008a. "Liquidity, Financial Cycles and Monetary Policy." *Federal Reserve Bank of New York Current Issues in Economics and Finance*, 14(1):1-7.

Adrian, T. and H. Shin. 2008b. "Financial Intermediaries, Financial Stability and Monetary Policy." Paper presented at the Federal Reserve Bank of Kansas City Symposium on "Maintaining Stability in a Changing Financial System", Jackson Hole, Wyoming.

Allen, F., and D. Gale. 2005. "From Cash-in-the-Market Pricing to Financial Fragility." *Journal of the European Economic Association*, 3: 535-546.

Bank for International Settlements. 2008. *78th Annual Report: 1 April 2007 – 31 March 2008.* Basel, Switzerland: Bank for International Settlements.

Bank of England. 2008. *Financial Stability Report.* Vol. 23. London: Bank of England.

Benmelech, E., and J. Dlugosz. 2009. "The Alchemy of CDO Credit Ratings." National Bureau of Economic Research Working Paper 14878.

Borio, C. 2008. "The Financial Turmoil of 2007: A Preliminary Assessment and Some Policy Considerations." Bank for International Settlements Working Paper 251.

Bernanke, B. S. 2008. "Risk Management in Financial Institutions." Speech delivered at the Federal Reserve Bank of Chicago's Annual Conference on Bank Structure and Competition, Chicago, Illinois.

Brunnermeier, M. K. 2008. "Deciphering the 2007-08 Liquidity and Credit Crunch." *Journal of Economic Perspectives*, 23(1): 77-100.

Brunnermeier, M. K., and L. Pedersen. 2009. "Market Liquidity and Funding Liquidity." *Review of Financial Studies*, 22(6): 2201-2238.

Caballero, R. J. 2001. *Macroeconomic Volatility in Reformed Latin America: Diagnosis and Policy Proposal*. Washington, D.C.: Inter-American Development Bank.

Calomiris, C. W., and C. M. Kahn. 1991. "The Role of Demandable Debt in Structuring Optimal Banking Arrangements." *American Economic Review*, 81(3): 495-513.

Coval, J. D., J. W. Jurek, and E. Stafford. 2008a. "Economic Catastrophe Bonds." *American Economic Review*, 29(3): 628-666.

Coval, J. D., J. W. Jurek, and E. Stafford. 2008b. Forthcoming. "Re-Examining The Role of Rating Agencies: Lessons From Structured Finance." *Journal of Economic Perspectives*.

Culp, C., L. 2002. "Contingent Capital: Integrating Corporate Financing and Risk Management Decisions." *Journal of Applied Corporate Finance*, 55(1): 46-56.

Diamond, D. W. 1984. "Financial Intermediation and Delegated Monitoring." *Review of Economic Studies*, 51(3): 393-414.

Diamond, D. W., and Raghuram G. Rajan. 2005. "Liquidity Shortages and Banking Crises." *Journal of Finance*, 60(2): 615-647.

Dittmar, A., and J. Mahrt-Smith. 2007. "Corporate Governance and the Value of Cash Holdings." *Journal of Financial Economics*, 83(3): 599-634.

Dudley, W. C. 2007. "May You Live in Interesting Times." Remarks at the Federal Reserve Bank of Philadelphia, Philadelphia, Pennsylvania.

Dudley, W. C. 2008. "May You Live in Interesting Times: The Sequel." Remarks at the Federal Reserve Bank of Chicago's 44th Annual Conference on Bank Structure and Competition, Chicago, Illinois.

European Central Bank. 2008. *Financial Stability Review*. Frankfurt am Main, Germany: European Central Bank.

Fernández-Ordoñez, M. 2008. "Economic Developments and the Financial Sector – a Spanish Perspective." Speech presented at 2008 International Monetary Conference – Central Bankers Panel, Barcelona, Spain.

Flannery, M. J. 2005. "No Pain, No Gain? Effecting Market Discipline via Reverse Convertible Debentures" In *Capital Adequacy Beyond Basel: Banking Securities and Insurance*, ed. Hal S. Scott. Oxford: Oxford University Press.

Froot, K. D. S. Scharfstein, and J. C. Stein. 1993. "Risk Management: Coordinating Corporate Investment and Financing Policies." *Journal of Finance*, 48 (5): 1629-1658.

Greenlaw, D. J. Hatzius, A. K Kashyap, and H. S. Shin. 2008. "Leveraged Losses: Lessons from the Mortgage Market Meltdown." U.S. Monetary Policy Forum Report 2.

Hart, O. and J. Moore. 1998. "Default and Renegotiation: A Dynamic Model of Debt." *Quarterly Journal of Economics*, 113(1): 1-41.

Hoenig, T. M. 2008. "Perspectives on the Recent Financial Market Turmoil." Remarks at the 2008 Institute of International Finance Membership Meeting, Rio de Janeiro, Brazil.

Gromb, D., and D. Vayanos. 2002. "Equilibrium and Welfare in Markets with Financially Constrained Arbitrageurs." *Journal of Financial Economics*, 66 (2-3): 361-407.

International Monetary Fund. 2008. *Global Financial Stability Report*. Washington, DC.: International Monetary Fund.

Kashyap, A. K., and J. C. Stein. 2004. "Cyclical Implications of the Basel-II Capital Standards." *Federal Reserve Bank of Chicago Economic Perspectives*, 28: 18-31.

Kelly, K. 2008. "Lost Opportunities Haunt Final Days of Bear Stearns: Executives Bickered Over Raising Cash, Cutting Mortgages." *Wall Street Journal*. May 27, A1.

Keys, B. T. Mukherjee, A. Seru, and V. Vig. 2008. "Did Securitization Lead to Lax Screening? Evidence from Subprime Loans." EFA 2008 Athens Meetings Paper. http://ssrn.com/abstract=1093137

Knight, M.. 2008. "Now You See It, Now You Don't: The Nature of Risk and the Current Financial Turmoil." Speech delivered at the Ninth Annual Risk Management Convention of the Global Association of Risk Professionals, New York.

Kyle, A. S., and W. Xiong. 2001. "Contagion as a Wealth Effect." *Journal of Finance*, 56(4): 1401- 1440.

Mian, A., and A. Sufi. 2008. "The Consequences of Mortgage Credit Expansion: Evidence from the 2007 Mortgage Default Crisis." National Bureau of Economic Research Working Paper 13936.

Morris, S., and H. S. Shin. 2004. "Liquidity Black Holes." *Review of Finance*, 8(1): 1-18.

Myers, S. C. 1977. "Determinants of Corporate Borrowing." *Journal of Financial Economics*, 5(2): 147-175.

Myers, S. C., and N. S. Majluf. 1984. "Corporate Financing and Investment Decisions When Firms Have Information That Investors Do Not Have." *Journal of Financial Economics*, 13(2): 187-221.

Myers, S. C., and R. G. Rajan. 1998. "The Paradox of Liquidity." *Quarterly Journal of Economics*, 113(3): 733-771.

Organization for Economic Cooperation and Development. 2008. "Financial Market Highlights– May 2008: The Recent Financial Market Turmoil, Contagion Risks and Policy Responses." *Financial Market Trends*, 1(94): 9-28.

Peek, J., and E. Rosengren. 2000. "Collateral Damage: Effects of the Japanese Bank Crisis on Real Activity in the United States." *American Economic Review*, 90(1): 30-45.

Rajan, R. G. 1994. "Why Bank Credit Policies Fluctuate: A Theory and Some Evidence." *Quarterly Journal of Economics*, 109(2): 399-442.

Rajan, R. G. 2005. "Has Financial Development Made the World Riskier." National Bureau of Economic Research Working Paper 11728.

Shleifer, A., and R. W. Vishny. 1992. "Liquidation Values and Debt Capacity: A Market Equilibrium Approach." *Journal of Finance*, 47(4): 1343-66.

Shleifer, A., and R. W. Vishny. 1997. "The Limits of Arbitrage." Journal of Finance 52(1): 35-55.

Stein, J. C. 1989. "Efficient Capital Markets, Inefficient Firms: A Model of Myopic Corporate Behavior." *Quarterly Journal of Economics*, 104(4): 655-669.

Stein, J. C. 2004. "Commentary." *Federal Reserve Bank of New York Economic Policy Review*, 10 (2): 27-29.

Tucker, P. M. W. 2008. "Monetary Policy and the Financial System." Speech delivered at the Institutional Money Market Funds Association Annual Dinner, London.

COMMENT

BY STEPHEN G. CECCHETTI, BIS, NBER AND CEPR

INTRODUCTION

Anil Kashyap, Raghuram Rajan and Jeremy Stein are among the deepest and most original financial economists working in the area of financial structure, and especially bank capital regulation, today. Both individually and in collaboration they have provided us with timely and insightful analysis on key issues in banking and policy. This paper is no exception. It starts with a lucid discussion of the main factors underlying the current financial crisis. The authors divide the drivers into two general categories: those associated with macroeconomic imbalances and those related to banks' inherent incentive structures. Combined, these can help explain the fragility of individual financial institutions, and why the problems we have encountered appeared to have been isolated before putting the entire financial system at risk.

The authors build on their analysis of banks' incentive structures to motivate a proposal for a new type of contingent capital scheme. This scheme provides banks with ready access to capital during episodes of systemic distress. The main benefit of this *microeconomic* tool is that it would reduce the *macroeconomic* externalities of an abrupt reduction in financial system leverage. I agree with many of the points the authors make, but I am left with a number of questions.

In this comment, I will begin with a discussion of the economics behind the crisis, then proceed to a description of the proposal, and finally explore some questions.

THE ECONOMICS BEHIND THE CRISIS

Kashyap, Rajan and Stein point to global macroeconomic imbalances as a fundamental causal factor behind the current financial crisis. They identify the build-up of private sector debt – demanded by the US and other industrialised economies and supplied by economies with current account surpluses, such as those in Asia – as creating the conditions for an unsustainable expansion in output that exceeded the economies' long-run capacity over an extended period. Against this backdrop, they see the emergence of financial innovation as a factor that helped channel, through complex structures, an abundant supply of credit to housing. Importantly, instrument complexity and opacity brought about a weakening of market discipline, which exacerbated agency problems. Coupled with banks' incentive structures, this led to high levels of leverage in the banking sector and, from a social point of view, to an excessive fragility of the financial system.

As Kashyap, Rajan and Stein point out, the natural capital structure for banks – little capital plus short-term (apparently) collateralised borrowing – leads individual institutions to react to losses in a manner that creates two externalities. The first concerns asset fire sales. An individual institution that is forced to sell will drive down the value of everyone else's assets. The second is the fact that as banks reduce leverage, lending to the real economy contracts. This, too, is self-reinforcing, as without access to credit non-financial firms are forced to cut expenditures, leading to a slowdown and further losses for banks. All of this makes it difficult, if not impossible, for a bank to raise capital in the midst of a systemic event.

THE SPECIFIC PROPOSAL

The authors have put forward a specific, and very natural, proposal for capital insurance. Since the problem is that capital skyrockets in cost exactly when banks need it most, they design a contract that injects capital at just the right time, shifting the risk to someone else. The authors have worked out a number of the details of their capital insurance proposal. Importantly, a bank would be given the option of buying insurance in lieu of higher mandatory capital requirements. Furthermore, the capital insurance would be offered only by long-only (ie unleveraged) institutions that do not face capital requirements themselves. The insurer is required to place the gross amount of the insurance in a custodial account (a "lock-box") to be held in the form of government securities or the equivalent. The payout is triggered by a fall in banking system-wide capital.

This proposal makes a very positive contribution to the current debate about how capital regulation can be improved. The authors rightly emphasise the need to broaden the scope of prudential regulatory policies to better capture risks.

You will not be surprised to hear me say that this is an area in which there has been substantial activity in recent months. For example, the Basel Committee on Banking Supervision has recently introduced improvements to the Basel II framework that strengthen the assessment of both the risks embedded in securitised instruments and the treatment of off-balance sheet exposures.

While continuous improvements of the regulatory guidelines within the framework of Basel II is essential, I am sympathetic to the following point made by Kashyap, Rajan and Stein:

> "[I]t is very difficult – probably impossible – to design a regulatory approach that reduces the probability of financial crisis to zero without imposing intolerably large costs on the process of intermediation in normal times. First, the viral nature of financial innovation will tend to frustrate attempts to simply ban whatever bad activity was the proximate cause of the previous crisis. Second, given the complexity of both the instruments and the organizations involved, it is probably naïve to hope that governance reforms will be fully effective."

Even so, improvements in the ability of regulatory tools to capture risk should extend to both systemic events and the risks to the real economy from the negative externalities of banks' individually rational actions.

In other words, we need practical proposals for strengthening the systemic dimension of prudential rules. Specifically, prudential tools need to be better calibrated to address risks to the system as a whole, and to become more responsive to the interdependencies between institutions and markets. The BIS has been emphasising this point for some time, arguing in favour of a better, rule-based, alignment of the microprudential perspective, with its emphasis on individual institutions, with the macroprudential perspective, which focuses on the behaviour of the system and its interaction with the business cycle. The current crisis only makes the point more pressing.[1]

A number of aspects of the macroprudential approach advocated by the BIS are beyond the scope of the Kashyap, Rajan and Stein paper. For example, this approach needs to be embedded in a holistic framework, which encompasses a wide range of policies and in which capital regulation is just one – albeit quite important – tool. In addition, the paper limits the discussion to a representative bank, whereas the cross-sectional dimension of the macroprudential framework calls for a differentiation across institutions according to their systemic importance and exposure to systematic risk.

The macroprudential approach has both a cross-sectional dimension and a time-series dimension. The former is simply to ensure that the failure of a single institution, or group of institutions, does not put the entire system at risk. The capital insurance proposal relates to the latter. There is a growing consensus that prudential regulation should seek to dampen the tendency of financial decisions to exacerbate macroeconomic cycles. Doing this requires introducing countercyclical elements that encourage banks to create true *buffers* that function as loss absorbers. Conceptually, we want banks to build up capital cushions during the calm and to drawn them down in the storm. As Kashyap, Rajan and Stein correctly point out, strict minimum capital requirements do the opposite, amplifying stresses because of the externalities of banks' behaviour.

I should note that proposals that emphasise ex ante provision of resources that can be used in bad times have been advanced by a number of people.[2] These typically imply some degree of countercyclicality in the level of capital banks are required to hold. Compared to the Kashyap, Rajan and Stein proposal, these alternatives have the advantage of leaning against the build-up of imbalance during the upswing of the cycle by restraining the expansion of financial system balance sheets overall.

1   See, for example, Crockett (2000), Knight (2006) and BIS (2002, 2005).
2   See, for instance, Gordy and Howells (2007), Flannery (2005), Goodhart and Persaud (2008), and Kashyap and Stein (2004), among others.

QUESTIONS

Returning to the specifics, this intriguing proposal raises a number of questions. I will focus on five, some of which are clearly acknowledged in the paper:

1. Who offers the insurance?
2. How much insurance would each bank purchase?
3. How is the trigger for payment measured and administered?
4. How is the insurance priced?
5. Does insurance economise on the capital committed to the banking system?

Who offers the insurance?

As I noted at the outset, the authors say that only unleveraged institutions should be allowed to supply this insurance. The problem with this is that there are many ways to borrow. Would a life insurance company or a pension fund, institutions with contingent liabilities that in many cases resemble nominal or index bonds, be qualified to write the insurance?

Another point is that, while the fact of the lock-box eliminates counterparty risk for the buyers of the insurance, the seller still faces the risk, meaning that if there is a systemic event triggering payment, the insurer faces a loss. This loss comes at what will surely be the worst possible time, when all financial institution balance sheets are already impaired. Does the capital insurance scheme simply shift the problem to another part of the financial system?

How much insurance would each bank purchase?

Would this depend on the characteristics of the individual institution, such as its size and degree of risk-taking, or on the potential economic costs from a systemic event? A calibration at the bank level that does not reflect the extent to which the individual bank may suffer from or exacerbate systemic distress runs the risk of encouraging socially suboptimal "herding" behaviour that would maximise the expected benefit from subscribing to the proposed capital insurance scheme.

How is the trigger for payment measured and administered?

For the scheme to work, we need a credible, real-time indicator of the aggregate state that is not revised. Any national income accounts-based quantity is clearly ruled out, as there are constant revisions. But why do the authors think that something like bank capital is less of a problem? Recall that the trigger for payment is the level of write-offs the banking system has experienced. The difficulty is that accounting standards and their enforcement may not be adequately immune to manipulations to make this quantity sufficiently credible. Admittedly, this criticism probably applies to capital regulation in general, so I may be holding the capital insurance proposal to an unrealistically high standard.

Related to this is the question of how the insurance scheme should evolve if clear signs of financial distress were to emerge prior to the realisation of a systemic event that triggers payouts to subscribers. During such an interim period, it might be tempting for supervisors to require that banks reassure markets by increasing their subscriptions to the insurance scheme. However, such behaviour is likely to amplify the concurrent rise in insurance premia, which could exacerbate individual banks' health and, eventually, even precipitate a crisis.

How is the insurance priced?

This is a critical point, on which I have three comments:

- Pricing system-risk insurance means estimating the probability of tail events, which are by definition infrequent. Not only is this extremely difficult, but the limited experience we have suggests that the market tends to underprice this risk in good times, which is to say when insurance providers are expected to be long on it.

- The primary rationale for the insurance system is to mitigate an externality. Doesn't that mean that the market price of the insurance will be too high from a social point of view, and thus need to be subsidised?

- If the market prices insurance properly, how different will the cost be from the cost of capital? Here I would make two points:

  i.   Since banks can chose whether to raise more capital or buy insurance, shouldn't they equate the (risk-adjusted) cost at the margin? Won't the insurance have the same price as capital?
  ii. It is true that since the suppliers of insurance only pay if a systemic event occurs, and not if the bank fails for idiosyncratic reasons, it would appear that they require a lower return. But, unlike equity holders, the insurance providers do not share in the profits during the good times. I hesitate to argue with these authors on a point of financial theory, but it seems to me that the difference in cost is likely to be small and could depend on the fact that in reality idiosyncratic risk is priced.

Does insurance economise on the capital committed to the banking system?

One of the appeals of the Kashyap, Rajan and Stein capital insurance scheme is that it is intended to economise on capital that is committed to the banking system, increasing the non-financial capital stock. There are two reasons to wonder if this is going to the case. First, there is the lock-box that forms such a critical element of the proposal. The idea is that you need to be certain the insurer can pay off if the catastrophic state occurs. What about the resources that are used to purchase the securities in the lock-box? I realise these have to be government securities – they need to be able to retain both their value and liquidity in a crisis – but what does that mean for the capital stock as a whole?

The second reason to question whether the proposal economises on capital allocated to the financial system comes from thinking about the pricing problem I just discussed. If, as I worry may be the case, the price of the insurance is close to that the risk-adjusted marginal cost of capital in the economy as a whole, then the savings may disappear. I fear that all of this leads me to wonder whether we shouldn't simply revert to the point where we are now: Insurance against systemic events is most efficiently supplied by the public authorities.

CONCLUDING REMARKS

My overall conclusion is that the proposal made by Kashyap, Rajan and Stein is welcome and should be considered along with others. While the various ideas may differ in details, they seem to agree on some basic principles that should guide the prudential framework. In broad terms, these principles are:

1) Strengthen macroprudential regulation and supervision by focusing on the stability and performance of the system as well as individual institutions. Proposals that link capital resources to the overall state of the economy and/or the health of the financial system are in line with this.

2) Safeguard stability by supplementing risk-sensitive prudential tools, which we all know can be bypassed through ingenious financial innovation, with simpler and more transparent rules. We urge bankers to pursue diversification in their investment portfolios. Shouldn't we expect regulators to do the same?

3) Continue to build on tools that make supervisory review more effective and enhance the capacity of markets to provide discipline.

Academics have a big role to play in this effort, and I think that the Kashyap, Rajan and Stein paper is one of the more thoughtful contributions in the right direction. And while it may seem that I have been very critical, let me close by saying that the proposal may be the best we can realistically hope for.

REFERENCES

Bank for International Settlements. 2002. "The Interaction between the Financial Sector and the Real Economy." In *72nd Annual Report*. Basel, Switzerland: Bank for International Settlements.

Bank for International Settlements. 2005. "The Financial Sector." In *75th Annual Report. Basel*, Switzerland: Bank for International Settlements.

Crockett, A. D. 2000. "Marrying the Micro- and Macro-prudential Dimensions of Financial Stability." Paper presented at the Eleventh International Conference of Banking Supervisors, Basel, Switzerland.

Flannery, M. J. 2005. "No Pain, No Gain? Effecting Market Discipline via Reverse Convertible Debentures." In *Capital adequacy beyond Basel: banking securities and insurance*, ed. Hal S Scott. Oxford: Oxford University Press.

Goodhart, C. and A. Persuad. 2008. "A Proposal for How to Avoid the Next Crash." *Financial Times*. January 31.

Gordy, M. and B. Howells. 2007. "Procyclicality in Basel II: Can We Treat the Disease without Killing the Patient?" *Journal of Financial Intermediation*, 15(3): 395–417.

Kashyap, A. and J. C. Stein. 2004. "Cyclical Implications of the Basel II Capital Standard." *Federal Reserve Bank of Chicago Economic Perspectives*, 28(1): 18–31.

Knight, M. D. 2006. "Marrying the Micro- and Macro-prudential Dimensions of Financial Stability: Six Years on." Paper presented at the 14th International Conference of Banking Supervisors, Mérida.

COMMENT

BY SEPPO HONKAPOHJA, BOARD MEMBER OF BANK OF FINLAND

This is a very useful paper covering three main themes: (i) analysis of the reasons for the over-exposure of banks, (ii) discussion of alternative principles for capital regulation and (iii) a specific proposal for reforming capital regulation. In my comments I have the perspective of a macroeconomist in discussing each of these topics, emphasizing the key messages by the authors and making some critical remarks as we move along.

I   OVER-EXPOSURE OF BANKS

A key initial insight of the paper is that the current financial crisis is due to a combination of two factors. First, substantial amounts of MBSs remained in the commercial and investment banks. In the upswing MBSs became popular, because low interest rates and a savings glut shifted the focus of investors on housing markets when they were looking for somewhat higher average returns. The second part of the explanation is that the risky MBSs were financed by short-term borrowing, so that in the wake of the decline in the housing market banks found it difficult to roll over the funding of their holdings of MBSs.

The deep explanations of the over-exposure and funding difficulties of banks come from agency problems that are inherent for banks. In internal incentive schemes of financial institutions it is difficult to separate genuine excess return from increased risk-taking. This problem arises because outcomes of investments are realized after long lags. In such cases it is difficult to tie reward to performance and the use of short-term reward schemes can lead to high levels of risk-taking as performance cannot be properly monitored.

Another central feature of financing of banks is that banks have relatively little equity in their balance sheets and their funding is relatively short-term in nature. The prevalence of debt finance is a natural response to agency problems in banking. It is difficult for equity holders to monitor banks because of the long time lag between investment and return and because many assets held by banks have high liquidity, which again makes monitoring by owners difficult.

A third aspect in the current crisis has been the fact that many of the new securities were complex, so that their risks were hard to assess during the upswing. When the downturn in housing prices took place, the implicit risks became exposed and this led to a strong decline in asset prices. A consequence of this decline were "fire sales" of assets by banks, which created further asset price declines and a negative externality on other banks. The whole banking system got into difficulties.

The fire-sale externality tends to be associated with banks' asset-side adjustments involving a lot of capital, which in turn has forced cuts in lending to businesses.

The authors call this a credit crunch externality. Customers of bank loans are hurt by banks' needs to reduce their balance sheets because of losses from declining asset prices.

In my opinion, there is a further externality and market failure. The losses led to liquidity problems for and solvency concerns about individual banks. These concerns have created a lack-of-trust externality between banks, which dried up interbank-funding markets. As is well-known, the failure of inter-bank markets has led to a further squeeze in bank lending to businesses and consumers.

2   PRINCIPLES FOR REGULATORY REFORM

The paper has a very thoughtful discussion of regulatory reforms in view of the current crisis. According to the authors, the current financial crisis originates from two problem areas, internal governance of banks and capital structures. Improvements to bank governance are seen in two main areas: (i) employee compensation should be tied to longer-term performance and (ii) profit measures should be risk-adjusted.

The authors suggest that these incentive problems and performance measure issues are not regulatory concerns but should instead be dealt with using improved internal governance. Clearly, internal governance of banks should focus on these two sets of issues. Nevertheless, it must be noted that employee, especially top management compensation is currently a huge public concern. For this reason, it cannot perhaps be left entirely to banks' internal reforms. If possible, some regulatory guidelines might be given to management compensation schemes. Moreover, risk-adjusted performance measures could be subjected to regulatory inspection.

Reform of banking capital structures is obviously a major topic in future reforms of financial regulation. The authors make useful criticisms of the straightforward idea of higher capital requirements. Such schemes are costly because of high costs of equity in banking, and higher capital requirements do not avoid the fire-sale externality. It should also be noted that traditional forms of capital regulation are not able to deal with the viral nature of financial innovation. Financial innovation is likely to revive once the current crisis is over and times are back to normal. It is going to be a challenge to financial regulators to deal with new instruments that will be eventually created. It will also be interesting to see how demands for different securities by investors are going change as a result of the current crisis. It is likely that investors want to have more transparent instruments.

The authors emphasize that one part of the regulatory response should be directed at ex post clean-up of a crisis. Government and private recapitalization of banks is an appropriate response to the fire-sale and credit crunch externalities that are a central part of a financial crisis. Recapitalizations of banks and the public guarantees of bank debt are indeed a major policy response in the current crisis. They are to be seen as a response not only to the credit-crunch externality discussed in the paper but also as a response to interbank market failure that has emerged in association with the solvency concerns.

The paper does not take up the issue of what to do weak banks, which can be a major part of the policy problems in a financial crisis. Importance of the issue of weak banks clearly depends on the severity of the crisis. In a mild crisis the problem is probably limited to a few isolated cases, whereas in a deep crisis a significant part of or possibly all of the banking system of a country gets into difficulties with solvency. In the latter case the government has to take a heavy-handed approach and restructure the country's banking system. This was the case, for example, in the Nordic crises of the 1990s. The Finnish, Norwegian and Swedish governments were forced to make heavy-handed restructurings of their banking systems.[1]

3   CAPITAL INSURANCE

The third theme of the paper is a proposed new scheme for capital regulation. It is suggested that a system of capital insurance be created to increase banks' capital in bad times. Banks would be required to buy insurance that pays off and thus props up banks' capital in states of the world in which the overall banking system is facing a crisis.

In this schemes insurers buy treasury bills and put them in a "lock box". Insurance money would be returned to insurer, with premia paid by banks and together with interest on the treasuries in the box if no systemic event occurs. However, if the crisis event occurs, then agreed sums of funds are transferred to bank's balance sheet. The scheme would invoke a trigger mechanism to decide on the insurance payments. As discussed in the paper, the scheme would also involve thresholds and caps to payments and also staggering of individual insurance contracts to ensure smooth functioning overall.

I have a number of comments on this proposal. One feature I like is that the proposed scheme would largely be a private solution to the banks' recapitalization problem. Insurance would presumably be provided by private institutions and not by the government. Having a private solution is in principle preferable, because public ownership of banks can create problems in market competition once a crisis is over. It should, however, be recognized that in some earlier crises private solutions were initially emphasized, but in deep crises (e.g. in the Nordic countries) the private solutions tended to be insufficient and governments had to take partial or full ownership of problem banks.

In my opinion the main problem with the proposal is that the supply side of capital insurance is not considered in detail. Only a brief discussion of potential

---

1   For an overview see, for example, Honkapohja, S. (2008), The Nordic Banking Crises of the 1990s, mimeo, September, Bank of Finland. Available at http://www.bof.fi/en/ suomen_pankki/organisaatio/johtokunta/honkapohja/ and as Bank of Finland Discussion Paper 5/2009.

suppliers is given. Pension funds and sovereign wealth funds are thought to be potential suppliers. It is also argued that quite naturally, investors subject to capital requirements could not be suppliers of capital insurance. This means, however, that pension funds in many countries could not be among the suppliers, as pension funds often have requirements or restrictions on forms of asset holdings. I also worry about the possible role of hedge funds here. In the current crisis hedge funds are strongly scaling down their operations. This suggests that they might not be interested in providing capital insurance.

One part of the proposal is the imposition of a trigger based on the aggregate of banks. This means that insurance paid out only in a sufficiently big crisis. Having the insurance payout based on a trigger computed from the aggregate of banks in a country is clearly a natural requirement as an individualized trigger is easily subject to manipulation. There can, however, be other difficulties in implementing a trigger based on the aggregate of banks. If the aggregate of banks is in trouble, then the crisis is likely to be systemic. In this event many or most banks are in trouble, which implies that the trigger-level aggregate losses are arising from correlated portfolios and realized systemic risks. Would suppliers of capital insurance be available for the renewal of individual insurance contracts that mature during a systemic financial crisis?

If it turns out that there are problems in finding private suppliers to the insurance scheme, one could consider public provision of capital insurance. Banks would pay premia to an insurance fund run by a government agency and payouts would be made up in a crisis situation and the payouts would have a cap based on the amount of insurance purchased. This would be somewhat analogous to a mandatory deposit insurance scheme in which deposits are insured up to an upper limit. If the government were the provider, then the outcome would be somewhat analogous to the current policies in which governments inject funds to increase banks' capital if a systemic crisis occurs.[2] The big difference would be the advance payments of insurance premia by banks and the automatic availability of funds for recapitalization.

The paper acknowledges that the capital insurance scheme would have its own moral hazard concerns. Even if the insurance payout is based on an aggregate criterion, it results in reduced incentives to hedge against a financial crisis. With the scheme in place, banks might be interested in taking on more systemic risks. The paper provides some discussion of the extent of this problem but it does not compare the extent of these moral hazard concerns in the proposed scheme and other ways of banks' recapitalization.

---

2   Current recapitalization policies by governments are conditional on the occurrence of a crisis, which is one feature common with an insurance scheme. Of course, the current schemes are discretionary and not an on-going arrangement with insurance premia paid in advance.

4   CONCLUDING REMARKS

This is a thoughtful and inspiring paper with useful analysis of different aspects of the current crisis. The authors are to be commended for proposing a new solution to the banks' recapitalization problem in a financial crisis. It must, however, be said that the proposed capital insurance scheme requires a lot of further analysis. In particular, the private supply side should be analyzed in more depth. It would also be important to properly assess the benefits and costs of the scheme in relation to other ways of solving the recapitalization problem. A general equilibrium framework would seem to be required for such an undertaking.

GENERAL DISCUSSION

Lorenzo Bini Smaghi asked **Raghuram Rajan** how to get financial markets to function again. Rajan responded that his inclination was as follows. Once the government decides to intervene, the government should go all the way: banks must be cleaned up, by a combination of recapitalization and purchases of bad assets. More public funds will be needed to accomplish this. **Alex Cukierman** argued that in a crisis as grave as the current crisis, there is no alternative to government intervention using taxpayers' money. He advanced the proposal that banks be taxed in a boom in order to fund government intervention in case of a grave crisis. Rajan replied that he worries that an insurance scheme run by the government, of the kind proposed by Cukierman, would under-price insurance, thereby creating a wealth transfer from taxpayers to banks. **Gabriel Stein** observed that capital insurance proposed by the authors seemed similar to deposit insurance. The key challenge for each policy is to minimize the costs to the taxpayer.

Francesco Giavazzi wondered if there is an externality when a bank terminates a loan. If there is, then what is the difference between a bank terminating a loan and General Motors terminating a contract with a supplier? Rajan responded that the difference was only a matter of degree. Nevertheless, the difference could be large due to systemic risk. **Stanley Fischer** remarked that the paper emphasizes internal agency problems in banks. He argued that marking-to-market was important in attenuating these agency problems. **Andrew Levin** wondered whether the state should regulate banks as it regulates public utilities. Rajan found the analogy between banks and public utilities unhelpful. We should let banks maximize profits, he said.

In response to the discussants, Rajan discussed in greater detail the supply of capital insurance. He emphasized that unlevered financial institutions should supply capital insurance. One can think of unlevered financial institutions as being owned by comparatively wealthy taxpayers. This observation shows that, under his proposal, risk would be shifted to wealthier taxpayers, rather than to all taxpayers. Furthermore, risk would be shifted *ex ante*. He added that state contingent capital is cheaper than direct capital, due to agency problems. One cannot access contingent capital *ex ante*. Finally, he acknowledged that accounting could be manipulated by banks that have bought capital insurance, but he believed that this problem could be minimized in a satisfactory way.

András Simor, Athanasios Orphanides, Francesco Giavazzi, Vitor Gaspar,
Erik Berglöf (from left to right)

SESSION 4

PANEL
THE EURO AND THE ENLARGEMENT –
CHALLENGES AHEAD

INTRODUCTION

BY FRANCESCO GIAVAZZI, IGIER, BOCCONI UNIVERSITY, CEPR AND NBER

"We are 27 countries in the European Union. In the euro area, we are 15. Of the 27, 25 have no opt-out clause. The challenge is to progressively absorb all the newcomers: none of them has an opt-out clause. At the same time it is imperative to preserve the credibility of the euro area as a whole by strictly respecting the conditions of entry, the Maastricht criterion." Jean-Claude Trichet:[1]

Enlargement will affect the euro area and the ECB in many ways. By virtually any metric, it will add to the region's diversity (whether the focus is on language, culture, or legal systems). From an economic perspective, a 25-country currency area will form the world's largest in terms of GDP, with a population of about 500 million, compared to around 300 million in the United States. The ratio of per capita incomes between the richest and poorest members would widen to nearly 13 from less than 4, based on recent data. The speed of integration of product, labor and financial markets may quicken, accelerating structural change. And each new euro-area member will bring with it a new fiscal agent and a parliament. Among other things, this expansion will increase incentives for free-riding, thereby complicating any constitutional changes that would require unanimity.

Naturally, the need to assess the preparedness of prospective members will repeatedly revive the issues that confronted the European Council ahead of EMU: What degree of convergence has been achieved, what is needed to satisfy the Treaty's provisions? Should those provisions be amended? So far the answer has been negative because "amendment" meant "relaxation": the experience with the current suggests however that there may be reason to make entry criteria more, not less stringent. Does this affect our view about the desirability of new criteria?

Will trends toward economic divergence for some existing euro-area members intensify or diminish as membership rises? How will the difficulty of coordination among 25 fiscal agents affect monetary policy? Will a larger number of more diverse members exposed to idiosyncratic shocks raise the chances of a national fiscal crisis, widen market yield spreads and, in the extreme, lead to a test of the Maastricht Treaty's "no-bailout" provisions?

Enlargement will be a particular challenge in the area of communication. Even today, no other central bank faces the task of communicating with the public at large in 16 different countries. Will the presence of NCB governors on the Governing Council of the ECB be enough? Diverse national histories may prompt different constituencies to view identical policy statements as accommodative or

---

1   Interview with S. G. Cecchetti and K. L. Schoenholtz (2009). *Europe and the Euro*, ed. A. Alesina and F. Giavazzi. Chicago: Chicago University Press.

restrictive. If the longest-run challenge of the ECB is to secure a popular base, then enlargement only intensifies that challenge.

The panel was asked to address in particular:

1. Entry criteria. The health of the banking system is not among the current entry criteria. In this light it is worth asking what would have happened had some of the "outs" been "in" during the current crisis. Consider for instance the effect of the exposure of Swedish banks to the Baltics, or of Hungary's exposure to a sudden stop in capital flows.

   Looking ahead, had these countries been in the euro area during the crisis, would they pose an additional difficulty for ECB monetary policy? Should the entry criteria be extended? Is there a tradeoff between the relaxation of criteria that are economically unsound (e.g. inflation in the light of the Balassa-Samuleson effect) and the introduction of new criteria, e.g. on the financing of the current account, or on banks' capital?

2. Large capital inflows. Massive capital inflows into some accession countries (e.g. Estonia) seem to have been distortionary, having created boom-bust cycles that domestic policies have been unable to offset. The same happened with Portugal and Greece just after they joined the euro. What is the lesson from these experiences?

3. Banking supervision. Are we sufficiently confident that cooperation between national supervisors would still work after enlargement? Does enlargement strengthen the argument for centralized euro area supervision?

4. A technical but important issue: different ways inflation is measured. In some accession countries (e.g. Estonia) inflation is still measured differently compared to the Euro area HICP. How does this affect the entry criteria?

5. Monetary policy in the meantime: exchange rate pegs (ERM2) or inflation targeting with flexible exchange rate?

PANEL STATEMENT

BY VÍTOR GASPAR, BUREAU OF EUROPEAN POLICY ADVISERS, EUROPEAN COMMISSION

I want to start by thanking Frank Smets for his invitation to participate in the ECB's Fifth Central Banking Conference "The Euro at Ten: Lessons and Challenges". Having been involved in the preparation of the first three ECB Central Banking Conferences it is, for me, personally very gratifying to be here. I also want to express my gratitude to colleagues from DG-ECFIN who provided me with the material I will use in my intervention.[1] Marco Buti and Servaas Deroose intended to be present here but, in the end, could not come due to pressing obligations linked to the on-going financial crisis.

This will be my only reference to the financial crisis. In contrast to Erik Berglöf, I will not focus on its implications for the challenges associated with euro enlargement. Nevertheless, I am prepared to argue that the financial crisis actually strengthens the argument that I will be putting forward in my intervention. I will not be following the sequence suggested by Francesco Giavazzi's five questions. I am convinced that, when I am finished, my answer to most of those questions will be clear. That said, it makes it more pressing and urgent.

Yesterday, I participated in a workshop in Brussels with the theme: "Five Years of an Enlarged EU: a Positive Sum Game". It was devoted to the impact of the EU's fifth enlargement. I am personally convinced that enlargement is one of the most successful policies of the EU. It has spread peace, prosperity, human rights and democracy across the European continent. At the same time, enlargement offers testimony to the EU's power of attraction. Enlargement has contributed to making the European Union the largest economic entity in the world. The European Union is characterized by its diversity.[2] Member States that joined during the two most recent enlargements are also very diverse among themselves. This diversity implies that there will be considerable differences in their policy approaches.

The same can be said about the euro area. The process of enlargement of the euro area is on-going. Of the ten Member States that joined with the fifth enlargement, four will have already joined the euro area by January 2009 (when the Slovak Republic becomes the 16th member of the euro area). The European Union Treaty provides a clear institutional path for euro adoption. Each Member State of the

---

1   Especially Marco Buti, Servaas Deroose, Massimo Suardi and Joachim Wadefjord. None should be held responsible for the intervention's shortcomings but myself.
2   Diversity has been a distinctive characteristic of European civilization for a long time. For example, Guizot (1840) writes: «Lorsque j'ai tenté de déterminer la physionomie propre de la civilisation européenne, comparée aux civilisations antiques et asiatiques, j'ai fait voir que la première était variée, riche, complexe, qu'elle n'était jamais tombée sous la domination d'aucun principe exclusif, que les divers éléments de l'état social s'y étaient combinés, combattus, modifiés, et qu'ils avaient été continuellement obligés de transiger et de vivre en commun.» (p. 380)

fifth and sixth enlargement, without exception, is expected, and is welcome, to adopt the euro. It can do so as soon as it meets the convergence criteria.

This allows me to make a comment in passing about the first question, raised by Francesco Giavazzi, concerning possible amendments to the convergence criteria. Convergence criteria aim at ensuring the formation of a stability oriented Economic and Monetary Union, based on the principle of an open market economy with free competition. As I said before, the institutional path for euro adoption – which includes the convergence criteria – is clear. Clarity is of particular importance for candidate countries. It sets out what each has to do in order to ensure admission to the euro area. One strong argument against considering revisions to the convergence criteria is precisely the uncertainty and disturbance that might cause in the candidate countries themselves. I do not want to discuss revisions to the convergence criteria further. In my view such a debate serves no useful institutional purpose.

Before continuing I want to mention, in passing, that participation in the euro area is associated with important benefits. These benefits can be organized into two groups: first, *integration benefits*. These relate to increased trade and financial integration. They derive from "One Money, One Market" mutually reinforcing integration dynamics.[3] The contributions to the panel "Optimum Currency Areas: The Academic View" will, no doubt, cover the relevant arguments and empirical evidence.[4] Second, *benefits from a coherent framework for stability-oriented macroeconomic policies*. In the euro area these are centred around monetary policy, assigned to an independent central bank – the European Central Bank – with the primary objective of maintaining price stability over the medium term. Stability-oriented macroeconomic policies provide the best environment for sustainable growth and development.

I have emphasized diversity across the new Member States. However, diversity does not prevent me from focusing on common challenges and guiding principles for policy-making. I will assume the viewpoint of a new Member State that shows the political will necessary to join the euro area. Notwithstanding diversity, most of the Member States, that have more recently joined the European Union, have average income levels well below the average of the EU. In the years since accession, they have converged fast. The gap with the average of the EU15 narrowed by about 10 percentage points and, in 2007, it reached 62%. During this period real GDP growth in the new Member States averaged 6.4% against 1.8% for the euro area. Catching up is progressing fast but there is still quite a long road ahead.

The challenge is to ensure steady, sustainable, non-inflationary growth. From the viewpoint of the countries concerned the prospect of participation in the euro area should be considered in this broader context.

---

3   See Mongelli (Forthcoming).
4   Given the composition of the panel, trade effects figured much more prominently than financial integration. Nevertheless the implications of the latter for the conduct of macroeconomic policy are very substantial.

I have studied the experience of adjustment to participation in the euro area, based on the experience of the founding participants.[5] I am still very much engaged in this line of research. I believe there is much to learn.

My tentative conclusion, from a policy perspective, is that it is useful to consider the challenges associated with adjustment to euro area participation, from the viewpoint of the new Member States, in three groups: first, achieving real and nominal convergence simultaneously. Second, managing the expansionary effect of trade and financial integration especially those associated with rapid credit growth in a context of financial deepening. Third, preserving external competitiveness, in order to contribute to stability and sustainability. The magnitude of the last challenge is illustrated by countries with substantial and enduring current account deficits, leading to rapid accumulation of net foreign liabilities.

While the above challenges are common, successful policies will have to take national specificities carefully into account. There is no "silver bullet" or universal panacea that could be applied blindly across the board. Thus, I would avoid dichotomies like ERM2 vs. inflation targeting with a floating exchange rate.[6] A successful participant in ERM2 will be able to maintain price stability. Similarly, an inflation targeting central bank in a small very open economy will have to respond to the exchange rate in order to maintain price stability.[7]

In spite of the diversity of situations, imposing a case-by-case approach, there are a number of general guiding principles that may be useful. Specifically, I want to list four:

First, it seems crucial to reinforce the conditions promoting free and open market competition favouring change and innovation and allowing profitable investment opportunities – including FDI. Such a principle, which is sound enough in general, is particularly important in the context of European integration and prospective participation in the euro area. The reason is that easier access to financing and the catching-up process itself lead to an easing of budget constraints in the short run. Such a temporary abode should not be used to protect inefficient providers of goods and services or to skew resource allocation to sectors sheltered from competition.

Second, prudent fiscal policy. This implies a fiscal policy based on automatic stabilizers ensuring a strong counter-cyclical stance. It also requires a focus on long-term sustainability and the quality of Public Finances.

Third, effective supervision of financial institutions and markets. It is essential to be aware and vigilant concerning systemic risks (including macro-financial risks).

---

5   Fagan and Gaspar (2008a) looked at the adjustment process of Ireland, Italy, Portugal and Spain. Fagan and Gaspar (2008b) also looked at the broader implications for two groups: "core" and "convergence" countries. Gaspar and St. Aubyn (2009) have also worked on the contrasting experiences of Portugal and Spain.

6   In reference to Francesco Giavazzi's question 5.

7   See Detken and Gaspar (2003) for a theoretical discussion.

Fourth, flexible labour and product markets facilitating structural adjustment while maintaining high levels of resource utilization.

Proverbs provide ample examples of best laid plans going awry. Difficulties in policy action follow from complex and conflicting theoretical and empirical evidence. Such difficulties are compounded in the face of significant structural adjustment. Different and contradictory arguments will be relevant, and the way to weigh them far from obvious. All of these challenges are clear and present for policy-makers from the new Member States in their path to the euro area. In the circumstances, it seems to be fundamental to resist the temptations of the present in order to lay out the foundations of future prosperity.

REFERENCES

Detken, C. and V. Gaspar. 2003. "Maintaining Price Stability under Free Floating: A Fearless Way Out of the Corner." European Central Bank Working Paper 241.

Fagan, G. and V. Gaspar. 2008a. "Adjusting to the Euro." In *Building the Financial Foundations of the Euro*, ed. Lars Jonung, Max Watson, and Christoph Walkner, 56-83. London: Taylor & Francis, Inc.

Fagan, G. and V. Gaspar. 2008b. "Macroeconomic Adjustment to Monetary Union." European Central Bank Working Paper 946.

Gaspar, V. and M. St. Aubyn. 2009. "Adjusting to the euro - the contrast between Portugal and Spain." http://www3.eeg.uminho.pt/economia/nipe/euro10years/papers/Miguel_St%20Aubyn.pdf.

Guizot, F.P.G. 1840. *Histoire de la civilisation en Europe*. Paris: Didier.

Mongelli, F.P. Forthcoming. "The OCA Theory and the Path to the EMU." In *Euro: The First Decade*, ed. M. Buti, S. Deroose, V. Gaspar and J. Nogueira Martins. Cambridge: Cambridge University Press.

PANEL STATEMENT

BY ATHANASIOS ORPHANIDES, GOVERNOR OF THE CENTRAL BANK OF CYPRUS

I appreciate the opportunity to participate in this panel on the euro and enlargement. Coming from one of the smallest new member states of our great union, and one that has just joined the euro area, I feel that we are well acquainted with the potential benefits of completing the journey towards our economic and monetary union as well as the challenges presented along the way. In my remarks, I will share with you some thoughts on these issues, drawing on our perspective and experience. Before I proceed, I should note that these thoughts are my own and do not necessarily reflect views of my colleagues on the Governing Council of the ECB.

As previous experience has shown, the new EU member states may find themselves confronted with a number of important challenges that test their economies in the run-up to ERM II and the adoption of the single currency. Apart from designing and pursuing the appropriate monetary and exchange rate policy that will eventually lead to the adoption of the euro, these challenges include strong consumption expenditure and significant credit growth following accession to the EU, higher inflation rates due to the convergence process, and destabilising capital flows triggered by interest rate differentials. The new member states may also be faced with inflated asset prices. As has already been exemplified, in order to mitigate the aforementioned challenges it is important for any new member state aspiring to adopt the euro to achieve a high degree of nominal and real convergence with the euro area before joining ERM II. Moreover, it is well established that the monetary and exchange rate regime in place and the response of a new member state to these challenges should not be seen in isolation from its initial starting conditions and historical/institutional evolution.

Regardless of the choice of monetary and exchange rate regime there are common challenges that the new member states will face on the road to euro adoption. A crucial role will be played by the initial conditions of the new member states. Per capita GDP and the general price level in the new member states are significantly below euro area levels. The very prospect of the catching up process presents a unique opportunity for raising the welfare of the citizens of the new member states but this is an opportunity that comes with challenges.

The initial level of development of a country, measured by its per capita GDP, and the speed of real convergence are the main determinants of relative inflation in the long-run – the Balassa-Samuelson effect. Therefore, the overall inflation rate in the new member states is expected to be higher during the catching up process. On the other hand, as the per capita income gap between the new member states and the euro area declines, we can expect the price level gap to decline as well. This price convergence can take place via a nominal appreciation of the exchange rate or via a relatively higher inflation rate, depending on the exchange rate regime.

Another major challenge for the new member states seeking to join the euro area is the considerable net capital inflows in the form of foreign direct investment (FDI) and portfolio investment. Most new member states have experienced strong non-FDI capital inflows encouraged by market expectations that these countries will join the euro area. In particular, they have been driven by initially higher domestic nominal interest rates and the expectation of yield convergence ahead of euro adoption, as well as by the favourable prospects for growth. In some new member states, these capital inflows continue to be the main source of financing, leading to a further build up of gross external debt as a proportion of GDP. Net inflows of FDI are also an important source of financing. In one case this constitutes about 20% of GDP. Compared with FDI, non-FDI flows may embody more serious risks since they are sensitive to interest rate differentials and risk premia, among other things. In any event, the risk of a sudden stop in capital flows should be kept in mind by the governments of new member states. The aim should be to pursue prudent policies that minimise these risks and insure against the worst of possible outcomes. In the present environment of malfunctioning international capital markets and funding difficulties in banking, such risks have increased.

A related challenge is that of managing the potential for a rapid expansion of credit. Indeed, a number a factors have led to such an expansion in the new member states in the last few years. On the demand side, the initial low level of credit availability and indebtedness, the rapid output growth, the rise in income expectations and the increased market confidence associated with EU entry have led to a greater willingness of economic agents to take on debt. On the supply side, the development of the banking sector after privatisation and the welcoming of foreign banks have increased the lending capacity of the banking sector. At the same time, rising competition among banks resulted in strong incentives for banks to expand their lending to households. With low initial credit to GDP ratios which afforded greater potential for growth, this implied considerably faster credit growth during the transition to equilibrium. Indeed, credit to households has risen the fastest in the five least developed new member states where the starting levels of credit were the lowest.

The fastest growing parts of the credit market have been household loans, particularly mortgage loans. The latter have been encouraged by deregulation in the property market, the rapid rise in property prices and expectations of further price increases which appear to have generated speculative buying, including by non-residents. Once again, the issue is how to properly pace the vast potential for welfare gains and the challenge for policy is how to prevent credit growth from becoming excessive, with the well known dangers of the resolution of the associated excesses.

Two other issues to take into account are whether the catching up process of the price level can be better managed inside or outside the monetary union, and whether the transition to the euro can be better managed with a floating or with a fixed exchange rate regime. Thus, the new member states are faced with the challenge of designing an appropriate exchange rate strategy that will eventually lead to the successful adoption of the euro. The EU position is that in the pre–accession phase no single strategy is prescribed. Accession countries are free to choose any regime they consider appropriate, ranging from a pegged exchange rate to inflation targeting.

We should acknowledge that alternative exchange rate strategies have different risks associated with them. However, recent experience has reaffirmed that successful adoption of the euro can be achieved with a number of these alternative strategies. For example, in the case of Cyprus and Malta, which joined the euro area in January of this year, the strategy was based on an exchange rate target. Although both countries used the same fluctuation band of ±15%, Cyprus allowed the exchange rate to fluctuate within the narrow band of ±2,25%, whereas Malta maintained the parity without fluctuations. In contrast, Slovakia, which is due to join the euro area on 1 January 2009, has relied on an inflation targeting strategy with wider variability in the exchange rate, tolerating fluctuations within a ±15% fluctuation band around the central exchange rate with the euro. Apart from the primary focus of the strategy, both price stability and exchange rate stability vis-à-vis the euro need to be achieved for successful integration into EMU.

Regardless of the choice of the monetary policy and exchange rate strategies during the transition to EMU, proper assessment of the timing of euro adoption presents some challenges. The new member states should examine very carefully the consequences of either pushing for early euro adoption or postponing membership. On one hand, early entry can provide the benefits of full membership of EMU. Delaying membership into the euro area risks exchange rate instability and should be avoided when a country is otherwise well-prepared to join. On the other hand, attempts to join before a country is ready can be problematic and it is useful to assess the risks from the perspective of where a country is in the catching up process. If the per capita GDP and price level gaps are still fairly large and the speed of catching up is fast, a country will have difficulty in controlling inflation once in the Monetary Union. Consequently, it might be advisable to postpone euro adoption until the gaps have narrowed.

Cyprus's aspiration to become a member of the EU started in the early 1990s and the debate as to which exchange rate policy would be the most appropriate was an important one. At the time, it was decided that the pursuit of an exchange rate strategy aimed at maintaining price stability through exchange rate stability was the appropriate regime that would lead to a smooth integration of Cyprus into EMU. This strategy involved linking the Cyprus pound to the ecu and later to the euro. Indeed, managing the exchange rate by pegging the Cyprus pound to a strong anchor delivered the desired price stability objective, in addition to high growth rates and low unemployment.

There are several critical elements for the success of this strategy. First, it was pursued by the Central Bank of Cyprus (CBC) with no devaluations even in the most adverse conditions. Thus, there was a clear and unambiguous policy stance which boosted credibility and facilitated future policies. The credibility of the CBC reinforced people's belief in this strategy and thus anchored inflation expectations. Second, the authorities followed prudent economic policies for most of the time which ensured the sustainability of the regime. In this respect, the credit and current accounts served as warning indicators signalling possible threats to the sustainability of the fixed rate regime. Third, in cases of imbalances the CBC resorted to the temporary use of non-traditional tools such as credit ceilings. The strategy was also reinforced and augmented by the prudent monitoring of money aggregates and the judicious screening of external balances. In particular, the current account deficit was closely monitored and served as an indicator of nascent inflationary threats, with tightening measures being adopted when imbalances in the current account appeared to accumulate even under conditions where the short-term outlook for inflation appeared benign. Thus, even though a stable exchange rate was the operational focus of policy during the transition to EMU, risks to price stability were always closely monitored and measures taken to avert their materialisation.

In summary, during the run-up to ERM II and the adoption of the single currency, the new member states could experience challenges that might expose their economies to some risks. To mitigate these challenges it is important for the new member states to achieve a high degree of nominal and real convergence with the EU economy before joining the ERM II. Even in the case of Cyprus and Malta, which had achieved a high degree of convergence, they still faced various challenges such as credit and housing booms and high capital inflows. During the transition period to the euro a crucial role will be played by the monetary and exchange rate regime that the countries follow. Nevertheless, it has been shown from the experience of the recent entrants to the euro area that regardless of the choice of regime, a country can successfully adopt the euro by displaying a strong commitment to following the appropriate strategies and having a clear reform agenda.

I would like to conclude by framing the issue at hand in a broader perspective. Ultimately, for the new member states, the challenges of successful completion of the journey towards the economic and monetary union are those of managing prosperity. Entry of a new state into the EU generates tremendous potential for wealth generation that should benefit all citizens of the union, both from old and new member states. The potential long-term benefits are arguably much greater for the citizens of new member states. It is an unavoidable element of human nature that new member state citizens may be impatient and wish to reap the full benefit that can be attained at the conclusion of the journey right away. The ultimate challenge for policy is to keep the long-run perspective and not allow impatience to result in accumulating imbalances that would delay attainment of the goal.

PANEL STATEMENT

BY ANDRÁS SIMOR, GOVERNOR OF MAGYAR NEMZETI BANK

I am glad to have been invited to this panel. It seems to me that 'euro enlargement' in the past couple of years featured prominently on the agenda of various European conferences and policy fora and, as such, ended up a bit over-discussed. However, the recent bout of the financial crisis has definitely put this topic in a new perspective. My impression is that a number of New Member States, as well as some of the old opt-outs, that were seriously affected by the crisis now wish that they were already in the euro area when this latest, most severe episode erupted. I would not be surprised if, as a consequence of the crisis, ambitions for speeding up the euro area entry process intensified in these countries. This panel discussion is a good opportunity for me to present the motivation, arguments and concerns that an 'out' country may have in this respect. Naturally, I can only speak on behalf of Hungary, or more precisely the Hungarian Central Bank. It may not be a typical view as this country was perhaps the most spectacularly affected by the crisis among the New Member States. Nevertheless, I think at least some elements of this view are shared by our Central Eastern European peers.

I would like to touch upon three major topics. First, how did the Hungarian Central Bank see the 'pros and cons' of a quick euro strategy before the crisis? Second, how did the crisis change this assessment? Finally, I would like to say a few words about the Maastricht criteria and the way we envisage to meet them.

The Hungarian Central Bank has long been a proponent of an 'as soon as possible' euro area entry strategy. We made our first comprehensive cost-benefit analysis back in 2001. The analysis suggested that Hungary constituted an optimal currency area with the euro area, at least to the extent that some peripheral euro area member countries did. The benefits appeared to be large, stemming from trade creation and the disappearance of a sizeable currency risk premium. At that time fiscal policy seemed broadly on track. We had just introduced inflation targeting which showed some early success in breaking inflation inertia. In the euro area itself, there were no signs of divergence, either. All this suggested that a quick euro area entry was doable and worth pursuing. The future looked rosy.

However, things turned out to be quite different. An unprecedented fiscal expansion in 2002-2006 shed a cruel light on the structural and institutional weaknesses of the Hungarian public finances and slowed down the disinflation process. The country was drifting away from meeting the Maastricht criteria and the expected date of entering the euro area was moving further and further out in the future. At the same time, news from the euro area caused some discomfort too, as growth in some less developed member countries slowed down so much that their real convergence stopped or even reversed.

Having had this experience, it is not surprising that when we did our review of the costs and benefits of the euro this year we were a bit more cautious than seven years ago. Although our basic conclusion remained the same, that is, we still think that Hungary should join the euro area as soon as possible, we had become more aware of some risks involved in the quick euro adoption strategy.

Let me elaborate on two of these risks. The first is entering the euro area without sufficient progress in structural reforms; the second is the problems caused by potentially large capital inflows after the common currency is introduced.

It is a commonly shared view that efficient labour and product markets, which help a country's dynamic adjustment to asymmetric shocks, are essential for success within a monetary union. In terms of labour and product market reforms Hungary still has a lot to do. Although nominal and real wages are more flexible than in the core euro area, the employment rate is one of the lowest in the EU. Our analysis suggests that this may be related to wrong incentives hindering labour supply, such as generous early retirement and maternity leave schemes and a very high tax wedge. These are in turn manifestations of a bigger problem, 'the premature welfare state', which is weighing heavily on potential growth on the one hand, and is a source of a chronic fiscal imbalance on the other. Our fiscal and labour market weaknesses are deeply interconnected and we have to address them together in a wide-ranging structural reform. Scaling back the overly generous welfare state is painful and the political willingness to do so is not so strong, so when this structural reform will take place is rather uncertain. The question is, can we afford to enter the euro area if this reform is not yet completed? This brings us to the territory of political economy, more precisely to the issue of whether the euro fosters or hinders structural reform. Although this issue has received a lot of attention recently in both theoretical and empirical work, my impression is that so far no consensus has emerged. What this means for the euro strategy of Hungary is that probably we should not risk entering the euro area until this crucial structural reform – that is, the scaling back of overly generous the welfare state in order to increase the labour supply, foster potential growth and stabilize public finances – is completed or is at least safely on track.

The second risk, which frequently took the centre stage in debates on euro accession, is that of large and potentially disruptive capital inflows. The starting point of the argument here is that the catching-up process of New Member States is about to continue for a long period even after they introduce the common currency. The catching-up entails a real appreciation, which, once the exchange rate is irrevocably fixed, translates into higher inflation and lower real interest rates. Low real interest rates may in turn trigger excessive demand fuelled by an unsustainable credit boom financed from foreign borrowing. When the inevitable correction comes, there is no independent monetary policy to smooth the adjustment and a serious bust follows the boom. Such boom-bust patterns were clearly observable in some first-wave euro area members like Portugal, Ireland and Spain. Better wait with euro adoption, the argument goes, until catching-up is more advanced and the equilibrium real appreciation is smaller. I have one observation to this argument. We cannot ignore the fact that the financial integration of the New Member States to a large extent has already taken place. The banking sectors in these countries are owned predominantly by euro area banks. In the past couple of years of abundant global liquidity, cross-border lending by parent banks in foreign currency was available in virtually unlimited quantities. This practically meant that foreign (euro or Swiss franc) interest rates had become the point of reference for domestic consumption and investment decisions well before the euro was introduced, pushing down the effective real interest rate. It is obvious by now that the credit boom that was envisaged to take place after euro area entry actually arrived much earlier. The only difference was that, not having the common currency yet, it left us with a sizeable currency mismatch. Staying out of the euro area did not prevent us from running into the boom. Now that we have to face the bust, it is not clear either whether having an independent monetary policy places us in a better position to smooth the adjustment. That is because the effectiveness of monetary easing and the subsequent depreciation is seriously limited by the negative wealth effect on the sizeable unhedged foreign currency liabilities the private sector had accumulated. In short, with integrated financial systems, large capital flows have been taking place in New Member States regardless of the fact that they have not yet introduced the euro. Euro adoption does not carry an extra risk in this respect. On the contrary, it may help eliminate potentially dangerous currency mismatches. It is important to see that in this respect, it would eliminate a source of instability from the point of view of the euro area parent banks as well.

Let me now turn to the implications the current crisis may have on euro adoption strategies. First, the crisis clearly illustrates that having your own currency may be more of a source of shocks than a shock-absorbing device. You may say that Hungary deserved what it gets now, but there are other countries with more sound fundamentals that are undergoing serious stress. Second, the crisis is an obvious indication that the years of abundant global liquidity are over. We are probably in the middle of a credit contraction globally and the chances of another credit-boom evolving in the foreseeable future are minimal. The risk of a credit-fuelled boom-bust, should a country enter the euro area in the next couple of years, is greatly reduced. Third, the crisis may have increased the disciplining power of financial markets. The deleveraging process that we are going through implies a thorough repricing of risk. Just like in other asset classes, there is increased differentiation among government bonds based on the issuers' risk profile. This is well illustrated by the unprecedented differences we currently see between CDS spreads on bonds of euro area sovereign issuers. Countries with weaker public finances, and Hungary is obviously one of them, will receive stronger incentives from the financial markets in the coming years to put their fiscal house in order. This means that the crisis may actually speed up the most important structural reform in Hungary, the much-needed scaling back of the overly generous welfare state. From the euro strategy perspective this would be good news, since, as I said before, we think that adopting the euro without going through this painful reform carries the risk of a prospective underperformance in the euro area.

All in all, this crisis has evidently demonstrated that the banking sectors of the euro area and the New Member States are deeply integrated, has greatly reduced the chances of credit booms in the forthcoming years and may exert an extra disciplining power in countries prone to fiscal misbehaviour in the future. For these reasons, I think it may act as a catalyst for the euro accession process.

Importantly, it should be *let to act* as a catalyst, that is, it should not be used as an excuse to make the entry criteria, or their interpretation, more stringent.

Finally, let me turn to the prospects of meeting the criteria in Hungary and, more specifically, what I think this implies for our euro strategy.

Currently, there is no official target date for euro adoption in Hungary. Popular support for the euro is relatively strong, and it probably intensified further after the recent currency turmoil. All the major political parties agree on the desirability of introducing the common currency. However, at the current juncture, Hungary does not meet any of the Maastricht criteria. Government and Central Bank officials, including myself, repeatedly expressed the view that the earliest date to start talking about a roadmap to euro area may be somewhere in 2009. Given Hungary's not too convincing track record regarding the fiscal balance and inflation, an ERM II entry is only reasonable when the prospective meeting of the Maastricht criteria is safely on track.

Hungary's Convergence Programme envisages meeting the fiscal deficit criterion by 2009. As a reaction to the recent bout of the global financial crisis and the deteriorating prospects for external financing, the government decided to withdraw the draft 2009 budget and rewrite it so that the deficit reduction next year is more pronounced. In addition, the IMF rescue package came with conditions which implied further expenditure-cutting measures. The Central Bank's latest inflation forecasts imply that the Maastricht inflation criterion may be met by 2010.

On the other hand, the financial turmoil has undoubtedly reached Eastern Europe. As a result, currently there is extreme uncertainty in the New Member States regarding the future course of such fundamental things as financial intermediation, credit growth, the exchange rate and real convergence in general. These are all very important factors that have to be taken into account when making a decision on the euro strategy or indeed on ERM II entry itself. It is therefore worth waiting with setting out very specific euro adoption plans for Hungary until the dust settles at least a little bit.

In the meantime, the Slovakian experience with the euro, starting next year but showing its implications already in the recent unfolding of the crisis, will provide a good natural experiment for the other New Member States, and will no doubt be closely watched.

GENERAL DISCUSSION

Much of the general discussion focused on the Balassa-Samuelson effect. The panellists were asked what a policy-maker in a country wishing to join EMU is to do when facing a five-percent-inflation-rate and a fixed exchange rate. **Vítor Gaspar** and **Athanasios Orphanides** both responded that a five-percent-inflation-rate does not represent price stability. Furthermore, Gaspar argued that evidence suggests the Balassa-Samuelson effect to be small. Orphanides reiterated that optimal policy in the transition to the EMU is country-specific. Nevertheless, some general principles are available. A candidate country must avoid a devaluation of its currency, and policy-makers in that country must watch the current account.

Jean Pisani-Ferry asked whether the current financial crisis implied that the enlargement of the euro area should slow down or accelerate. **Erik Berglöf** responded that, in his judgment, there was no conflict between any institutional reforms that may be sparked by the crisis and the enlargement of the euro.

Jaume Ventura, André Sapir, Wolfgang Schill, Andrew Rose, Martin Feldstein (from left to right)

SESSION 5

PANEL
OPTIMAL CURRENCY AREAS – ACADEMIC VIEWS

INTRODUCTION

BY WOLFGANG SCHILL, ECB

Let me welcome Martin Feldstein, Andrew Rose, André Sapir and Jaume Ventura. Thank you very much for joining this session whose aim is to seek an academic view on what lessons we can draw from the optimal currency area theory during these ten years.

When looking through a couple of recent surveys of the literature on optimal currency areas I was reminded again how much of the work stands on the shoulders of Mundell, McKinnon and Kenen and in how much detail they were trying to carve out the characteristics they thought were crucial for judging whether two economies should form a currency union or not.

Taking the risk of oversimplifying, along the lines of their arguments, a monetary union among a group of partner countries can function well if: (i) labour mobility and/or wage and price flexibility is high, (ii) the countries are relatively small and open to trade, (iii) the production and consumption structures are similar, (iv) the degree of diversification is high so that overall, and (v) the probability of asymmetric shocks should be low.

However, as compelling one might think these arguments are, during the 1970s and 1980s we have seen the popularity of this strand of work falling. Despite the simplicity of the OCA theory, its normative implications were complex to follow through. As we might hear in a few minutes there are still quite different judgements within the academic community which prominent or less prominent place this work deserves within the universe of economic theory.

Nevertheless, while almost forgotten, a renaissance for the OCA theory took place in the second half of the 1980s. The main driver was that plans towards a European Monetary Union became more and more concrete.

A little bit later, Frankel and Rose started to turn the earlier argumentation of the OCA theory upside down. Again risking oversimplification, they replaced a static approach with a dynamic one, and proposed that participation in a monetary union will by itself foster trade and integration to a degree that it changes the economic structures of the countries concerned. Thereby business cycles would become more highly correlated, asymmetric shocks less likely, and a country specific monetary policy less needed. As a consequence, the much emphasised costs of giving up tailor made monetary policy would be significantly reduced.

Finally, one should not hide or forget, that at around the same time a competing hypothesis was advanced – by Krugman in particular. The argument here was that participation in a monetary union would foster specialisation and concentration, and thereby give way to exactly opposite effects, namely more idiosyncratic business cycles, more differentials in growth, employment and inflation and – sooner or later more and more political tensions.

Now, some time has passed since these heated debates. European Economic and Monetary Union and the Euro have been in place for almost a decade. Therefore, one could argue that the discussion is far less theoretical than it might have been at times and a new empirical dimension is emerging as new data is collected. So it is probably exactly the right time to again review the arguments, taking into account the experience so far.

Since almost ten years have successfully passed with the euro, natural questions to pose to the panellists relate to the future. For example:

(i)   What are the longer term challenges national policy makers face when participating in a large and diversified economic and monetary union?
(ii)   What are the longer term challenges for monetary policy operating in such an environment? And
(iii)   Which structural policies and reforms could be most effective to foster the smooth functioning of EMU?

PANEL STATEMENT

BY MARTIN FELDSTEIN, HARVARD UNIVERSITY

I am very pleased to be a participant in this ECB Central Bank Conference on the tenth anniversary of the creation of the euro and of the European Economic and Monetary Union (EMU). While it is difficult to specify the conditions for an optimal currency area, it is clear that the eurozone has been a very successful currency area. The euro was launched without serious problems and the ECB has succeeded in achieving the low inflation rate that is its single policy mandate. The desire of other countries to join the eurozone is further evidence that it is doing something right.

Rather than trying to define an optimal currency area or to state the conditions for an optimal currency area, I think it is better to ask the question: When is it in the interest of an outsider to join an existing currency union? And when is it in the interest of the existing members to add that outsider? Of course, this can be applied to the initial decision of any two or more countries to form a currency union.

I will begin by reviewing the advantages of a currency union from the point of view of the potential entrant and of the receiving group. I will then discuss two negative aspects of a currency union and examine the economic conditions that affect the seriousness of these negative aspects.

TRADITIONAL ADVANTAGES OF A CURRENCY UNION

Since this session is subtitled "Academic Views," I will begin with the three standard textbook advantages of a monetary union.

Currency convenience. A traveler in the eurozone does not have to carry a different currency for each country that he will visit. This is an advantage to potential joiners, to the receiving group, and to outsiders like myself. The importance of this is not large in today's world of credit cards and ATMs.

Price comparability. With a single currency, a shopper in one country can easily compare the price of a particular good in different places, thereby minimizing the cost of purchase and strengthening the efficiency of the market. This too is a potential gain both to the joiner and to the existing group. But I have never understood why this is considered significant. The housewife in Madrid cannot shop for her daily bread in Frankfurt while the wholesale buyer has always been able to compare the prices of steel that were stated in Spanish pesetas and German marks with the help of a pocket calculator.

Cross border investment. A single currency eliminates the direct exchange rate risk of cross-border investment within the currency union. This also is a potential gain to both the joiner and the existing group. Each can invest in the other without worrying about the potential loss if the exchange rate changes adversely. To the extent that this causes cross-border investment to occur that would not otherwise have happened, it presumably increases the efficiency of the international allocation of capital. But the amount of this gain is reduced to the extent that firms would otherwise hedge that currency risk by borrowing in the host country to finance their cross-border fixed investment and would use currency futures to hedge the currency risk of cross-border portfolio investment.

TRANSITION GAINS

The academic literature on monetary unions focuses on the *continuing* advantages and disadvantages of membership. In practice the creation of the European Monetary Union demonstrated that there can be significant transition gains for some of the joining countries.

Before they joined the EMU, several countries had high inflation rates and correspondingly high rates of interest. The requirement to reduce inflation and interest rates as conditions of membership gave these countries the political ability to make these healthy changes. Once in the EMU, the lack of independent national monetary policies preserved the low inflation.

The EMU membership criteria imposed on those who would join the EMU also included a reduction in the fiscal deficit and in the national debt. Although not all applicants satisfied these standards at the time of entry, their attempts to do so did initially help to reduce government spending and to limit fiscal deficits.

FIVE ADDITIONAL PERSISTENT GAINS FOR JOINERS

As I look at the EMU experience I see five additional ongoing gains that accrue to those who join.

Inflation Discipline. Although not every monetary union has a commitment to low inflation, the EMU has had one from the beginning with the ECB's single goal of price stability. Countries with a tradition of high inflation, often driven by union wage demands, benefited from the discipline imposed by EMU membership. Unions recognized that wage increases in excess of productivity gains could not be absorbed by an exchange rate adjustment but would lead to a loss of competitiveness and reductions in employment.

This gain to the joiners who had previously had high inflation rates did bring with it a risk to the low inflation members. Since monetary policy in the EMU is set by a consensus of all member countries, there was the danger that an increase in the number of countries with a history of high inflation could lead to a more inflationary monetary policy for the union as a whole. Fortunately that has not happened in the EMU.

Exchange Rate Discipline. Any monetary union automatically prevents member countries from seeking to gain competitive advantage by currency devaluations or to offset excess wage increases in this way. This is closely related to the inflation discipline but goes beyond it since it is implicit in any monetary union. It is a gain to those countries that had a history of devaluations but a risk to those existing member countries to the extent that there comes to be increased pressure to devalue the common currency.

Lender of Last Resort. Commercial banks always have the potential need for a lender of last resort when they experience a liquidity problem. Under those circumstances, central banks do provide liquidity against illiquid collateral. In this age of global banking, the needs of a domestic bank or of a group of domestic banks may exceed the appropriate lending ability of the national central bank and the fiscal capacity of the national government. This is an even greater problem if the commercial bank needs foreign exchange. Shifting from the resources of a single national bank to the resources of the central bank of the monetary union provides a more powerful lender of last resort. This is an advantage to any country that joins but is a potential risk to the existing members if the resulting lending is against overvalued collateral.

Expertise. Although some small countries have a rich supply of wise economists and skilled bankers, not all of them do. The complex decisions of monetary policy and banking supervision can benefit from the larger pool of talent that can serve on the monetary policy board of a multi-country union and on the supervisory and research staffs of the central bank.

Political Union. A monetary union need not be a precursor of a political union. But the EMU and the euro were seen by many in Europe as ways of strengthening the European union and developing support for a stronger political union. If individuals carry euros in their pockets instead of French francs or Italian lira, they would be more likely to think of themselves as Europeans. If they saw the power of the central banks shift from their own national capitals to Frankfurt, they would see the European Union as a more significant political force. For those who favored this transition to a stronger political union, the creation of the monetary union and the single currency were advantages.

DISADVANTAGES OF A CURRENCY UNION

The currency union implies a single monetary policy and a single exchange rate for all member countries. A country that joins a currency union therefore gives up the opportunity to select a monetary policy that it regards as optimal for its own circumstances. Similarly, the country's exchange rate cannot respond to the market forces by which changes in technology, taste, and the behavior of other countries affect its international competitiveness.

A country that considers joining a currency union must weigh these disadvantages against the advantages that I have described in the earlier part of these remarks. This balancing will differ from country to country. Each country must consider the extent to which it can expect to gain from those advantages and the extent to which it would be disadvantaged by the single monetary policy and single exchange rate.

The adverse effect of the single monetary policy and single exchange rate will depend primarily on four conditions.

Industrial similarity. If all of the countries in the currency union had the same industrial composition and were subject to the same shocks to technology and demand, the lack of individualized monetary policy and differential exchange rate movements would be irrelevant. A country that considers joining should evaluate the extent to which a monetary policy designed for the currency union as a whole would be the best one for itself. We see in the EMU substantial differences among countries in the distribution of industries that are reflected in differences in unemployment rates and in trade balances.

Labor Mobility. A fall in demand in a particular country or region will lead to less unemployment if the labor force is geographically mobile and can shift to other areas where demand is stronger. This is one way in which the United States has been able to cope with cyclical and structural changes in demand. The ability to achieve such labor mobility in a currency union depends on several features. The variety of languages clearly inhibits labor mobility within the euro area. Labor regulations, union restrictions, and licensing rules may also impede such geographic mobility.

Fiscal Structure. Fiscal policy is important in two ways: the role of the central fiscal authority and the freedom of the individual national fiscal authorities. In the United States, the central government collects about two thirds of all taxes and an even larger part of cyclically sensitive income and profits taxes. When demand falls in a particular part of the country, the amount of taxes paid from that region to the central government falls. This automatic fiscal policy dampens the local decline in net income and therefore stimulates demand relative to what it would otherwise be. That helps to compensate for the lack of an independent monetary authority for the region. In a currency union with a very small central fiscal authority, like the EMU, there is no such fiscal counterbalance to local swings in domestic demand.

Members of the currency union can of course vary national taxes and spending to provide a local stimulus to offset declines in demand. But this ability to run deficits creates a problem for the currency union as a whole. Because there is a single currency, large fiscal deficits in any single country do not create the market feedback in the form of higher interest rates or a weaker currency as it would if the deficit country had its own currency. Although there are some relatively small differences in national interest rates, the primary effect of any country's fiscal deficit is diluted and spread over the entire currency union, causing the common interest rate to rise and the overall currency to decline.

While this is an advantage for the country that alters its domestic policy, it is a disadvantage for the currency union as a whole. That led to the Stability and

Growth Pact that, in principle, limits the extent of any country's fiscal deficit. Some rule of that type is a necessary feature of any currency union in which fiscal actions remain decentralized among the member governments. That limit on each country's fiscal policy is a further disadvantage for countries that consider joining a currency union.

Willingness to Sacrifice. The potential success of a currency union depends on the willingness of the member countries to accept what the monetary authority regards to be best for the group of countries as a whole. At times, that will mean a policy that is directly counter to the interest of specific countries within the currency union. The willingness of those countries and of their voting publics to support a common policy that is clearly against their interest is a critical feature that will govern the long-term success and survival of any currency union.

THE CURRENT CHALLENGE

The first decade of the EMU has been a clear success. But it is about to be challenged by more difficult conditions: a financial crisis and sharply declining economic activity on a scale that exceeds anything that Europe experienced in the past decade.

Not all EMU countries will be affected equally by the evolution of the European economy or by the policies of the ECB. Some governments or political parties within countries will wish that they had more control over their monetary policy or more ability to pursue a very aggressive fiscal policy.

Because of a limited willingness to make sacrifices for the benefit of other EMU nations or for the EMU as a system, some of those governments or politicians may seek to exit the EMU or may threaten that they will do so unless policies are changed.

In short, the next few years will be a very challenging time for the ECB and for the European political process.

PANEL STATEMENT[1]

BY ANDREW K. ROSE, UNIVERSITY OF CALIFORNIA, NBER AND CEPR

ABSTRACT

This short paper reviews the recent literature linking monetary union, international trade, and business cycle synchronization. I survey the literature using the quantitative technique of meta-analysis, which allows me to estimate the effects of EMU taking into account the entire extant literature. Twenty-six recent studies have investigated the effect of currency union on trade, using actual European data of relevance. Taking all these studies into account, EMU has raised trade inside the Eurozone by at least 8% and perhaps 23%. Twenty different studies have estimated the effect of trade on the synchronization of business cycles. Aggregating across these estimates, an increase of bilateral trade between two countries raises the synchronization of their business cycles by an economically and statistically significant effect. I estimate that a one percent increase in bilateral trade increases the correlation coefficient of detrended output by .02. Taken together, the estimates suggest that EMU has created a virtuous circle; by increasing trade and the synchronization of business cycles, EMU reduces the need for national monetary policy. That is, EMU seems along the path to becoming an optimum currency area.

INTRODUCTION

Fifteen European countries are currently involved in the world's largest and most interesting currency union, EMU. Yet most economists (especially those from the other side of the Atlantic) do not think that when EMU was created it was an optimum currency area (hereafter "OCA"). At the birth of EMU in 1999, national business cycles appeared to be imperfectly synchronized across the members of EMU, and few thought that trade would rise substantially with monetary union. Together, these lead most to believe that EMU did not satisfy the requirements of an OCA, using either the classic model of Mundell (1961) or the more modern version of Alesina and Barro (2002). In this short paper, I wish to argue that even though EMU was not created as an OCA, it is moving in that direction.

My argument relies on two recent empirical literatures, which I survey briefly. The first estimates the effect of European Monetary Union (EMU) on trade; the second estimates the effect of trade on the cross-country synchronization of business cycles. I use meta-analysis to provide a quantitative summary of both literatures.

---

1   The data set, sample output, and a current version of the paper are available at my website faculty.haas.berkeley.edu/arose.

These literatures deal with questions that are intrinsically important to the EMU/OCA nexus, and inter-related. Any reduction of the transactions costs associated with trade inside the Eurozone by EMU is of general interest. Indeed, one of the few undisputed benefits of EMU is its trade-promoting effect, so quantifying its size is an important exercise. The second linkage is also of interest. If increased trade raises the coherence of business cycles across countries, it thereby reduces the need for national monetary policy. If *both* links work in practice, then a currency union like EMU which does not look like an optimal currency area *ex ante* may become one *ex post*. This can occur if the trade increase stemming from currency union actually makes the currency union optimal, by reducing or eliminating the need for a national monetary policy to reduce idiosyncratic business cycles. Frankel and Rose (1997, 1998) lay out the argument in detail.

A BRIEF HISTORY OF THE LITERATURE

In the summer of 1999, I began to circulate a paper that estimated the effect of currency union on trade; *Economic Policy* subsequently published this paper in 2000. This paper exploited a panel of cross-country data covering bilateral trade between a large number of countries. Since most of the variation was across pairs of countries rather than time, I used a conventional "gravity" model of trade to account for factors that drive trade (other than monetary arrangements). This equation has now become the standard vehicle for the literature, and takes the form:

$$T_{ijt} = \beta_1 D_{ij} + \beta_2 (Y_i Y_j)_t + \Sigma_k \beta_k Z_{ijt} + \Sigma_t \delta_t T_t + \gamma CU_{ijt} + u_{ijt},$$

where: T_{ijt} denotes the natural logarithm of trade between countries i and j at time t, $\{\beta\}$ is a set of nuisance coefficients, D_{ij} denotes the log of distance between i and j, Y denotes the log of real GDP, Z denotes other controls for bilateral trade, CU_{ijt} is a dummy variable that is one if countries i and j are in a currency union at t and zero otherwise, and u is a well-behaved disturbance term. The coefficient of interest is γ, which represents the partial effect of currency union on trade, *ceteris paribus*.

The surprising and interesting finding was that currency union seemed to have a strong and robust effect on trade. Even using the standard linear gravity model that accounts for most variation in trade patterns, my point estimate was that the coefficient for a currency union dummy variable (which is unity when a pair of countries share a common currency and zero otherwise) has a point estimate of around =1.21. This implies that members of currency unions traded over three times as much as otherwise similar pairs of countries *ceteris paribus*, since exp(1.21) >3. While there was no benchmark from the literature, this estimate seemed implausibly large to me (and others). Almost all the subsequent research in this area has been motivated by the belief that currency union cannot reasonably be expected to triple trade. I provided a meta-analysis of the work as it existed in March 2004 in my 2005 paper with Stanley.

One of the problems with almost all the work that Stanley and I surveyed was that it estimated the effect of currency unions on trade using monetary unions that preceded EMU. This choice was made of necessity; since the euro only started to circulate in 2002, there was essentially no European data of relevance available. However, the currency unions that existed before the Eurozone involved countries that were either small or poor (or both). Clearly the relevance of such currency unions for EMU was unknown.

Some four years have now passed since I finished my 2005 survey (with Stanley), and much work has been done. I am now aware of 26 studies that estimate the currency union effect on trade – γ in equation (1) above – *using data directly relevant for EMU.* It seems appropriate to see what these studies say, taken as a whole.

META-ANALYSIS: THE EFFECT OF CURRENCY UNION ON TRADE

Meta-analysis is a set of quantitative techniques for evaluating and combining empirical results from different studies. Essentially one treats different point estimates of a given coefficient as individual observations. One can then use this vector of estimates to: estimate the underlying coefficient of interest, test the hypothesis that the coefficient is zero, and link the estimates to features of the underlying studies. Since there are currently a number of studies that have provided estimates of γ, the effect of currency union on trade, meta-analysis seems an appropriate way to summarize the current state of the literature. Stanley (2001) provides an excellent recent review and further references.

One begins meta-analysis by collecting as many estimates of a common effect as possible. To my knowledge, there are twenty-six papers that provide estimates of the effect of currency union on bilateral trade (γ) using data of relevance. These articles are tabulated in Table 1 (I note parenthetically that I am a co-author of none.) I also present the studies' preferred estimate of γ, along with its standard error. In each case, I present the estimate of γ that seems to be most preferred or representative (if a preferred estimate is not available) by the author(s) of the study. While I have strong views about the value of some of these estimates (or lack thereof), I weigh each estimate equally, simply because there is no easily defensible alternative weighting scheme.

The most basic piece of meta-analysis is a test of the null hypothesis γ=0 when the twenty-six point estimates (and their standard errors) are pooled across studies. This classic test is due originally to Fisher (1932) and uses the p-values from each of the (26) underlying γ estimates. Under the null hypothesis that each of the p-values is independently and randomly drawn from a normal [0, 1] distribution, minus twice the sum of the logs of the p-values is drawn from a chi-square. The hypothesis can be rejected at any standard significance level, since under the null hypothesis the test-statistic of 785 is drawn from chi-squared (52).[2]

---

2 Edgington's small sample correction leads to the same conclusion.

Table I Recent Studies of Currency Union and Trade

			Gamma	SE
1	Bun and Klaassen	2002	0.33	0.1
2	de Souza	2002	0.17	0.24
3	de Nardis and Vicarelli	2003	0.061	0.027
4	Cabasson	2003	0.63	0.24
5	Micco, Stein, Ordonez	2004	0.089	0.025
6	Barr, Breedon and Miles	2004	0.25	0.033
7	Baldwin and Taglioni	2004	0.034	0.015315
8	Faruqee	2004	0.082	0.018
9	de Nardis and Vicarelli	2004	0.093	0.039
10	Clark, Tamirisa, and Wei	2004	0.22	0.38
11	Baldwin, Skudelny, and Taglioni	2005	0.72	0.06
12	Yamarik and Ghosh	2005	1.8285	0.30475
13	Adam and Cobham	2005	1.029	0.039486
14	Baxter and Koupritsas	2006	0.47	0.22
15	Flam and Nordstrom	2006b	0.139	0.02
16	Berger and Nitsch	2006	-0.001	0.036
17	Gomes, Graham, Helliwell, Kano, Murray and Schembri	2006	0.069	0.011
18	Baldwin and Taglioni	2006	-0.02	0.03
19	Baldwin and Di Nino	2006	0.035	0.01
20	Flam and Nordstrom	2006a	0.232	0.024
21	Tenreyro and Barro	2007	1.899	0.351
22	Bun and Klaassen	2007	0.032	0.016
23	de Nardis, De Santis and Vicarelli	2007	0.04	0.01278
24	Brouwer, Paap, and Viaene	2007	0.067	0.025769
25	Flam and Nordstrom	2007	0.248	0.046
26	de Nardis, De Santis and Vicarelli	2008	0.09	0.033962

I tabulate meta-estimates of the currency effect on trade in Table 2. I provide both "fixed effect" and "random effect" meta-estimates that are common in the area. The former are based on the assumption that a single fixed effect underlies every study, so that, in principle, if every study were infinitely large, every study would yield an identical result. This is the same as assuming there is no heterogeneity across studies. By way of contrast, the random effects estimator assumes that the studies are estimating different treatment effects, drawn from a distribution whose mean is of interest.[3]

3   http://www.cochrane-net.org/openlearning/HTML/mod13.htm. To elaborate: the fixed effect assumption is that differences across studies are only due to within-study variation. By way of contrast, random effects models consider both between-study and within-study variability and assume that the studies are a random sample from the universe of all possible studies.

Table 2 Meta-analysis of impact of currency union on trade

	Estimation Technique	Pooled Estimate of γ	Lower Bound of 95%	Upper Bound of 95%
Fixed		0.08	0.07	0.09
Random		0.21	0.15	0.27

Manifestly, there is considerable heterogeneity; the fixed and random effect estimators are not similar in magnitude. However, both estimates are both economically substantial; the smaller fixed effect estimate of γ indicate that currency union raises trade by about 8% (as ln(.08)-1=.08), while the random effect estimate indicates that the effect is more like 23%.

$$BCS_{ijt} = \alpha + \beta * \ln(trade_{ijt}) + controls + \varepsilon_{ijt}$$

There is little indication that any single study is especially influential in driving these results. If the studies are omitted from the meta-analysis one by one, one finds the (fixed-effect) point estimates for γ tabulated in Table 3, along with a 95% confidence interval.

It seems that EMU has had a measurable effect already on trade. In the spirit of trying to stay modest, the few years since EMU began have already seen trade rise within the Eurozone by at least 8%. Since EMU is a relatively young institution, it seems likely (though uncertain) that this effect will grow with time. I also note that this conclusion is consistent with writers who have surveyed the literature in a more qualitative fashion. The best known of these is Baldwin (2006), who writes "The bottom line of this literature is that the euro probably did boost intra-Eurozone trade by something like five to ten percent on average, although the estimates size of this effect is likely to change as new years of data emerge."[4]

---

4   Probably the most relevant is Frankel (2008), who writes "If one estimates the effects of the euro versus other monetary unions in a large sample that includes all countries and all years, thereby bringing to bear as much information as possible on questions such as the proper coefficients on common border and common language in a gravity model, then the effect of the euro in the first eight years is seen to be large, and comparable with the effect of the other non-euro monetary unions."

Table 3 Checking for influential studies in the meta-estimate of γ

	Study Omitted	Gamma	Lower Bound of 95%	Upper Bound of 95%
1	Bun and Klaassen	0.08	0.07	0.09
2	de Souza	0.08	0.07	0.09
3	de Nardis and Vicarelli	0.08	0.07	0.09
4	Cabasson	0.08	0.07	0.09
5	Micco, Stein, Ordonez	0.08	0.07	0.09
6	Barr, Breedon and Miles	0.08	0.07	0.09
7	Baldwin and Taglioni	0.09	0.08	0.10
8	Faruqee	0.08	0.07	0.09
9	de Nardis and Vicarelli	0.08	0.07	0.09
10	Clark, Tamirisa, and Wei	0.08	0.07	0.09
11	Baldwin, Skudelny, and Taglioni	0.08	0.07	0.09
12	Yamarik and Ghosh	0.08	0.07	0.09
13	Adam and Cobham	0.07	0.06	0.08
14	Baxter and Koupritsas	0.08	0.07	0.09
15	Flam and Nordstrom	0.08	0.07	0.09
16	Berger and Nitsch	0.08	0.08	0.09
17	Gomes, et al	0.09	0.08	0.10
18	Baldwin and Taglioni	0.09	0.08	0.09
19	Baldwin and Di Nino	0.10	0.09	0.10
20	Flam and Nordstrom	0.08	0.07	0.09
21	Tenreyro and Barro	0.08	0.07	0.09
22	Bun and Klaassen	0.09	0.08	0.10
23	de Nardis, De Santis and Vicarelli	0.09	0.08	0.10
24	Brouwer, Paap, and Viaene	0.08	0.07	0.09
25	Flam and Nordstrom	0.08	0.07	0.09
26	de Nardis, De Santis and Vicarelli	0.08	0.07	0.09

INCREASED TRADE ENHANCES BUSINESS CYCLE SYNCHRONIZATION

I now turn to the link between international trade and business cycle synchronization. It is now standard to use the following equation:

where BCS a measure of business cycle synchronization between countries i and j during time period t. Countries might choose their monetary regime, such as a fixed exchange rate, to both simultaneously enhance trade and affects BCS, so β is almost always estimated with instrumental variables.

Frankel and Rose (1997, 1998) show that theoretically β is ambiguously signed; it depends on what kind of trade is spurred by integration, and what sorts of shocks hit the economy. However, *if* β is positive, then currency unions may endogenously become optimal. In particular, if currency raises trade significantly, then by indirectly raising BCS it reduces the need for a national monetary policy to offset idiosyncratic domestic shocks, thus making the currency union sustainable.

The chief measurement issue is determining an empirical analogue for business cycle synchronization (BCS). This is typically (though not always) measured as a correlation coefficient that is estimated between detrended levels of activity for countries i and j, over some reasonable period of time.[5] Since EMU has only existed for a short period of time, no study, to the best of my knowledge, creates BCS measures using only post-EMU data.

The coefficient of interest is β, which measures the effect of trade on BCS. This has been estimated by twenty different studies. These studies, along with their estimates of β (and its standard error) are tabulated in Table 4. While twenty studies are not enough to give one a truly large sample, it still seems worthwhile to use meta-analysis to aggregate their estimates quantitatively.

---

5   Different measures of real activity are available (real GDP; the unemployment rate; industrial production ...), as are detrending techniques (HP-filtering; Baxter-King filtering; first-differencing; linear detrending ...). These do not seem to have an appreciable difference on the results in practice.

Table 4 Recent Studies of Trade and Business Cycle Synchronization

			Beta	SE
1	Baxter and Kouparitsas	2005	0.134	0.032
2	Bower and Guillenmineau	2006	0.02055	0.00528
3	Calder	2007	0.013	0.004
4	Calderon Chong and Stein	2007	0.015	0.003055
5	Choe	2001	0.027	0.008333
6	Clark and van Wincoop	2001	0.09	0.03
7	Crosby	2003	0.048	0.063
8	Fidrmuc	2004	0.021	0.044872
9	Fiess	2007	0.123	0.062
10	Frankel and Rose	1998	0.086	0.015
11	Gruben, Koo and Mills	2002	0.059	0.017206
12	Imbs	2003	0.03089	0.020058
13	Imbs	2004	0.074	0.022289
14	Inklaar, Jong-a-Pin and de Haan	2005	0.115	0.041071
15	Kose and Yi	2005	0.091	0.022
16	Kose, Prasad and Terrones	2003	0.0107	0.0045
17	Kumakura	2006	0.0575	0.0354
18	Kumakura	2007	0.05555	0.01232
19	Otto, Voss and Willard	2001	0.0461	0.090999
20	Shin and Wang	2004	0.07665	0.07665

Table 5 Meta-analysis of impact of trade on business cycle synchronization

	Estimation Technique	Pooled Estimate of γ	Lower Bound of 95%	Upper Bound of 95%
Fixed		0.020	0.016	0.023
Random		0.043	0.031	0.054

The hypothesis that β is statistically insignificantly different from zero is grossly rejected; under the null hypothesis of no effect, the test-statistic of 277 is drawn from chi-squared (40).[6] The meta-estimates of the effect of trade on BCS are presented in Table 5. As with the effect of currency union on trade, there is considerable heterogeneity and the fixed and random effect estimators are not close. I continue to be conservative, and focus on the lower, fixed-effect, estimate of $\beta \approx .02$. While this is considerably lower than I estimated in my 1998 paper with Frankel, it is still economically significant. If EMU has thus been associated with a trade increase of say 8% and each 1% increase in bilateral trade leads to an increase in BCS of .02, then EMU leads to an increase in the correlation coefficient of detrended outputs of (.02*8=) .16. Since the sample average of BCS is around .22, this represents an economically relevant increase in the synchronization of business cycles across the members of EMU. While this reduction in idiosyncratic national business cycles is substantial, whether it is enough to obviate the need for a national monetary policy is, of course, a different question.

SUMMARY AND CONCLUSION

The objective of this paper was to provide a brief quantitative survey of two related literatures. The effect of EMU on trade has now been examined by some 26 studies; I use meta-analysis to aggregate these together. If one weighs each of the studies equally, the literature has not yet come to a consensual view concerning the effect of EMU; a conservative estimate is that EMU has already lead to an increase in trade of some 8%, but a more substantive effect of 23% is also plausible. The hypothesis that it has had had no effect at all can be easily rejected by the literature taken as a whole.

I also ask what can be learned from the twenty papers that estimate the effect of international trade on business cycle synchronization (BCS). The meta-estimates here are also heterogeneous, though again the idea that trade has no effect on BCS seems grossly inconsistent with the data. A conservative estimate is that each 1% increase in trade between a pair of countries seems to raise the correlation coefficient for their detrended outputs by around .02.

EMU seems to have had a combination of two effects: the direct consequence of increased trade, and an indirect benefit through the effect of this trade expansion on business cycle synchronization. This means that EMU may have created

6   Again, Edgington's technique changes nothing.

a virtuous circle that might make currency union closer to being sustainable. Whether the effect is big enough to make Europe an optimal currency area remains to be seen. A modern currency union between large rich countries like EMU has no historical precedent, and too little time has passed since the introduction of the euro for the trade and BCS effects to be clearly estimated. That said, EMU seems clearly to be moving along the path to becoming an optimum currency area.

I close with a caveat. EMU has had and is having an enormous number of economic consequences, and I have ignored almost all of them in this brief paper. Countries choosing whether or not to enter (or stay in) EMU have to consider its effect on the efficiency of capital and labor markets, the quality of monetary policy inside EMU, risk-sharing, and so forth. The non-economic issues associated with sovereignty and political influence within the EMU may be of equal or greater importance. Still, the two literatures I have surveyed provide some grounds for an optimistic, though early, view of EMU.

REFERENCES

Adam, C., and D. Cobham. 2007. "Exchange Rate Regimes and Trade" Rate Regimes and Trade. *Manchester School*, 75(1): 44-63.

Alesina, A. and R.J. Barro. 2002. "Currency Unions." *Quarterly Journal of Economics*, 107(2): 409-436.

Baldwin, R. 2006. "The Euro's Trade Effects." European Central Bank Working Paper 594.

Baldwin, R.E., and V. Di Nino. 2006. "Euros and Zeros: The Common Currency Effect on Trade in New Goods. National Bureau of Economic Research Working Paper 12673.

Baldwin, R., and D. Taglioni. 2004. "Positive OCA Criteria: Microfoundations for the Rose Effect." http://hei.unige.ch/~baldwin/RoseEffect/OCA_BaldwinTaglioni17Mar04.pdf.

Baldwin, R., and D. Taglioni. 2006. "Gravity for Dummies and Dummies for Gravity Equations." National Bureau of Economic Research Working Paper 12516.

Baldwin, R., F. Skudelny, and D. Taglioni. 2005. "Trade Effects of the Euro." European Central Bank Working Paper 446.

Barr, D., F. Breedon and D. Miles. 2004. "Life on the Outside." *Economic Policy*, 18(37): 573-613.

Baxter, M. and M. Kouparitsas. 2005. "Determinants of Business Cycle Comovement: A Robust Analysis" *Journal of Monetary Economics*, 52(1): 113-157.

Baxter, M., and M. A. Koupritsas. 2006. "What Determines Bilateral Trade Flows?" National Bureau of Economic Research Working Paper 12188.

Berger, H., and V. Nitsch. 2008. "Zooming Out: The Trade Effect of the Euro in Historical Perspective." *Journal of International Money and Finance*, 27(8): 1244-1260.

Bower, U., and C. Guillenmineau. 2006. "Determinants of Business Cycle Synchronisation Across Euro Area Countries." European Central Bank Working Paper 587.

Brouwer, J., R., and J. M. Viaene. 2007. "The Trade and FDI Effects of EMU Enlargement." *Journal of International Money and Finance*, 27(2): 188-208.

Bun, M.J.G. and F.J.G.M. Klaassen. 2002. "Has the Euro Increased Trade?" Tinbergen Institute Discussion Paper 02-108/2.

Bun, M.J.G. and F.J.G.M. Klaassen. 2007. "The Euro Effect on Trade is not as Large as Commonly Thought." *Oxford Bulletin of Economics and Statistics*, 69(4): 473-496.

Cabasson, D. 2003. "Survey about Monetary Unions." www.economics.adelaide.edu.au/workshops/ doc/monetary.pdf

Calder, C. 2007. "Trade, Specialization and Cycle Synchronization." World Bank. Unpublished.

Calderon, C., A. Chong and E. Stein. 2007. "Trade Intensity and Business Cycle Synchronization; Are Developing Countries Any Different?" *Journal of International Economics*, 71(1): 2-21.

Choe, J.I. 2001. "An Impact of Economic Integration through Trade" *Journal of Asian Economics*, 12(4):569-586.

Clark, P., N. Tamirisa, and S.J. Wei. 2004. "Exchange Rate Volatility and Trade Flows." International Monetary Fund Occasional Paper 235.

Clark, T. and E. van Wincoop. 2001. "Borders and Business Cycles." *Journal of International Economics*, 55(1): 59-85.

Crosby, M. 2003. "Business Cycle Correlations in Asia-Pacific" *Economics Letters*, 80(1): 35-44.

de Nardis, S. and C. Vicarelli. 2004. "Currency Unions and Trade" *Review of World Economic*, 139(4): 625-649.

de Nardis, S. and C. Vicarelli. 2003. "The Impact of the Euro on Trade." European Network of Economic Policy Research Institutes Economics Working Paper 17.

de Nardis, S., R. De Santis and C. Vicarelli. 2007. "The Euro's Effects on Trade in a Dynamic Setting." Institute for Studies and Economic Analyses Working Paper 80.

de Nardis, S., R. De Santis and C. Vicarelli. 2008. "The Single Currency's Effects on Eurozone Sectoral Trade" Institute for Studies and Economic Analyses Working Paper 88.

de Souza, L.V. 2002. "Trade Effects of Monetary Integration in Large, Mature Economies." Kiel Working Paper 1137.

Faruqee, H. 2004. "Measuring the Trade Effects of EMU." International Monetary Fund Working Paper 154.

Fidrmuc, J. 2004. "The Endogeneity of the Optimum Currency Area Criteria, Intra-Industry Trade, and EMU Enlargement." *Contemporary Economic Policy*, 22(1): 1-12.

Fiess, N. 2007. "Business Cycle Synchronization and Regional Integration." *World Bank Economic Review*, 21(1): 49-72.

Flam, H., and H. Nordstrom. 2008. "The Euro and Single Market impact on Trade and FDI." http://www-2.iies.su.se/~flamh/Euro%20FDI%20Revisited%20 Revised%20081212.pdf

Flam, H., and H. Nordstrom. 2006a. "Euro Effects on the Intensive and Extensive Margins of Trade." Institute for International Economic Studies Seminar Paper 750.

Flam, H., and H. Nordstrom. 2006b. "Trade Volume Effects of the Euro." Institute for International Economic Studies Seminar Paper 746.

Frankel, J.A. 2008. "The Estimated Effects of the Euro on Trade: Why Are They Below Historical Effects of Monetary Unions Among Smaller Countries?" National Bureau of Economic Research Working Paper 14542.

Frankel, J.A. and A.K. Rose. 1997. "Is EMU More Justifiable *Ex Post* than *Ex Ante?*" *The European Economic Review*, 41(3-5): 753-760.

Frankel, J.A. and A.K. Rose. 1998. "The Endogeneity of the Optimum Currency Area Criteria" *Economic Journal*, 108(449): 1009-25.

Gomes, T., C. Graham, J. Helliwell, T. Kano, J. Murray and Lawrence Schembri. 2006. "The Euro and Trade." http://www2.dse.unibo.it/soegw/paper/ GomGraHelKanoMurrayS.pdf.

Gruben, W.C., J. Koo and E. Mills. 2002. "How Much Does International Trade Affect Business Cycle Synchronization?" Federal Reserve Bank of Dallas Working Paper 203.

Imbs, J. 2003. "Co-Fluctuations." http://www.hec.unil.ch/jimbs/Research/ Cofluct2001.pdf

Imbs, J. 2004. "Trade, Finance, Specialization and Synchronization." *Review of Economics and Statistics*, 86(3): 723-734.

Inklaar, R., R. Jong-a-Pin and J. de Haan. 2005. "Trade and Business Cycle Synchronization in OECD Countries – a Re-examination." CESIfo Working Paper 1546.

Kose, A. and K.M. Yi. 2005. "Can the Standard International Business Cycle Model Explain the Relation between Trade and Comovement?" Federal Reserve Bank of Philadelphia Working Paper 03.

Kose, A., E.S. Prasad and M.E. Terrones. 2003. "Volatility and Comovement in a Globalized World Economy: An Empirical Exploration." International Monetary Fund Working Paper 246.

Kumakura, M. 2006. "Trade and Business Cycle Co-Movements in Asia-Pacific." *Journal of Asian Economics*, 17(4): 62-645.

Kumakura, M. 2007. "Trade, Production and International Business Cycle Comovement." Osaka City University. Unpublished.

Lane, P. R. 2006. "The Real Effects of EMU." Institute for International Integration Studies Discussion Paper 115.

Mancini-Griffoli, T. and L.L. Pauwels. 2006. "Is There a Euro Effect on Trade?" Graduate Institute of International Studies at Geneva HEI Working Paper 04.

Micco, A., E. Stein and G. Ordonez .2004. "The Currency Union Effect on Trade" *Economic Policy*, 18(37): 315-356.

Mongelli, F.P., E. Dorrucci and I. Agur. 2005. "What Does European Institutional Integration Tell Us About Trade Integration?" European Central Bank Occasional Paper 40.

Mongelli, F.P. and J.L. Vega. 2006. "What Effect is EMU Having on the Euro Area and its Member Countries? An Overview" European Central Bank Working Paper 599.

Mundell, R.A. 1961. "A Theory of Optimum Currency Areas." *American Economic Review*, 51(4):657-665.

Otto, G., G. Voss and L. Willard. 2001. "Understanding OECD Output Correlations." Reserve Bank of Australia Discussion Paper 2001-5.

Rose, A.K. and T.D. Stanley. 2005. "A Meta-Analysis of the Effect of Common Currencies on International Trade." *Journal of Economic Surveys*, 19(3): 347-365.

Shin, K. and Y. Wang. 2004. "Trade Integration and Business Cycle Synchronization in East Asia." *Asian Economic Papers*, 2(3):1-20.

Stanley, T.D. 2001. "Wheat from Chaff: Meta-Analysis as Quantitative Literature Review." *Journal of Economic Perspectives*, 15(3): 131-150.

Tenreyro, S., and R.J. Barro. 2007. "Economic Effects of Currency Unions" *Economic Inquiry*, 45(1): 1 – 23.

Yamarik, S., and S. Ghosh. 2005. "A Sensitivity Analysis of the Gravity Model." *International Trade Journal*, 19(1): 83-126.

PANEL STATEMENT

BY ANDRÉ SAPIR, UNIVERSITÉ LIBRE DE BRUXELLES

THE OCA THEORY

Mundell (1961) is a short and beautiful paper. In less than ten pages, and without a single mathematical formula or graph, it presents the optimum currency area (OCA) theory, which is rightly regarded as the theoretical underpinning for Europe's single currency. It is fit, therefore, that the celebration of the euro's tenth anniversary should reflect upon the contribution of the OCA theory to the euro's success.

The general question raised by Mundell (1961) is whether national currencies should be flexible - or what is the optimum number of currencies - for the purpose of stabilization. Writing in the early Sixties, just after the creation of the European Common Market, Mundell also poses the corollary question of whether its members should "allow each national currency to fluctuate, or would a single currency area be preferable?" (p. 657).

The answer to the general question, he finds, depends on the extent of factor mobility. "The argument for flexible exchange rates *based on national currencies* is only as valid as the Ricardian assumption about factor mobility. If factor mobility is high internally and low internationally a system of flexible exchange rates *based on national currencies* might work effectively enough." (p. 661, emphasis added). Hence, the question about whether or not the Common Market should adopt a single currency "is essentially an empirical problem" concerning the degree of factor mobility among its members (p. 662).

Contrary to what is often alleged, Mundell (1961) does not claim that the degree of factor mobility is the sole criterion for determining the optimum number of currencies. Three other criteria are implicit in the paper, which relate to the fact that the loss in terms of stabilization due to the creation of a single currency is higher when (1) macroeconomic shocks are more asymmetric between countries; (2) the size of countries is large, and therefore the exchange rate instrument is more powerful for offsetting such shocks, a point later emphasized by McKinnon (1963); and (3) other adjustment mechanisms, including possibly a common fiscal system later emphasized by Kenen (1969), are less able to deal with asymmetric.

After the initial conceptual work of the 1960s, the OCA theory was nearly all but forgotten during the next two decades.[1] It was revived in the early 1990s, around

---

1   A major exception is Mundell (1973).

the time of the Maastricht Treaty, which laid out the timetable for Economic and Monetary Union (EMU) and the criteria countries would have to fulfil before adopting the single currency. The revival came in the form of empirical evidence concerning mostly Europe, which had lacked so far, rather than as challenges to the existing theory.

Most of the empirical literature on the OCA theory deals with the issue of asymmetric shocks. The general result is that the countries which belonged to the European Union in the 1990s (EU-15) fall into two groups: a 'core', comprising of Germany, France, the Benelux countries, Austria and Denmark, where shocks are highly correlated and the speed of adjustment is relatively fast; a 'periphery', comprising of Italy, Spain, Greece, Portugal, Ireland, Finland, the United Kingdom and Sweden, where shocks are larger and more idiosyncratic, and the speed of adjustment is slower.[2,3]

MAASTRICHT

The Maastricht criteria bear little resemblance to the OCA criteria. Whereas the latter emphasize the importance of economic integration and of real convergence among the candidate countries to monetary integration, the former insists instead on nominal convergence. What matters for Maastricht is inflation, exchange rates, interest rates and public finance, not asymmetric shocks due to structural differences.

Why this apparent discrepancy, or even contradiction, between the OCA and the Maastricht criteria? One possible explanation is that EMU is driven by political rather than by economic considerations, and that its founding fathers feared the political consequences of a division of the European Union into a 'core' and a 'periphery' that might have resulted from the use of OCA criteria. Though there may be some truth in this line of reasoning, it is clearly unreasonable to believe that economic considerations were totally absent in the preparation of the Maastricht criteria.

What then might be possible economic explanations for ignoring the OCA criteria? One reason is that macroeconomic shocks were considered to be less likely inside the monetary union because of the elimination of shocks induced by national central banks. A second is that it was hoped that shocks would become less asymmetric because the introduction of a single currency would induce real convergence by boosting intra-industry trade, as suggested by Frankel and Rose (1997). A third reason is that the exchange rate instrument had anyway lost its usefulness as a tool for offsetting shocks due the liberalization of capital controls. A final reason is that, although EMU lacks a common fiscal instrument, national automatic stabilizers were possibly viewed as sufficiently capable of absorbing

---

2   See, in particular, Bayoumi and Eichengreen (1993, 1996 and 1997).
3   Forni and Reichlin (2001), however, strike an important note of dissent with their finding that the 'core' consists not of nations but of regions belonging to different countries.

asymmetric shocks, especially after the introduction of the Stability and Growth Pact, which was meant to increase the room for manoeuvre in bad times.[4]

Although these economic considerations probably go some way in explaining why the framers of the Maastricht Treaty decided to ignore the OCA criteria, they cannot explain why other criteria were used instead. The reason is simple enough. European monetary union has never been about simply creating a single currency. Rather it has always been about creating a stable common currency, a currency like the D-Mark. The Maastricht criteria are therefore essentially designed to ensure that countries joining the euro are able to live within an environment of low inflation, similar to what Germany, and the countries in DM-area, enjoyed before monetary unification.

OCA THEORY VS. MAASTRICHT

Based on the Maastricht criteria, 11 of the EU-15 countries were judged ready to adopt the euro on 1 January 1999, and Greece was admitted two years later. Since the other three EU members were actually not interested in joining the euro at the time, it can be safely concluded that the Maastricht criteria did not split the European Union into two groups.[5]

On the other hand, had the OCA theory criteria been in force, only the DM-area countries (Germany, France, the Benelux and Austria) would have qualified initially, and the EU would have been split into a 'core' and a 'periphery', with Italy, Spain, Greece, Portugal, Ireland and Finland out in the cold.

The possibility of such a split was real, even with the Maastricht criteria, which might have been interpreted with an 'OCA theory twist' for fear that a wide EMU may be too risky initially in terms of asymmetric shocks. The eventuality of a narrow EMU was a topic of much concern in the run up to the introduction of the euro, especially among economists from the 'periphery'. For instance, Viñals (1996) addresses the potential consequences of a narrow EMU on the excluded countries and finds that "there is a real risk of an unfavourable effect on the economies of [these] countries, provoked by financial markets turning their backs on their currencies. If this were to happen, there would be a danger that the countries excluded from EMU would undergo unwanted currency depreciations and higher interest risk premia that would adversely affect inflation and the budget deficit" (pp. 1108-9). The paper concludes that a European monetary union going beyond the 'core' countries is absolutely necessary. "At stake is not only the chance to create a monetary union that is adequately representative of Europe, but also the preservation of the integrity of the Single Market." (p. 1109).

Since the wide EMU approach prevailed, one may be tempted to ask whether it was a mistake to ignore the OCA criteria after all. One way to answer this

4   These explanations are developed in Buti and Sapir (1998).
5   This was true at least until the 2004 enlargement.

question is to look at the perception of euro area members by financial markets reflected in 5-year credit default swap (CDS) rates on government bonds. During 'good times', broadly speaking the first nine years of the euro, financial markets made very little difference between the 'core' and 'periphery' countries. As late as 29 December 2007, the 5-year CDS rates ranged between 10 and 20 for all euro area countries. Since the acceleration of the financial crisis in September 2008, huge spreads between the two groups of countries have appeared. At the time this conference took place in mid-November 2008, the rates for government bonds from Greece, Ireland and Italy were already above 100 and around 75 for Spain and Portugal, compared to 25-35 for France, Germany and the Netherlands.[6] Not surprisingly, differences reassert themselves during 'bad times'.

CONCLUSION

The OCA theory criteria are clearly relevant and important for entry into a monetary union. In practice, however, they are difficult to use for two reasons. First, there is the issue of whether it is countries or regions overlapping several countries that are the relevant units when judging the importance of asymmetric shocks. Second, the risk of asymmetric shocks measured prior to the formation of a monetary union may be very different from the risk actually encountered after the creation of the single currency. In the case of the European monetary union, the OCA theory criteria may have had the added disadvantage that their application might have created an economic and political problem by splitting the European Union into a 'core' and a 'periphery'. Ignoring these criteria has not prevented, however, certain fundamental differences between countries belonging to the euro area from reappearing during the 'bad times' that emerged with the financial crisis of 2008. This suggests that entry criteria are necessarily imperfect and that more attention needs to be devoted to systemic surveillance of countries after entry in order to limit problems in 'bad times'.

REFERENCES

Bayoumi, T. and B. Eichengreen. 1996. "Operationalising the Theory of Optimum Currency Areas". Paper presented at the Centre for Economic Policy Research Conference on Regional Integration, La Coruna, Spain.

Bayoumi, T. and B. Eichengreen. 1997. "Ever Closer to Heaven? An Optimum-Currency-Area Index for European Countries." *European Economic Review* 41 (3-5): 761-70.

Buti, M. and A. Sapir, ed. 1998. *Economic Policy in EMU*. Oxford: Oxford University Press.

Forni, M. and L. Reichlin. 2001. "Federal Policies and Local Economies: Europe and the US." *European Economic Review*, 45(1): 109-34.

6   The rate was 25 for Finland, 50 for Belgium and 75 for Austria.

Frankel, J and A. Rose. 1997. "Is EMU More Justifiable Ex Post Than Ex Ante?" *European Economic Review*, 41(3-5): 753-60.

Kenen, P.B. 1969. "The Optimum Currency Area: An Eclectic View". In, *Monetary Problems of the International Economy*, ed. R.A. Mundell and A. Swoboda. Chicago: University of Chicago Press.

McKinnon, R. 1963. "Optimum Currency Areas". *American Economic Review*, 53(4): 717-25.

Mundell, R. A. 1961. "A Theory of Optimum Currency Areas." *American Economic Review*, 51 (6): 657-65.

Mundell, R.A. 1973. "Uncommon Arguments for Common Currencies." In *The Economics of Common Currencies*, ed. H.G. Johnson and A.K. Swoboda. London: Allen & Unwin.

Viñals, J. 1996. "European Monetary Integration: A Narrow or a Wide EMU?" *European Economic Review*, 40 (3-5): 1103-09.

PANEL STATEMENT

BY JAUME VENTURA, CREI AND POMPEU FABRA UNIVERSITY

About half a century ago, Robert Mundell raised a novel question: when is it optimal for a set of countries to adopt a common currency? This seemed an esoteric problem at the time, the kind of theoretical stuff only academics care about. But events since have made it clear that this problem is also very relevant for policymakers who mostly care about practical matters. Not surprisingly then, some of the best minds in the profession have devoted substantial time trying to answer Mundell's question. As a result of their efforts, there is today a massive body of theoretical and applied research on optimal currency areas. This research has greatly improved our understanding of many aspects of this problem, and it constitutes a prime example of how theory and policy interact in a fruitful way.

But my objective here is neither to review nor to praise past research. To the contrary, I want to point at where this research has missed the mark and then discuss some of the potential directions that I think this research should take in the future. It is obvious to everybody that a currency union has microeconomic effects, as it reduces the costs of transactions between countries. The most interesting question has always been what the costs of a currency union are. Existing research has been lopsided, focusing almost exclusively on the central bank's role in managing the business cycle in the presence of price and wage rigidities. In fact, the problem of choosing the optimal currency area has been framed in terms of how a currency union limits the ability of the central bank to fulfill this role. This is certainly an important aspect of the optimal currency area problem. But it is not the only one. The central bank also has the role of ensuring financial stability by acting as a lender-of-last-resort when systemic risk and contagion in the financial system threaten to bring the economy to a halt. And yet, we know very little about how a common currency affects the ability of the central bank to effectively play this important role. Perhaps surprisingly, the literature on optimal currency areas has by and large neglected this aspect of the problem. It seems safe to assume though that recent events have convinced most of you that this is a gap in our knowledge that we desperately need to fill.

I   LIQUIDITY MANAGEMENT IN NORMAL TIMES: DEALING WITH NOMINAL RIGIDITIES

The bulk of existing research in the optimum currency areas problem has adopted what I would label as a "monetary-policy" view of liquidity management. According to this view, central banks should aim at keeping the interest rate low and steady and provide the economy with the liquidity it needs as economic activity grows and the financial system evolves.

This simple recipe need some qualification, though. As a result of shocks to preferences and technology, the growth rate of economic activity fluctuates. It has become commonplace to refer to these fluctuations in the growth rate as business cycles. In the absence of frictions, these cycles would constitute optimal responses of the economy to shocks, and should not concern central banks. But there are frictions to watch for, namely, wage and price rigidities. These rigidities sub-optimally magnify the business cycle and open up the door for the central bank to play a useful stabilizing role. By lowering the interest rate when economic activity is growing sluggishly, and raising it when economic activity is growing too fast; the central bank can neutralize the effects of nominal rigidities and smooth the business cycle. Despite occasional claims to deny this, this view of liquidity management as a tool to moderate business cycles quite accurately depicts the behavior of central banks in normal times.

This view of liquidity management leads to a very natural answer to Mundell's question. Namely, the borders of an optimal currency area are determined by a trade-off between the microeconomic benefits of a single currency and the macroeconomic losses from a one-size-fits-all monetary policy. The stronger are the trade linkages among the members of the currency union, the larger are the microeconomic benefits that a currency union delivers. The less synchronized are the business cycles of the members of the currency union, the larger are the macroeconomic losses that the union generates. It is not surprising therefore that most research on optimal currency areas has focused on studying the theoretical determinants of these gains and losses. A more applied branch of this research has focused on measuring these gains and losses in specific cases, in order to assess whether the conditions for a welfare-improving currency union exist. As mentioned already, I will not try to review this extensive research here.

A very interesting line of this literature has asked whether the conditions that guarantee a successful currency area are endogenous to the creation of the currency area itself. In a nutshell, the idea here is that the adoption of a single currency might foster trade among its members and synchronize their business cycles. Even if a currency area does not look optimal ex-ante, it might turn out to be optimal ex-post as its creation creates the conditions that are required for its success. This way of looking at the optimal currency area issue is both original and insightful. In his presentation to this panel, Andy Rose has just provided a nice summary of some of the findings of this line of research.

Before going beyond the "monetary-policy" view, I cannot resist to briefly mention an important issue that I think deserves much more attention than it has received. I am referring here to the role of externalities in the choice of monetary policy. Globalization has expanded market borders well beyond political borders. And yet the current political structure gives governments the incentives to adopt a local approach to economic policy that disregards the costs and benefits that fall on the other side of the political border. As the mismatch between market borders and political borders grows, externalities becomes more severe and the quality of policy making declines. Cooperation among existing central banks is only a partial and inefficient way of coping with this problem. The creation of a currency union and a single central bank seems to me a much more effective way to handle externalities in policy making. This consideration, however, has not been emphasized enough by existing research on optimal currency areas.

But as I said at the beginning, I want to talk about future research and not past research. And it seems to me that future research should work at complementing the "monetary-policy" view of liquidity management with another view that, somewhat paradoxically, is much older. This is the "financial-stability" view of liquidity management, and I turn to it next.

2   LIQUIDITY MANAGEMENT IN CRISIS PERIODS: DEALING WITH SYSTEMIC RISK

Much before Keynes convinced the profession of the need for active macroeconomic management to deal with the business cycle, central banks were entrusted with the mission of safeguarding financial stability by providing enough liquidity to banks during crisis periods. This traditional role of central banks as the lender-of-last-resort has been essentially ignored by the literature on optimal currency areas. And yet, it has important implications for the design of an optimum currency area and it has obviously taken a prominent place recently.

The "financial-stability" view of liquidity management recognizes the dangers of one of the most useful activities of banks, namely, maturity conversion. This consists of borrowing short-term from savers and lending long-term to investors. Maturity conversion is useful because it allows the economy to efficiently use existing liquidity. Firms typically need liquid assets to finance real investments that will generate profits or cash-flows a few years ahead. Borrowing long-term allows firms to carry on these investments with the confidence that they will not run out of cash before the investments deliver their fruits. Families and other creditors typically save to insure against unexpected shocks such as unemployment or illness. Lending short-term allows families to operate with the confidence that they will be able to use their savings when they are most needed. Therefore, the banks fulfill a useful service to their clients by borrowing short from families and lending long to firms.

The problem, of course, is that the maturity mismatch between assets and liabilities subjects banks to the risk of a liquidity shortage. This happens if a large fraction of the creditors of a bank want their savings back on short notice and the bank does not have enough liquid assets because it has made loans with a long maturity. In general, such a situation should not concern central banks since the interbank market will take care of this problem. Banks with a liquidity shortage will borrow from those that have excess liquidity using their loans as a collateral. There is no reason to think that, in normal times, the banking system as a whole has a shortage of liquidity.

But two types of problem can arise in this market that create the possibility of an aggregate liquidity shortage or financial crisis and require the central banks to play its role of lender-of-last-resort. The first type of problem is a situation of panic or generalized lack of confidence. This happens when the liquidity shortage affects most banks in the system simultaneously and the interbank market dries up. Without an injection of liquidity by the central bank, banks would be unable to face the demands of their creditors. The system needs additional liquidity and only the central bank can create it. Quick and decisive intervention by the central bank might avoid a banking crisis that could have very negative consequences for the real economy. As soon as the panic is over, the central bank can safely withdraw the additional liquidity from the market and avoid potential inflationary consequences. If properly executed, this intervention should not have fiscal costs. To the contrary, the central bank might charge an interest rate to banks for the liquidity provided and even make a gain.

But even better, panics might not even happen if creditors anticipate this type of intervention by the central bank. After all, panics are nothing but the bad outcome of a coordination game. Creditors panic and run to the banks because they think other creditors will do the same and leave them with nothing. If nobody ran today, there would be enough for everybody tomorrow and no need to panic at all. To convince investors not to run, the central bank only needs to give assurances to creditors that there will be enough liquidity for everybody tomorrow even if others run today. This type of reasoning provides the logic behind deposit insurance and other type of ex-ante policies that protect the banking system from the possibility of aggregate liquidity shortages. Whether central banks can ever achieve enough credibility to ensure that no panics will arise is still an open question. For our purposes, it suffices to notice that having a central bank that is willing and able to provide liquidity during crises periods not only reduces the negative effects of these crises, but it also lowers the probability of them happening in the first place. And all of this without fiscal costs!

The second type of problem is a situation in which there is too little information in the market and, as a result, the quality of the loans owned by a given bank is unknown to other banks. This is likely to happen in periods of fast financial innovation in which many of the products that banks own are new, opaque and therefore difficult to adequately price. In this case, the standard "lemons" problem arises and banks are naturally reluctant to lend to each other, correctly fearing that the bank asking for loans is insolvent. Once again, we find that the interbank market dries up and some banks are no longer capable to satisfy their creditors. The problem becomes one of systemic risk if, as it is the case in modern financial systems, the balance sheets of banks are interconnected. As one bank goes down, doubts arise about connected banks that might lead them to fail as well. This leads to a new round of doubts and failures that spreads the liquidity shortage throughout the system. Very soon most of the banking system is under suspicion and a systemic collapse is looming. Without quick and decisive intervention by the central bank, this collapse might occur and bring along severe costs in terms of economic activity.

The details of how to handle this type of crisis are less known. Moreover, there are no miracle cures. This is not a coordination problem anymore, but one of asymmetric information. If the market does not know the quality of bank assets, neither does the central bank. Accepting those assets as collateral by the central bank might therefore involve heavy fiscal losses. Direct infusion of liquidity at the cost of the taxpayer is also a possibility. It is still possible that, in this second type of crises, quick and decisive intervention by the central bank might also avoid a banking crisis that could have very negative consequences for the real economy. But we do not know very well the costs of such intervention. To start with, the fiscal costs might be large. Is it fair that taxpayers suffer because of the misbehavior of managers and the inability of shareholders to control them? Moreover, if anything has been learned recently, is that agency problems are much more severe than we ever anticipated. What are the effects on incentives of a policy of bailing out banks at the cost of the taxpayer? The creation of new and opaque assets with the intent of going around existing regulation might make bank managers rich. But somewhat paradoxically, it also cloggs the financial system and might lead to a sudden shortage of liquidity. Bailing out banks might limit the effects on real activity of this type of crises, but it might worsen incentives and make them more likely in the medium and long-run. We do not know yet what is the optimal way to handle this second type of crises, but it is safe to work with the hypothesis that it will involve some sort of rescue package together with a toughening of regulation.

It goes without saying that the "monetary-policy" and "financial-stability" views of liquidity management are not only not incompatible, but they are complementary. Each of them describes one important aspect of central banking and only together they provide a complete picture of the behavior of central banks. And yet, we find that up to now the "financial-stability" view of liquidity management has not played any significant role in the research on optimal currency areas. I venture to say here that, once the research in this area takes into account the role of the central bank as a lender-of-last-resort, there will be one new and important factor entering the basic trade-off for a currency union, in addition to trade linkages and synchronization of business cycles. This additional factor is the interconnectedness of financial systems.

In the absence of a currency union, what are the problems that can arise when various central banks try to simultaneously manage a common crisis? Regardless of whether the crisis is due to a panic (coordination-problem type of crisis) or misbehavior of managers (asymmetric information type of crisis), it is crucial that the central bank be able to inject liquidity wherever the financial system needs it. The problem, of course, is that this might be outside the political borders. It will be of very little help to inject liquidity only in domestic banks if the later balance sheets are heavily interconnected with those of foreign banks who are not receiving the liquidity they need. A quick and decisive intervention is difficult if many central banks have to agree first on how and when liquidity is provided. One can go back in history to find many instances in which a crisis keeps growing as policymakers spend their time bickering on who should do what and when, and worrying more about the impact of their actions on public perceptions than about actually solving the problem.

The situation is even worse when the solution of the crisis involves fiscal costs. This adds an important negative externality in policy making that can lead to two perverse effects. The first one is that it can lead to a war of attrition, that is, a situation in which corrective action is delayed because of disagreement on how to share the costs. In this sort of situation (which is not unlike the case of a strike), all parties involved want other parties to pay most of the cost of intervention. While disagreements are sorted out, the status quo remains and the crisis grows larger. By the time the different parties agree to a solution, the problem is much larger than it was at the beginning. This is obviously inefficient and costly. Why is it not possible then to reach an agreement quickly? The answer is asymmetric information. Everyone is suffering because of the delay, but everyone is holding its position in the hope that the situation will be so unsustainable to others that they will concede and accept to pay most of the costs. The agreement is only possible when the costs have grown so large that they are unbearable to some of the parties.

The second problem is that, once the agreement is reached, it is likely to be inefficient and difficult to enforce. The liquidity banks receive might depend on the nationality of their shareholders rather than their real needs. Needed but costly interventions might not take place if most of the benefits go abroad. Not needed and also costly interventions might take place, if most of the costs are financed by foreign taxpayers. When redistribution across national lines becomes an issue, efficiency takes the back seat and this leads to short and long term negative effects. Despite official talk to the contrary, central banks are not immune to domestic politics and the electoral effects of their policy choices.

For all these reasons, a currency union looks much more attractive when we are reminded of the central bank's role as a lender of las resort.

3 FINAL REMARKS

As I mentioned at the beginning of my intervention, my goal was not to review or praise past research. Instead, I have made the observation that existing research on optimal currency areas has missed the mark in one important respect: the need to evaluate how a currency union affects the central bank's ability to fulfill its role of lender-of-last-resort. I hope I have made a convincing case for research to proceed in this direction and that some of the tips provided here will be useful to researchers in the area. Thank you for your kind attention.

GENERAL DISCUSSION

Vítor Gaspar asked **André Sapir** why in his panel presentation Sapir used current account balances, and not fiscal balances, to explain risk premia on long-term government debt within the euro area. Sapir responded that the current account balances explain the risk premia, while the fiscal balances do not. Furthermore, Gaspar asked **Martin Feldstein** to comment on the fact that risk premia on long-term government debt in the euro area have only appeared recently. We had ten good years, replied Feldstein, and pressures within the euro area are beginning to show up only now.

Tommasso Aquilante asked **Andrew Rose** whether data on trade in services were included in the empirical studies that Rose considered in his panel presentation. Aquilante conjectured that trade in services faces higher barriers than trade in goods. **Andrew Levin** remarked that services are less cyclical than goods. Rose responded that little data on trade in services was available. **Stanley Fischer** wondered whether **Jaume Ventura**'s model of externalities in lending-of-last-resort activities implied that banking supervision had to be done by an EMU-wide institution. Andrew Levin wondered whether there is evidence to support the view that small countries and small companies have gained relatively more from the European common currency.

Assaf Razin asked everyone to compare Hungary and the United Kingdom. Hungary seems capable of achieving low and stable inflation only by joining EMU. By contrast, the United Kingdom can depreciate itself out of the current recession. Razin believed that reflecting upon this comparison would be crucial for understanding the monetary integration in Europe.

Su Ning, Guillermo Ortiz, Ben Bernanke, Jean-Claude Trichet, Stanley Fischer,
Lucrezia Reichlin (from left to right)

SESSION 6

PANEL
INTERNATIONAL INTERDEPENDENCIES
AND MONETARY POLICY – POLICY VIEWS

INTRODUCTION

BY LUCREZIA REICHLIN, LONDON BUSINESS SCHOOL

I am honoured to chair the Policy Panel of this conference, celebrating the 10th anniversary of the euro. The panellists do not need introduction. I welcome here Ben Bernanke, Chairman of the Federal Reserve, Stanley Fisher, Governor of the Bank of Israel, Su Ning, Deputy Governor of the People's Bank of China, Guillermo Ortiz, Governor of the Banco de México, and Jean-Claude Trichet, President of the European Central Bank.

It is an odd time for celebration. In the midst of a financial crisis and with a recession glooming ahead, we may be facing the hardest test not only for the single European currency, but also for the world's financial architecture.

Let me suggest some questions for discussion. This conference has analyzed the experience of the euro area as a currency union in the last ten years. Looking ahead, what are, in your view, the key issues when it comes to the link between financial integration, financial development, and currency and monetary arrangements?

The process of real integration, financial integration and the financial development we have witnessed, both at the regional level and at the global level, pose some new challenges for monetary policy. How have these developments affected the prospects of existing and possible future currency unions and fixed exchange rate regimes?

Furthermore, there are some topics that are particularly important today. One key policy issue is whether there is a need for new local or global financial regulation to prevent potential financial instability linked to financial integration. Financial integration also raises new problems for banking and corporate finance.

Finally, let me put on the table the issue of the role of a central bank as provider of liquidity and lender of last resort in a monetary union, and the connected problem of the interplay between fiscal and monetary policy.

PANEL STATEMENT

BY BEN S. BERNANKE, CHAIRMAN OF THE BOARD OF GOVERNORS, US FEDERAL RESERVE SYSTEM

I am pleased to be here in Frankfurt today to celebrate the 10th anniversary of the euro. The euro's introduction was a remarkable achievement. As an academic, I did a bit of consulting for the European Monetary Institute, the European Central Bank's (ECB) predecessor, on monetary transmission mechanisms; I thus played a part, albeit an extremely small one, in this grand project. I mention this only as a reminder that the creators of the euro drew on monetary expertise from around the world, an early example of the international cooperation that has since proven to be one of the hallmarks of the ECB. Indeed, the run-up to the euro's establishment and the experience of the past decade have been associated with an unprecedented degree of policy coordination among the sovereign states within the euro area, including cooperation in the areas of fiscal and regulatory policies as well as monetary policy.

The current financial crisis and global economic slowdown likewise have been an occasion for unprecedented international policy coordination, within Europe but also globally. For example, in its regulatory capacity, the Federal Reserve has worked closely with regulators and supervisors from a number of European nations, and we are active participants in the international Financial Stability Forum and the standard-setting bodies operating under the aegis of the Bank for International Settlements. My focus today, however, will be cooperation in monetary policy and, especially, in the meeting of the liquidity needs of our increasingly globalized financial markets.

As you know, financial markets remain under severe strain. The proximate cause of the financial turmoil was the end of the U.S. housing boom and the attendant losses on mortgages and mortgage-related assets by many institutions. However, more fundamentally, the turmoil was the product of a global credit boom, characterized by a broad underpricing of risk, excessive leverage by financial institutions, and an increasing reliance on complex and opaque financial instruments that have proven to be fragile under stress. The unwinding of this boom (and the associated financial losses) has led to the withdrawal of many investors from credit markets and deleveraging by financial institutions, both of which have acted to constrict available credit to households and businesses. This credit squeeze is, in turn, a principal cause of the economic slowdown now taking place in many countries.

Central bankers have been working closely together throughout this period of financial turmoil. Personally, I have found the opportunity to share views regularly with President Trichet and other leading central bankers at various international meetings extremely valuable. We are all in frequent contact by phone as well. Our consultations allow us to keep abreast of developments in other countries, to compare our analyses of developing trends, and to draw on each other's experience and knowledge.

The merits of coordinated monetary policies have been discussed by policymakers and academics for decades, but in practice, such coordination has been quite rare. However, on October 8, the Federal Reserve announced a reduction in its policy interest rate jointly with five other major central banks – the Bank of Canada, the Bank of England, the ECB, Sveriges Riksbank, and the Swiss National Bank (SNB) – with the Bank of Japan expressing support. Last month's joint action was motivated by the abatement of inflationary pressures and increased indications of economic slowing in our respective economies. In addition, the coordinated rate cut was intended to send a strong signal to the public and to markets of our resolve to act together to address global economic challenges.

As you know, however, monetary policy actions have not resolved the ongoing strains in financial markets, including interbank funding markets. The Federal Reserve has responded to the strong demand for funding by banks and primary dealers by dramatically increasing the amount of term funding that it auctions to banks, providing new lending facilities for nonbanks, supplying high-quality securities for use in repurchase agreement (repo) markets and for other collateralized lending, and funding purchases of commercial paper. Elsewhere, including Canada, the euro area, and the United Kingdom, central banks have introduced or expanded similar measures to boost the provision of liquidity in their local currencies. In addition to these measures, governments in many countries broadened deposit insurance coverage and announced plans to inject capital into their banking systems and to guarantee bank debts. All of these steps are consistent with the principles agreed to by the Group of Seven finance ministers and central bank governors in their October 10 communiqué.

Although the range of mechanisms we have used has been broad, our provision of liquidity conforms to a central bank's traditional role as the lender of last resort. However, a novel aspect of the current situation is that the balance sheets of financial institutions have increasingly come to include instruments denominated in foreign currencies. The need for currencies outside an issuing country's markets arises primarily from the global role played by key international currencies, such as the dollar and the euro. For example, over the past decade, international loans and deposits have grown tremendously, as has the issuance of international debt securities – that is, bonds, notes, and money market instruments sold outside the borders of the borrower's country and sometimes denominated in foreign currencies. These developments have posed new challenges for conventional central bank liquidity and lender-of-last-resort policies. For example, injecting euros or sterling into national money markets may not be sufficient to restore market function in these economies when funding shortages are in dollars.

Indeed, a significant feature of the recent financial market stress is the strong demand for dollar funding not only in the United States, but also abroad. Many financial institutions outside the United States, especially in Europe, had substantially increased their dollar investments in recent years, including loans to nonbanks and purchases of asset-backed securities issued by U.S. residents.[1] Also, the continued prominent role of the dollar in international trade, foreign direct investment, and financial transactions contributes to dollar funding needs abroad. While some financial institutions outside the United States have relied on dollars acquired through their U.S. affiliates, many others relied on interbank and other wholesale markets to obtain dollars. As such, the recent sharp deterioration in conditions in funding markets left some participants outside the United States without adequate access to short-term dollar financing.

The emergence of dollar funding shortages around the globe has required a more internationally coordinated approach among central banks to the lender-of-last-resort function. The principal tool we have used is the currency swap line, which allows each collaborating central bank to draw down balances denominated in its foreign partner's currency. The Federal Reserve has now established temporary swap lines with more than a dozen other central banks.[2] Many of these central banks have drawn on these lines and, using a variety of methods and facilities, have allocated these funds to meet the needs of institutions within their borders.[3] Although funding needs during the current turmoil have been the most pronounced for dollars, they have arisen for other currencies as well. For example, the ECB has set up swap lines and repo facilities with the central banks of Denmark and Hungary to provide euro liquidity in those countries. The terms of many swap agreements have been adjusted with the changing needs for liquidity: The sizes of the swaps have increased, the types of collateral accepted by these central banks from financial institutions in their economies have been expanded, and the maturities at which these funds have been made available have been tailored to meeting the prevailing needs. Notably, in mid-October, the Federal Reserve eliminated limits on the sizes of its swap lines with the ECB, the Bank of England, the SNB, and the Bank of Japan so as to accommodate demands for U.S. dollar funding of any scale. Taken together, these actions have helped improve the distribution of liquidity around the globe.

This collaborative approach to the injection of liquidity reflects more than the global, multi-currency nature of funding difficulties. It also reflects the importance of relationships between central banks and the institutions they serve. Under swap agreements, the responsibility for allocating foreign-currency liquidity within a jurisdiction lies with the domestic central bank. This arrangement makes use of the fact that the domestic central bank

---

1   See Patrick McGuire and Goetz von Peter (2008), "International Banking Activity amidst the Turmoil," BIS Quarterly Review, June; also see ECB (2008), "The International Role of the Euro (923.7 KB PDF)," July. The ECB report noted that investment banks based in the United States and financial institutions based in the United Kingdom have been among the top non-euro-area issuers of euro-denominated bonds; it also said that banks in Europe and some firms located mainly in the United Kingdom with business concentrated in the securitization of residential mortgages have been among the top non-U.S. issuers of dollar-denominated bonds.

2   The central banks include those in Australia, Brazil, Canada, Denmark, the euro area, Korea, Japan, New Zealand, Mexico, Norway, Singapore, Sweden, Switzerland, and the United Kingdom.

3   Some other countries with extensive accumulated stocks of dollar reserves have made these dollars available in their economies through auctions and regional arrangements.

is best positioned to understand the mechanics and special features of its own country's financial and payments systems and, because of its existing relationships with domestic financial institutions, can best assess the strength of each institution and its needs for foreign-currency liquidity. The domestic central bank is also typically best informed about the quality of the collateral offered by potential borrowers.

The efforts by central banks around the world to increase the availability of liquidity, along with other steps taken by central banks and governments, have contributed to tentative improvements in credit market functioning. However, the continuing volatility of markets and recent indicators of economic performance confirm that challenges remain. For this reason, policymakers will remain in close contact, monitor developments closely, and stand ready to take additional steps should conditions warrant. In times like these, we are especially aware of the importance of having close working relationships with our central bank colleagues around the world. These relationships are fostered by the ties established in forums like this one and in the many venues where policymakers regularly gather.

The 10th anniversary of the euro is an opportunity not only to celebrate an impressive and historic achievement, but also to reaffirm our commitment to cooperation as we address the challenges of an increasingly integrated global economy. Central bankers and other policymakers around the world must continue to work together to address disruptions in credit markets and to promote a vibrant global economy.

PANEL STATEMENT

BY STANLEY FISCHER, GOVERNOR OF THE BANK OF ISRAEL

As a policymaker from a small open economy, I shall focus on the question of whether the increase in global financial integration – that is, capital account integration – of the last half-century has moved or should move the monetary policy regime in a small open economy such as ours in a particular direction. The answer is based on the work of Mundell and McKinnon in the 1960s, including their fundamental research on optimal currency areas.

Essentially the question comes down to the joint choice of exchange rate and monetary policy regimes. For a country completely open to international capital flows, I believe in the corner solution approach to the exchange rate regime, based on the impossible trinity. But that strong statement has to be combined with the recognition (i) that the real exchange rate cannot be a matter of indifference to the policymakers of a small open economy, and (ii) that to say that the exchange rate should be flexible is not necessarily to say that it should be totally free floating.

In practice, for an economy open to international capital flows, the choice needs to be made between a pegged exchange rate regime – which leaves very little room for a monetary policy focused on domestic goals, and a flexible exchange rate regime, which requires the specification of a monetary policy regime. The experience of the last twenty years supports the view that an inflation targeting regime has many advantages, provided that it is understood that we are talking about *flexible* inflation targeting.

Modern monetary policy is typically given three goals – and here I quote from the draft revised Bank of Israel law, which draws on the laws of other central banks including the ECB and the Bank of England, and which we hope will be accepted by the government and the Knesset:

- The primary goal of monetary policy is to maintain price stability, typically as defined by the government. In our case, the inflation target range is 1-3 percent per annum, with the center of the range – 2 percent per annum – being taken as the point target. There may be a slight preference for stating the target as a number – generally 2 percent – with a tolerance range of plus/minus 1 percent, as a way of avoiding giving the impression that any rate between 1 and 3 percent is equally satisfactory.

- To support the other goals of government economic policy, particularly growth and employment, so long as that does not conflict with the primary goal of maintaining price stability.

- To contribute towards ensuring the stability of the financial system.

The *flexibility* in flexible inflation targeting consists of allowing the central bank to choose the time path by which it intends to return to the target inflation rate or range when the inflation rate deviates from target. This flexibility is needed because a monetary policy that seeks to return inflation to the target range as rapidly as possible may well destabilize the path of real output, and thus conflict with the second and possibly the third goals of monetary policy.

The debate about the inflation targeting approach to monetary policy can become heated. On one side are proponents of the dual mandate approach, which says that both inflation and output should receive equal weight as goals of monetary policy. In making the argument, proponents usually argue against a monetary policy approach that would imply that inflation is the only goal of monetary policy. If there were ever proponents of this approach, they are now very rare, for the flexible inflation targeting approach – which gives weight to both output and inflation over the short and medium term – is the more generally accepted view. The equal weight view has the difficulty that in the medium and longer term, monetary policy has very little influence on growth. Thus a monetary policy that strives to achieve a growth target that cannot be reached, is likely to produce increasing inflation – at which point the flexible inflation targeting approach allows the policymaker to give medium- and longer-term preference to achieving the inflation goal, which is what monetary policy can achieve over that time horizon. On the other side, flexible inflation targeting is attacked by proponents of a twin-pillar monetary policy, one that focuses not only on the behavior of inflation but also on that of the money supply. This latter approach seems fully consistent with flexible inflation targeting, and it may well be a matter of tradition and preference as to whether that fact is recognized or not.

What should a central bank that is following a flexible inflation targeting approach do if the exchange rate is at a level that is problematic from the macroeconomic viewpoint, that is, from the viewpoint of growth? There are several possibilities:

1. Ignore the problem – which is easier for a large relatively closed country than for a small open economy;

2. Say this is a problem for fiscal policy. This may be the right answer from an analytic viewpoint, but it is not a good answer in the real world of policymaking. The truth is that all of us would be very happy if fiscal policy would stick to medium-term guidelines that produce a desired path of government spending, the deficit, and the debt, with appropriate counter-cyclical elements, without expecting it also to take care of the real exchange rate;

3. Try to use capital controls. These may work for a short time, though even that is doubtful, and in any case they will not work for any length of time. Further, reverting to the use of capital controls sends a disturbing signal to foreign investors and domestic residents alike.

4. An inflation targeting country that has significant pass-through from the exchange rate to inflation will in practice react to *changes* in the exchange rate in a way that is likely to be stabilizing for the real exchange rate;

5. The central bank may by coincidence find itself in a position similar to that of the Bank of Israel earlier this year, when the need to add to reserves coincided with a significant strengthening of the real exchange rate. Our own examination of the adequacy of our foreign exchange reserves had for some time been signaling that we needed to increase our reserves, which by each of three tests we applied[1] were too small by about $10 billion, to a range of $35-40 billion. We decided to begin acquiring reserves at a time when the exchange rate of the shekel had appreciated significantly, which made the decision to buy foreign exchange easier. We decided *not* to set a target range for the exchange rate, but rather to buy at a steady rate each day, and not to vary the daily rate of purchases based on day-to-day exchange rate changes. This judgment was based on lessons we have drawn from experience in countries with open capital accounts during the 1990s and in other periods, when governments that intervened in the markets in order to achieve a given exchange rate frequently found themselves losing against more sophisticated private sector market participants.

Clearly, no country can rely on its decisions on desired reserves coinciding with its views on possible deviations of the exchange rate from its medium term equilibrium. Ours was a fortunate coincidence, which led to a policy response that has by and large been successful, in that the exchange rate against the dollar has gradually returned to a range that is more consistent with our macroeconomic situation than it was in March. I should also note that we originally started buying a very small amount daily -- $25 million in March 2008 – but when the exchange rate strengthened rapidly in July, we increased our daily purchases to $100 million a day. We have maintained that daily rate of purchases – and given global economic instabilities in the last several months, we are very pleased to have added significantly to our reserves.[2]

6. The central bank may also have to intervene from time to time to deal with disorderly markets. Some time ago we developed a set of criteria by which we would define a situation of foreign exchange market failure. We had not seen such a situation for many years, but early this year, in mid-March, we found our foreign exchange market showing signs of market failure as previously defined. Accordingly we intervened in the market (this was before we instituted the program of reserve acquisitions described above) and succeeded in restoring its efficient operation.

The argument so far has been simple: a small open economy in the modern world should operate with a floating exchange rate and a flexible inflation targeting approach to monetary policy. But we have to recognize that the current crisis

---

1   The three were: the test that says reserves should be at least equal to foreign exchange liabilities falling due within the next twelve months; a reserve adequacy test in terms of months of imports; and an internal calculation based on potential uses of reserves, and the probabilities with which we were likely to find ourselves needing to use the reserves in each of the possible situations.
2   When the initial $10 billion of purchases were completed at the beginning of December, we recalculated the desired level of reserves, and as a result of increased market volatility, decided to continue the program until we reach a reserve range of $40-44 billion.

has revealed the difficulty for many countries of operating successfully in a world with massive and volatile capital flows, of the type we have seen in the last year.

It had seemed, based on the experience of the 1990s, that countries that had accumulated sufficient reserves could manage to ride out periods of global economic instability by using their reserves to defend against capital outflows. But it is clear from the situations of Russia and Korea in the last few months that even very large reserves are not sufficient to ensure stability in the face of rapid reversals of capital flows.

Countries can augment their reserves by obtaining access to contingent credit lines. In the 1990s both Mexico and Argentina at different times had such lines provided by the private sector, but when the going got tough, these lines evaporated or became very hard to activate. The IMF has several times tried to develop a contingent credit line facility, including during the last two months. However there have been difficulties in the design of such facilities, none of which has ever been used. It must be possible to design such a facility in a way that countries will be willing to use it to augment reserves – but to do that, member countries of the Fund that are opposed to the use of low-conditionality facilities will have to change their views, for until now this group has generally succeeded in placing conditions on activation of contingency facilities that have rendered them unusable.

Perhaps the most interesting development with regard to augmenting foreign exchange reserves in the face of a lack of liquidity in this crisis has been the swap lines that the Fed has extended not only to the central banks of the leading industrialized countries, but also to four emerging market country central banks – those of Brazil, South Korea, Mexico, and Singapore. The Fed is the only financial institution that can extend dollar liquidity in unlimited amounts, and its willingness to provide large-scale liquidity assistance to central banks of countries that are judged to be following responsible policies, may well represent an important step in the evolution of the international financial system and its ability to deal with crises.

The other approach to the impossible trinity is to opt for a pegged exchange rate, thereby losing the capacity to conduct a monetary policy aimed at affecting the domestic economy. Hong Kong SAR has clearly succeeded in this enterprise, withstanding a coordinated attack on the currency in 1997, and not having been seriously challenged since then. Nonetheless very few countries have been able to live with a pegged rate, even within a currency board arrangement, in the last twenty years. At this moment we are seeing major difficulties confronting Latvia.

One can argue that countries that have not succeeded in maintaining a pegged exchange rate have simply not been willing to implement the necessary monetary policy. However the issue is not one of monetary policy alone – it is also an issue for all of macroeconomic policy, for given the massive capital inflows to Latvia and the other Baltics, and absent an active monetary policy, fiscal policy as well as monetary policy would have had to be aimed at maintenance of the currency board arrangement. That means that a country that wants to peg its exchange rate may well find itself without any effective policy tools that can be used for domestic purposes. It is accordingly no surprise that given the scale of capital flows in the last two decades, so few countries have succeeded in maintaining a pegged rate for a long period.

That takes us to the last possibility – the hardest of hard pegs, joining a currency bloc. Joining a currency bloc is a far more serious step than merely changing monetary policy. For some countries, giving up the national money is a traumatic step. More fundamentally, the country that joins a currency bloc is likely beginning a series of far-reaching structural changes in its economy, including in its production and trading patterns.

To be sure, even such a step is not irreversible. Countries can in principle leave a currency bloc, possibly not of their own volition. And not all currency blocs are equally strong. The European Monetary Union is the strongest of such blocs, quite likely the strongest international currency bloc ever. Its strength, and its attraction in a time of fully integrated capital markets, is evident from the fact that as a result of the current crisis, some countries that had decided to stay out of EMU appear to be rethinking that issue.

That fact, and this tenth anniversary, are testimony to the founders, builders, and guardians of the Euro area, who have within a short time created a currency that has earned the trust of its users within the Euro area and outside it. It is an impressive and historical achievement.

PANEL STATEMENT

BY SU NING, DEPUTY GOVERNOR OF THE PEOPLE'S BANK OF CHINA

I am very pleased to be invited to address the audience on the topic of challenges confronting China's monetary policy and China's policy measures in the context of globalization.

I CHALLENGES OF GLOBALIZATION FOR CHINA'S MONETARY POLICY

China has been actively engaged in the economic globalization process after its accession into the WTO, and has integrated into the international community becoming an important part of the world economy. Globalization has brought forth both opportunities and challenges to China. With respect to monetary policy, the challenges are as follows.

First, China's BOP imbalances against the background of global economic imbalances have become a major factor constraining the independence and effectiveness of China's monetary policy. With dual surplus on the trade account and the capital account, in order to keep the RMB exchange rate at an adaptive equilibrium level, the People's Bank of China (PBC) has to purchase foreign exchange and inject base money. These operations have piled up massive liquidity, stimulated excessive investment, pushed up asset prices and have eventually affected price stability.

Second, increasing sensitivity of domestic prices to international price movements has made it more difficult for the PBC to maintain price stability. In recent years, prices of commodities, food and assets have gone up across the board, shoring up inflationary pressure all over the world and exerting a noticeable impact on domestic prices in China. Globalization has complicated the factors that affect prices; therefore, how to predict price trend, how to differentiate the effects of various factors, how to appropriately apply monetary policy are new issues encountered by the PBC when performing its mandate of maintaining price stability.

Third, the global financial crisis will have repercussions on China's economic and financial stability. Despite relatively strong independence of China's economy, it inevitably cannot be obviated from the international financial crisis when the world is increasingly globalized. After the breaking out of the Asian financial crisis, China went through economic slowdown and heightened financial risks. The adverse impact of the recent global financial crisis triggered by the U.S. sub-prime crisis on China's economic growth and financial stability cannot be taken lightly.

2 MONETARY POLICY RESPONSES TO THE CHALLENGES FROM GLOBALIZATION

To address the challenges brought by globalization, the PBC has taken a series of measures in recent years.

First, the PBC has adopted comprehensive measures to promote the equilibrium of balance of payments and enhance the independence of its monetary policy. China's BOP imbalances have deep-rooted reasons related to globalization, and is a part of global imbalance. To address the root causes of its BOP imbalances, China needs to restructure the economy. But to solve the issue, it also requires a global economic restructuring through joint efforts from the international community. China has strengthened the coordination and cooperation of its monetary and exchange rate policy with fiscal, trade, industrial, investment and other macro-economic policies in recent years and, as part of its wider efforts to restructure the economy, has implemented a basket of restructuring policies to expand consumption, increase imports and open up the domestic market. Meanwhile, the PBC has improved its liquidity management in the banking system, conducted sterilization operations to siphon excessive liquidity resulting from purchase of foreign exchange through multiple monetary policy instruments, thus buying time for economic restructuring. The PBC has also actively participated in the IMF-initiated multilateral consultations involving China, the U.S., Japan, the euro zone and Saudi Arabia to discuss policy responses to promote an orderly solution of global imbalance.

Second, the PBC has made its monetary policy more preemptive and better targeted and has maintained prices at a basically stable level. The PBC has reinforced monitoring and analysis of price movements, analyzing the influence of internal factors on prices as well as closely studying how domestic prices are affected by price movements of commodities in the international market, international economic and financial developments and monetary policy changes in other countries. The PBC has made great efforts to improve the price monitoring system and to analyze the impact of short-term supply shocks and imported factors on domestic prices, in order to accurately predict medium- and long-term price movements and enhance the preemptiveness and effectiveness of monetary policy. When addressing the latest round of inflation, the PBC made in-depth analysis of the causes and, after identified different influences of imported factors on prices, supply constraints and resources prices adjustments, the PBC was able to make correct judgments on the general movements of price and adopt well-targeted policies accordingly. Currently, the PBC is closely following the price developments in order to secure medium- and long-term price stability through flexible monetary policy.

Third, the PBC has put the role of financial adjustment into full play to promote stable and rapid economic growth. When facing risks of slowdown, the PBC works to avoid a sharp decline in economic growth by stimulating domestic growth potential through macroeconomic policies. Recently, facing with unfavorable fallout of the global financial crisis, the PBC has timely adjusted its monetary policy stance and has taken flexible measures in response.

In September and October, the PBC reduced the reserve requirement ratio twice, and cut interest rate three times. The PBC has also designed a series of policies to extend greater credit support to some key sectors in the economy to bolster growth. At present, China's credit growth is moderate in general, and China's economy continues to grow at a relatively rapid pace.

Fourth, the PBC has continued to push forward financial reform, strengthen risk prevention and establish a risk management mechanism so as to maintain financial stability. Efforts have been made to enhance the overall strength, competitiveness and risk management of China's financial sector. Measures have been taken to improve the monitoring over major financial markets such as money, capital and insurance markets and their interaction with monetary policy so as to establish and improve regulation, assessment and early warning systems to prevent systemic risks. The PBC will establish a deposit insurance system, improve the investor protection system and insurance policyholder protection system, and standardize the market exit mechanism of financial institutions. The PBC will strengthen liquidity monitoring and management in conducting its due role of lender of the last resort.

Fifth, the PBC has promoted international coordination of monetary policy and international financial cooperation. China is actively involved in international financial cooperation and conduct in-depth discussion on global economic and financial issues and policy coordination issues with other governments and central banks through various frameworks.

Currently, the international financial market is still in violent turbulence, posing unprecedented challenges to all monetary authorities. In order to ward off the impact of the international economic malaise, the Chinese government has decided to adopt proactive fiscal policy and moderately loose monetary policy. Recently, the central government unveiled a 4-trillion yuan economic stimulus package comprising of ten measures aimed to expand domestic demand and promote economic growth. Going forward, the PBC will strive to improve the preemptiveness, scientific approach and effectiveness of monetary policy, flexibly use monetary instruments in order to promote stable and rapid economic development and financial stability. Meanwhile, the PBC will further reinforce international policy coordination and cooperation, and join force with the international community in dealing with the financial crisis.

PANEL STATEMENT

BY GUILLERMO ORTIZ MARTÍNEZ, GOVERNOR OF BANCO DE MÉXICO

I   INTRODUCTION

This paper discusses the convenience of adopting coordinated policy actions among financial authorities around the globe, in the context of the current world financial turmoil, originated in the U.S. economy and spread to the global financial sector.

The literature on international coordination of macroeconomic policies in general, and of monetary policy in particular has analyzed the benefits and costs of policy coordination among countries. As it is well known, shocks and the policy response to these shocks in one country could have effects in other economies. In this context, it is interesting to assess if some degree of policy coordination may improve efficiency by the internalization of the so-called externalities.

Most of the literature on international policy coordination focuses on the gains and incentives to cooperate in "normal times", when markets are functioning relatively well. Under these circumstances the individual net benefits from adopting cooperative policy measures are perceived to be relatively small for each country. In contrast, the experience of the recent episode of "financial strain" showed that the relative gains from policy coordination in this type of environment are substantially higher. Thus, countries are more willing to cooperate and adopt collective policy actions during episodes of severe "financial stress".

In this sense, one of the lessons from the recent crisis is that there is not an appropriate international infrastructure to encourage international cooperation in "normal times" that can also facilitate a prompt implementation of coordinated actions during episodes of "financial stress". Thus, it is important to improve the international arrangements for cooperation among authorities around the world.

This paper is structured as follows: section 2 reviews the theoretical framework that has been used in the analysis of policy coordination among countries, which is useful for analyzing the incentives to cooperate in "normal times"; section 3 analyzes the convenience of adopting collective policy actions in periods of "financial stress" and describes the implementation of policy coordinated actions during the current global financial crisis; and, section 4 discusses the need to improve the institutional framework for international cooperation. Conclusions are presented in section 5.

2   THEORETICAL   FRAMEWORK   ON   INTERNATIONAL   POLICY
COORDINATION

Countries are subject to different types of shocks in the global economy and the policy response to these shocks plays a key role in transmitting its effects across countries. According to Meyer, Doyle, Gagnon and Henderson (2002), in general, there are two main types of shocks: international shocks, with either symmetric or asymmetric effects on different countries, and country-specific shocks, that broadly speaking can be transmitted from one country to another depending on the existing trade and financial links across economies.

In recent years, the globalization process has tightened trade and financial links across countries. For instance, Kose, Prasad, Rogoff and Wei (2006), and Rogoff (2006) document that cross border financial claims and direct foreign investment have significantly increased over the last two decades. Bordo and Murshid (2002) show that a globalization process involves a larger variety of international shocks, and a faster and stronger transmission of country-specific shocks and policies across economies.

Under these circumstances, the question that arises is whether an inward-looking approach to policy design is optimal or some degree of international policy coordination may improve the outcome? A theoretical framework to analyze this question can be found in the traditional game theory approach. The first author to apply techniques of game theory to address the issues of policy coordination among countries was Hamada (1976), who developed a two-country model where policymakers' objectives were price stability and balance of payments equilibrium, and the level of credit expansion was the policy instrument. Hamada showed that in equilibrium countries do not cooperate and they can not achieve their objectives simultaneously. Thus, the non-cooperative solution would be suboptimal. Some refinements of this policy game are contained in Hamada (1979 and 1985), and in Canzoneri and Henderson (1991), among others.

In general, as in the case of a non-cooperative game, without coordination each country takes for granted other countries' policy parameters and implied responses in order to design its own strategy (Nash equilibrium). As Taylor (2008) has pointed out, in the case of monetary policy actions one can easily imagine central bank policymakers taking for granted the policy rules of other central banks and deciding the best monetary policy response to achieve price and output stability, which leads to a global non-cooperative rule.

In the case of zero-sum games, where what one player gains the other loses, there would be no case for cooperation (Fudenberg and Tirole, 1995). However, in the case of policy coordination among countries, things are different because of the existence of externalities. In this sense, the theoretical literature on international policy coordination emphasizes the fact that macroeconomic policies in one country affect welfare in other countries, that is, the design and implementation of policy actions has externalities for other countries (Meyer, Doyle, Gagnon and Henderson, 2002). Another important externality is the effect that cooperation has in the design of policies on expectations, particularly, the possibility that cooperation could lead expectations towards a more desirable outcome.

A framework for international policy cooperation would therefore internalize these external effects and lead to higher global welfare than the non-cooperative case. In this regard, a significant body of literature on international cooperation shows that when policymakers do not cooperate, the results are not optimal, but when they cooperate, the solution is Pareto superior (see Cooper 1985; Corden 1985; Canzoneri and Gray 1985, Currie and Levine, 1985).

However, as it is well known, in the presence of externalities, optimization by an individual agent does not take into account potential positive or negative effects on other economies, that is, they do not collect all the benefits and costs of their actions. When countries decide whether to cooperate or not with other countries, they do not fully internalize all the effects of their actions. As a result, for each country the individual net benefit from cooperating with the rest of the world is usually smaller than the social benefit.

Furthermore, even though policy cooperation among countries may imply welfare gains, the absence of a commitment device has made cooperation an unlikely event. Only when the payoff for cooperation is large and is shared by the different countries, and a non-zero probability is assigned to a very bad outcome associated with a non-cooperative solution, the mechanisms to cooperate are successful. Otherwise, there are always incentives to deviate from these commitments. In addition, since policy makers are, in general, appointed for fixed terms, it is possible for authorities to underestimate the probability of this rare event taking place during their tenure and therefore assume that the corresponding probability is zero. Therefore, this structure of incentives implies that in many cases, international policy cooperation is only feasible when there is a supranational authority that can make credible threats to induce commitment among countries (Meyer, Doyle, Gagnon and Henderson, 2002).

Finally, some quantitative literature on policy coordination has also stressed that the gains of policy coordination among countries may be fairly small. Oudiz and Sachs (1984) were the first to estimate the gains from international cooperation. They used the reduced forms of econometric models and quadratic country welfare functions, and found small gains from policy coordination. Frankel (1989) also estimated the welfare gains between cooperative and non-cooperative outcomes, and found similar results. Recently, Obstfeld and Rogoff (2002) used an open economy macroeconomic model to analyze cooperation and found that the gains from policy coordination are small. Several other authors have used similar models to analyze the welfare gains from policy coordination and found similar results (see Corsetti and Pesenti 2001, Zheng and Pappa 2005, Tchakarov 2004, among others).

Usually these models have focused on the coordination of monetary policy actions among countries, highlighting the role of these policies in stabilizing macroeconomic fluctuations. However, as it was emphasized by Lucas (1985), the gains from reducing business cycles fluctuations *per se* are fairly limited.

Thus, the benefits from policy coordination seem to be quite small, that is, the cooperative outcome does not seem to substantially improve the non-cooperative one. In this sense, as Taylor (2008) has recently pointed out, the perception that gains from cooperation are small and the complexity associated with the adoption of coordinated policy actions among different countries, have discouraged policymakers around the world to embrace cooperative policies. Thus, countries have relied on inward-looking policies.

3 THE CASE FOR COOPERATION

The theoretical framework described in the previous section is useful to explain the absence or very little cooperation that we have seen in "normal times", that is, when domestic and international markets are functioning relatively well. However, this inward-looking approach, to some extent, has allowed the accumulation of some distortions and imbalances in the global economy. In this sense, it can be argued that the current financial crisis was preceded by little cooperation in some areas.

For instance, the rise in commodity prices was viewed by several central banks as an exogenous shock to their economies and responded accordingly. However, the fact is that, from a global perspective, this shock resulted, to some extent, from a lax global stance of monetary policy. As Frankel (2008) has pointed out, low global real interest rates reduced the cost of carrying inventories and tended to raise commodity prices. It can be considered as a clear example of how international coordination may have helped to moderate the effect of the recent expansionary phase of the global business cycle on the prices of commodities.

Another example is the absence of a prudential regulatory framework for the financial system at an international level, which allowed a substantial relaxation of credit standards. In addition, it appears today that not enough attention was given to supervising the involvement of non-financial firms in financial markets, particularly with respect to the use of sophisticated derivative instruments that implied some risks.

These considerations suggest that when policymakers assess the convenience of embracing a cooperative global policy, they seem to ignore the possibility (assign a zero probability) that extremely adverse events, like the current crisis, could take place during their tenure. Thus, when deciding whether to cooperate or not, the adoption of a risk management approach (assigning a non zero probability to extreme adverse events) may change the incentives in favor of a global cooperative policy.

Despite the discussion on the issues that led to the current financial crisis, this experience is useful to illustrate that coordination under episodes of "financial stress" is clearly convenient. For instance, once the financial crisis started and spread to the global economy, central banks and other financial authorities immediately started to respond with domestic measures to provide liquidity to their financial systems. Even if these individual responses were in the right direction, they were not enough to prevent a further deterioration of conditions in financial markets. Eventually this situation led to the bankruptcy of Lehman Brothers in mid-September. This event significantly changed the perception of risk in financial markets, and the probability of a major disruption in international financial markets increased. Then, in the weeks following this event, it became clear that non-coordinated policies were not enough to restore confidence in financial markets and reduce the risk of a further deterioration of economic conditions.

In this sense, the possibility of a disruption in financial markets increased the relative gains from collective policy actions among authorities from different countries. Here it is important to note that conditions in financial markets started to improve when markets perceived a coordinated effort among central banks and financial authorities across the world, which confirms the convenience of embracing coordinated actions at an international level in periods of severe financial stress.

Among the coordinated policy actions adopted by central banks and other financial authorities are: a) the coordinated global interest rate cut at the beginning of October, when the Fed, along with other central banks around the world, cut its reference interest rate; b) the *swap* lines among central banks, as a collective action to supply dollar liquidity to financial markets; c) the new credit lines offered recently by the IMF; and, d) the coordinated efforts across countries to capitalize financial institutions around the globe. These coordinated actions helped to restore investors' confidence in financial markets and the probability of a severe disruption in financial markets apparently has decreased.

In the case of emerging markets, the effects of the crisis have been transmitted to these economies through several channels. First, the financial crises and the subsequent slowdown in economic activity in advanced economies has impacted emerging countries though real channels, such as the reduction in export growth, the drop in labor remittances, and the deterioration in households and firms confidence. On the other hand, the financial distress has both direct and indirect effects on emerging markets financial sectors. Direct channels of contagion could arise when domestic financial institutions have significant exposure to foreign assets, and/or when they rely on foreign funding. Indirect channels of contagion, in turn, are exposed through several factors such as a tightening of financial conditions in domestic debt markets, excess volatility in asset prices (exchange rate, stock market, domestic bond market), and a slowdown of bank credit and an increase in its costs.

However, it is interesting to note that emerging markets had not been significantly affected until mid-September (collapse of Lehman Brothers). However, the aggravation of the financial crisis tested the resilience of these economies. By October 24, asset prices and their volatility in these economies had been affected considerably. For example, from Sep. 12 to Oct. 24, EMBI spreads increased 395bp in Mexico and 400bp in Brazil; domestic currencies depreciated 26% in Mexico and 30% in Brazil; stock markets decreased 34% in Mexico and 40% in Brazil; and, 10-year domestic bond yields increased 284bp in Mexico and 448pb in Brazil.

The experience from emerging markets is useful again to illustrate the importance of coordinated actions. Despite some individual measures adopted in each country, the announcement of the facilities to access liquidity in dollars for emerging markets on October 29 (*swap* lines between the Fed and the central banks of Brazil, South Korea, Mexico and Singapore, and new credit lines offered by the IMF) coincides with an improvement in the performance of financial variables in emerging markets. In particular, after the adoption of these coordinated policy actions, an important reduction in sovereign interest rate spreads and in volatility in asset prices was observed.

In view of the performance of financial markets after the implementation of these collective policy efforts, coordination among authorities around the globe has been certainly welcome. Therefore it is interesting to consider, as the markets return to "normal times", the convenience of maintaining some of these mechanisms in the future as part of a framework to help countries (and, in general, the world economy) cooperate and to some extent insure against episodes of financial disruption.

4   NEED TO IMPROVE THE INSTITUTIONAL FRAMEWORK FOR COOPERATION

The recent global financial crisis has made it clear that the cooperative efforts adopted in forums such as the BIS, IMF, and the Financial Stability Forum, among others, in terms of exchanging views and providing information about the global economy, have been insufficient in providing a framework for cooperation. Thus, it is important not only to strengthen the role of these institutions but also to build a wider international infrastructure that facilitates higher levels of cooperation among countries in "normal times".

However, it is important to note that the adoption of coordinated efforts in "normal times", does not necessary imply that all central banks should embrace exactly the same monetary policy actions. As it was mentioned before, international shocks can have asymmetric effects on countries, that is, the same shock can affect several countries in different ways. Under these circumstances, the appropriate policy response would not be the same for all countries. For instance, in the particular cases of Mexico and Canada, both countries are highly integrated to the U.S. economy, which might make a case for a currency union in North America. However, several international shocks have asymmetric effects on these economies (i.e. shocks to prices of certain commodities), thus, central banks should have enough flexibility to respond independently to these types of shocks.

Coordination in "normal times" means the implementation of an appropriate institutional mechanism that can make possible the adoption of coordinated actions by central banks and other financial authorities around the world. This institutional mechanism could be used to: a) provide the infrastructure to facilitate the prompt implementation of collective policies in periods of severe "financial stress" in the global economy, when the rapid adoption of coordinated policy actions is a necessary measure to restore the normal functioning of markets; and, b) provide a framework to discuss and analyze, during "normal times", coordinated efforts to insure against the occurrence of enormously traumatic events, like the current financial crisis. This framework must facilitate the exchange of information in a transparent way, the improvement of the regulatory framework of financial institutions, and the monitoring of the world economy in order to avoid the accumulation of huge distortions and imbalances as in the previous years. Finally, the presence of emerging market authorities in the design and implementation of this global cooperative framework should increase, as their role in the world economy has increased in recent years.

5   FINAL REMARKS

The current episode of financial strain in the global economy provides some important lessons for central banks and financial authorities around the world. First, it makes clear that the current institutional framework for cooperation is not enough to avoid the accumulation of imbalances and distortions that paved the way for the liquidity and credit problems that have affected financial markets since the second half of 2007. Second, it illustrates that the net payoff that countries can have under coordination depends on the state of their economies and of the world economy. For instance, the incentives to cooperate are higher in periods of severe "financial stress" than in "normal times". Third, it shows the need to rethink the role of international policy coordination, not only as a vehicle to address financial stress episodes, as the current one, but to conveniently define a framework for international policy cooperation that could also work in "normal times".

It is clear that working towards an environment of international coordination on macroeconomic policies is a complex task. However, it is also evident that this challenge will help to build a more stable international financial environment.

REFERENCES

Bordo, M. and A. P. Murshid. 2002. "Globalization and Changing Patterns in the International Transmission of Shocks in Financial Markets." National Bureau of Economic Research Working Paper 9019.

Canzoneri, M. and J. Gray. 1985. "Monetary Policy Games and the Consequences of Non-Cooperative Behaviour." *International Economic Review*, 26(3): 547-564.

Canzoneri, M. and D. Henderson. 1991. *Monetary Policy in Interdependent Economies: A Game Theory Approach*. Cambridge, MA: MIT Press.

Cooper, R. 1985. "Economic Interdependence and Coordination of Economic Policies." In *Handbook of International Economics*, ed. R.W. Jones and P. Kenen, 1195-1239. Oxford : North-Holland Publishing Co.

Corden, W. M. 1985. "Macro-Economic Policy Coordination." In *Inflation, Exchange Rate and the World Economy: Lectures on International Monetary Economics*, ed. W. Max Corden. Oxford: Oxford University Press.

Corsetti, G. and P. Pesenti. 2001. "International Dimensions of Optimal Monetary Policy." Federal Reserve Bank of New York Staff Report 124.

Currie, D. and P. Levine. 1985. "Macroeconomic Policy Design in an Interdependent World." In *International Economic Policy Coordination*, ed. W. H. Buiter and R. C. Marston. Cambridge, MA: Cambridge University Press.

Frankel J. 1989. "Obstacles to International Macroeconomic Policy Coordination." National Bureau of Economic Research Working Paper 2505.

Frankel J. 2008. "The Effect of Monetary Policy on Real Commodity Prices." In *Asset prices and Monetary Policy*, ed. J. Y. Campbell. Chicago, IL: University of Chicago Press.

Fudenberg, A. and J. Tirole. 1995. *Game Theory*. Cambridge, MA: The MIT Press.

Hamada, K. 1976. "A Strategic Analysis for Monetary Interdependence." *Journal of Political Economy*, 84(4): 677-700.

Hamada, K. 1979. "Macroeconomic Strategy Coordination under Alternative Exchange Rates." In *International Economic Policy*, ed. Rudiger Dornbusch and Jacob Frenkel. Baltimore, MD: John Hopkins University Press.

Hamada, K. 1985. *The Political Economy of International Monetary Interdependence*. Cambridge, MA: MIT Press.

Kose, A., E. Prasad, K. Rogoff and S. J. Wei. 2006. "Financial Globalization: A Reappraisal." International Monetary Fund Working Paper 189.

Liu, Z. and E. Pappa. 2005. "Gains From International Monetary Coordination: Does It Pay to Be Different." European Central Bank Working Paper 514.

Lucas, R. 1985. *Models of Business Cycles. Yrjo Jahnsson Lectures*. Oxford, England: Basil Blackwell.

Meyer, L., B. Doyle, J. Gagnon and D. Henderson. 2002. "International Coordination of Macroeconomic Policies: Still Alive in The New Millennium?" Board of Governors of the Federal Reserve System International Finance Discussion Paper 723.

Obstfeld, M. and K. Rogoff. 2002. "Global Implications of Self-Oriented National Monetary Rules." *The Quarterly Journal of Economics*, 117(2): 503-535.

Oudiz, G. and J. Sachs. 1984. "Macroeconomic Policy Coordination Among the Industrial Economies." *Brookings Papers on Economic Activity*, 1984(1): 1-75.

Rogoff, K. 2006. "The impact of Globalization on Monetary Policy." Presented at the Federal Reserve Bank of Kansas City Symposium on "The New Economic Geography: Effects and Policy Implications," Jackson Hole, Wyoming.

Taylor, J. 2008. "The Impacts of Globalization on Monetary Policy." Presented at the Banque de France Symposium on "Globalization, Inflation and Monetary Policy," Paris, France.

Tchakarov, I. 2004. "The Gains from International Monetary Coordination Revisited." IMF Working Paper 04/01.

PANEL STATEMENT

BY JEAN-CLAUDE TRICHET, PRESIDENT OF THE ECB

I would like to express my gratitude for having the opportunity to host this panel of distinguished experts and colleagues. Dear Ben, dear Stanley, dear Ning, and dear Guillermo: I greatly appreciate your willingness to participate in this conference despite the tremendous challenges we are all currently faced with. I would also like to use this opportunity to thank the conference organisers for a superb job and indeed all conference participants for their important contributions.

It is perhaps unfortunate that the current crisis distracts our minds from the subject of the Conference: the euro coming of age. In different conditions, I would have argued – as I did in the past – that, far from suppressing growth and entrenching divergences, the euro has spurred a spectacular drive of job creation virtually everywhere in the Union. By helping and fostering a long-due redressing of economic priorities and processes, the euro has enabled many countries participating in Monetary Union to do their best to compete successfully. We see signs that this restructuring is spreading to other parts of the Union that have been less successful so far in taking up the challenge.

Under normal circumstances, European Monetary Union – international integration in its most intimate form – would have been the subject of these remarks.

With the current crisis in the background, however, I want to address a different form of convergence and cooperation in the international arena, which involves central banks and crisis management.

Of course, this brings me quite far. With ever stronger global integration of goods and services trade and, in particular, financial markets there are increasingly stronger linkages among the world regions. As a result, economic and financial crises in one world region increasingly spill over to other regions. At the same time, corrective policy action in one region creates conditions and economic incentives that are felt and are acted upon elsewhere. How should policymakers around the world deal with this fact? In particular, is there a case for international coordination of macroeconomic policies?

I will try to give a tentative answer to these important questions. I will argue that we need to be careful with what we understand by international policy coordination. Policy coordination does not mean, of course, a unique policy stance for the entire world. Coordinated policy action is not a surrogate for domestic macroeconomic prudence. We are all convinced that monetary policies geared towards domestic price stability, sound public finances and flexible economic structures create the conditions for an international financial architecture that can last.

Are there areas in which policy cooperation can help strengthen domestic macroeconomic policies? My short answer is "Yes, there are". Before giving you concrete examples of beneficial cooperation, let me take a brief theoretical detour, which will make clear why aiming for a globally unified policy stance is undesirable, whereas other types of cooperation are more promising. In an influential paper a few years ago Obstfeld and Rogoff questioned the conventional wisdom that increased integration of goods and financial markets strengthens the case for policy stance coordination.[1,2] Their theoretical results even suggest that the need for policy stance coordination decreases with the level of international integration. The basic intuition is that integrated goods and financial markets provide a powerful risk-pooling mechanism, leaving policymakers free to focus on minimising the distortions that might hamstring their respective domestic economies. As I noted on previous occasions, the path of policy over the business cycle in the euro area relative to the United States has differed for a number of reasons – and this despite the common conviction that maintaining price stability is the prerequisite for sustainable job creation and economic success. The most important reasons for different policy paths are differences in underlying economic structures and differences in the timing, nature and duration of economic shocks.[3]

This being said, there is an interesting sideline in Obstfeld and Rogoff's paper, which seems to me to be very relevant for the current situation and which would be a fruitful area for future research. The result I mentioned earlier – that tight international linkages do not necessarily strengthen the case for international policy coordination – holds for what I would define as "normal times". In Obstfeld and Rogoff's words it holds "unless risk aversion is very high".[4] In the current generation of theoretical models, risk aversion is generally considered a constant parameter. I think that recent years and months have taught us an important lesson: attitudes toward risk not only vary over time – for example, following long-term trends – but they do so by waves and oscillations around trends. Phases of excessive risk taking can be followed by sudden reversals driven by abrupt global confidence shocks such as the one experienced in mid-September 2008.

The entirely exceptional joined interest rate cuts on 8 October 2008 and – in similar tense conditions – on 13 September 2001 have to be seen in this context. In both cases there was extraordinary uncertainty about the economic outlook and there was strong evidence that upside risks to price stability had diminished in many world regions at the same time. Joint action was first and foremost predicated on the need to respond to the same shock, a shock that was being transmitted around the globe with lags measurable in hours. This created the room for interest rate cuts, in all cases consistent with the mandate of the respective central banks. We

---

1   Obstfeld and Rogoff (2002).
2   A classic contribution to the literature on policy coordination, reflecting the conventional wisdom, can be found in Oudiz and Sachs (1984).
3   See Trichet (2006) and Trichet (2007).
4   Obstfeld and Rogoff (2002), p. 503.

chose to coordinate the timing of announcement because we wanted to mutually reinforce our message of confidence to the markets.

That being said, reflecting upon our very close relationship, I see all the hours spent on exchanging ideas with my fellow governors, reflecting on facts and prospects, has progressively consolidated an element of intimate confidence that is a major asset for the present and future. We have built a remarkable common ground of shared experience, mutual understanding and trust – in which today's consultation does not need a long preamble because it follows naturally from yesterday's discussion – that has facilitated action in many directions.

We have intimately cooperated in ways that cannot be easily integrated into theoretical models. For example, there is a continuous exchange of information that helps all of us to better understand the nature of the crisis and its intricate international propagation patterns. We have cooperated intimately as regards the provision of liquidity in order to restore the normal functioning of interbank money markets around the world.

Since December 2007, the ECB, in cooperation with the US Federal Reserve System and other central banks, has been conducting term auction facilities – so-called TAF operations – in which it provides USD liquidity on behalf of the US Fed to euro area banks against ECB eligible collateral. These operations do not have a direct impact on euro liquidity conditions and are aimed at improving global funding conditions. In this respect I would like to stress that to my knowledge this was the first joint action of that kind ever taken by central banks to relieve pressures in the short term funding markets.

The world can count on a continuation of this fruitful cooperation among central banks and it can also count on the fact that this cooperation occurs fully in line with our respective mandates and, in exceptional times like these, can even strengthen their achievement.

REFERENCES

Obstfeld, M. and K. Rogoff. 2002. "Global Implications of Self-Oriented National Monetary Rules." *Quarterly Journal of Economics,* 117(2): 503-535.

Oudiz, G. and J. Sachs. 1984. "Macroeconomic Policy Coordination among the Industrial Countries." *Brookings Papers on Economic Activity*, 1:1-64.

Trichet, J. C. 2006. "Monetary Policy Activism." European Central Bank Monthly Bulletin, 8(11): 67-83.

Trichet, J. C. 2007. "The Euro Area and its Monetary Policy." Presented at the Conference on "The ECB and its Watchers IX," Frankfurt am Main, Germany.

GENERAL DISCUSSION

Francesco Giavazzi asked the panellists whether the current financial crisis would foster more cooperation within Europe in the area of financial regulation and supervision. **Alex Cukierman** posed a similar question about fiscal policy. **Jean-Claude Trichet** responded that Europeans should take advantage of the pressure due to the crisis in order to consider pan-European banking supervision. As far as fiscal policy is concerned, the Stability and Growth Pact remains fundamental for the functioning of EMU. **Ben Bernanke** believed formal cooperation in fiscal policy within EMU to be unlikely. On the other hand, he thought that informal convergence of fiscal policies across EMU is likely. Such convergence is desirable because of international spillovers entailed by fiscal policy. According to **Stanley Fischer**, the invisible hand of intellectual climate makes a significant fiscal expansion likely all over the world. **Guillermo Ortiz** remarked that emerging markets must be cautious and they cannot engage in a persistent fiscal expansion.

Jürgen Stark delivering the closing address

CLOSING ADDRESS

CLOSING ADDRESS

BY JÜRGEN STARK, EXECUTIVE BOARD MEMBER OF THE ECB

I wish to thank all of you for joining this 5th ECB Central Banking Conference here in Frankfurt. It has been a privilege for us – and here I am speaking also on behalf of my colleagues on the Executive Board of the ECB – to host this event, with such distinguished panellists and participants during this busy and extremely difficult time.

In my view, the past one and a half days have been a great success. Your expertise, experience and thought-provoking ideas, as well as your contributions to the discussions have enriched the intellectual and political debate on monetary union in Europe – its achievements, its challenges and its future.

It has not been the aim of this conference to celebrate the ECB and its achievements. However, it is worth recalling that, contrary to what was expected by a number of critical observers in the run-up to Economic and Monetary Union (EMU), the euro has been a remarkable achievement. Let me also remind you in this context that the ECB is obliged to maintain price stability.

With inflation averaging only slightly above 2% in the euro area in the face of several significant adverse supply shocks, we have witnessed a decade of relatively stable prices. Likewise, longer-term inflation expectations have remained broadly anchored at levels in line with price stability during this time. Such anchoring reflects favourably on the high degree of credibility enjoyed by the ECB's monetary policy. This success is also a tangible proof of the institutional robustness, coherence and unity of the Eurosystem – of its capacity to act in a truly European spirit on the basis of shared values, high standards and common principles. This has in turn led to striking progress in economic and financial integration in the euro area.

Ten years on, even those early critics admit that the euro has performed better than expected. And meanwhile, today's critics are saying that the ECB's monetary policy over this period has not really been tested, that it's just been lucky. Not true. The past ten years have not been plain sailing. Far from it. From the outset, the ECB has been confronted with a high degree of uncertainty and a series of severe shocks: the aftermath of the Asian crisis in the late 1990s; the bursting of the dot.com bubble; 9/11; and sharp rises in oil and food prices worldwide.

Over this same period, the euro area has also had internal imbalances to contend with. An issue that was intesively discussed yesterday. These imbalances remain a challenge. While EMU highlights the need for flexible economies, the euro cannot be blamed for the emergence of those imbalances. Rather, this largely reflects a lack of adjustment in a number of Member States. This is particularly true for those euro area countries whose adjustment mechanisms and responsiveness to exogenous shocks is still rather slow. To allow euro area economies to develop their growth potential and to reap the full economic benefits of EMU, it remains indispensable that the countries concerned bring their structural reforms and fiscal consolidation measures more into line with the conditions and rules of monetary union.

Overall, the ECB has done well to overcome these difficulties. However, the current global financial distress poses challenges of a significant and unprecedented nature to the ECB and other central banks around the globe. With this crisis, EMU is now ultimately experiencing a real test.

In these demanding times, some widely-recognised core principles have helped the ECB to weather the storm. The Maastricht Treaty assigns a clear and unambiguous mandate to the ECB to maintain price stability. It also grants the ECB full independence from political influence to fulfil this mandate. Besides these instiitutional safety belts, monetary policy needs to be forward-looking, medium-term oriented and underpinned by a comprehensive analytical framework. Given the monetary nature of inflation over the longer term, such a framework must include a thorough analysis of monetary and credit developments to allow for well-informed and consistent decision-making. Finally, one principle – that has gained much attention during the current crisis – is to keep the determination of the monetary policy stance distinguished from the management of liquidity in money markets.

All these principles are captured in the ECB's monetary policy strategy. And globalisation does not fundamentally alter these principles – which give guidance, in particular, in critical times. To weaken or even abandon these principles would undermine our commitment and credibility. And, in the end, we would risk losing orientation.

Our strategy has provided a consistent and coherent framework not only for internal analysis and policy decision-making but also for external communication. Using the same framework for internal and external purposes has helped the ECB to ensure that its monetary policy remains consistent, credible and effective. One key element here is that the ECB, from the outset, has been transparent about its mandate, strategy, and decisions, as well as about what monetary policy can do and, even more importantly, what it cannot do. In this sense, expectations about transparency requirements should be in line with the actual strategy followed by the central bank.

Without compromising on its mandate, the ECB has demonstrated a willingness and capacity to react rapidly to exceptional circumstances. It has taken a large number of extraordinary measures to support the functioning of the money market and interbank intermediation. These measures could be perceived as innovative:

- it has provided full allotment at a fixed interest rate in all its refinancing operations;

- it has expanded the range of eligible collateral in this context; and,

- in close cooperation with other central banks, it has taken measures to improve global funding conditions in various currencies.

Allow me to add here, on a personal basis, a word of caution: we, as central bankers, have the obligation to remain prudent. First, not to set the wrong incentives for market participants. Second, central banks need to be aware of any operational and reputational risks associated with the adoption of new measures and less traditional instruments, notably for the balance sheet of the Eurosystem and, ultimately, for the credibility of the ECB's monetary policy. Not to mention the potential impact on central bank independence. The reputation of the ECB is firmly based on the credibility of its commitment to price stability. This credibility must by no means be put at stake.

Likewise, in its monetary policy decisions, the ECB has not shied away from taking some highly unusual but appropriate steps. Within the space of less than one month, on 8 October and 6 November, the ECB lowered its key rates by 100 basis points in total. These moves were remarkable and unique in the ECB's ten-year history – in terms of magnitude, timing and rapidity. Importantly, the latest policy decisions remained fully in line with the ECB's mandate and the principles I mentioned just now.

Those who say that we were or still are "behind the curve" should consider all the decisions the ECB has taken since the financial crisis has intensified and broadened. In this respect, let us not forget that a central bank has only one instrument at hand, namely monetary policy. It cannot be held accountable for meeting more than one objective. Any such attempt would overburden monetary policy. For this reason, the Treaty provides for a clear and efficient allocation of policy responsibilities, with price stability being exclusively and primarily assigned to an independent ECB as its primary objective.

Not surprisingly, our debates yesterday and today have triggered the question of how to safeguard EMU and build on its achievements at a time when the world's financial landscape is changing dramatically. In fact, the current financial turmoil – the origins and implications of which we discussed in detail – is likely to dampen demand in the euro area and the rest of the world for quite some time. It may well turn out to be a litmus test for the functioning of EMU, both in economic and institutional terms.

Having carefully listened to the presentations, I remain confident that monetary union will withstand the test of time. As illustrated during the conference, the euro has already brought real benefits to the 320 million people in the euro area. It has been the main driver behind the remarkable increase in economic and financial integration as well as the transformation of the financial system over the past decade. It has made the euro area economically more stable for both investors and consumers.

In particular, financial integration has promoted cross-border portfolio flows in the euro area and thus enabled consumers and investors to share and diversify risks. As illustrated yesterday, EMU has increased banking integration.

Another interesting finding is that key policy initiatives at the European level, notably within the context of the Financial Services Action Plan, have made a significant contribution to fostering banking and regulatory integration.

However, in my view, there is room for improvement, especially as regards cooperation and coordination between national supervisors and regulators in Europe. As the Vice-President emphasised in his opening address yesterday, there is a growing understanding of the need to strengthen the pan-European character of financial stability arrangements for crisis prevention and resolution.

However, during the ongoing financial turmoil, the euro area and the EU as a whole have proved their capacity to act decisively and promptly under difficult circumstances. National measures have been coordinated in a pragmatic manner with a view to enhancing their effectiveness through mutual reinforcement.

As regards the role of central banks in banking supervision, recent tensions in financial markets have confirmed that close cooperation and active exchanges of information between central banks and supervisory authorities are indispensable. In particular, the financial turmoil has revealed areas in which cooperation could be strengthened. In fact, central banks contribute to financial stability.

But improved coordination and institutional innovations, while necessary, are not sufficient to make the euro area economy more resilient to adverse shocks. To enhance the adjustment capacity of the euro area economy, the current situation should serve as a catalyst for the resolute implementation of the necessary reforms. This would enable the Member States of the EU to fully exploit the benefits of economic and financial integration, with positive effects on growth potential and job creation in the euro area.

Having said all this, we should not forget how Europe would look today without the euro. An issue that was only marginally addressed during the conference. It goes without saying that the euro area countries would be significantly worse off. Multiple crises would arise simultaneously. Currency crises would go hand in hand with banking crises and real economy disruptions at country level. These currency crises might also spill over to other countries in the region. Not to forget political tensions between countries. By eliminating contagion via the exchange rate channel, the euro has mitigated the risk of contagion stemming from national economic or financial crises. In this sense, the euro has been a very important stabilising element in difficult times.

It is therefore not surprising that many central and eastern European countries would like to join the euro area on a fast-track procedure to be better shielded from global financial tensions and crises. This is understandable, given that many of them have already made progress towards adopting the euro. But we have also heard clear words of caution. Let me take the opportunity to emphasise that the euro area is not a closed shop. Following three enlargement rounds since the start of monetary union in January 1999, and with Slovakia joining the euro area as its 16th member on 1 January 2009, there is no reason to believe that the door might one day be closed.

But there is no shortcut. In fact, the difficulties that some countries face today are related to their failures to adjust, failures that go back a long way. As a result, domestic and external imbalances have emerged, with adverse effects on the sustainability of the catching-up processes in those countries. The fast introduction of the euro would not resolve the underlying problems – but could weaken EMU.

Structural adjustments as well as nominal and real convergence are therefore needed prior to the adoption of the euro. This means that the countries concerned must achieve a sustainable level of nominal convergence at high standards in terms of meeting the convergence criteria.

The adoption of the euro without adjustment is not possible. To regard entry into EMU as an easy way to solve or circumvent the current challenges surrounding the catching-up processes would be wrong. And a premature entry might aggravate current problems and put the credibility of EMU at risk. Policymakers have to be aware that the adoption of the euro represents a regime shift and thus, as Governor Constancio pointed out yesterday, need to learn the rules of the game in advance.

The ECB has demonstrated its ability to act even under extraordinary circumstances – without compromising its price stability mandate. This has strengthened the ECB's credibility.

If the ECB is to continue to deliver price stability over the medium term, then the financial system has to be stable and function smoothly. It is first and foremost through that financial system that monetary policy impulses are transmitted to future price developments. It is indispensable to restore confidence and bring the global financial system back on a solid footing. It is crucial to understand the implications of globalised financial markets for the design of institutional arrangements for the prevention and resolution of financial crises.

Let me conclude: We are going through a period when solid institutions are needed around the globe. And solid institutions are expected to be disciplined. As such, central banks provide an anchor of confidence and stability in difficult times. This must not be put at risk by weakening or even "lifting" this anchor.

PROGRAMME

Opening address:
Lucas Papademos

Session 1
European Monetary Union after ten years: what has EMU brought to consumers and the corporate sector? Prices and quantities

Chair: **Gertrude Tumpel-Gugerell**
Executive Board Member, European Central Bank

Main Speaker:
Charles Wyplosz and Francesco Paolo Mongelli
Professor, Graduate Institute of International Studies, Geneva

Discussants:
Francesco Caselli
Professor, London School of Economics

Vítor Manuel Ribeiro Constâncio
Governor, Banco de Portugal

Session 2
European Monetary Union after ten years: what has EMU brought to consumers and the corporate sector? The evolution and the role of financial markets

Chair:
José Manuel González Páramo
Executive Board Member, European Central Bank

Speakers:
Philip Lane
Professor, Trinity College Dublin

Sebnem Kalemli-Ozcan
Associate Professor, University of Houston, European Central Bank Duisenberg Fellow

Simone Manganelli
Principal Economist, Financial Research Division, European Central Bank

Elias Papaioannou
Assistant Professor, Dartmouth College

José Luis Peydró-Alcalde
Economist, Financial Research Division, European Central Bank

Discussants:
Marco Pagano
Professor, University of Naples

Axel A. Weber
President, Deutsche Bundesbank

Dinner address:
Jean-Claude Trichet
President, European Central Bank

FRIDAY, 14 NOVEMBER 2008

Session 3
Challenges for monetary policy and financial stability from globalisation

Chair:
Lorenzo Bini Smaghi
Executive Board Member, European Central Bank

Main Speaker:
Raghuram G. Rajan
Professor, University of Chicago Graduate School of Business

Discussants:
Stephen G. Cecchetti
Professor, Brandeis University

Seppo Honkapohja
Board Member, Bank of Finland

Session 4
Panel: the euro and the enlargement: challenges ahead

Introduction:
Francesco Giavazzi
Professor, Università Bocconi

Panellists:
Vitor Gaspar
Acting Director-General of the Bureau of European Policy Advisers
European Commission

Athanasios Orphanides
Governor, Central Bank of Cyprus

András Simor
Governor, Magyar Nemzeti Bank

Session 5
Panel: optimal currency areas - an academic view

Introduction:
Wolfgang Schill
Director General Economics, European Central Bank

Panellists:
Martin Feldstein
Professor, Harvard University

Andrew Rose
Professor, University of California, Berkeley

André Sapir
Professor, Université Libre de Bruxelles

Jaume Ventura
Senior Researcher, Centre de Recerca en Economia Internacional,
Pompeu Fabra University

Session 6
Panel: international interdependencies and monetary policy - a policy maker's view

Introduction:
Lucrezia Reichlin
Director General Research, European Central Bank

Panellists:
Ben Bernanke
Chairman of the Board of Governors, US Federal Reserve System

Stanley Fischer
Governor, Bank of Israel

Su Ning
Deputy Governor, People's Bank of China

Guillermo Ortiz
Governor, Banco de México

Jean-Claude Trichet
President, European Central Bank

Closing address:
Jürgen Stark
Executive Board Member, European Central Bank